P9-CEK-387

INTERMEDIATE

2008–2009 YEARBOOK

The Education Center, Inc.
Greensboro, North Carolina

The Mailbox® 2008–2009 Intermediate Yearbook

Managing Editor, *The Mailbox* Magazine: Peggy W. Hambright

Editorial Team: Becky S. Andrews, Diane Badden, Kimberley Bruck, Karen A. Brudnak, Pam Crane, Chris Curry, Sarah Foreman, Margaret Freed (COVER ARTIST), Tazmen Hansen, Marsha Heim, Lori Z. Henry, Krystle Short Jones, Kitty Lowrance, Sherry McGregor, Jennifer Nunn, Mark Rainey, Greg D. Rieves, Kelly Robertson, Hope Rodgers, Eliseo De Jesus Santos II, Rebecca Saunders, Rachael Traylor, Sharon M. Tresino, Zane Williard

ISBN10 1-56234-924-4
ISBN13 978-1-56234-924-0
ISSN 1088-5552

Printed in the United States of America.

The Education Center, Inc.
P.O. Box 9753
Greensboro, NC 27429-0753

Contents

Skills for the Season

We All Rock!

Participating in a discussion

In advance, gather a class supply of different rocks and place them in a container. Have the class sit in a circle and pass the container from left to right. Invite each student to select a rock. Then ask each child, in turn, to share his rock and the reasons he chose it. Lead the class to determine that just as each rock is unique, each student has unique qualities as well. To wrap up, ask each student to share a quality or trait that makes him unique.

Pam Clifton, West County Middle School, Leadwood, MO

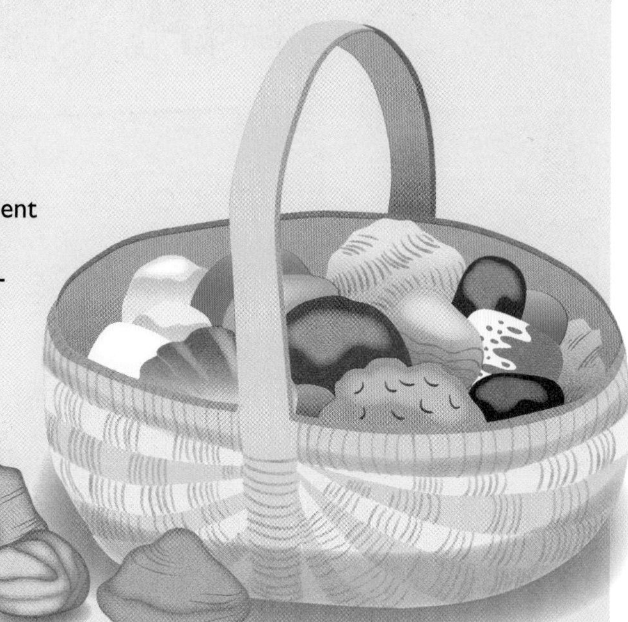

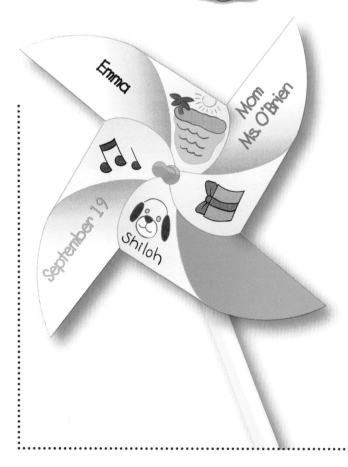

Personalized Pinwheels

Following directions

Have students make these breezy projects to share information about themselves with their new classmates. Give each child a copy of page 10 and the materials listed. Have her follow the steps to create a personalized pinwheel. Pin the pinwheels on a bulletin board so students can learn all about their new crop of classmates.

Kim Minafo, Apex, NC

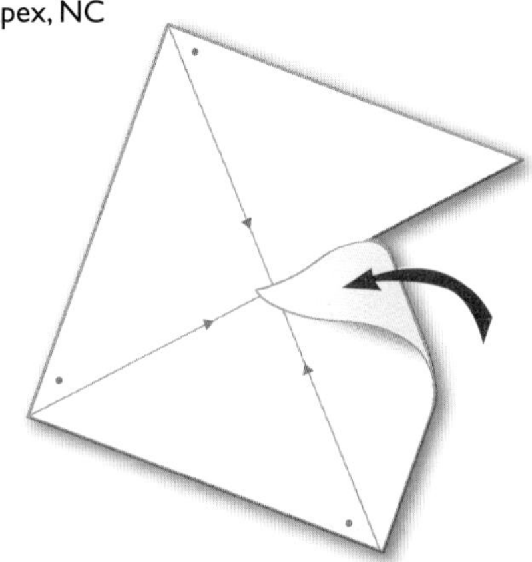

Name ______________________________

Don't Forget It!

Write the place value for 8 in each number. Then use the code to write the matching letter in the box.

1. 193,486,205 ten thousands [T]
2. 307,198,456 ____________ [ ]
3. 958,063,117 ____________ [ ]
4. 674,229,800 ____________ [ ]
5. 236,850,779 ____________ [ ]
6. 507,483,269 ____________ [ ]
7. 439,062,181 ____________ [ ]
8. 714,906,823 ____________ [ ]
9. 198,245,670 ____________ [ ]
10. 814,635,702 ____________ [ ]
11. 123,078,991 ____________ [ ]
12. 685,123,479 ____________ [ ]
13. 914,685,027 ____________ [ ]

Code

Place Value	Letter
ones	X
tens	E
hundreds	A
thousands	O
ten thousands	T
hundred thousands	G
millions	D
ten millions	I
hundred millions	U

What is the most important thing to bring to school?

To answer the question, write each boxed letter from above on its matching numbered line below.

__ 8   __ 5 __ 11 __ 2 __ 9   __ 4 __ 13 __ 1 __ 12 __ 6 __ 10 __ 3 __ 7

Name ________________________________

Circle every proper noun that should be capitalized.
Underline each common noun.

1. dr. floss is my dentist. At every checkup he reminds me to floss.

2. The stylist who cuts my hair is named ms. clip.

3. mr. pipe is our plumber. He lives on leaky lane.

4. If I am sick, I see dr. well. He wants to keep me healthy and in school.

5. david digit is our banker. His house is on division street.

6. If we need someone to help clean the house, we call mr. sweep.

7. ms. english is my tutor. She lives in grammar, texas.

8. mike lube changes the oil in our car. He works at a place called quick change shop.

9. ima plant is our gardener. She is from new jersey, which is the garden state.

10. The best cookie maker I know is mom, and she lives with me on baker street.

11. bea a. teacher wrote a book titled *homework, homework, and more homework.*

12. The comedian named i. m. funny likes to tell jokes and make people laugh.

I know a lot of people with names that seem to match their jobs!
2019

Count the total number of proper nouns and the total number of common nouns. Do these two numbers match the numbers on the girl's jersey?

Name ______________________________

Breakfast Bars

Use the graph to answer each question.

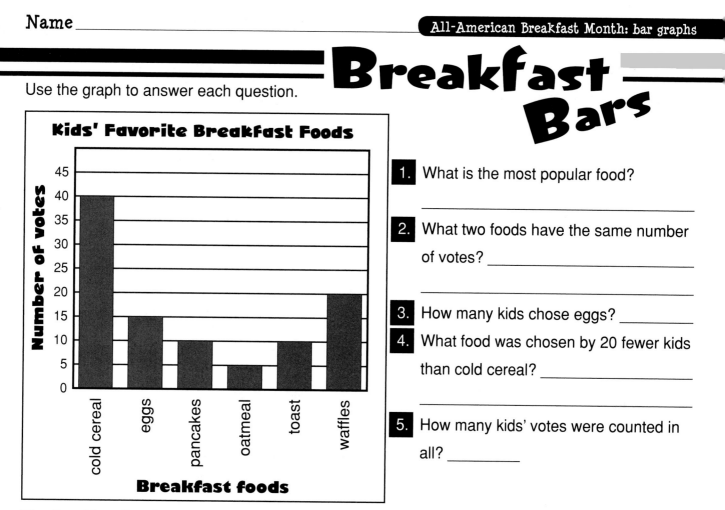

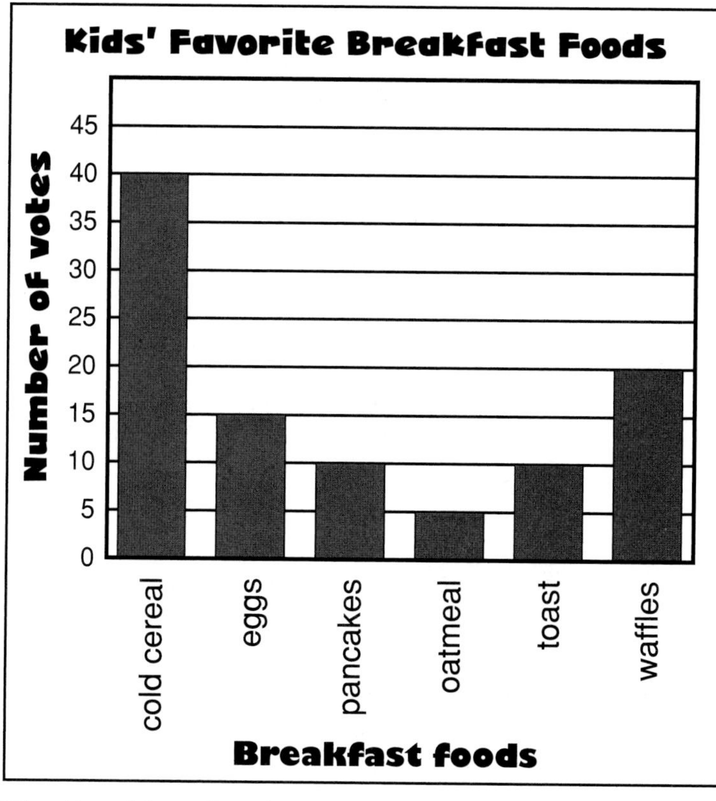

1. What is the most popular food?

   ____

2. What two foods have the same number of votes? ______________________________

   ____

3. How many kids chose eggs? __________
4. What food was chosen by 20 fewer kids than cold cereal? ______________________________

   ____

5. How many kids' votes were counted in all? __________

The Breakfast Bar Cereal Company decided to make six new cereals to sell. Complete the bar graph below using the data provided.

New Cereals

Names	Boxes Made
Apple Max	4,500
Berry Blast	2,500
Cherry Cheers	1,750
Nutty News	1,250
Peachy Puffs	3,750
Raisin Raves	3,250

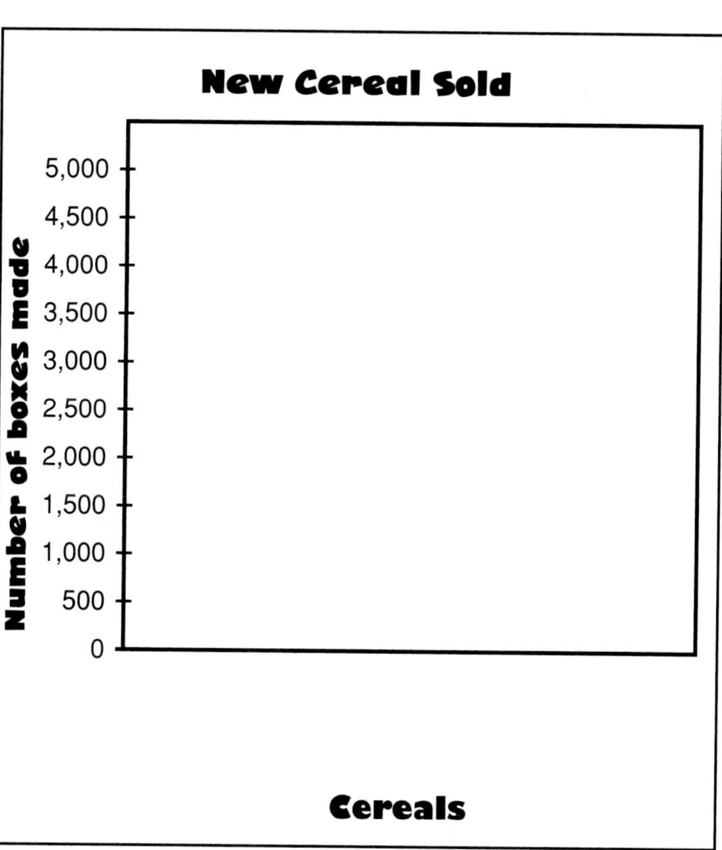

Pinwheel Pattern and Directions

Use with "Personalized Pinwheels" on page 6.

Steps:

1. Cut out the square. Starting at the corners, cut along each dotted line toward the center, stopping at the ▲. Fold the corners marked with a ● toward the center.
2. In section 1, write your name. On the folded part of section 1, draw your favorite place.
3. In section 2, list two people who are important to you. On the folded part of section 2, draw your favorite thing to do.
4. Color the inside of section 3 your favorite color. On the folded part of section 3, draw your favorite book character.
5. In section 4, write your birthday. On the folded part of section 4, draw your favorite food.
6. Push the pin through the overlapping corners and through the center of the pinwheel. Then push the pin in the side of the pencil eraser. Uncrease the folds.

Materials

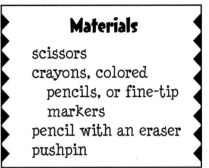

scissors
crayons, colored pencils, or fine-tip markers
pencil with an eraser
pushpin

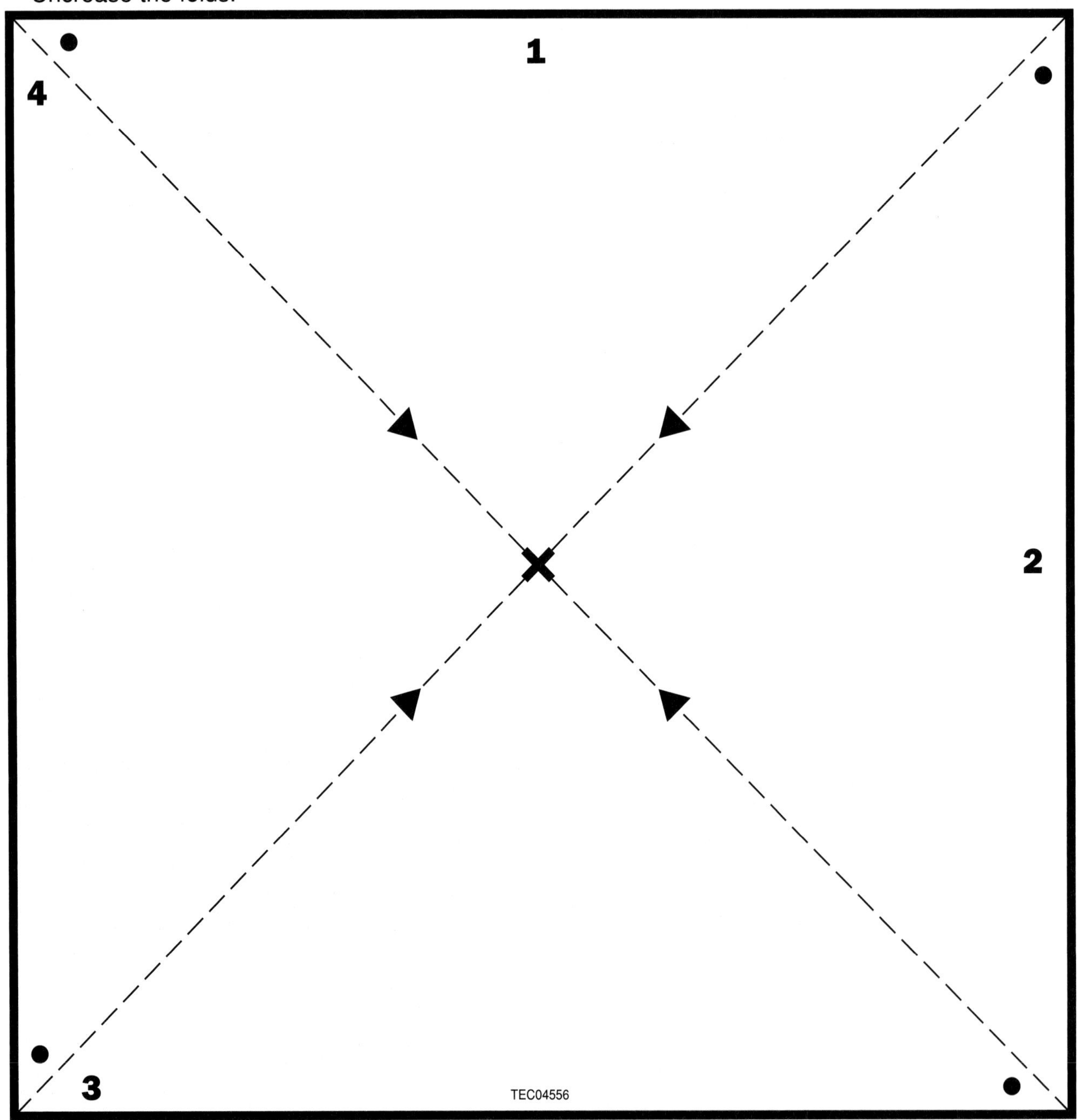

SKILLS FOR THE SEASON

Fall Fun
Reading comprehension, grammar, writing

Keep early finishers engaged by having your school librarian gather in advance several informational books about different seasonal topics. (See the list shown.) Place the books at a table along with a class supply of page 17. Have each early finisher read a book of her choice and then choose a predetermined number of activities from page 17 to complete. As she finishes an activity, she checks off the corresponding box on her copy of the page.

Leigh Anne Newsom, Cedar Road Elementary, Chesapeake, VA

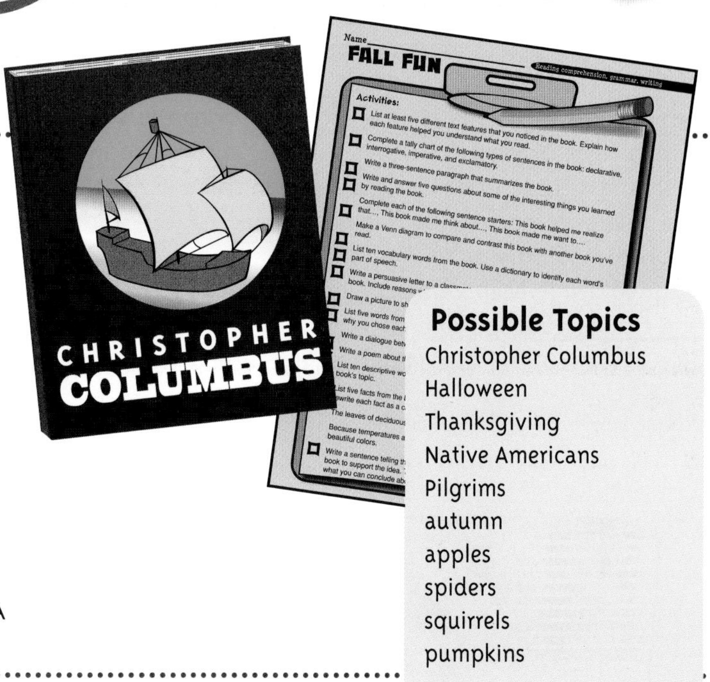

Possible Topics
Christopher Columbus
Halloween
Thanksgiving
Native Americans
Pilgrims
autumn
apples
spiders
squirrels
pumpkins

My jack-o'-lantern is tall and skinny. It has triangular eyes, straight eyebrows, and a round green nose in the middle of its face. Its smile is big, making it easy to notice its two teeth. Can you find my jack-o'-lantern?

Personalized Pumpkins
Descriptive writing

Start by having each student cut a pumpkin shape from orange construction paper. Instruct the child to decorate his cutout to look like a unique jack-o'-lantern and then write a paragraph describing it. After collecting the paragraphs and displaying the pumpkins, give each student a different child's description to match to a jack-o'-lantern. Finally, have each child check to see whether his own paragraph was correctly matched with his pumpkin!

Teresa Vilfer-Snyder, Fredericktown Intermediate, Fredericktown, OH

Exploring Circles

Relationship between circumference and diameter

Object	C	d	C ÷ d
orange	9 in.	3 in.	3
apple	8 in.	2.5 in.	3.2
pumpkin	20 in.	6.5 in.	3.08

Obtain an apple, an orange, and a small round pumpkin. Instruct volunteers to find each item's circumference by wrapping string around it and then measuring the string's length with a ruler or yardstick. Have students record the measurements in a chart. Next, cut each item in half and have volunteers use rulers to measure each item's diameter. After students add these measurements to their charts, have each child use a calculator to divide each item's circumference by its diameter. Discuss the results, guiding students to conclude that the circumference of a circle is about three times its diameter.

Joanne Sowell, Futral Road Elementary, Griffin, GA

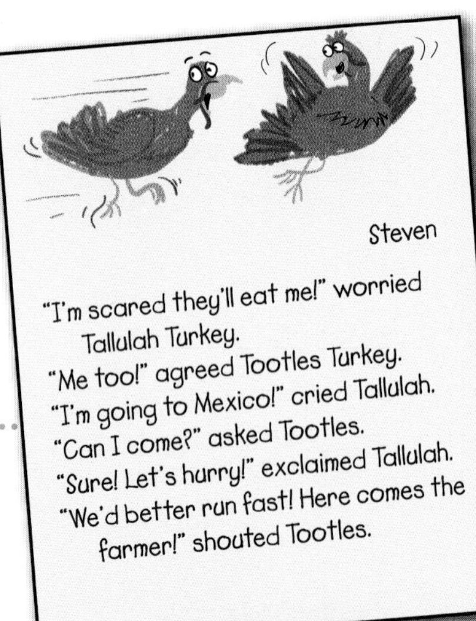
Steven

"I'm scared they'll eat me!" worried Tallulah Turkey.
"Me too!" agreed Tootles Turkey.
"I'm going to Mexico!" cried Tallulah.
"Can I come?" asked Tootles.
"Sure! Let's hurry!" exclaimed Tallulah.
"We'd better run fast! Here comes the farmer!" shouted Tootles.

Turkey Talk

Writing dialogue

Discuss with students what a turkey might feel or might say to a friend just before Thanksgiving. Have each student write a conversation between two turkeys on a farm to reveal their thoughts. After students illustrate their work, post the completed papers on a display titled "Talking Turkey."

Janel Flynn, Barnstable Horace Mann Charter School, Marstons Mills, MA

Authors Are Everywhere

Geography

To celebrate Geography Awareness Week (November 16–22), have students find out where different authors live. Instruct each student to check the book jacket of his library book or one from the class library to determine where the author is from. (If this information is not on the jacket or inside covers, have him choose a different book.) As students share the locations, tally them by state in a chart. Then display a large U.S. map so students can point out the regions the authors represent.

Kim Minafo, Apex, NC

State	Tally
New York	𝍸 I
California	𝍸 III
Delaware	I
Wyoming	I
Montana	I
South Carolina	III
Illinois	𝍸

Name ____________________

Rake It In!

Write a cause or an effect for each statement below. For the last two, write your own cause and effect statements about raking leaves.

1. **Cause:** Every leaf had fallen from the trees in the yard.
   Effect: ____________________

2. **Cause:** ____________________
   Effect: Forest and Autumn spent all day Saturday raking leaves.

3. **Cause:** Every trash bag was filled with leaves.
   Effect: ____________________

4. **Cause:** Forest and Autumn's dad decided to pitch in and help.
   Effect: ____________________

5. **Cause:** ____________________
   Effect: Forest and Autumn had fun jumping in the leaf piles.

6. **Cause:** ____________________
   Effect: Autumn and Forest had to rake the leaves into piles again.

7. **Cause:** ____________________
   Effect: ____________________

8. **Cause:** ____________________
   Effect: ____________________

Name ____________________

DOOR TO DOOR

Write and solve a multiplication problem for the phrase on each house. In each row, use your answer from the first problem to complete the next problem.

Name ____________________

A Vote For...

Use the clues to complete the chart.
Then answer the questions.

Clues

- [ ] Three homerooms voted. There are 30 students in each homeroom.
- [ ] Delphi received 24 votes in all.
- [ ] Everyone voted in Homeroom 1 and Homeroom 2. Two students were absent and unable to vote in Homeroom 3.
- [ ] In Homeroom 1, Amos got twice as many votes as Delphi. Both Bernie and Camilla got five fewer votes than Delphi.
- [ ] Homeroom 2 gave Camilla 13 votes and Bernie 11 votes. Amos got twice as many votes as the difference between Bernie and Camilla's votes. Delphi got the rest of the votes.
- [ ] In Homeroom 3, Delphi got half of the votes. Bernie got half as many votes as Delphi. Camilla got 2 votes. Amos got the remaining votes.

Election Results

	Amos	Bernie	Camilla	Delphi
Homeroom 1				
Homeroom 2				
Homeroom 3				
Total				

1. Who won the election? ____________________
2. Which homeroom do you think the winner is from?
   Why? ____________________

____

Name ____________________

A Filling Feast

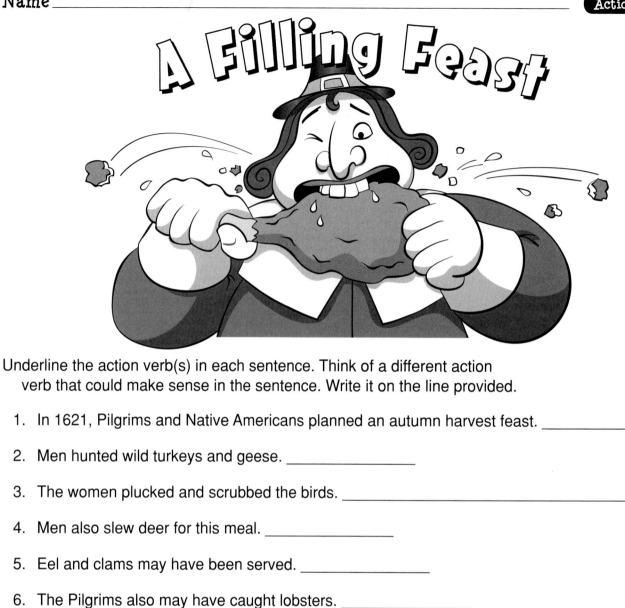

Underline the action verb(s) in each sentence. Think of a different action verb that could make sense in the sentence. Write it on the line provided.

1. In 1621, Pilgrims and Native Americans planned an autumn harvest feast. ____________
2. Men hunted wild turkeys and geese. ____________
3. The women plucked and scrubbed the birds. ____________
4. Men also slew deer for this meal. ____________
5. Eel and clams may have been served. ____________
6. The Pilgrims also may have caught lobsters. ____________
7. They may have seasoned their food with liverwort. ____________
8. Perhaps the children gathered walnuts and chestnuts. ____________
9. The children may have also picked grapes and plums for the feast. ____________
10. Someone might have pulled carrots from the ground. ____________
11. Someone else might have peeled and chopped onions. ____________
12. The Pilgrims did not bake pumpkin pies. ____________
13. They also did not boil and mash potatoes. ____________
14. They did not even eat corn on the cob, ham, or cranberry sauce. ____________
15. Even without a modern menu of food, they enjoyed a great meal! ____________

Name ______________________________

FALL FUN

Activities:

- [ ] List at least five different text features that you noticed in the book. Explain how each feature helped you understand what you read.
- [ ] Complete a tally chart of the following types of sentences in the book: declarative, interrogative, imperative, and exclamatory.
- [ ] Write a three-sentence paragraph that summarizes the book.
- [ ] Write and answer five questions about some of the interesting things you learned by reading the book.
- [ ] Complete each of the following sentence starters: This book helped me realize that..., This book made me think about..., This book made me want to....
- [ ] Make a Venn diagram to compare and contrast this book with another book you've read.
- [ ] List ten vocabulary words from the book. Use a dictionary to identify each word's part of speech.
- [ ] Write a persuasive letter to a classmate, trying to convince that person to read the book. Include reasons why you think this person would like the book.
- [ ] Draw a picture to show something you learned from the book.
- [ ] List five words from the book that you feel summarize the book's topic. Explain why you chose each word.
- [ ] Write a dialogue between two people discussing the book's topic.
- [ ] Write a poem about the book's topic.
- [ ] List ten descriptive words from the book. Use them in a paragraph to describe the book's topic.
- [ ] List five facts from the book. Then, using information you learned from the book, rewrite each fact as a cause-and-effect sentence. For example:

  The leaves of deciduous trees have beautiful colors in the fall.
  Because temperatures are cooler in the fall, the leaves of deciduous trees have beautiful colors.
- [ ] Write a sentence telling the main idea of the book. Next, list three details from the book to support the idea. Then, based on the details, write a sentence explaining what you can conclude about the main idea.

Note to the teacher: Use with "Fall Fun" on page 11.

SKILLS FOR THE SEASON

Reindeer Glyph

Math concept review

Help students review important math skills with this seasonal glyph! Give each child a copy of page 23. Have the student cut the page apart and follow the directions to create a one-of-a-kind reindeer. Then have her finish coloring her reindeer and mount it on construction paper to display in the room.

Mary Stinchfield, Northbridge Middle School, Whitinsville, MA

Name Mary

Reindeer Glyph Directions

Complete each step to create your reindeer.

Step 1: Add the digits in your birthdate to find the number of prongs to add to each antler. (For example, if you were born on the 12th of your birth month, add the digits as follows: $1 + 2 = 3$.)

Step 2: Assume $x = 2$. Solve each problem. Circle the answer closest to your age to find out the color of your reindeer's eyes.
$3x + 3$ = green $3x + 4$ = black $3x + 5$ = brown $3x + 6$ = blue

Step 3: Circle the statement that is true about your age to find out what to draw on your reindeer's neck.
My age is a multiple of 2.—bells
My age is not a multiple of 2.—bow

Step 4: Circle the statement that is true about your first name to find out the color of your reindeer's nose.
The number of letters in my first name is divisible by 3.—green
The number of letters in my first name is not divisible by 3.—red

Step 5: If A = 1, B = 2, C = 3, etc., add the letters in your last name to find out how to draw the tail on your reindeer.
The total is divisible by 5.—tail pointed up
The total is not divisible by 5.—tail pointed down

Step 6: Write your birthday as a decimal multiplication problem to find out how to draw your reindeer's legs. (Example: October 2, 1998 = 10.2×0.98)
The product is between 0 and 3.—1 bent leg
The product is greater than 3 but less than 6.—2 bent legs
The product is between six and 9.—3 bent legs
The product is greater than 9.—4 bent legs

Seasonal Souvenirs

Studying countries or states

In advance, make several copies of the gift tag patterns on page 24. Give each pair of students three or four tags. The partners label each tag to themselves and from a different state or country. After the partners research each state or country and discover its products, they then select one item they would like to receive as a holiday present. They draw and label a picture of that object on the back of the matching gift tag. If desired, attach a ribbon to each tag and hang the tags on a classroom Christmas tree or wreath.

Julie Alarie, Williston, VT

TO: Julie and Taylor
FROM: Brazil

Pickup truck

Color Code

square = red
trapezoid = orange
parallelogram = yellow
equilateral triangle = green
isosceles triangle = blue

Geometric Blizzard

Polygons

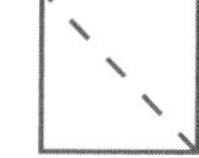

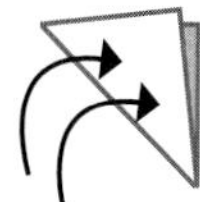

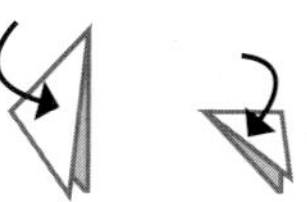

Begin this fun activity by displaying the list of polygons shown in the color code. Have each child fold a square sheet of unlined paper as shown. Then have him draw on each edge of the folded paper half of each shape listed. He may draw as many shapes as he likes as long as he includes at least one of each. After the child cuts out each shape and unfolds his resulting snowflake, have him outline each type of shape according to the color code.

Jennifer Otter, Oak Ridge, NC

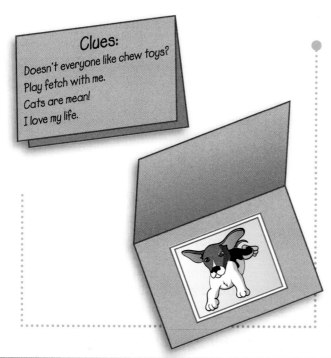

Clues:
Doesn't everyone like chew toys?
Play fetch with me.
Cats are mean!
I love my life.

Dr. Dolittle's Sentences

Types of sentences

To beat the mid-winter doldrums, celebrate the January 14 birthday of Hugh Lofting, the creator of Doctor Dolittle. Have each student secretly cut out a magazine picture of an animal, glue the picture to the bottom half of a sheet of construction paper, and then fold over the top of the page as shown. Next, have the student write on the outside of her folded paper four clues, one for each type of sentence, the animal might give about itself. Finally, have the student read the clues aloud and challenge classmates to identify her animal. For an added challenge, have students write clues as simple, compound, and complex sentences.

Julie Alarie, Williston, VT

Halfway Day

Introducing fractions

Try this alternative to the 100th Day of school to get students excited about fractions. On the day that is exactly halfway through the school year, celebrate Halfway Day by centering all the day's activities around the theme of "half." For example, have students write half of an assignment in manuscript and the other half in cursive. Give students the first half of each spelling word and have them complete the second half. Or have students pair up on assignments, with one child writing the first half of each answer and the other writing the second half. For a bit of added fun, allow students to dress up for Halfway Day by wearing one half dressy clothes and one half casual clothes.

Lauren Mahan, Lt. Peter M. Hansen School, Canton, MA

Computer

Name ____________________ **Volume**

Whose Gifts?

Find the volume of each package. Then write a matching name on each gift tag.

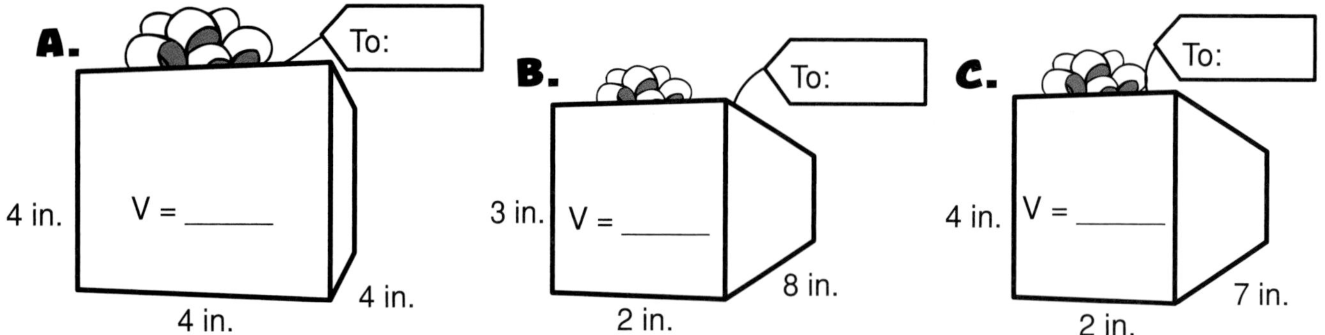

D. To:
5 in. V = ______
6 in.
4 in.

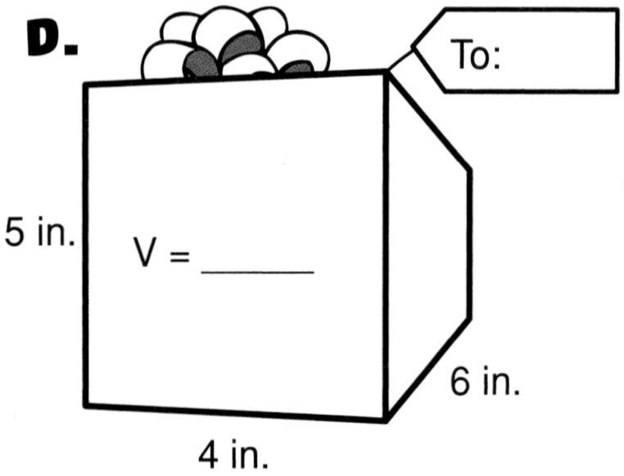

E. To:
3 in. V = ______
4 in.
3 in.

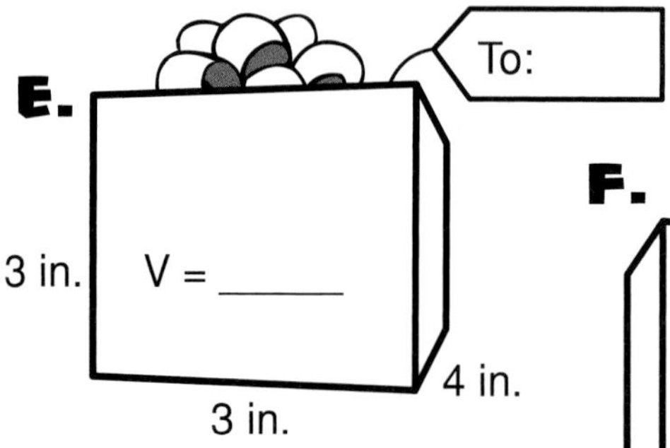

F. To:
V = ______
5 in.
2 in.
5 in.

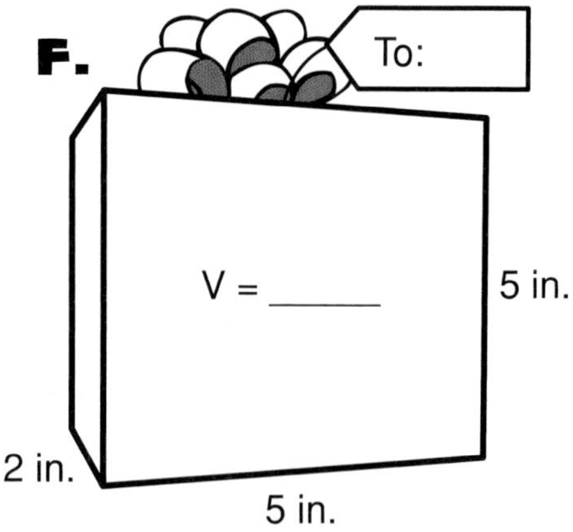

G. To:
V = ______
4 in.
5 in.
3 in.

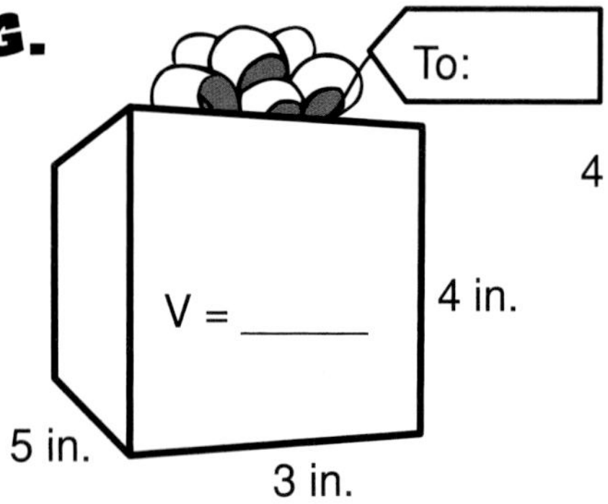

H. To:
V = ______
4 in.
3 in.
2 in.

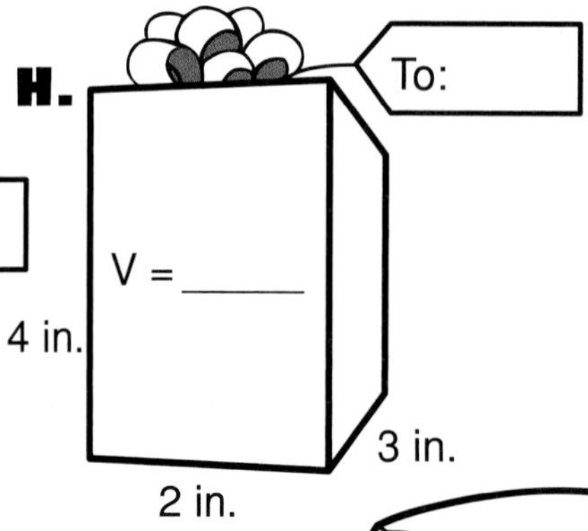

I. To:
5 in. V = ______
6 in.
1 in.

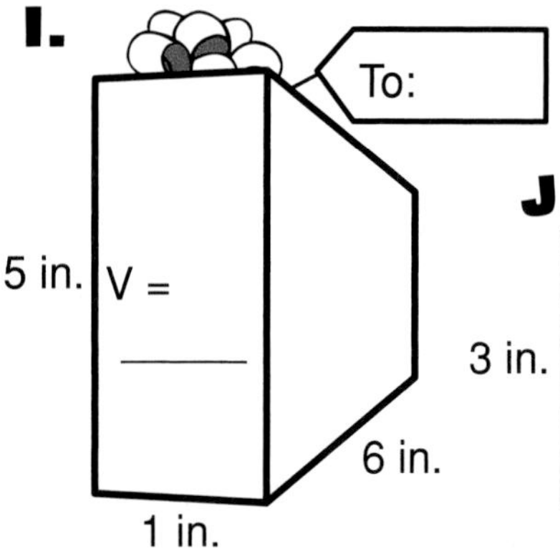

J. To:
3 in. V = ______
5 in.
3 in.

Amy	36 in.^{3}
Matt	48 in.^{3}
Jen	64 in.^{3}
Todd	30 in.^{3}
Jeff	45 in.^{3}
Ian	50 in.^{3}
Will	60 in.^{3}
Brad	56 in.^{3}
Kel	120 in.^{3}
Meg	24 in.^{3}

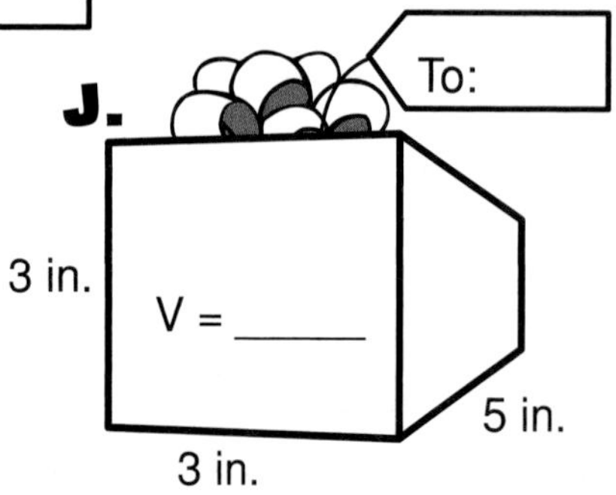

Name ____________________

The Countdown Begins!

10, 9, 8, 7, 6...

Graph each set of ordered pairs. Connect each plot in order in each set. Find the mistake in each set and then correct it.

Set 5
Start at (23, 6)

(28, 6)
(29, 10)
(29, 4)
(28, 3)
(27, 3)
(29, 0)
(27, 0)
(25, 3)
(25, 0)
(23, 0)
(23, 6)

Set 4
Start at (0, 6)

(3, 6)
(3, 4)
(4, 4)
(4, 7)
(7, 6)
(7, 3)
(6, 2)
(4, 2)
(4, 0)
(3, 0)
(3, 2)
(1, 2)
(0, 3)
(0, 6)

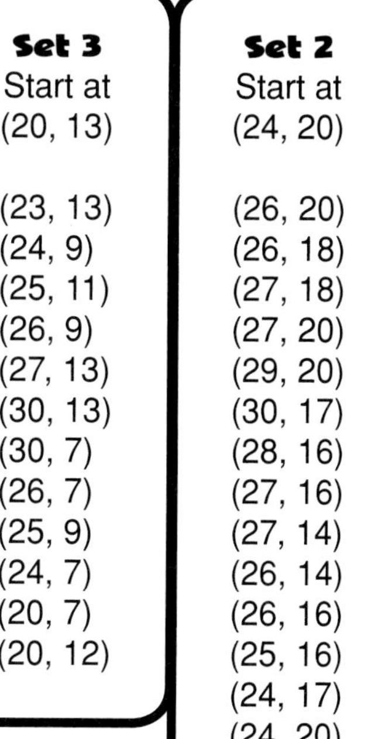

Set 3
Start at (20, 13)

(23, 13)
(24, 9)
(25, 11)
(26, 9)
(27, 13)
(30, 13)
(30, 7)
(26, 7)
(25, 9)
(24, 7)
(20, 7)
(20, 12)

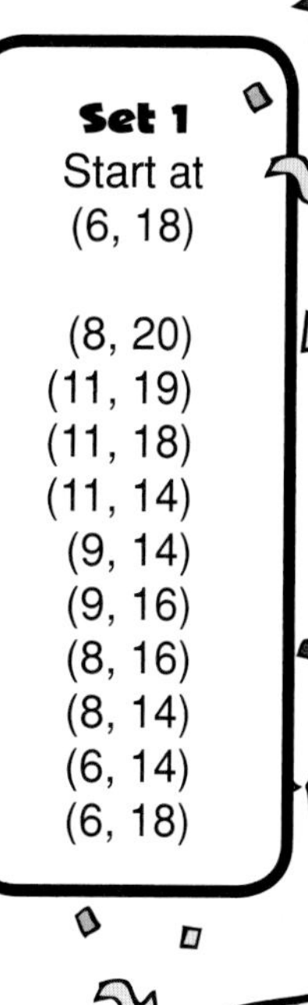

Set 2
Start at (24, 20)

(26, 20)
(26, 18)
(27, 18)
(27, 20)
(29, 20)
(30, 17)
(28, 16)
(27, 16)
(27, 14)
(26, 14)
(26, 16)
(25, 16)
(24, 17)
(24, 20)

Set 1
Start at (6, 18)

(8, 20)
(11, 19)
(11, 18)
(11, 14)
(9, 14)
(9, 16)
(8, 16)
(8, 14)
(6, 14)
(6, 18)

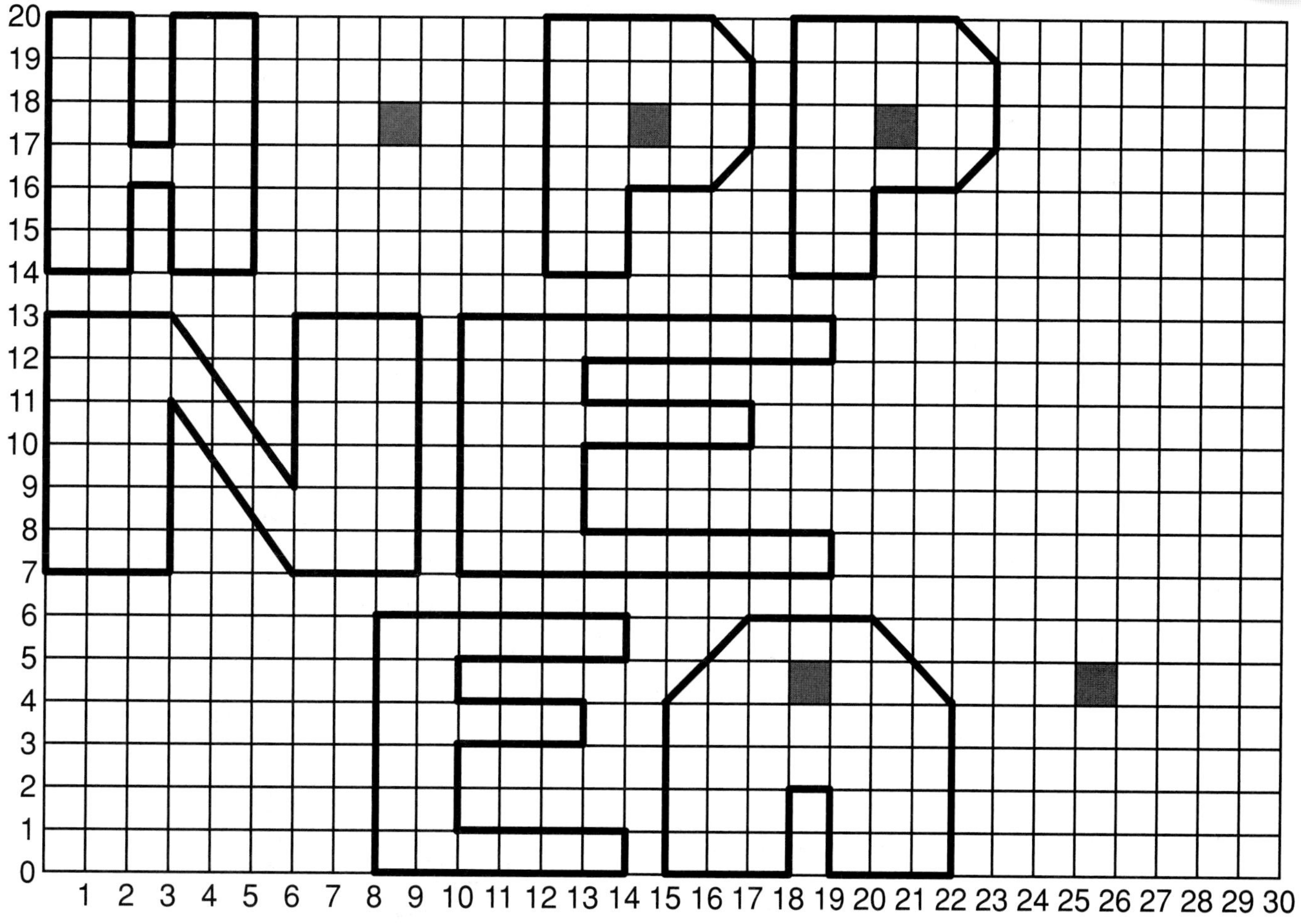

Name ______________________________

Snow School

Before reading the story, write a word in each blank. Then read the story you created. Underline each simile once and each metaphor twice.

One morning as I walked to school, I noticed something like

a(n) ____________________ (object) in a(n) ____________________ (place).

Snow began to fall! It seemed that with every block I passed, the snow began to fall harder and quicker. It was coming down as fast as

a(n) ____________________ (animal) at a track race. When I reached the

playground, it was a(n) ____________________ (place) made of snow.

By this time I was a really cold ____________________ (animal) and couldn't

wait to get inside the school building. Like a(n) ____________________ (vehicle),

I ran to the front door. Then I saw the most amazing thing. The entire school,

inside and out, was a snow-covered ____________________ (imaginary place).

The principal was dressed in so many layers of clothing, he was like a(n)

____________________ (animal). The hallway was a(n) ____________________ (name of a ride)

filled with kids. Each one had a sled and was taking turns sledding down the hallway. They were

like a bunch of ____________________ (animals) at the North Pole.

Suddenly, in a loud booming voice, the principal announced, "Go home! School is closed!" Every student just continued playing in the hallway. No one wanted to go home! We all stayed at school for hours. When the sky was a dark ____________________ (piece of clothing), we finally decided to head home.

Name ______________________

Reindeer Glyph Directions

Complete each step to create your reindeer.

Step 1: Add the digits in your birthdate to find the number of prongs to add to each antler. (For example, if you were born on the 12th of your birth month, add the digits as follows: 1 + 2 = 3.)

Step 2: Assume $x = 2$. Solve each problem. Circle the answer closest to your age to find out the color of your reindeer's eyes.

$3x + 3$ = green $3x + 4$ = black $3x + 5$ = brown $3x + 6$ = blue

Step 3: Circle the statement that is true about your age to find out what to draw on your reindeer's neck.

My age is a multiple of 2.—bells
My age is not a multiple of 2.—bow

Step 4: Circle the statement that is true about your first name to find out the color of your reindeer's nose.

The number of letters in my first name is divisible by 3.—green
The number of letters in my first name is not divisible by 3.—red

Step 5: If A = 1, B = 2, C = 3, etc., add the letters in your last name to find out how to draw the tail on your reindeer.

The total is divisible by 5.—tail pointed up
The total is not divisible by 5.—tail pointed down

Step 6: Write your birthday as a decimal multiplication problem to find out how to draw your reindeer's legs. (Example: October 2, 1998 = 10.2 x 0.98)

The product is between 0 and 3.—1 bent leg
The product is greater than 3 but less than 6.—2 bent legs
The product is between six and 9.—3 bent legs
The product is greater than 9.—4 bent legs

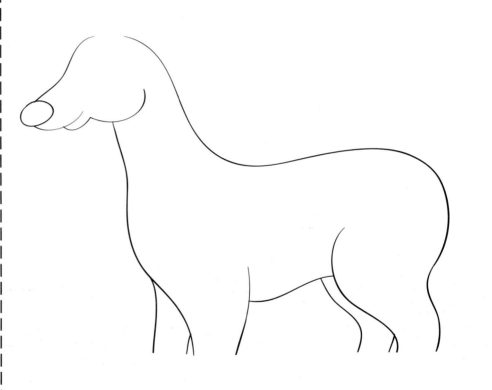

Note to the teacher: Use with "Reindeer Glyph" on page 18.

Name ______________________

Gift Tag Patterns

Use with "Seasonal Souvenirs" on page 18.

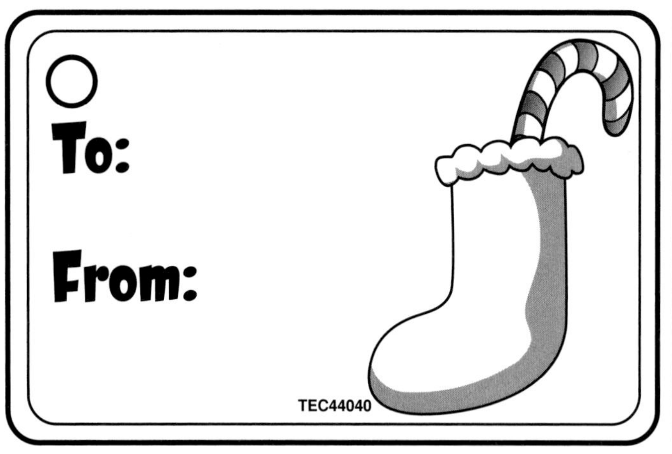

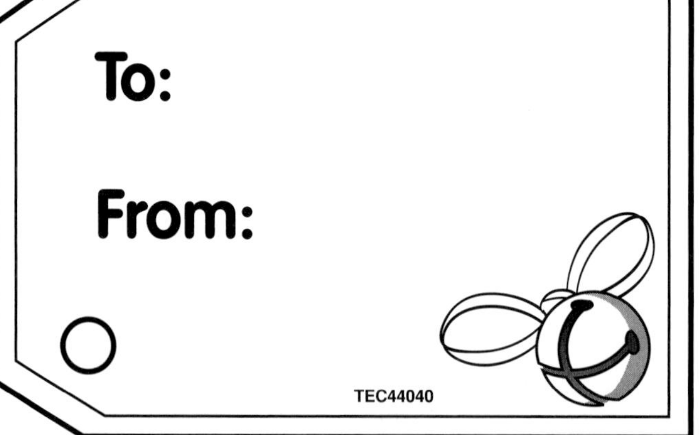

SKILLS FOR THE SEASON

Let's Talk!
Oral presentations

Host a classroom talk show to celebrate Black History Month. Have each child choose a famous Black American from a copy of the list on page 31 and then research her person to answer questions such as those shown. When each child is finished, assume the role of a talk show host. Then interview each child, in turn, as she pretends to be her chosen person.

Kristen Proehl, Westwood Elementary, Greenwood, IN

Questions

- When and where were you born?
- Where did you go to school?
- When you were growing up, what was your family like?
- What are your interests?
- Are you married? Do you have any children? If so, tell us about them.
- What did you do to become famous?

$2^2 + 2 \times 2 - 1 =$

$4 + 2 \times 2 - 1 =$

$4 + 4 - 1 =$

$8 - 1 = 7$

An Orderly Groundhog
Order of operations

For some Groundhog Day (February 2) fun, have each child use only twos to write a math problem on the outside of a copy of the groundhog card from page 31. Direct him to include in his problem parentheses, exponents, multiplication, division, addition, and subtraction. Then have him color the illustration, cut out the card, fold it as shown, and solve his problem inside. As time permits, have students trade groundhog cards and solve each other's problems.

Jennifer Otter
Oak Ridge, NC

TIP
You can also use the groundhog card for a writing activity.

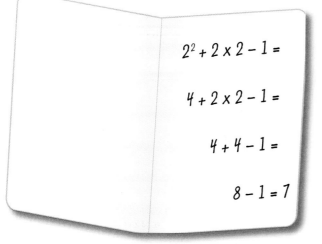

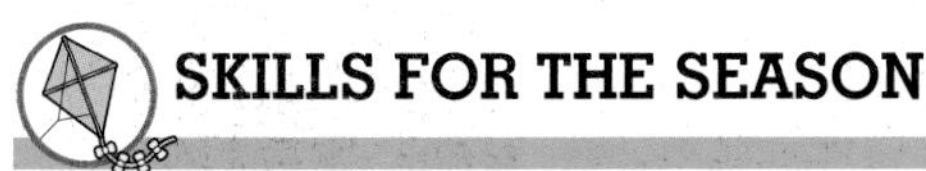

Is That a Fact?

Identifying facts and opinions

In honor of Presidents' Day (the third Monday in February), make a copy of the 20 president-related statements on page 32. Then have each student number a sheet of paper from 1 to 20. Read the statements aloud one at a time, pausing for each child to write an *F* on her paper if the statement is a fact or an *O* if it is an opinion. Then discuss the correct answers.

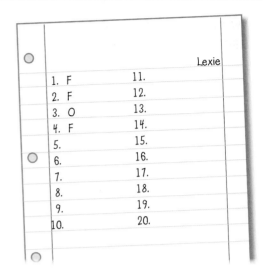

Lexie

1. F
2. F
3. O
4. F
5.
6.
7.
8.
9.
10.
11.
12.
13.
14.
15.
16.
17.
18.
19.
20.

A Historical Quilt

Writing a report

This March project results in a unique National Women's History Month display. Have each child research a different woman from the list on page 32. Direct him to write a brief report about the woman's life and draw a portrait of her. Then have him glue his report and portrait to a nine-inch construction paper square and add details that represent stitching. Display the completed projects so they look like a quilt.

Elizabeth Adasse and Jennifer Nigro
P.S. 499 Queens College School for Math, Science, and Technology
Flushing, NY

Where's the Gold?

Prepositional phrases

Give students practice with prepositions this St. Patrick's Day by having them write stories about a leprechaun who hides a pot of gold. Direct each writer to use prepositional phrases to provide specific details about where the leprechaun's gold is hidden. Also instruct him to underline the prepositional phrases he uses. Then invite him to share his story with the class.

Jennifer Otter, Oak Ridge, NC

Micah

Larry the Leprechaun wanted the perfect hiding place for his huge pot of gold. First, he tried hiding it on top of the refrigerator, but the pot was too big. Then he tried hiding it underneath his bed, but it wouldn't fit there either. He finally decided to hide his pot of gold in his garage. He put it in a corner behind his enormous workbench where nobody could see it. He figured if anyone came looking for his gold, they would search throughout his house first and would not even think to look in the garage. Larry really hoped his gold was in a safe place!

Name ____

Opposites Attract

Write each pair of antonyms on the lines. Color the heart half next to each word you use. Some words will not be used.

frequent
bravery
permanent
vague
natural
common
cowardice
accept
refuse
artificial
love
safety
temporary
departure
rare
seldom
danger
arrival
absent
you

1. ______________________________
2. ______________________________
3. ______________________________
4. ______________________________
5. ______________________________
6. ______________________________
7. ______________________________
8. ______________________________
9. ______________________________
10. ______________________________
11. ______________________________
12. ______________________________

present
stingy
jolly
generous
serious
ton
clear

Be Mine

What does the elephant's valentine say?

To find out, write each unused word from above in order on the lines below.

I __________ __________ a __________!

Name ____________________

PRESIDENTIAL TRIVIA

Read each sentence. Color the symbol next to the best meaning of the boldfaced word.

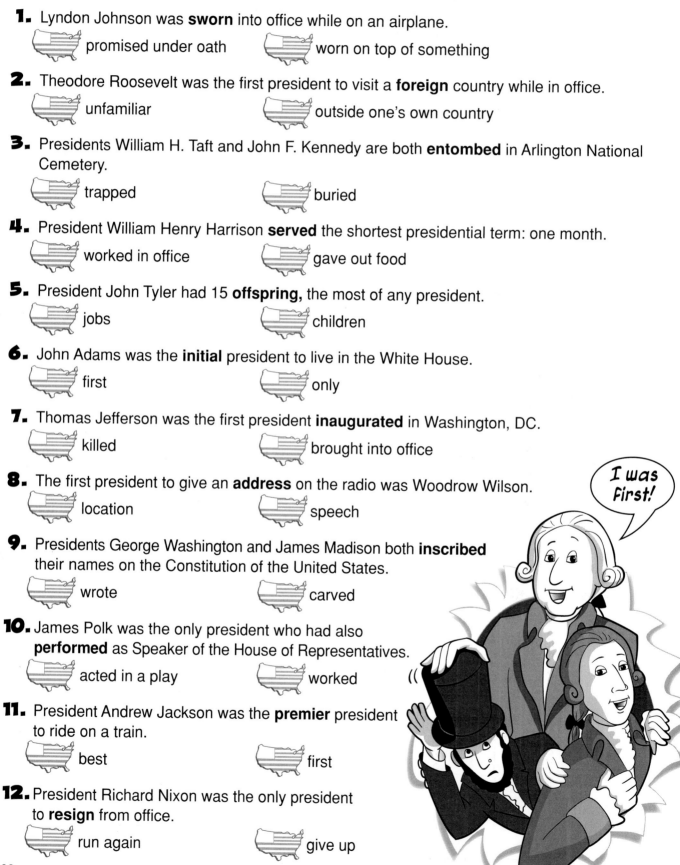

1. Lyndon Johnson was **sworn** into office while on an airplane.
- promised under oath
- worn on top of something

2. Theodore Roosevelt was the first president to visit a **foreign** country while in office.
- unfamiliar
- outside one's own country

3. Presidents William H. Taft and John F. Kennedy are both **entombed** in Arlington National Cemetery.
- trapped
- buried

4. President William Henry Harrison **served** the shortest presidential term: one month.
- worked in office
- gave out food

5. President John Tyler had 15 **offspring,** the most of any president.
- jobs
- children

6. John Adams was the **initial** president to live in the White House.
- first
- only

7. Thomas Jefferson was the first president **inaugurated** in Washington, DC.

- killed
- brought into office

8. The first president to give an **address** on the radio was Woodrow Wilson.
- location
- speech

9. Presidents George Washington and James Madison both **inscribed** their names on the Constitution of the United States.
- wrote
- carved

10. James Polk was the only president who had also **performed** as Speaker of the House of Representatives.
- acted in a play
- worked

11. President Andrew Jackson was the **premier** president to ride on a train.

- best
- first

12. President Richard Nixon was the only president to **resign** from office.

- run again
- give up

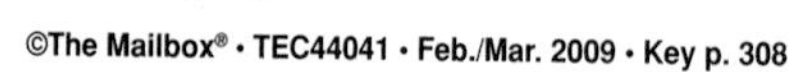

Name ____________________

Reaching the Rainbow

Draw a factor rainbow for each number shown. Color the leprechaun's hat if the number on it is a prime number.

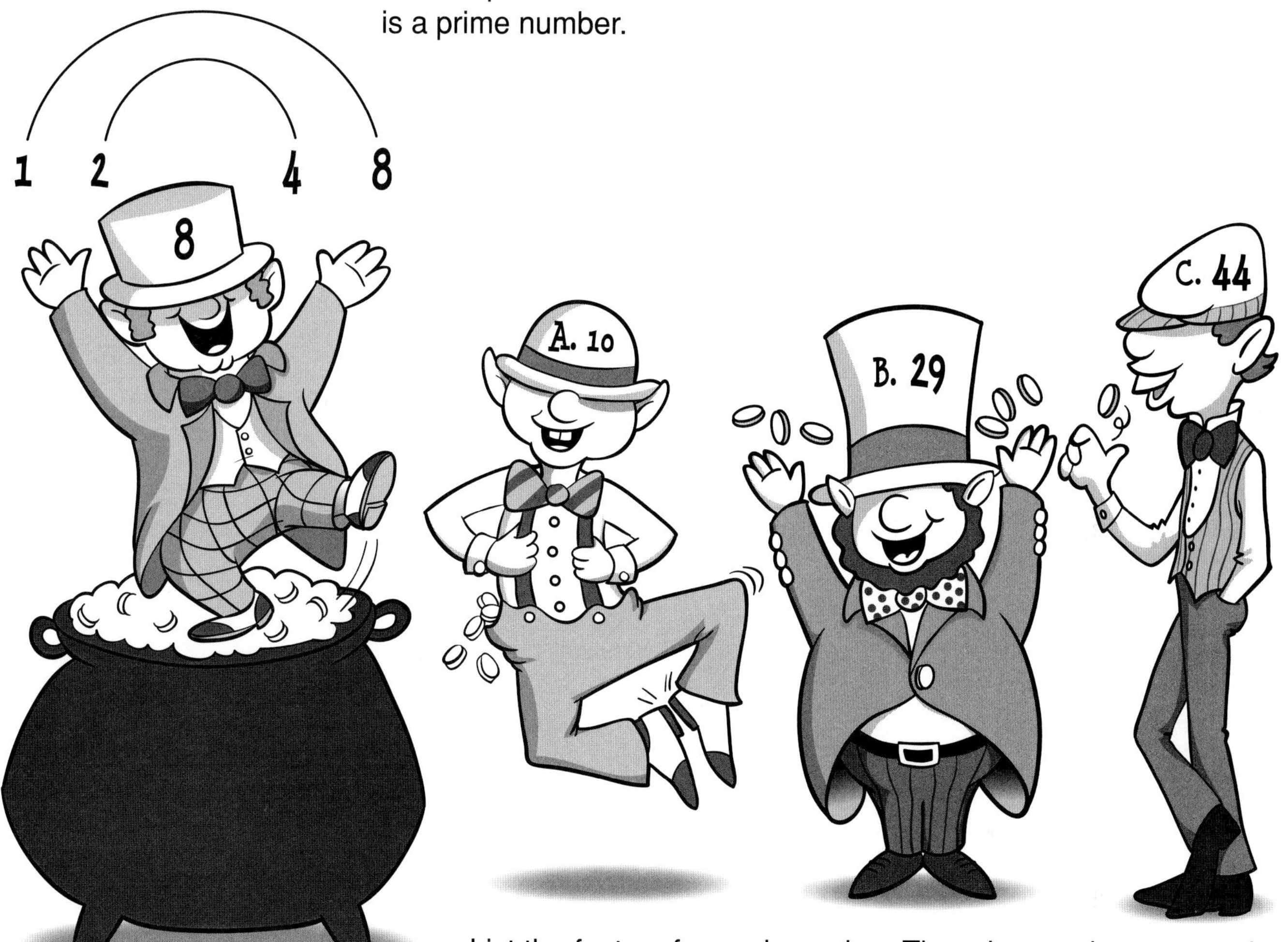

List the factors for each number. Then draw a clover around the greatest common factor of each number pair.

D.		E.		F.		G.		H.		I.	
12	36	50	27	40	16	25	54	31	62	46	24

Name ______________________________

Windy Conditions

Measure to the nearest $\frac{1}{2}$ inch.

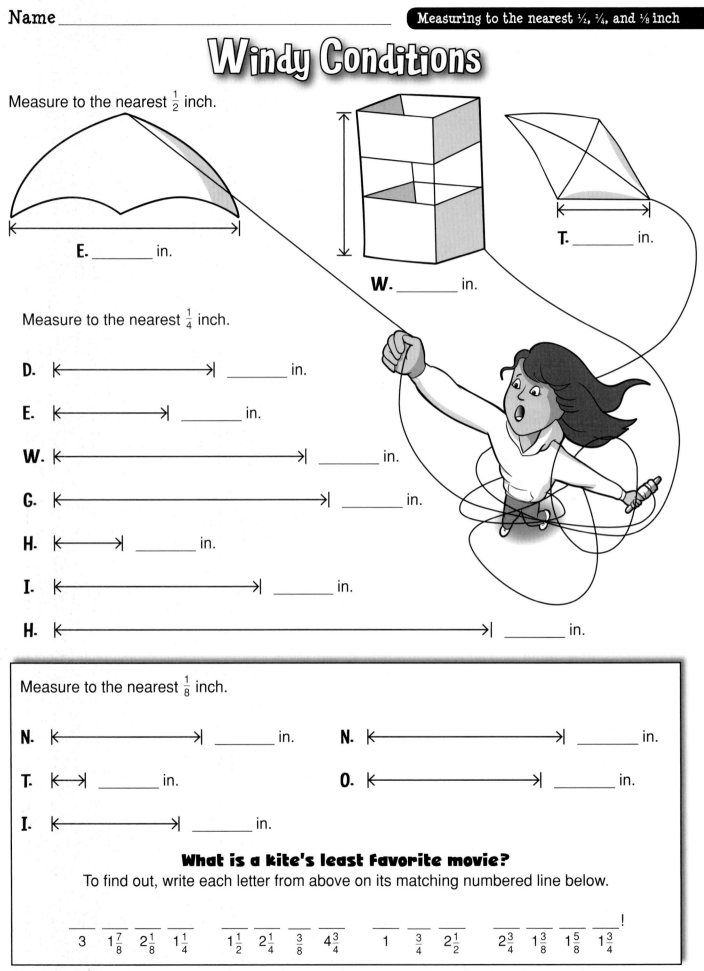

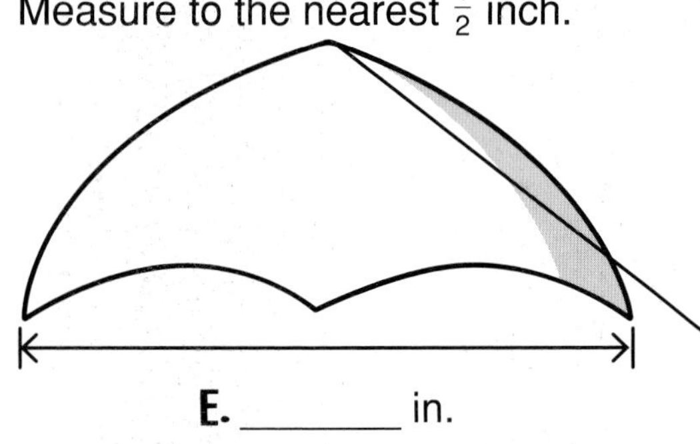

E. ______ in.

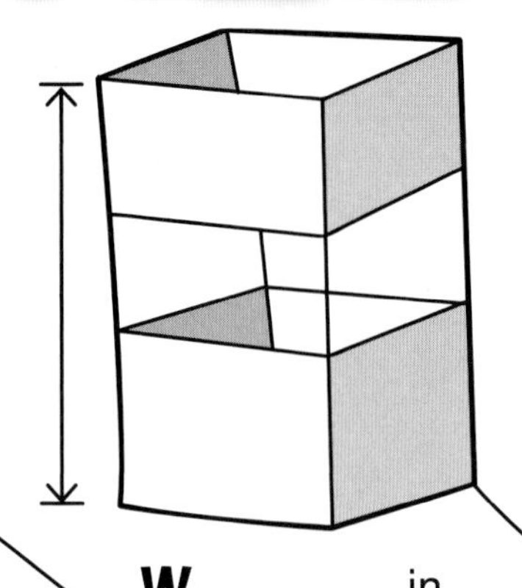

W. ______ in.

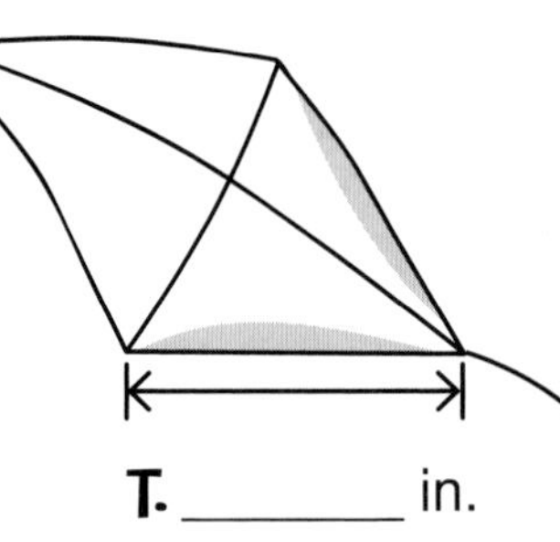

T. ______ in.

Measure to the nearest $\frac{1}{4}$ inch.

D. 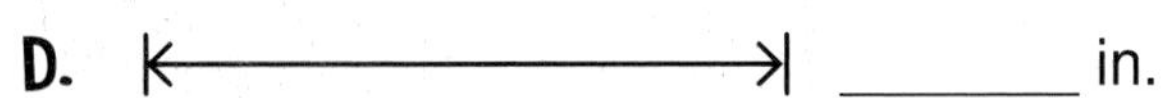 ______ in.

E.  ______ in.

W. 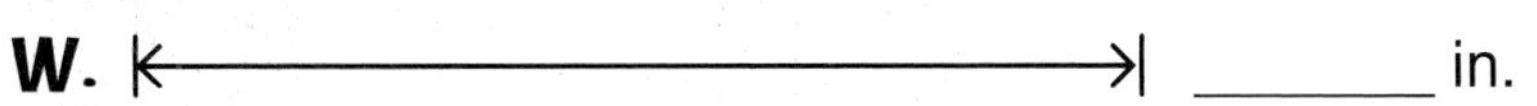 ______ in.

G. ______ in.

H. 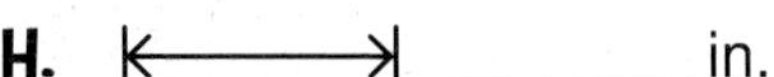 ______ in.

I. ______ in.

H. ______ in.

Measure to the nearest $\frac{1}{8}$ inch.

N. ______ in.

N. ______ in.

T. ______ in.

O. ______ in.

I. ______ in.

What is a kite's least favorite movie?

To find out, write each letter from above on its matching numbered line below.

___ ___ ___ ___   ___ ___ ___ ___   ___ ___ ___   ___ ___ ___ ___!

3 $1\frac{7}{8}$ $2\frac{1}{8}$ $1\frac{1}{4}$ $1\frac{1}{2}$ $2\frac{1}{4}$ $\frac{3}{8}$ $4\frac{3}{4}$ 1 $\frac{3}{4}$ $2\frac{1}{2}$ $2\frac{3}{4}$ $1\frac{3}{8}$ $1\frac{5}{8}$ $1\frac{3}{4}$

Groundhog Card

Use with "An Orderly Groundhog" on page 25.

TEC44041

Famous Black Americans

Hank Aaron
Kareem Abdul-Jabbar
Maya Angelou
Louis Armstrong
Halle Berry
Guion S. Bluford Jr.
George Washington Carver
Bill Cosby
Miles Davis
Frederick Douglass
Morgan Freeman
Mae C. Jemison
Barbara Jordan
Michael Jordan
Jackie Joyner-Kersee
Martin Luther King Jr.
Thurgood Marshall
Willie Mays
Toni Morrison
Shaquille O'Neal
Rosa Parks
Colin Powell
Jackie Robinson
Will Smith
Harriet Tubman
Booker T. Washington
Denzel Washington
Oprah Winfrey
Tiger Woods
Andrew Jackson Young Jr.

Note to the teacher: Use with "Let's Talk!" on page 25.

Presidential Fact or Opinion?

1. George Washington's false teeth were made of ivory and other materials.
2. John Adams worked from 4 AM until 10 PM every day.
3. The most magnificent home in America was designed by Thomas Jefferson.
4. James Madison was the first president to wear long pants.
5. James Monroe was the first president to often be seen in public without a wig.
6. John Quincy Adams had both a pet alligator and a pool table in the White House.
7. Andrew Jackson should not have been elected president.
8. Martin Van Buren was the first president to be born as an American citizen.
9. William Henry Harrison was too stubborn to wear a coat during his inauguration speech.
10. John Tyler was probably not a good public speaker.
11. James K. Polk stretched the U.S. border from the Atlantic to the Pacific.
12. Zachary Taylor was called "Old Rough and Ready."
13. Millard Fillmore was a terrible cook.
14. Franklin Pierce was the most handsome president.
15. James Buchanan had a herd of elephants.
16. Abraham Lincoln received over 10,000 death threats.
17. Abraham Lincoln was a much better president than Andrew Johnson.
18. Ulysses S. Grant was the greatest general ever.
19. Rutherford B. Hayes was the first president to use a telephone.
20. James Garfield was more important after he died.

Note to the teacher: Use with "Is That a Fact?" on page 26.

Famous American Women

Jane Addams
Susan B. Anthony
Clara Barton
Halle Berry
Mary McLeod Bethune
Amelia Earhart
Florence Griffith Joyner
Helen Keller
Dolley Madison
Toni Morrison
Annie Oakley
Sandra Day O'Connor
Rosa Parks
Condoleezza Rice
Sally Ride
Betsy Ross
Sojourner Truth
Harriet Tubman
Venus Williams
Oprah Winfrey
Kristi Yamaguchi

 Note to the teacher: Use with "A Historical Quilt" on page 26.

SKILLS FOR THE SEASON

Roll a Person, Place, or Thing!

Writing sentences, nouns

April is National Humor Month. To celebrate, give each pair of students two dice and a copy of page 40. Have the partners follow the directions on the page to write a silly sentence about the corresponding person, place, and thing they circled. Allow students to continue rolling the dice and writing sentences for several minutes. Then provide time for the partners to share their sentences with the class. Expect giggles!

VaReane Heese, Springfield Elementary, Omaha, NE

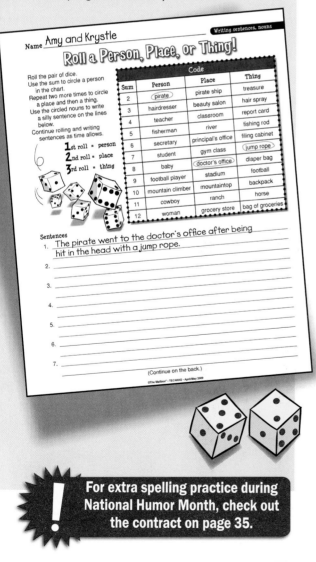

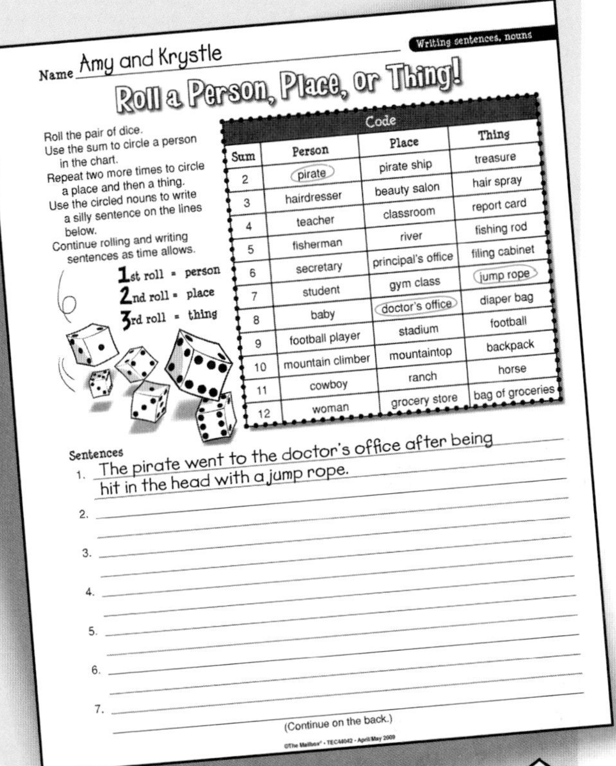

Name Amy and Krystle

Writing sentences, nouns

Roll a Person, Place, or Thing!

Roll the pair of dice.
Use the sum to circle a person in the chart.
Repeat two more times to circle a place and then a thing.
Use the circled nouns to write a silly sentence on the lines below.
Continue rolling and writing sentences as time allows.

1st roll = person
2nd roll = place
3rd roll = thing

Code

Sum	Person	Place	Thing
2	(pirate)	pirate ship	treasure
3	hairdresser	beauty salon	hair spray
4	teacher	classroom	report card
5	fisherman	river	fishing rod
6	secretary	principal's office	filing cabinet
7	student	gym class	(jump rope)
8	baby	(doctor's office)	diaper bag
9	football player	stadium	football
10	mountain climber	mountaintop	backpack
11	cowboy	ranch	horse
12	woman	grocery store	bag of groceries

Sentences

1. The pirate went to the doctor's office after being hit in the head with a jump rope.
2.
3.
4.
5.
6.
7.

(Continue on the back.)

©The Mailbox® • TEC44042 • April/May 2009

You Ought to Be in Pictures!
Symmetrical Snapshots

A Fine "A-fair"!

Reviewing math skills

Celebrate Mathematics Awareness Month this April with a simple math fair! Have each student select a math topic that has been covered during the school year. Then have the student create a display that explains the topic in a creative way. Once all projects are complete, invite other classes to visit your fair and hear students explain their displays.

Isobel L. Livingstone, Rahway, NJ

For extra spelling practice during National Humor Month, check out the contract on page 35.

You're a Lifesaver!

Compound and complex sentences

Practice sentence skills to celebrate Mother's Day this year. Have each student make a list of favorite candy bars and a second list of other favorite candies. Direct her to use three candy bar names in separate compound sentences to describe her mother or another older friend or relative. Then have her use the names of three candies from the second list in separate complex sentences to describe the same person. After she has written the six sentences, have her design a card to look like a piece of candy she mentioned. Then have her copy all six sentences inside the card to give to her mom for Mother's Day.

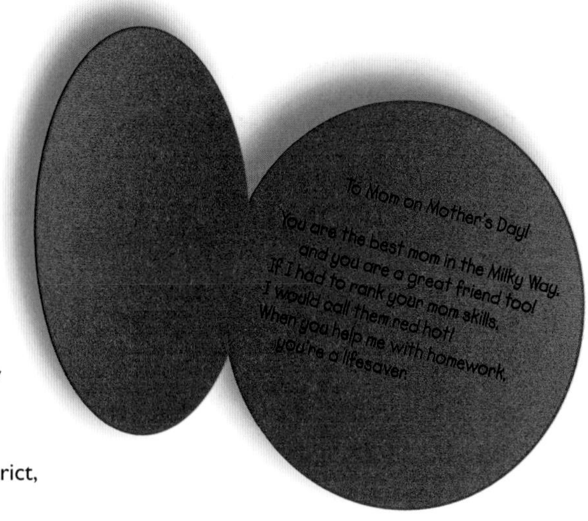
To Mom on Mother's Day!
You are the best mom in the Milky Way,
and you are a great friend too!
If I had to rank your mom skills,
I would call them red hot!
When you help me with homework,
you're a lifesaver.

adapted from an idea by Renee Cooperman, Kenmore Town of Tonawanda School District, Kenmore, NY

______________ Is Number One!

______________ hide.
______________ fun.
______________ pride.
She is number one!

______________ days.
______________ sun.
______________ obeys.
She is number one!

______________ seen.
______________ ton.
______________ routine.
She is number one!

She's Number One!

Writing poetry

Celebrate National Poetry Month in April or Teacher Appreciation Week in May with this fun activity! To begin, have each student fold two sheets of paper in half and then glue them together as shown. On another sheet of paper, have each student list things she likes about her favorite teacher. Display the poem format shown. Then have the student write each section on a different page of the booklet, using ideas from her list in the blanks. Have the student decorate the booklet before giving it to her favorite teacher.

Cinco de Mayo Math

Expressions

To celebrate Cinco de Mayo, have each student create a large sombrero cutout similar to the one shown. Have him program the hat with a three- or four-digit multiple of five. Then provide each child with several red, green, and white paper circles. Have the student program each circle with an expression that equals the number on his hat. Encourage him to use at least one fraction and one decimal. Finally, have students glue their expressions to the bottom of their hats as shown. Post the completed sombreros around the room.

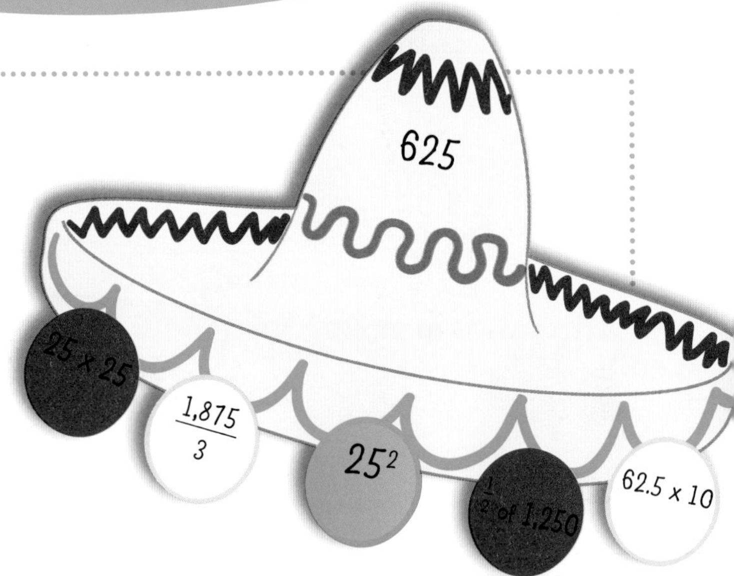
625
25 x 25
1,875 / 3
25²
½ of 1,250
62.5 x 10

Name ____

Side-Splitting Spelling

Draw a star next to your assigned spelling list. Then write the number of activities you must complete in the space provided.

What do you call a funny chicken?
A "comedi-hen"!

List A	List B
joy	smirk
glee	chuckle
jest	giggle
gag	laugh
joke	droll
grin	mirth
smile	amuse
quip	antic
humor	comic
cheer	happiness
prank	entertain

List C

monkeyshines	hilarious	diversion	merriment
jocularity	buffoonery	humorous	facetious
joviality	witticism	comical	

I must complete _____ activities.

Ha! Ha! Ha!

1. Use at least three of your words to write a funny joke for the "comedi-hen" to tell to her friends.
2. Cut out a comic strip from the newspaper. Cover the words in the strip. Use as many of your spelling words as possible to write a new story to go with the pictures.
3. List your words in alphabetical order. Label each word's part of speech.
4. Use all your words to write a story about the funniest thing that has ever happened to you. You may exaggerate the story to add more humor if needed.
5. Ask five people what makes them laugh or smile. Then cut and decorate a sheet of construction paper to resemble a happy face. List each person's response on the back. Underline any spelling words that are used.

Ha! Ha! Ha!

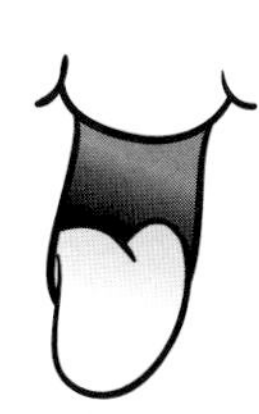

Note to the teacher: Give each student a copy of the contract. Assign the student a list of words. Then have him complete a specified number of activities.

Name________________

GOOFY GRAPHS

Read each set of data and its graph. Then answer the questions.

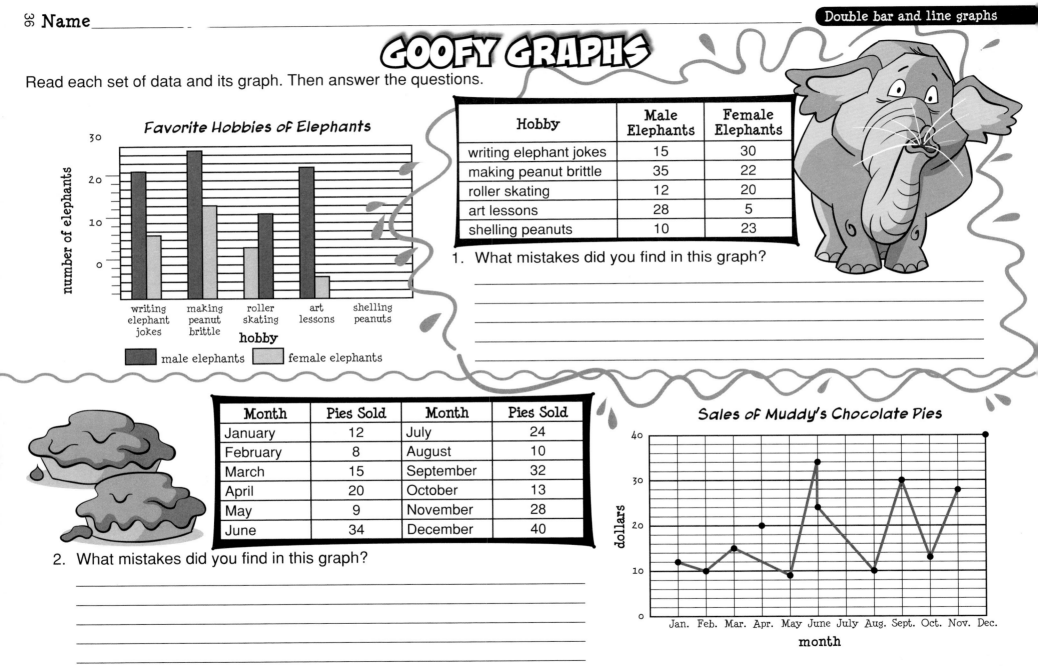

Favorite Hobbies of Elephants

number of elephants: 30, 20, 10, 0

writing elephant jokes · making peanut brittle · roller skating · art lessons · shelling peanuts

hobby

male elephants · female elephants

Hobby	Male Elephants	Female Elephants
writing elephant jokes	15	30
making peanut brittle	35	22
roller skating	12	20
art lessons	28	5
shelling peanuts	10	23

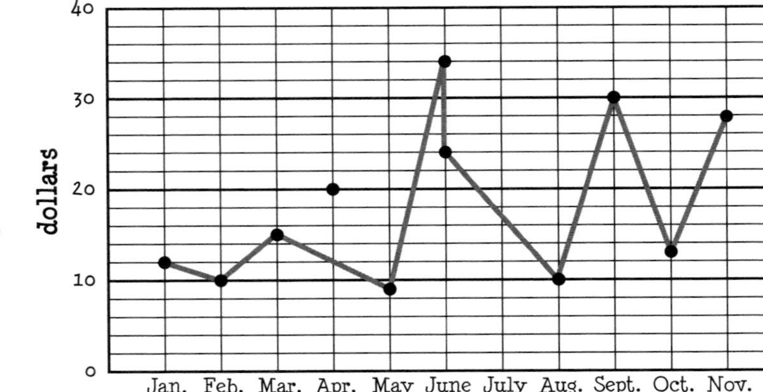

1. What mistakes did you find in this graph?

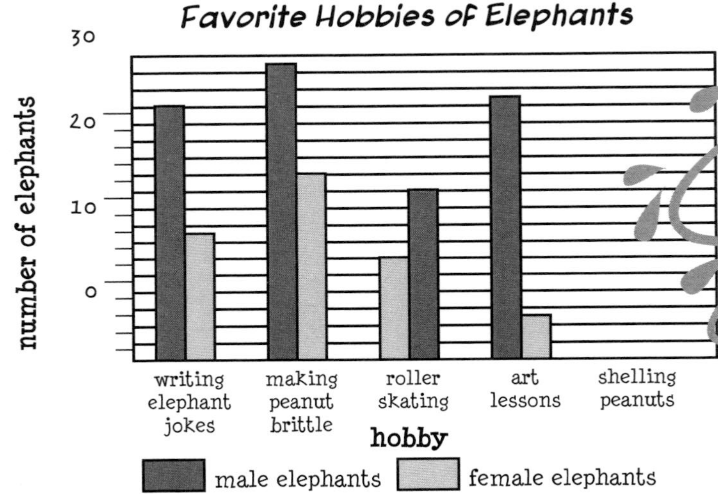

Month	Pies Sold	Month	Pies Sold
January	12	July	24
February	8	August	10
March	15	September	32
April	20	October	13
May	9	November	28
June	34	December	40

2. What mistakes did you find in this graph?

Sales of Muddy's Chocolate Pies

dollars: 40, 30, 20, 10, 0

Jan. Feb. Mar. Apr. May June July Aug. Sept. Oct. Nov. Dec.

month

Name ______________________________

In the News

Unscramble each verb in parentheses. Then write the verb and its correct tense on the blank.

Recycling Race

Last week, the fourth graders (lodh) __hold, held__ (1) a special Earth Day event. On Monday, they (igenb) ____________ (2) to see who could collect the most plastic jugs and aluminum cans. "Each student is (nirbg) ____________ (3) in items from home," Judy said. Thousands of plastic jugs and metal cans (era) ____________ (4) collected. A city recycling truck (emet) ____________ (5) the students at school and (kate) ____________ (6) the items to the recycling center. The student who (ingbr) ____________ (7) in the most to recycle won a prize. Even though Collin (iwn) ____________ (8) the event, Principal Smith (llet) ____________ (9) the students, "You all (od) ____________ (10) a good job."

A Classy Cleanup

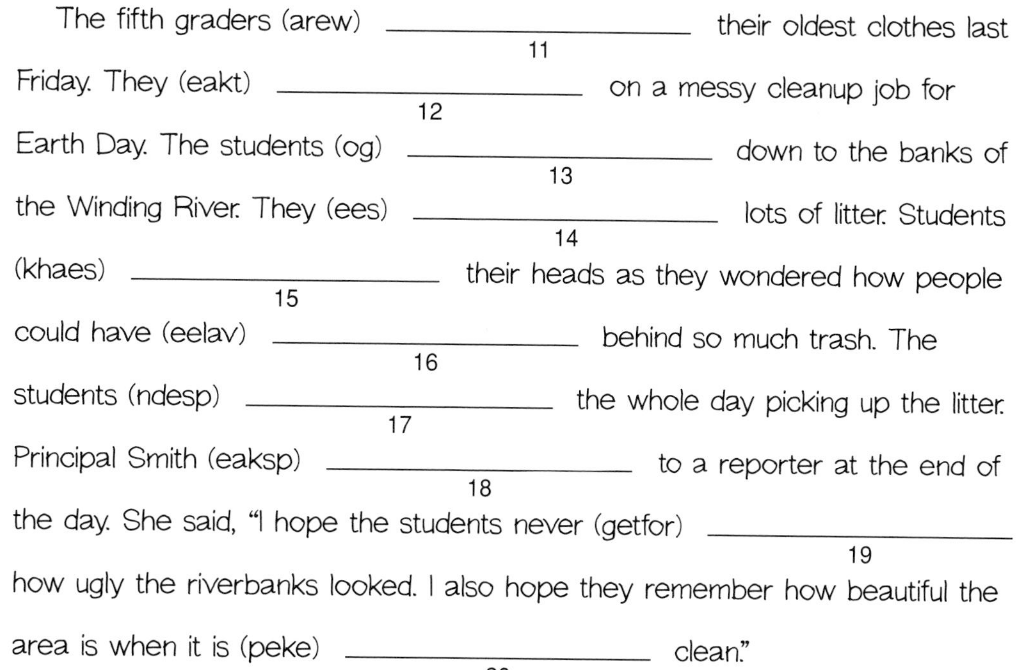

The fifth graders (arew) ____________ (11) their oldest clothes last Friday. They (eakt) ____________ (12) on a messy cleanup job for Earth Day. The students (og) ____________ (13) down to the banks of the Winding River. They (ees) ____________ (14) lots of litter. Students (khaes) ____________ (15) their heads as they wondered how people could have (eelav) ____________ (16) behind so much trash. The students (ndesp) ____________ (17) the whole day picking up the litter. Principal Smith (eaksp) ____________ (18) to a reporter at the end of the day. She said, "I hope the students never (getfor) ____________ (19) how ugly the riverbanks looked. I also hope they remember how beautiful the area is when it is (peke) ____________ (20) clean."

Bonus Box: On the back of this page, write each underlined verb in its future tense.

Name ____________________ **Probability**

Candy Dandies

Find the probability of drawing a piece of candy labeled with the type of number described. Write each answer in simplest form.

Example: prime $\frac{1}{2}$

1. divisible by 7 ______
2. sum of its digits greater than 7 ______
3. not divisible by 5 ______
4. less than 20 ______
5. not divisible by 2 ______
6. larger digit in its tens place than its ones place ______

7. ends in 6 ______
8. not divisible by 10 ______
9. from 80 to 100 ______
10. with 9 tens ______
11. less than 100 ______
12. from 30 to 40 ______
13. divisible by 3 ______

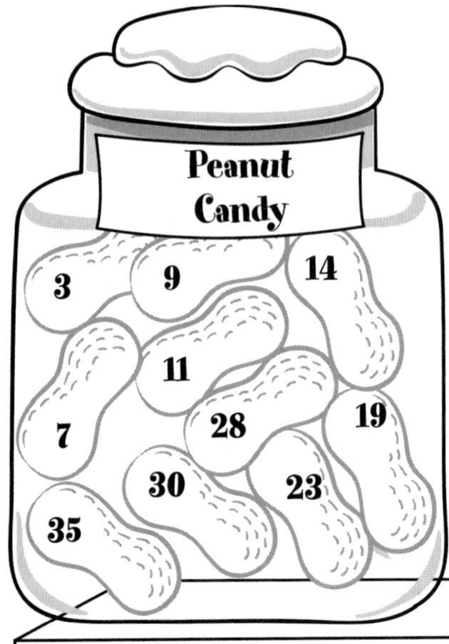

14. divisible by 5 ______
15. divisible by 4 ______
16. multiple of 3 ______
17. difference between its digits greater than 0 but less than 4 ______
18. greater than 40 ______
19. ones digit 4 times greater than its tens digit ______
20. two-digit palindrome (the same number whether written backward or forward) ______

Name ______________________________

Mother's Day Messages

Tell whether each underlined word is an adjective or an adverb by circling the letter in the correct column. Then write the word being modified.

	Adjective	Adverb	Modified Word
1. Mom, I love the way you look at me so thoughtfully.	S	M	
2. I love the way you care for our unusual family.	E	C	
3. Thanks for working so hard at your job.	Y	R	
4. I will never forget the many times when you helped me with homework.	D	H	
5. I think you cook many tremendous meals.	R	T	
6. Of all the important people in the world, you are my favorite.	M	G	
7. At the end of a long day, it's great when you hug me tightly.	N	U	
8. You are so talented, and you have many motherly skills.	T	B	
9. When I have chores to do, you watch closely to make sure I get them done.	I	È	
10. I appreciate your unending smile and the way that you support me.	O	F	
11. You carefully clean the house daily.	C	A	
12. Mom, I will never find another mother who is as great as you!	L	D	

How do you say *mother* in other languages?

To find out, write each circled letter from above on its matching numbered line or lines below.

French = ___ ___ ___ ___
1 9 5 2

German = ___ ___ ___ ___ ___ ___
6 7 8 8 2 3

Swedish = ___ ___ ___ ___ ___
1 10 4 2 5

Spanish = ___ ___ ___ ___ ___
1 11 4 3 2

Danish = ___ ___ ___
6 10 3

Dutch = ___ ___ ___ ___ ___ ___
1 10 2 12 2 5

Mom

Name ____________________

Roll a Person, Place, or Thing!

Roll the pair of dice.
Use the sum to circle a person in the chart.
Repeat two more times to circle a place and then a thing.
Use the circled nouns to write a silly sentence on the lines below.
Continue rolling and writing sentences as time allows.

1st roll = person
2nd roll = place
3rd roll = thing

Code			
Sum	**Person**	**Place**	**Thing**
2	pirate	pirate ship	treasure
3	hairdresser	beauty salon	hair spray
4	teacher	classroom	report card
5	fisherman	river	fishing rod
6	secretary	principal's office	filing cabinet
7	student	gym class	jump rope
8	baby	doctor's office	diaper bag
9	football player	stadium	football
10	mountain climber	mountaintop	backpack
11	cowboy	ranch	horse
12	woman	grocery store	bag of groceries

Sentences

1. ____________________

2. ____________________

3. ____________________

4. ____________________

5. ____________________

6. ____________________

7. ____________________

(Continue on the back.)

 Note to the teacher: Use with "Roll a Person, Place, or Thing!" on page 33.

SKILLS FOR THE SEASON

Bags of Praise

End of school

Try this self-esteem builder for the end of the school year or anytime you want to encourage students. Prepare a class list on lined paper, skipping a line between names. Next, have each student personalize a small paper bag and place it on his desk. Give him a copy of the class list and have him write a compliment beside each classmate's name, signing his name if desired. Then have him cut apart the list and place each compliment in the corresponding classmate's bag. (If desired, look over each child's comments before he puts them in the bags.) Your students will love receiving these kudos!

Lois McLaughlin, High Point, NC

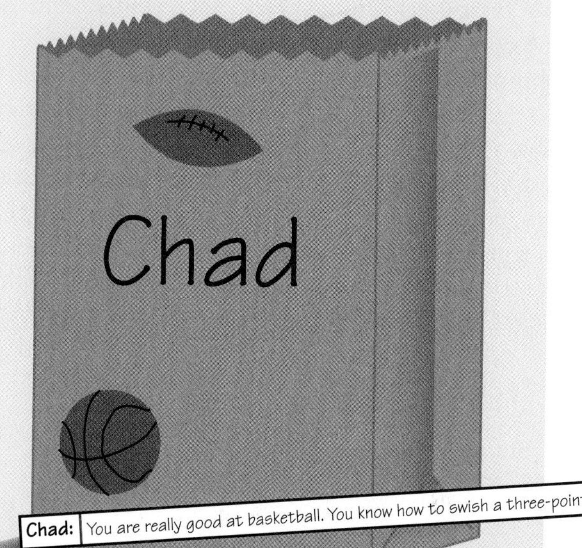

Chad
Chad: You are really good at basketball. You know how to swish a three-pointer.

Signers of the Declaration of Independence
John Adams (Massachusetts)
Samuel Adams (Massachusetts)
Josiah Bartlett (New Hampshire)
Elbridge Gerry (Massachusetts)
Button Gwinnett (Georgia)
Lyman Hall (Georgia)
John Hancock (Massachusetts)
Benjamin Harrison (Virginia)
John Hart (New Jersey)
Joseph Hewes (North Carolina)
Thomas Heyward Jr. (South Carolina)
William Hooper (North Carolina)
Stephen Hopkins (Rhode Island)
Francis Hopkinson (New Jersey)
Samuel Huntington (Connecticut)
Thomas Jefferson (Virginia)
Francis Lightfoot Lee (Virginia)
Richard Henry Lee (Virginia)
Francis Lewis (New York)
Philip Livingston (New York)
Thomas Lynch Jr. (South Carolina)
Thomas McKean (Delaware)
Arthur Middleton (South Carolina)
Lewis Morris (New York)
Robert Morris (Pennsylvania)
John Morton (Pennsylvania)
Thomas Nelson Jr. (Virginia)
William Paca (Maryland)
Robert T. Paine (Massachusetts)
John Penn (North Carolina)
George Read (Delaware)
Caesar Rodney (Delaware)
George Ross (Pennsylvania)
Benjamin Rush (Pennsylvania)
Edward Rutledge (South Carolina)
Roger Sherman (Connecticut)
James Smith (Pennsylvania)
Richard Stockton (New Jersey)
Thomas Stone (Maryland)
George Taylor (Pennsylvania)
Matthew Thornton (New Hampshire)
George Walton (Georgia)
William Whipple (New Hampshire)
William Williams (Connecticut)
James Wilson (Pennsylvania)
John Witherspoon (New Jersey)
Oliver Wolcott (Connecticut)
George Wythe (Virginia)
What is the probability of selecting the name "John" if you randomly select a name from the list?

Signers' Likelihood

Probability

Combine math and a bit of U.S. history with this fun activity. Give each pair of students a copy of page 47, which lists the 56 signers of the Declaration of Independence. Ask students a probability question about the list, such as the one shown. Discuss whether the statement is impossible, unlikely, equally likely, likely, or certain to occur. Next, have each student pair create similar probability questions about the Declaration of Independence's signers. Then have the partners trade papers with another twosome and answer each other's questions.

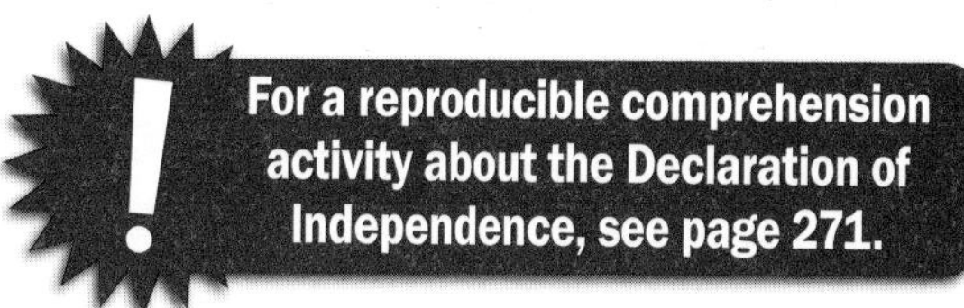
For a reproducible comprehension activity about the Declaration of Independence, see page 271.

Light the Way!

Research

Build research and writing skills with a bright, highly motivating topic—lighthouses! Have each student choose a lighthouse from a copy of page 48 to research. Then, to create her own replica of the lighthouse, instruct her to stack a large foam cup, the bottom third of a 16-ounce red plastic cup, and a clear nine-ounce plastic cup as shown. Then have her decorate the foam cup to look like her lighthouse. If desired, allow her to paint the clear cup with clear glitter glue to simulate the lighthouse's light. Have her glue her lighthouse on a paper plate and decorate the plate with various arts and crafts materials as shown. As students present their lighthouse reports, have them share their replicas.

Gemma M. Goodwin, Shady Lane Elementary, Westville, NJ

I Am...

End of school

Use this star-powered idea to get students thinking about all the things they are good at doing. Display the poetry frame shown. Then model a superstar poem about yourself on the board. Next, give each student a large construction paper star and have him write a similar poem about himself on the cutout. When students are finished, have them share their poems with the class. If desired, post the superstar poems on a display titled "We Are Superstars!"

Renee Cooperman, Kenmore Town of Tonawanda School District
Kenmore, NY

An "I Am" Poem
Line 1: "I am a superstar at"
Line 2: Three *-ing* verbs
Line 3: Three nouns
Line 4: Four-word phrase
Line 5: Five-word phrase

Andre
I am a superstar at
Running, swimming, and fishing.
Math, art, and board games.
Sports in gym class.
Teaching my friends
new things.

Tall-Tale Travels

Narrative writing

Challenge your students to stretch their imaginations by planning an unbelievable summer vacation. Give each child a copy of a grid like the one shown and have her select items by drawing an X in any five of the grid's squares. Next, have her write a tall tale about her summer vacation using the selected items. After students share their stories, let the class vote on which tale was stretched the tallest!

Farrah Milby, Weddington Hills Elementary, Concord, NC

Tall Tale Travels

sunny day	the beach	shark	frozen lemonade	surfboard
airplane	stingray	monkey	pool	slice of watermelon
sunflower	RV	ice cream cone	fishing reel	mountains
map	cell phone	tent	fish	campfire
water park	sunscreen	backpack	roller coaster	fast food

Name ______________________

School's Out!

Find the area and perimeter of each empty classroom.

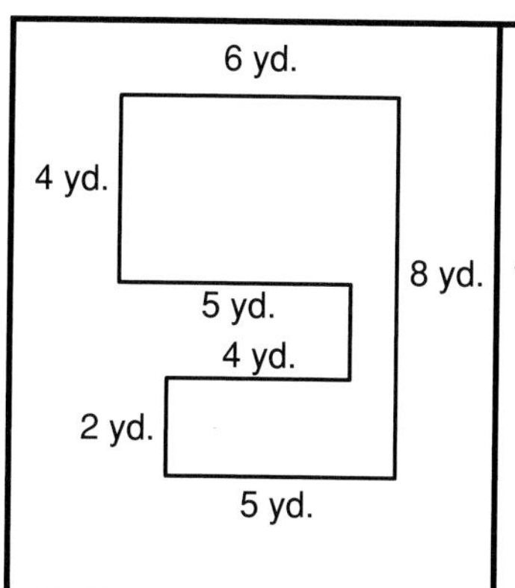

N. Area = ________
Perimeter = ________

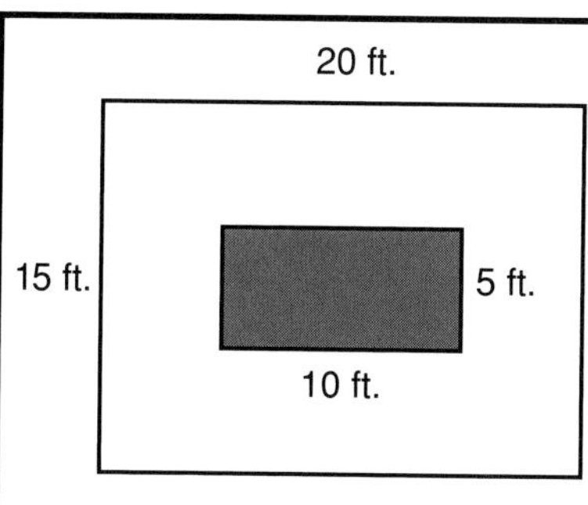

F. Area = ________
Perimeter = ________

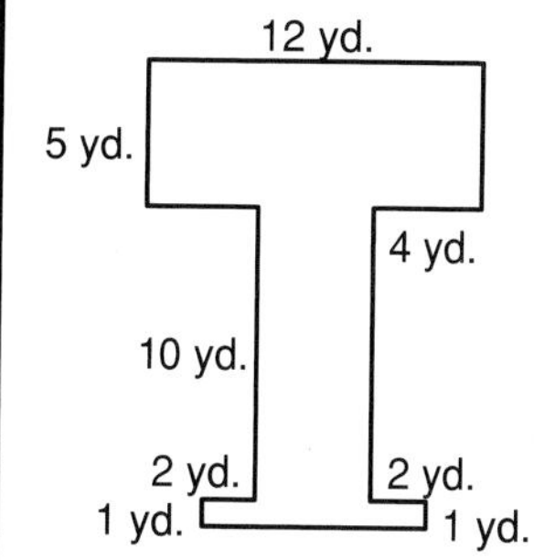

O. Area = ________
Perimeter = ________

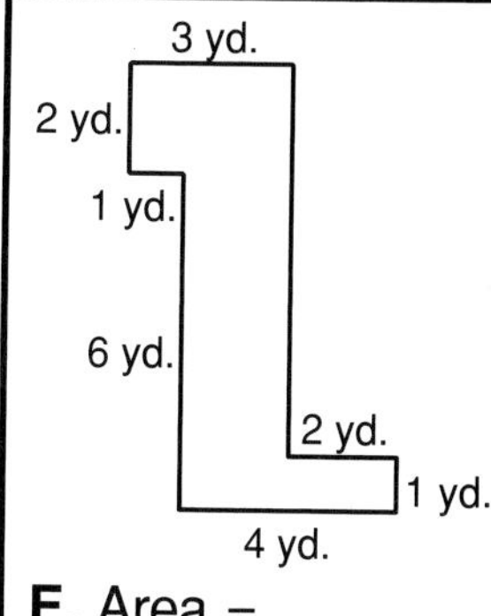

E. Area = ________
Perimeter = ________

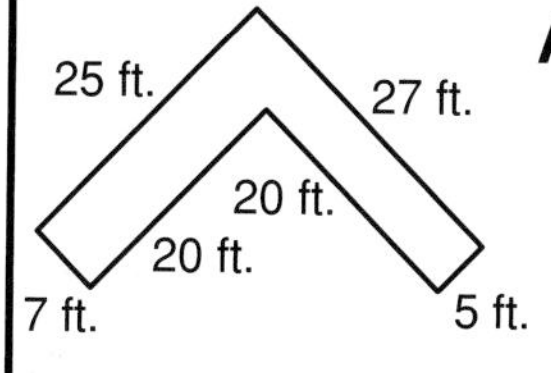

A. Area = ________
Perimeter = ________

100 ft.

28 ft.

T. Area = ________
Perimeter = ________

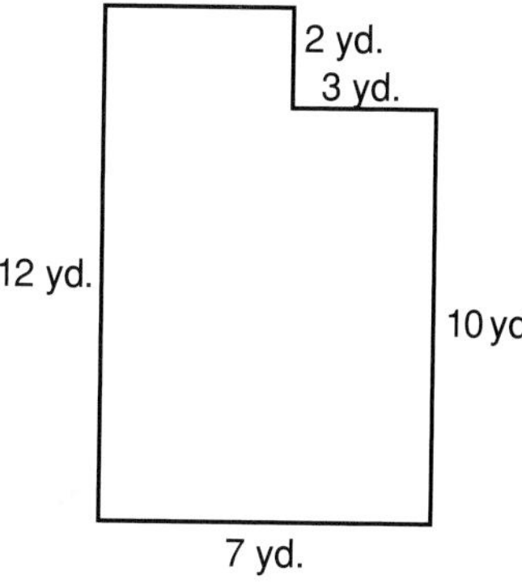

R. Area = ________
Perimeter = ________

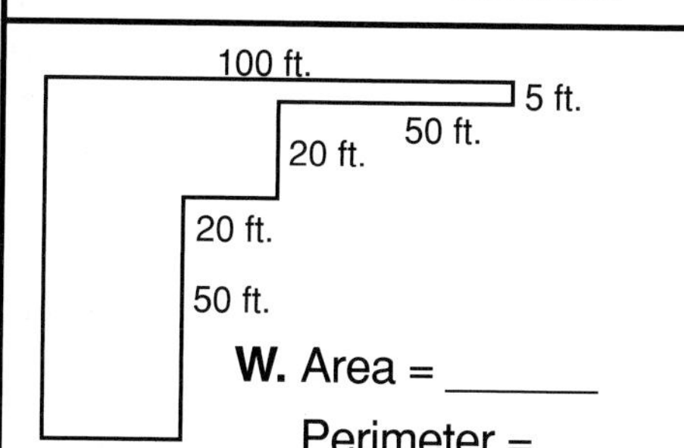

W. Area = ________
Perimeter = ________

D. Area = ________
Perimeter = ________

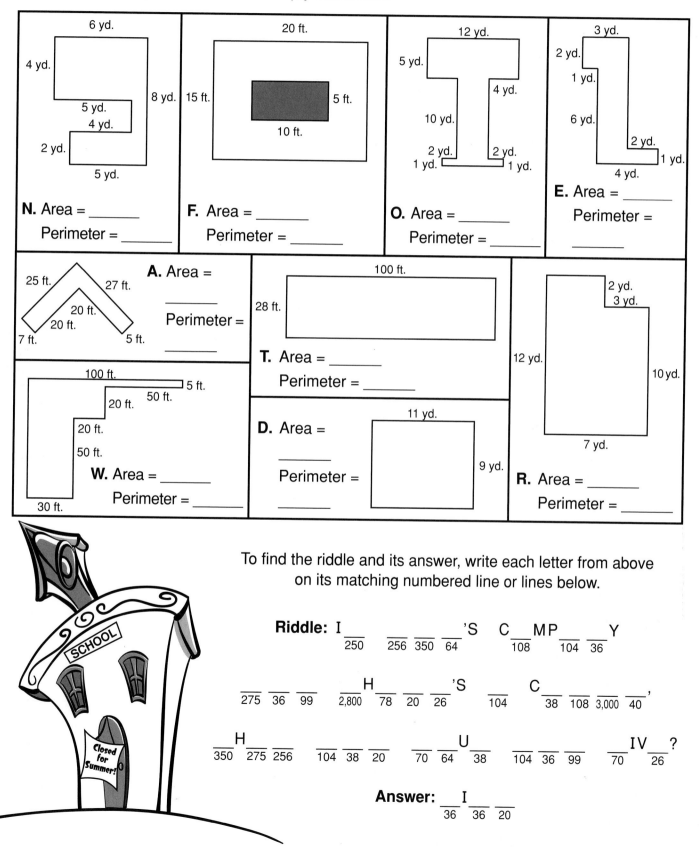

To find the riddle and its answer, write each letter from above on its matching numbered line or lines below.

Riddle: I __(250) __(256) __(350) __(64)'S C __(108) M P __(104) __(36) Y

__(275) __(36) __(99) __(2,800) H __(78) __(20) __(26)'S __(104) C __(38) __(108) __(3,000) __(40),

__(350) H __(275) __(256) __(104) __(38) __(20) __(70) __(64) U __(38) __(104) __(36) __(99) __(70) I V __(26)?

Answer: __(36) I __(36) __(20)

 Name________________________

Dismissed!

Read each clue below. Form a word that matches the clue by drawing a line to connect a prefix or suffix to a base word. Then write the word next to its clue.

anti- •	• -able	hope •	• -dom	non- •	• cut
bend •	• -age	king •	• formed	pre- •	• -er
bi- •	• cycle	length •	• -ful	self- •	• fat
block •	• freeze	mad •	• -hood	teach •	• happy
develop •	• honest	mal- •	• -ness	un- •	• help
dis- •	• -ment	mis- •	• print	use •	• -less
ex- •	• president	neighbor •	• wise		

Clues

1. a substance to help protect against freezing ____________
2. able to bend ____________
3. a vehicle with pedals and two wheels ____________
4. the act of blocking ____________
5. the act of developing ____________
6. not truthful ____________
7. a former elected official ____________
8. full of hope ____________
9. a region ruled by a king or queen ____________
10. in the direction of length ____________
11. the state of being mad ____________
12. formed badly ____________
13. to print incorrectly ____________
14. the state of being neighbors ____________
15. not having fat solids ____________
16. cut before ____________
17. helping one's self ____________
18. one who teaches ____________
19. not happy ____________
20. without use ____________

Name ____________________

The Flip-Flop Shop

Write a possible solution for each problem below. Use a word from the flip-flops in each solution. You may use each word only once.

act

calculate

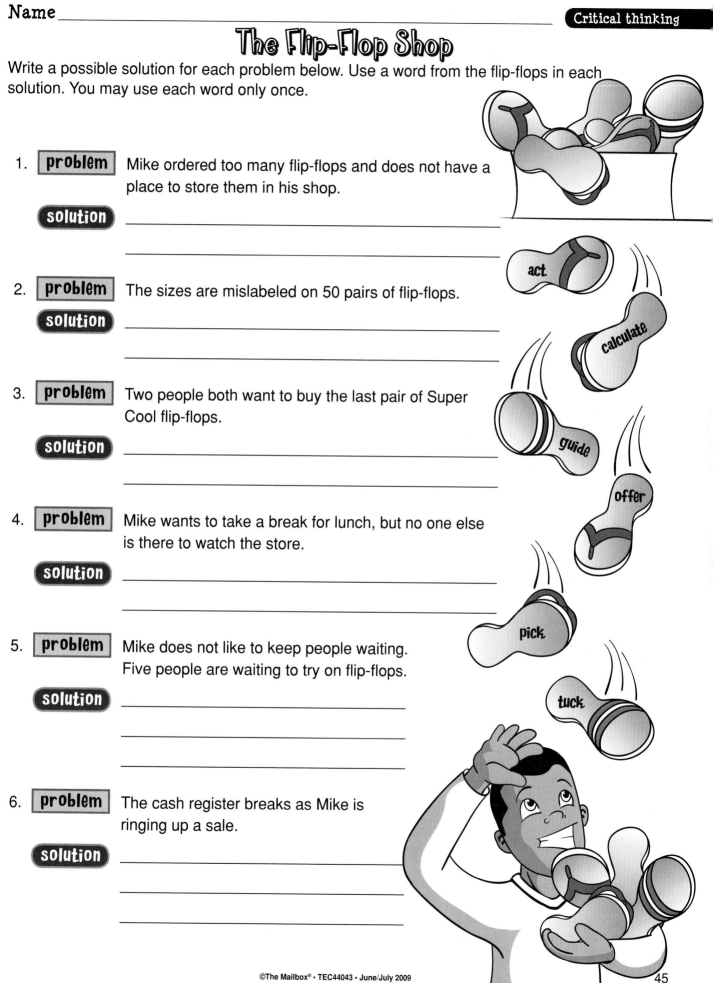

guide

offer

1. **problem** Mike ordered too many flip-flops and does not have a place to store them in his shop.

solution ____________________

____

2. **problem** The sizes are mislabeled on 50 pairs of flip-flops.

solution ____________________

____

3. **problem** Two people both want to buy the last pair of Super Cool flip-flops.

solution ____________________

____

4. **problem** Mike wants to take a break for lunch, but no one else is there to watch the store.

solution ____________________

____

5. **problem** Mike does not like to keep people waiting. Five people are waiting to try on flip-flops.

solution ____________________

____

____

6. **problem** The cash register breaks as Mike is ringing up a sale.

solution ____________________

____

____

Name ____________________

Surf's Up!

Draw the lines of symmetry. On the blank, write whether the figure has point symmetry, rotational symmetry, or line symmetry.

1. 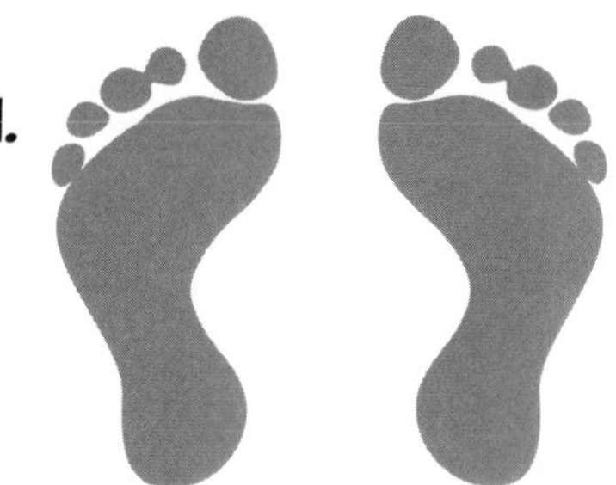

____

2. 

____

3. 

____

List all the lines of symmetry on each surfboard.

4. 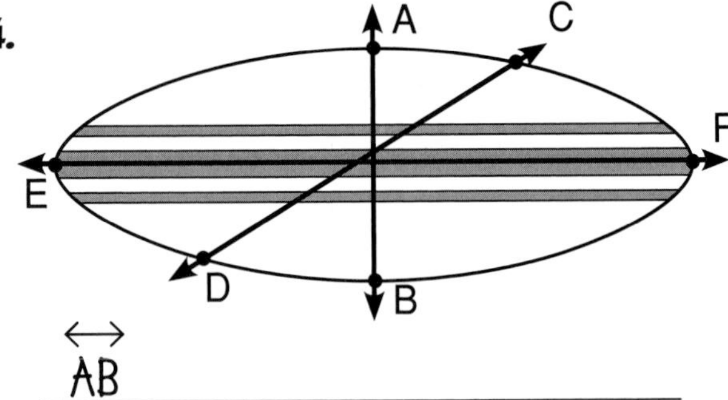

____

5. 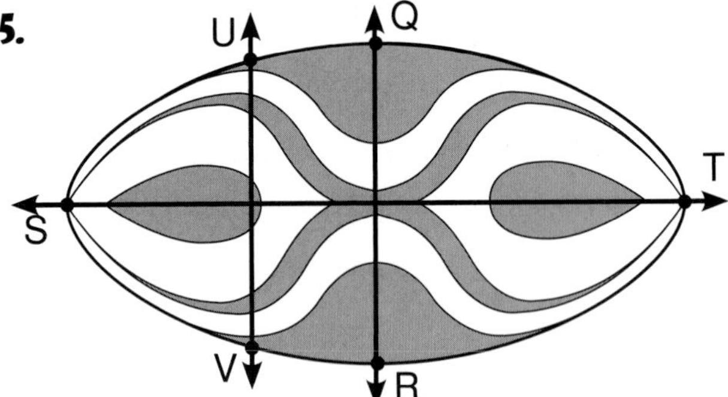

____

6. 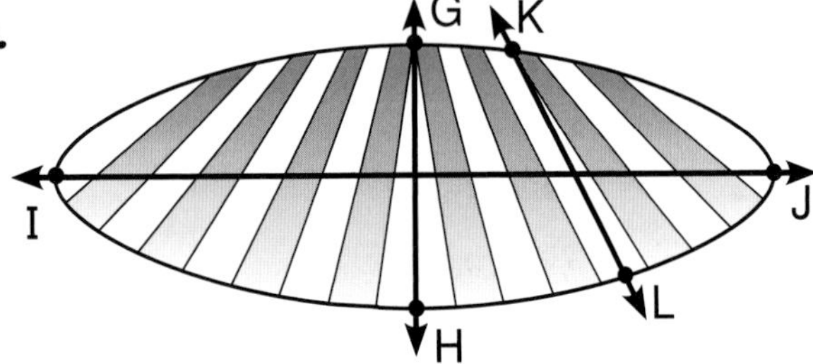

____

7. 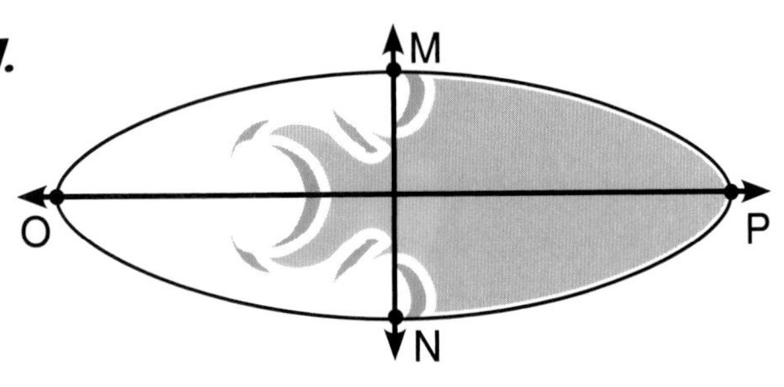

____

8. 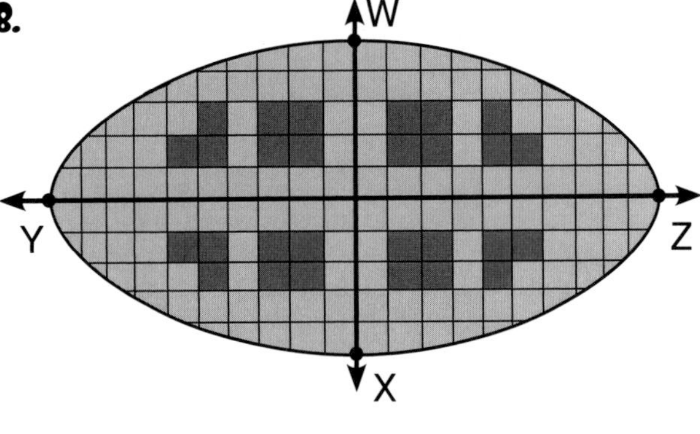

____

Bonus Box: On the back of this page draw your own surfboard. Draw and label a line for each type of symmetry you use.

Signers of the Declaration of Independence

John Adams (Massachusetts)
Samuel Adams (Massachusetts)
Josiah Bartlett (New Hampshire)
Carter Braxton (Virginia)
Charles Carroll (Maryland)
Samuel Chase (Maryland)
Abraham Clark (New Jersey)
George Clymer (Pennsylvania)
William Ellery (Rhode Island)
William Floyd (New York)
Benjamin Franklin (Pennsylvania)
Elbridge Gerry (Massachusetts)
Button Gwinnett (Georgia)
Lyman Hall (Georgia)
John Hancock (Massachusetts)
Benjamin Harrison (Virginia)
John Hart (New Jersey)
Joseph Hewes (North Carolina)
Thomas Heyward Jr. (South Carolina)
William Hooper (North Carolina)
Stephen Hopkins (Rhode Island)
Francis Hopkinson (New Jersey)
Samuel Huntington (Connecticut)
Thomas Jefferson (Virginia)
Francis Lightfoot Lee (Virginia)
Richard Henry Lee (Virginia)
Francis Lewis (New York)
Philip Livingston (New York)
Thomas Lynch Jr. (South Carolina)
Thomas McKean (Delaware)
Arthur Middleton (South Carolina)
Lewis Morris (New York)
Robert Morris (Pennsylvania)
John Morton (Pennsylvania)
Thomas Nelson Jr. (Virginia)
William Paca (Maryland)
Robert T. Paine (Massachusetts)
John Penn (North Carolina)
George Read (Delaware)
Caesar Rodney (Delaware)
George Ross (Pennsylvania)
Benjamin Rush (Pennsylvania)
Edward Rutledge (South Carolina)
Roger Sherman (Connecticut)
James Smith (Pennsylvania)
Richard Stockton (New Jersey)
Thomas Stone (Maryland)
George Taylor (Pennsylvania)
Matthew Thornton (New Hampshire)
George Walton (Georgia)
William Whipple (New Hampshire)
William Williams (Connecticut)
James Wilson (Pennsylvania)
John Witherspoon (New Jersey)
Oliver Wolcott (Connecticut)
George Wythe (Virginia)

Note to the teacher: Use with "Signers' Likelihood" on page 41.

United States Lighthouses

This is a list of some of the historic lighthouses in the United States.

California
Battery Point Lighthouse

Connecticut
Sheffield Island Lighthouse

Delaware
Harbor of Refuge Lighthouse

Florida
Jupiter Inlet Lighthouse

Georgia
Tybee Island Light Station

Illinois
Grosse Point Lighthouse

Indiana
Michigan City Lighthouse

Maine
Pemaquid Point Lighthouse

Maryland
Thomas Point Shoal Lighthouse

Massachusetts
Boston Lighthouse

Michigan
Beaver Island Light Station

Minnesota
Split Rock Lighthouse

New Hampshire
Portsmouth Harbor Lighthouse

New Jersey
Sandy Hook Lighthouse

New York
Thirty Mile Point Lighthouse

North Carolina
Cape Hatteras Lighthouse

Ohio
Marblehead Lighthouse

Oregon
Heceta Head Lighthouse

Rhode Island
Block Island Southeast Lighthouse

South Carolina
Hunting Island Lighthouse

Texas
Port Isabel Lighthouse

Virginia
Cape Henry Lighthouse

Washington
Alki Point Lighthouse

Wisconsin
Raspberry Island Lighthouse

 Note to the teacher: Use with "Light the Way!" on page 42.

Classroom Displays

CLASSROOM DISPLAYS

Start the year with this high-flying display. On the first day of school, have each student decorate and cut out a copy of the airplane pattern on page 51. Display the completed planes around an enlarged copy of the pattern. Later, change the title to "It's 'Plane' to See That This Work Is Great!" Then use the updated display to highlight samples of students' best work.

Cyndi Smith, Fairview Elementary, Carthage, MD

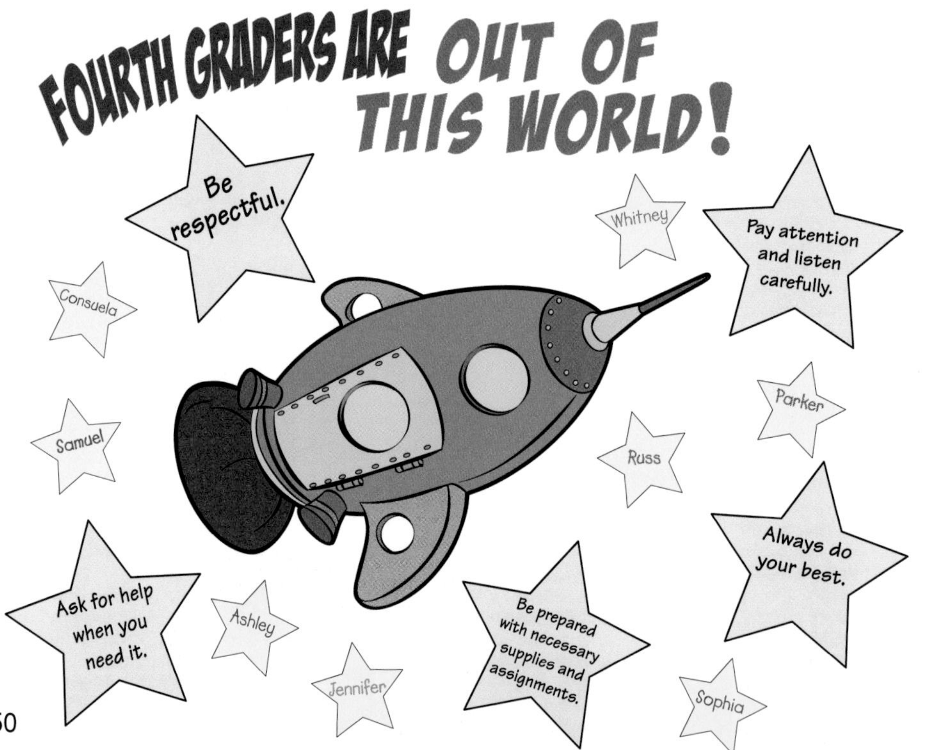

Post an enlarged copy of the rocket ship pattern from page 52. Then mount five large star cutouts (enlarge the star pattern from page 52) on the board. Brainstorm with students rules that will make the year a successful one. After students choose the five most important rules, write each rule on a star. Then have each child sign, cut out, and post a copy of the star pattern, as shown.

adapted from an idea by Linda Masternak Justice, Kansas City, MO

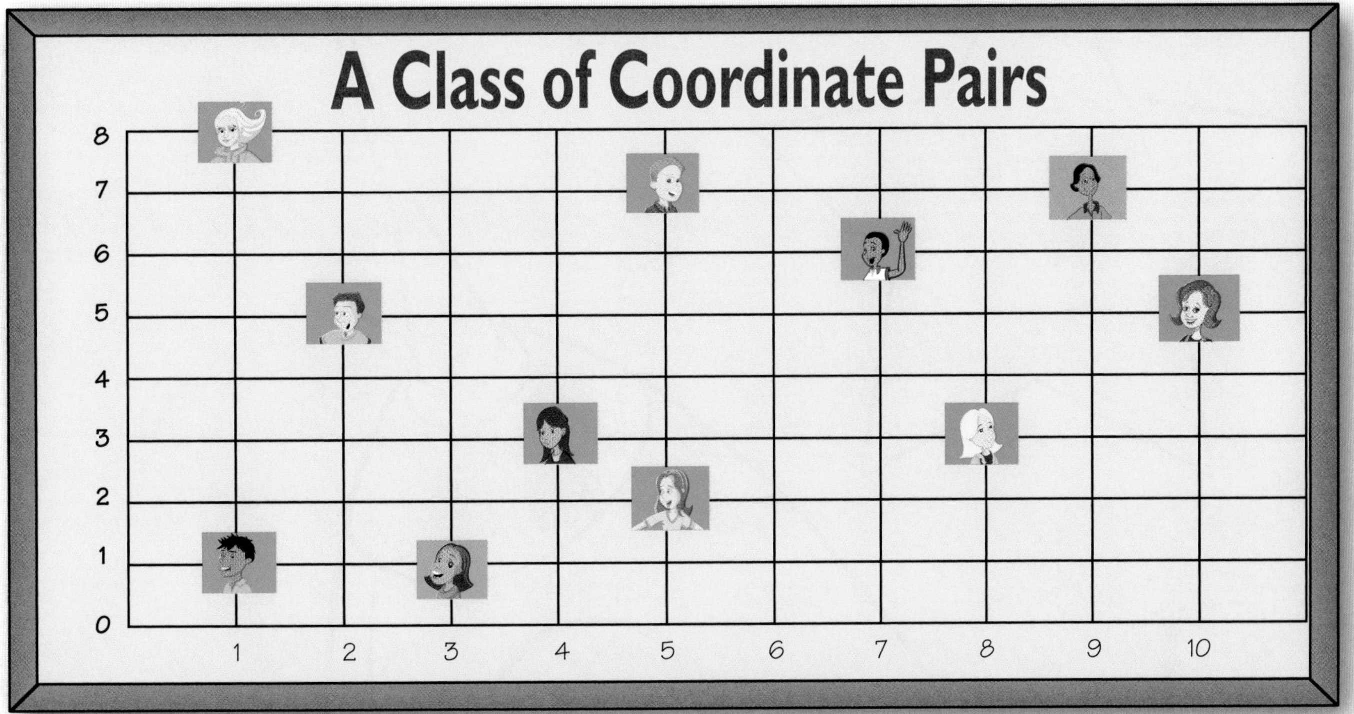

This picture-perfect display is a super way to review coordinate graphing and help students get to know their classmates. On a board, draw and label a graph similar to the one shown. Post a photo of each student on the graph. Then give each student a copy of your class roll and have him list the corresponding coordinate pair beside each name.

adapted from an idea by Denise Givens, Coral Ridge Elementary, Fairdale, KY

Airplane Pattern

Use with "It's 'Plane' to See That This Class Is Great!" on page 50.

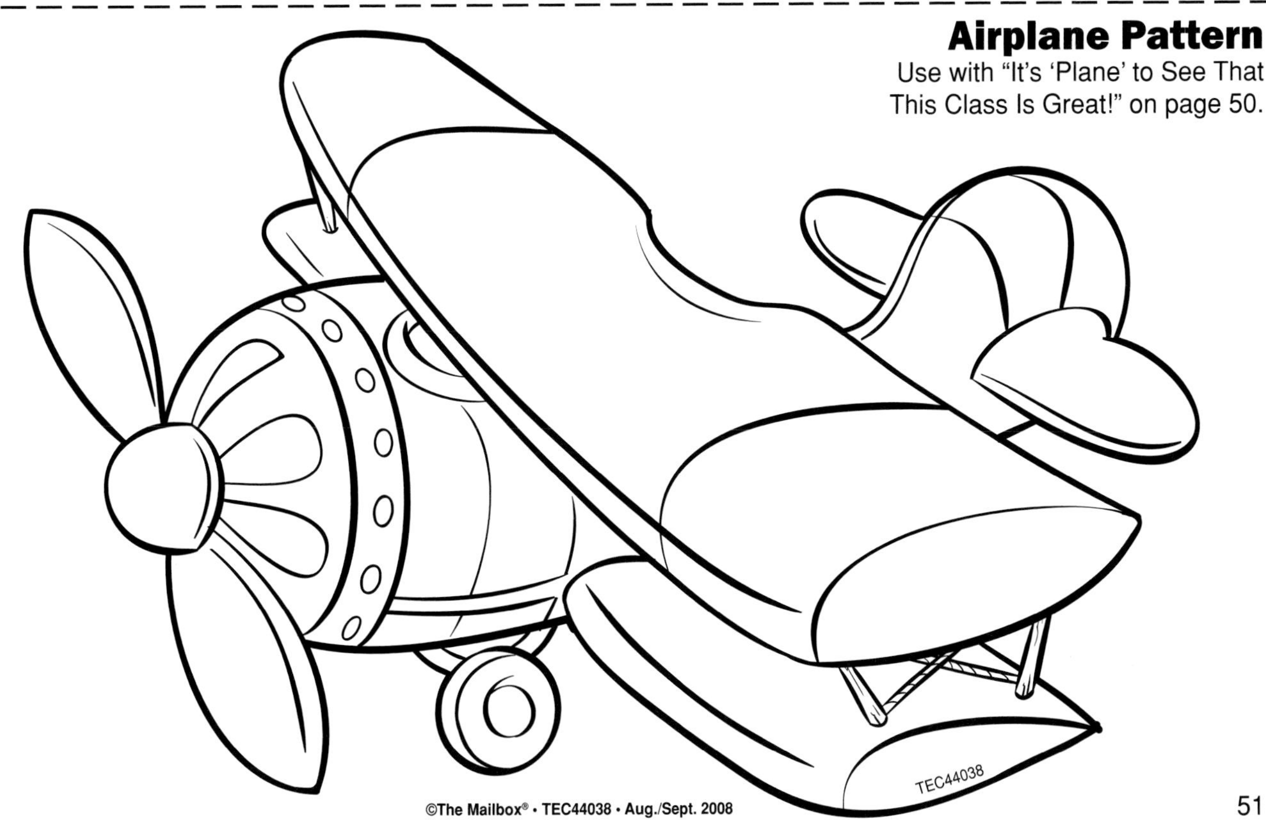

Rocket Ship and Star Patterns

Use with "Fourth Graders Are Out of This World!" on page 50.

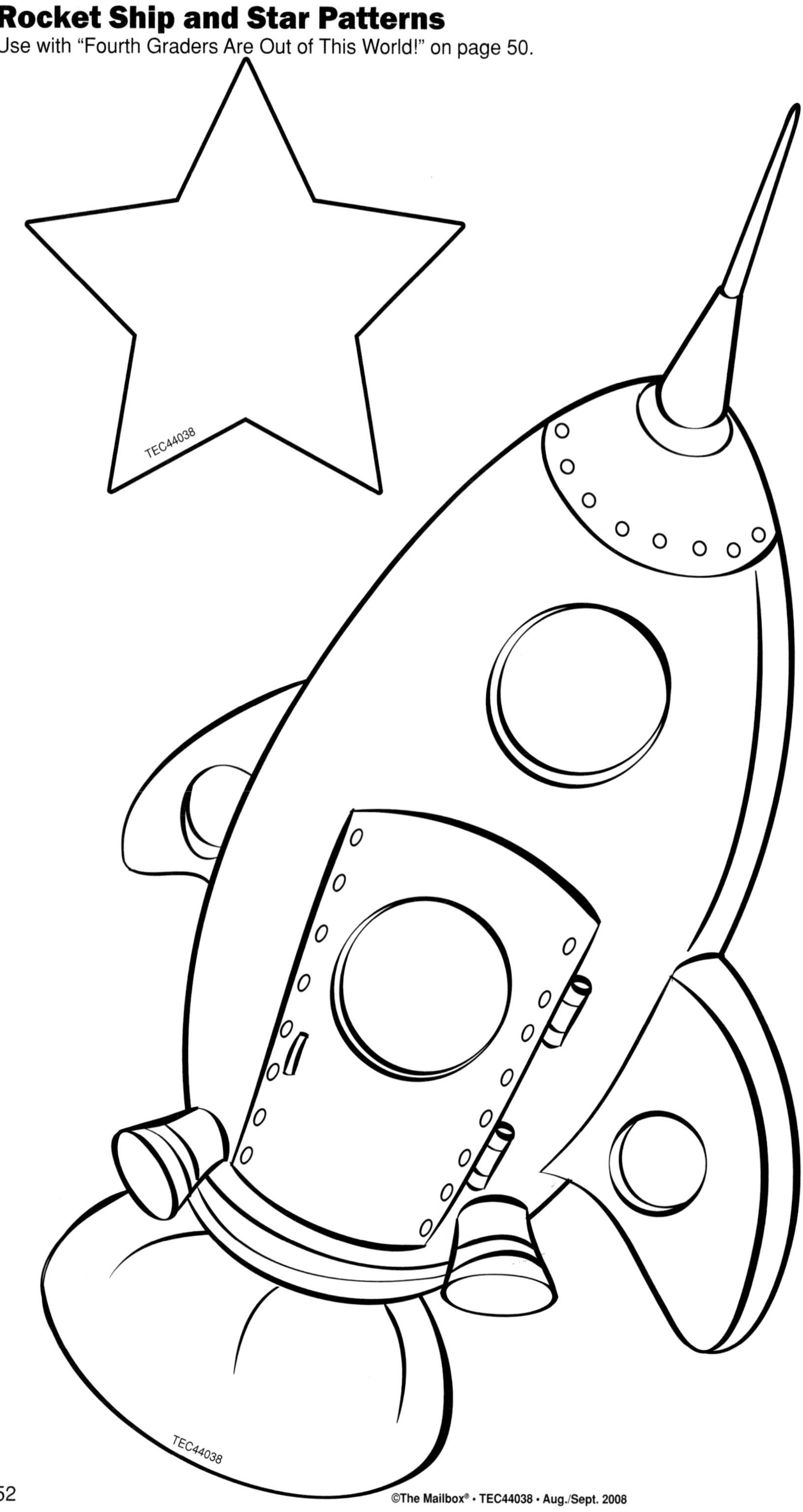

Corral student work samples to showcase on this display! Post an enlarged copy of the cowboy pattern on page 55. Attach a piece of twine to the board so it looks like the cowboy's lasso. Then post student papers inside the lasso.

Beverly Langland, Jacksonville, FL

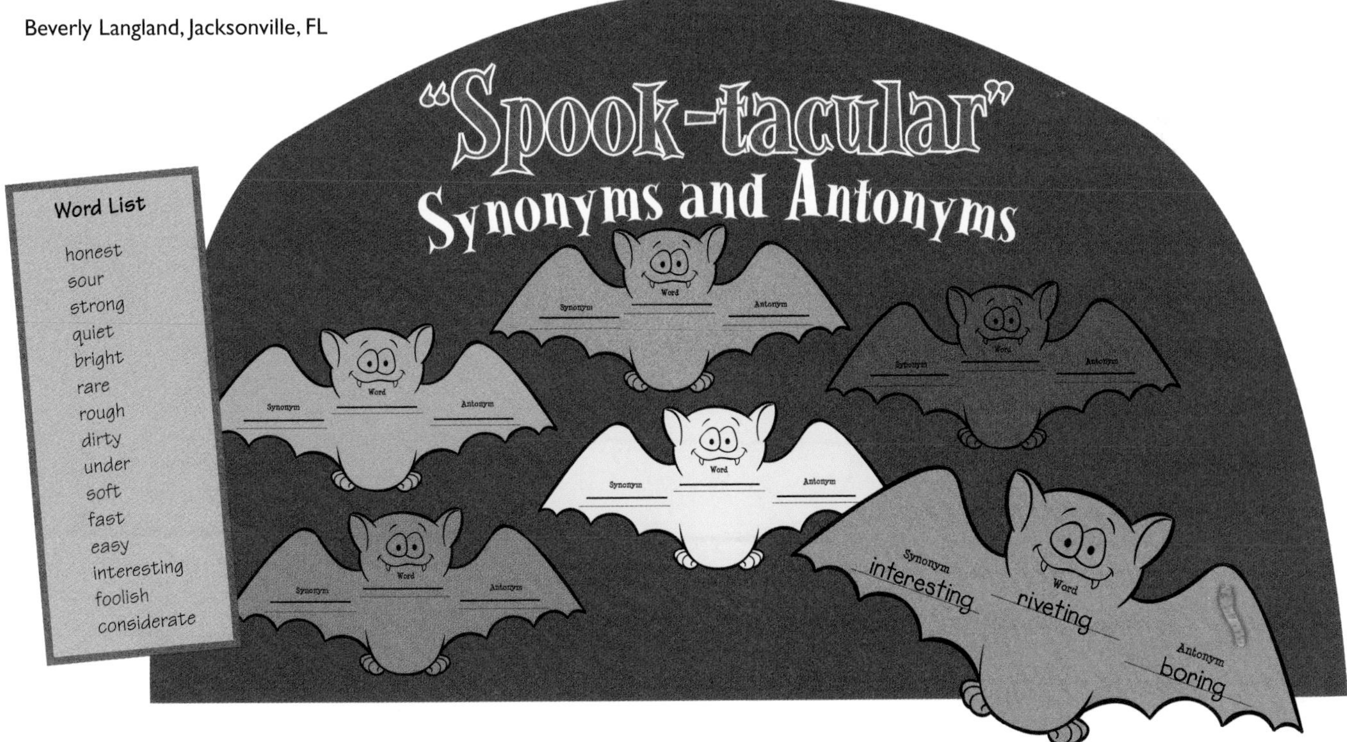

The bats in this cave give students plenty of synonym and antonym practice. Have each child choose a different word from the list shown to write on a copy of the bat pattern from page 54. Have the student use a thesaurus to find a synonym and an antonym for his word and label his bat accordingly. After students lightly color and cut out their bats, post them on a large cave cutout.

Teri Nielsen, Tracey's Elementary, Tracys Landing, MD

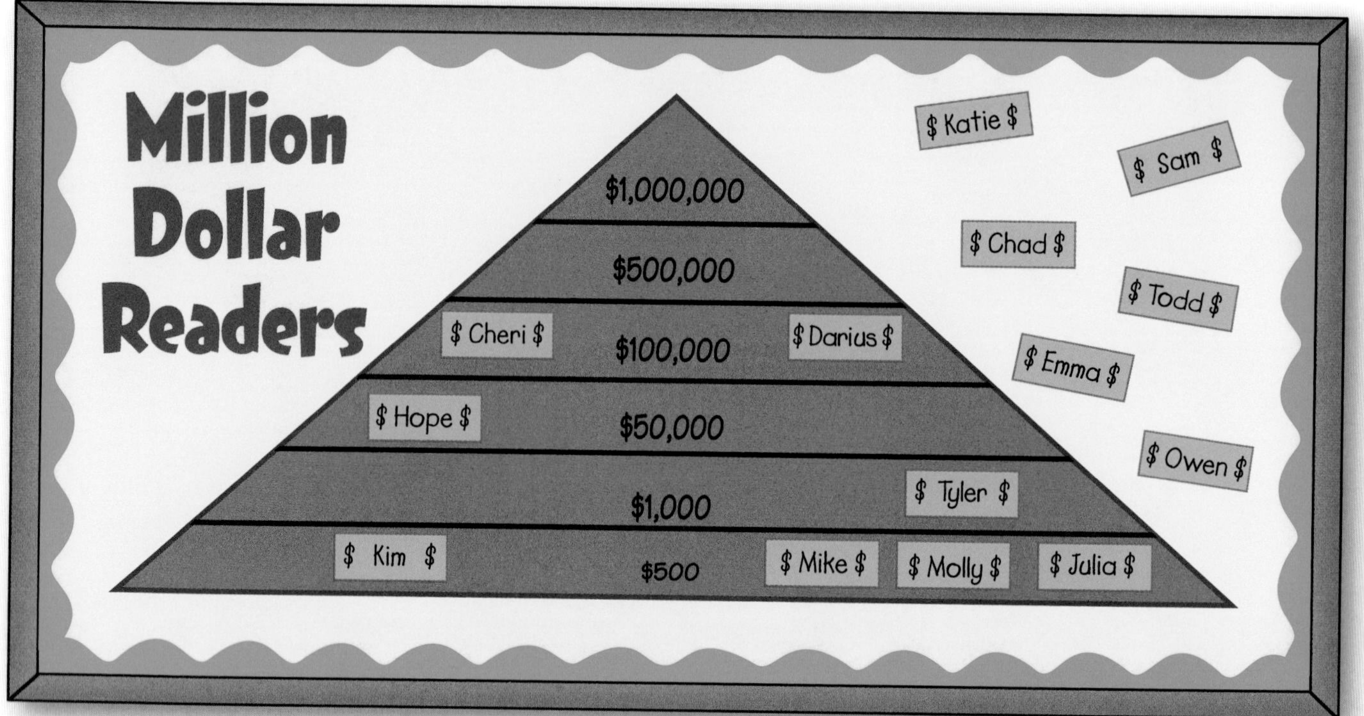

Encourage students to read with this motivating display. Post a large pyramid labeled as shown. Have each child personalize a green rectangle (dollar bill) as shown. Then laminate the bills for durability and display them around the pyramid. After a student reads his first book, move his bill onto the pyramid's bottom level. For each additional book he reads, he moves his bill up one level. When a child's bill reaches the top level, reward him with a small treat.

Cindy Koehler, Summit Hill Elementary, Alpharetta, GA

Bat Pattern

Use with "'Spook-tacular' Synonyms and Antonyms" on page 53.

Cowboy Pattern

Use with "A Fall Roundup of Good Work!" on page 53.

CLASSROOM DISPLAYS

Have each student cut out a holiday lightbulb from colorful paper and position it so the base is at the top. On her cutout, have her write a holiday poem in a format of her choice. Display the poems as a string of lightbulbs by connecting the lightbulbs with curling ribbon and stapling them in place as shown.

Rebecca McCright
B.T. Washington Elementary
Midland, TX

We're One Sweet Class!

To promote class unity, mount a large red candy cane cutout on a door or wall. Next, discuss with students ways they have stuck together to achieve a goal. Then, on a white paper strip that fits the candy cane, have each student write about a different time the class worked together. Attach the labeled strips to the candy cane.

Melissa Walker
Alexander Wilson Elementary
Graham, NC

We worked together when we were trying to earn the Class of the Month award in the library. We reminded each other to return our books on time.

When the Weather Outside Is
Frightful,
What Makes You Feel
Delightful?
When the weather gets cold and snowy, I make a huge mug of hot cocoa and put marshmallows in it. After I make my cocoa, I curl up on the couch under a cozy blanket. Then I look out the window and watch the snow fall. The blanket and hot cocoa keep me warm no matter how cold it gets outside!
Tamara

For this winter display, have each student write on a blank card a paragraph about something she does when winter weather arrives. Mount the completed cards on colorful paper and display them with a snowpal cutout.

Sora Miriam Zucker, Beth Jacob Day School, Brooklyn, NY

Honor Dr. Martin Luther King Jr. with this peace-promoting display. Discuss with students the quote shown. Next, give each child a copy of page 58. Have him write in the modified peace symbol three ways he can promote peace. When he is finished writing, invite him to decorate the shirt and then cut it out.

Dana Sanders, Hamilton Crossing Elementary, Cartersville, GA

T-Shirt Pattern

Use with "Give Peace a Chance" on page 57.

CLASSROOM DISPLAYS

30 WAYS TO SAY...

This Valentine's Day, teach students that there's more than one way to say, "I love you!" Post a large heart cutout with an enlarged copy of page 60 attached to it. Have each student write "I love you" in one of the featured languages on a small heart cutout and then decorate the cutout's edges. Next, on a blank card, have each child write about how she can demonstrate her love for someone without saying the words. Display the cutouts and cards as shown.

Tara Powell
Corpus Christi Elementary
Wilmington, DE

I Love You!

Je t'aime
French

Ti amo
Italian

Ash miliu tave
Lithuanian

S'ayapo
Greek

Ngo oi ney
Cantonese

Ta gra agam ort
Gaelic

I can show my mother I love her by helping her with my little brother and sister when she is tired.

Volim te
Serbian

Ich liebe Dich
German

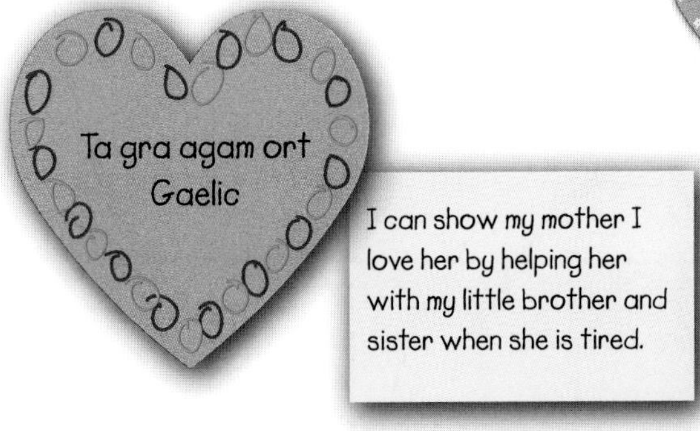

Problem
Solving
Is
"De-light-ful"

For this easy-to-adapt display, post a large laminated lightbulb cutout labeled with a wipe-off marker as shown. Surround the lightbulb with examples of students' problem-solving papers. To display your students' best work samples for mixed subjects, just change the title to "Great Work Is 'De-light-ful.'"

Shaune Scott
Ryder Elementary Charter School
Miami, FL

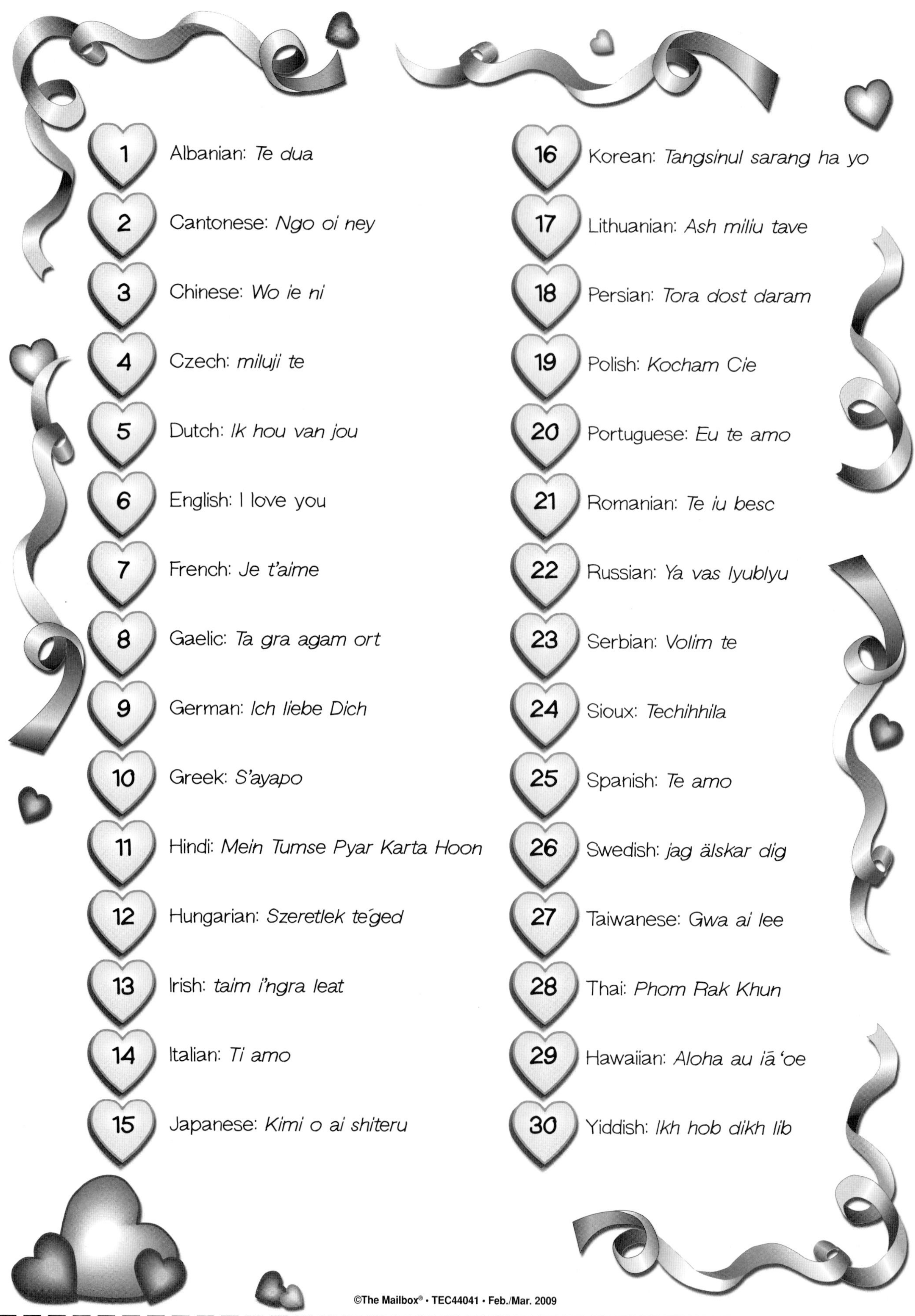

1 Albanian: *Te dua*

2 Cantonese: *Ngo oi ney*

3 Chinese: *Wo ie ni*

4 Czech: *miluji te*

5 Dutch: *Ik hou van jou*

6 English: I love you

7 French: *Je t'aime*

8 Gaelic: *Ta gra agam ort*

9 German: *Ich liebe Dich*

10 Greek: *S'ayapo*

11 Hindi: *Mein Tumse Pyar Karta Hoon*

12 Hungarian: *Szeretlek te'ged*

13 Irish: *taim i'ngra leat*

14 Italian: *Ti amo*

15 Japanese: *Kimi o ai shiteru*

16 Korean: *Tangsinul sarang ha yo*

17 Lithuanian: *Ash miliu tave*

18 Persian: *Tora dost daram*

19 Polish: *Kocham Cie*

20 Portuguese: *Eu te amo*

21 Romanian: *Te iu besc*

22 Russian: *Ya vas lyublyu*

23 Serbian: *Volim te*

24 Sioux: *Techihhila*

25 Spanish: *Te amo*

26 Swedish: *jag älskar dig*

27 Taiwanese: *Gwa ai lee*

28 Thai: *Phom Rak Khun*

29 Hawaiian: *Aloha au iā 'oe*

30 Yiddish: *Ikh hob dikh lib*

 Note to the teacher: Use with "30 Ways to Say…*I Love You!*" on page 59.

CLASSROOM DISPLAYS

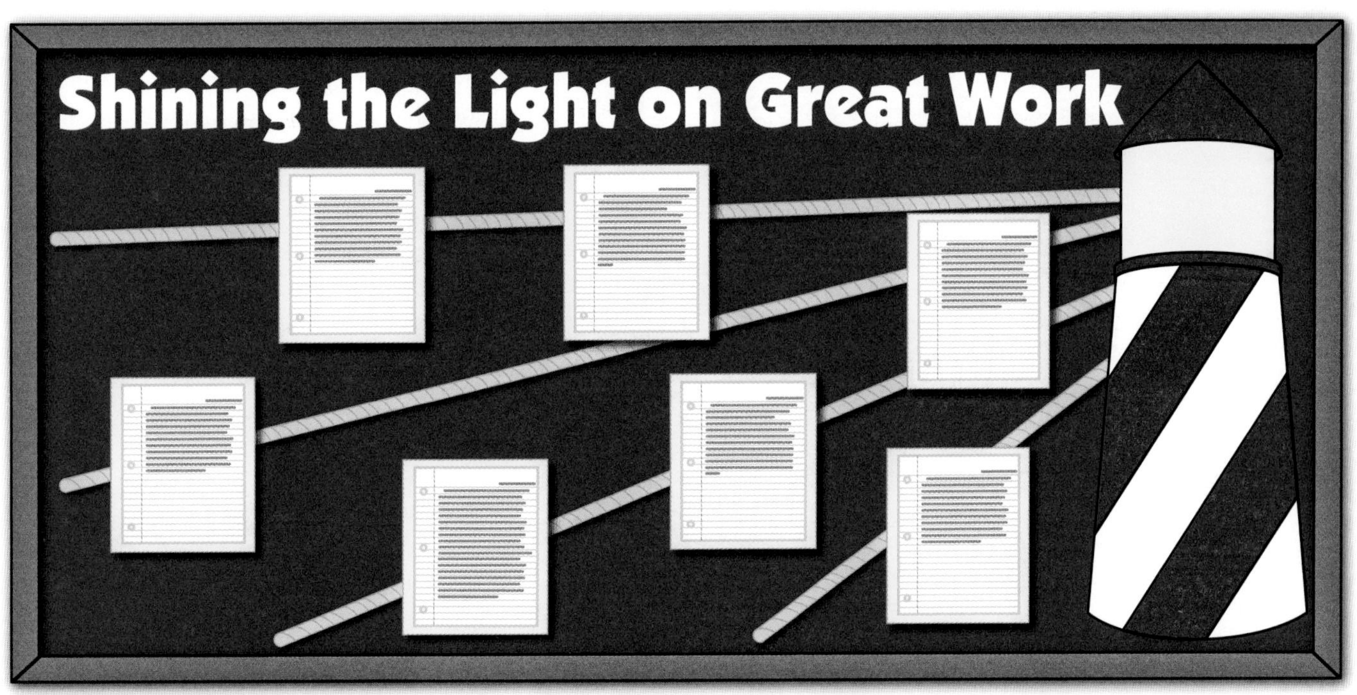

Shine some light on students' best work with this illuminating display. Post on a board a large lighthouse cutout. Then attach lengths of yellow yarn (beams of light) and students' mounted work samples as shown.

HUMOROUS POEMS TO MAKE YOU HOOT!
Andy
Haiku
I dressed too fast and
realized at school that my
sneakers did not match!

April is National Poetry Month *and* National Humor Month. Incorporate both observances into this fun-filled display. Instruct each student to write a humorous poem on a copy of page 63. Then have him draw a goofy face on his owl, color the bird, and cut it out. Display the finished projects as shown.

Colleen Dabney, Williamsburg, VA

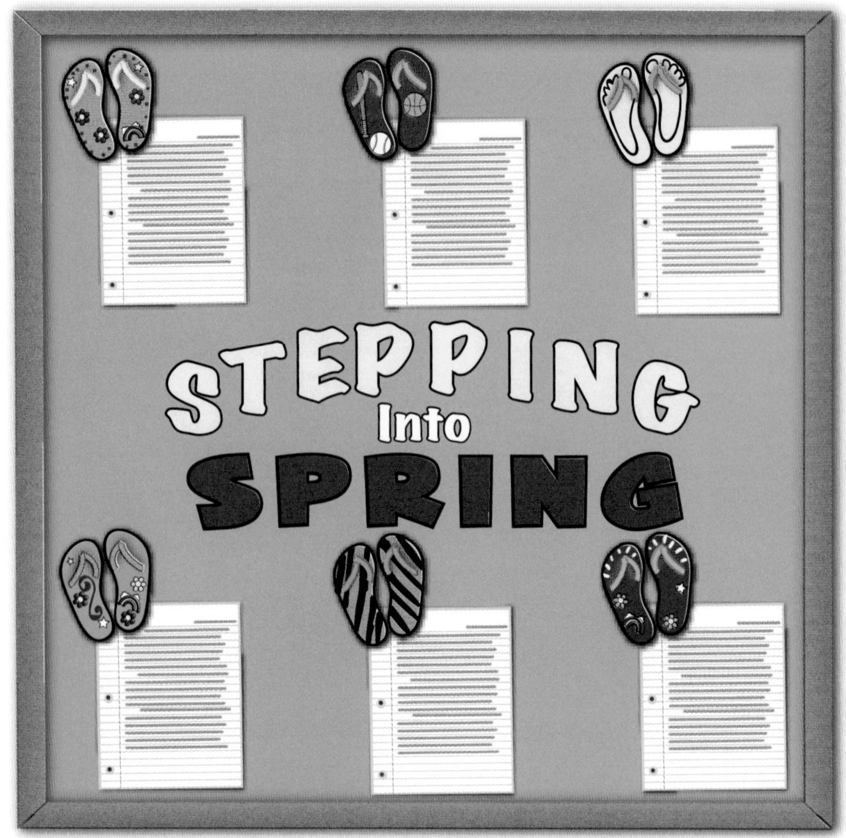

To begin, have each child write about her favorite springtime things. When she's finished, have her cut out a construction paper copy of the flip-flop patterns below and poke a sharpened pencil in her cutouts where indicated. For each flip-flop, she cuts a pipe cleaner in half and threads the pieces (straps) through the holes as shown. Then she decorates her flip-flops as desired. Display each child's flip-flops along with her writing.

Connie Thompson
Falling Branch Elementary
Christiansburg, VA

TIP
To alter the display, change the title to "Stepping Into Summer" and have students write about their summer plans.

Flip-Flop Patterns

Use with "Stepping Into Spring" on this page.

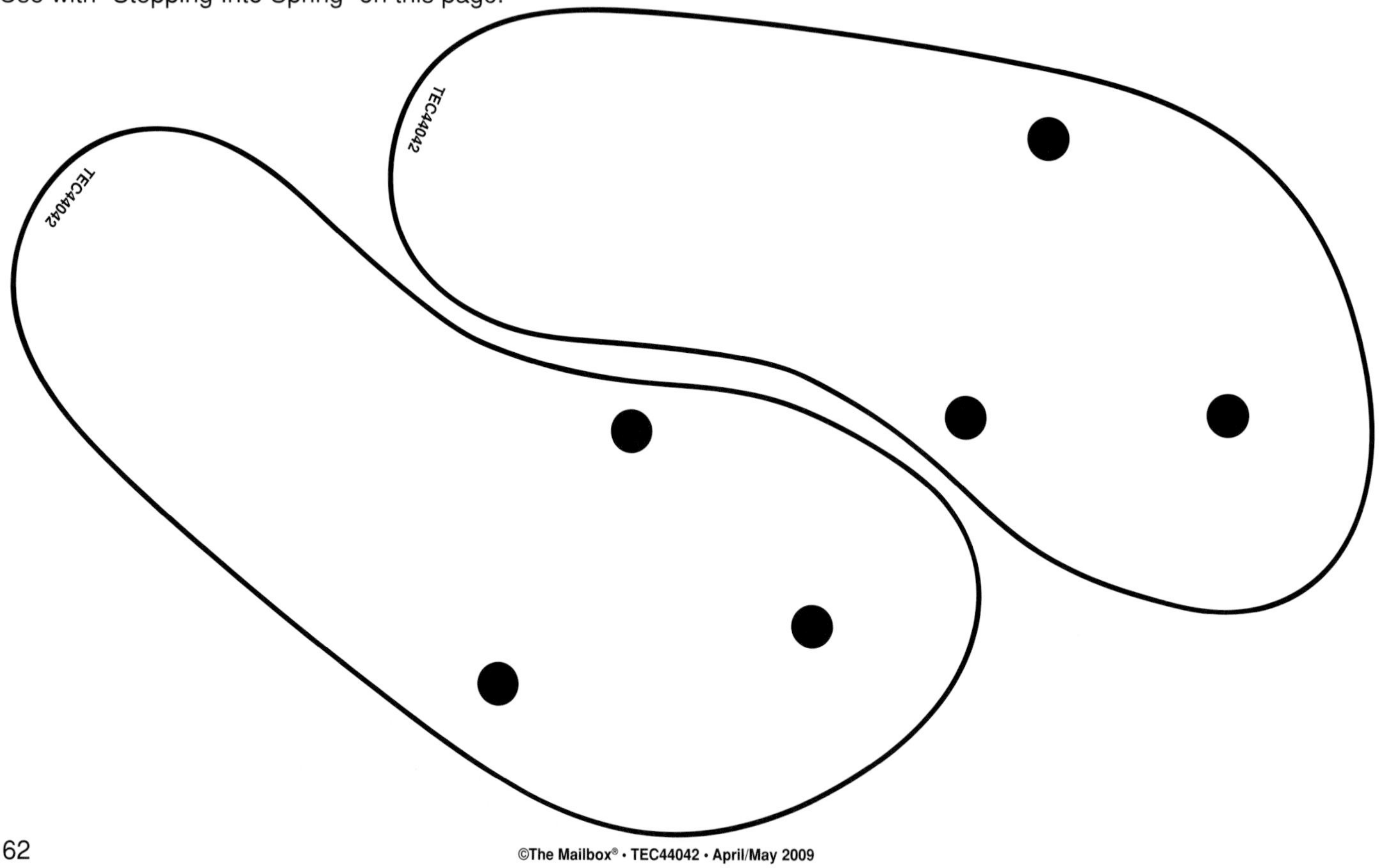

TEC44042

TEC44042

Owl Pattern

Use with "Humorous Poems to Make You Hoot!" on page 61.

CLASSROOM DISPLAYS

To create this year-end display, have each child cut out a copy of the overalls pattern on page 65 and label it with five things he enjoyed learning this year. Then have him decorate his cutout as desired.

Laura Whalen, Suder Elementary, Jonesboro, GA

Have each student celebrate summer by writing a haiku poem on a yellow paper star. Write each child's name on a piece of white ribbon. Then display each star and ribbon as shown.

adapted from an idea by Colleen Dabney, Williamsburg, VA

Program and color, as shown, an enlarged copy of the parrot pattern on page 66. Make smaller colorful copies of the pattern using the color code. Then, on a matching color of bird, have each student write the title of a book he has read this year that he thinks a classmate would enjoy. At the end of the year, encourage students to take home several cutouts from the display to use as summer reading suggestions.

adapted from an idea by Colleen Dabney
Williamsburg, VA

Color Code
red = fantasy
orange = traditional literature
yellow = realistic fiction
green = informational
blue = biography
purple = autobiography

Overalls Pattern

Use with "Overall, It's Been a Great Year!" on page 64.

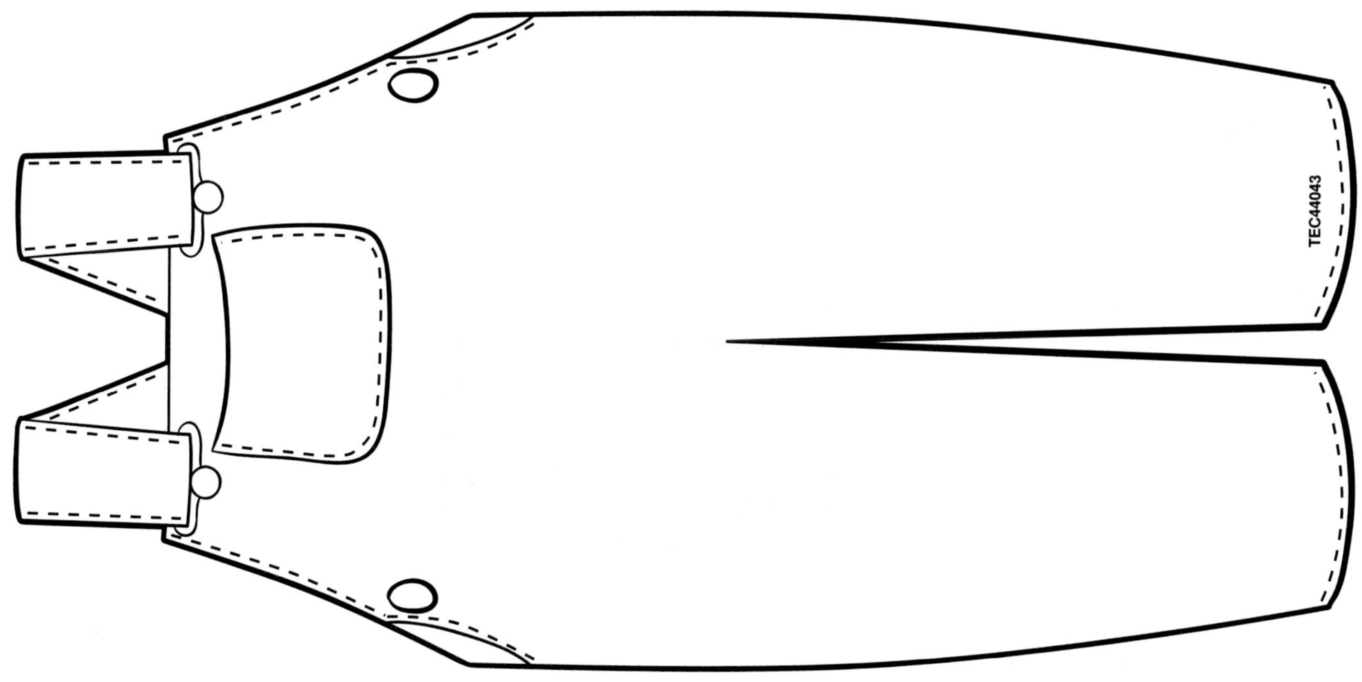

Parrot Pattern

Use with "Soar With Summer Reading!" on page 65.

Language Arts

Language Arts TIPS & TOOLS

Simple Switch
Types of sentences

Begin this activity by writing a simple declarative sentence on the board. Show students how to change the sentence into interrogative, imperative, and exclamatory sentences as shown. Then have students help you identify the punctuation and key words and phrases used in each sentence. Next, give each pair of students a copy of page 73. Instruct each twosome to select a phrase from the page and use it to write a similar set of four sentences. When the duos are finished, have them share their sentences in random order. Challenge the listeners to identify each sentence's type and the clues that helped them.

Lauren E. Cox, Four Oaks Elementary, Four Oaks, NC

He went to the museum. (declarative)

When did he go to the museum? (interrogative)

Please tell him to go to the museum. (imperative)

You won't believe what happened to him at the museum! (exclamatory)

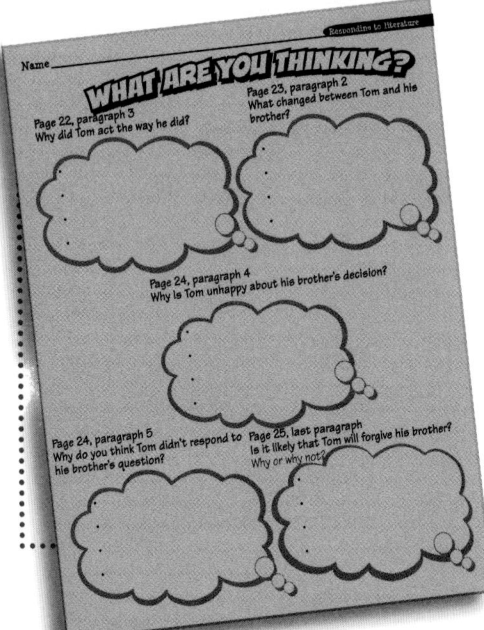

What Are You Thinking?
Comprehension

Here's a terrific way to build higher-level comprehension skills. Above each thought bubble on a copy of page 74, write a page number, a paragraph number or other identifier, and an open-ended inferential question, as shown. Then give each child a copy of the page. While the student reads, have her list in the bubbles her responses and the text evidence that supports them. Use the page anytime you want to give students a quick comprehension builder.

Elisse Arnell, Merrick, NY

Places, Please!

Capitalization, punctuation

It's easy to adapt this hands-on independent activity to practice a variety of skills. Label sentence strips with sentences that feature the skill you want students to review. Cut each strip apart as shown, and store its pieces and an answer key in a resealable bag labeled with the skill. A student removes the pieces from the bag, arranges them in order, and then copies the sentence correctly on his paper. For further practice, have the student also write one or more original sentences that follow the capitalization and punctuation rules shown on the sentence strip.

LaVone Novotny, Marion, OH

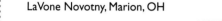

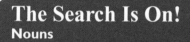

Lynn | , | the best athlete | at our school | , | wants to be | an astronaut | .

The Search Is On!

Nouns

Use this team game to review the kinds of nouns students have studied. Display a points chart that includes the noun types being reviewed. Instruct each team to open its reading texts to any two-page spread. At your signal, give the teams five minutes to find and list as many examples of the targeted nouns (with no repeats) as possible. When time is up, have each team share its list. Award points; then play another round using a different two-page spread. The team with the most points after a desired number of rounds wins.

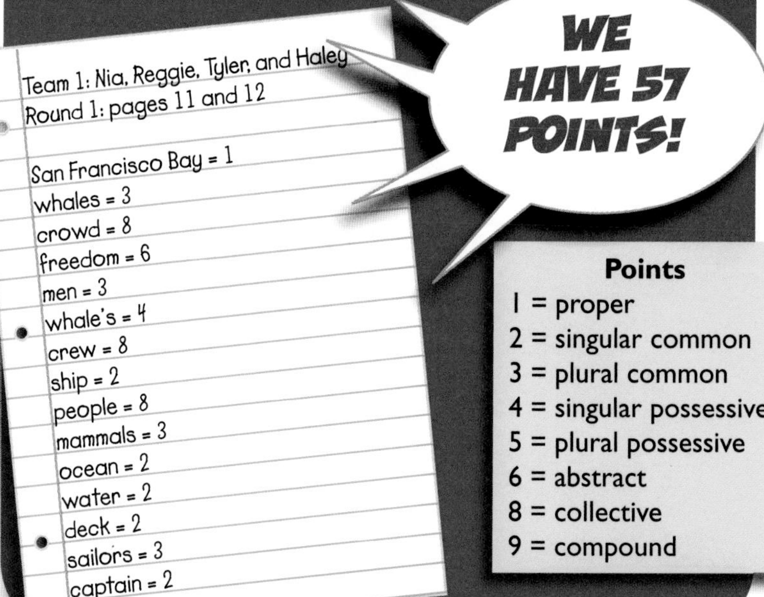

Team 1: Nia, Reggie, Tyler, and Haley
Round 1: pages 11 and 12
San Francisco Bay = 1
whales = 3
crowd = 8
freedom = 6
men = 3
whale's = 4
crew = 8
ship = 2
people = 8
mammals = 3
ocean = 2
water = 2
deck = 2
sailors = 3
captain = 2
WE HAVE 57 POINTS!

Points

1 = proper
2 = singular common
3 = plural common
4 = singular possessive
5 = plural possessive
6 = abstract
8 = collective
9 = compound

manage

Team Bee

Spelling

To play this fun no-elimination game, give each group of students a small whiteboard (or notepad) and a marker. Next, call out a spelling word and allow the groups 30 seconds to spell the word on their boards. If requested, provide a definition or use the word in a sentence. When time is up, have groups hold up their boards. Award a point to each team whose word is spelled correctly. Repeat with additional words until one team reaches a predetermined number of points.

Marcia Worth-Baker
South Orange, NJ

Name________________________________

Doors to Understanding

Topic: ________________________________

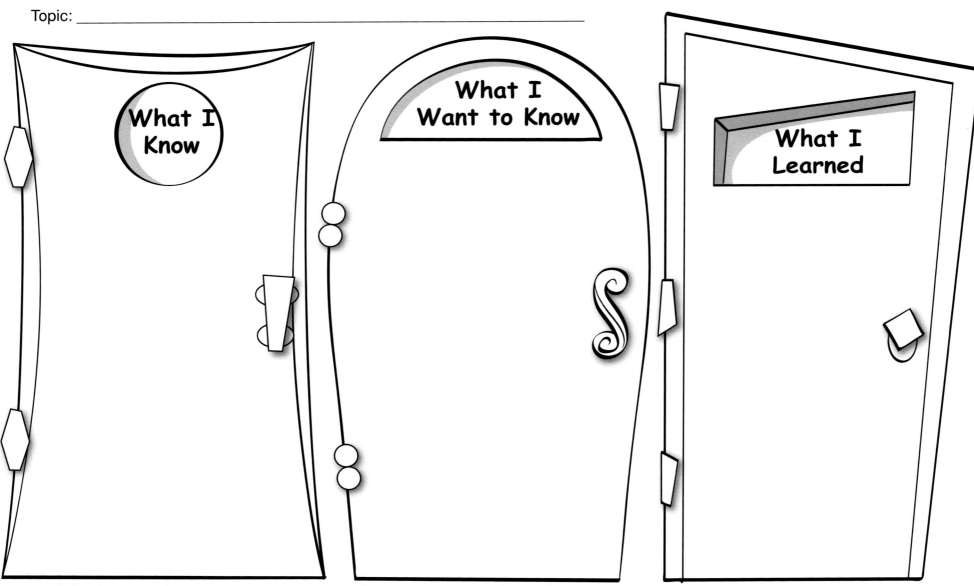

What I Know

What I Want to Know

What I Learned

Name ______________________________

Babysitting Blues

Color each rattle by the code.

Code
simple = blue
compound = purple
complex = green

1. I used to enjoy babysitting!
2. I make $5.00 an hour, and I like having a job.
3. Last week I took care of the Ferguson triplets.
4. I got a terrible headache because they cried all evening.
5. Fern Ferguson cried the most since she bumped her head.
6. Mrs. Ferguson must pay me more, or I'll never babysit for her again.
7. Frankie Ferguson is usually sweet, but he was terrible last week.
8. I will have to bring a friend with me next week.
9. Although I was tired after my babysitting job, I watched a movie later.
10. The Ferguson triplets are quite a handful!

Bonus Box: On the back of this page, write three sentences about a job you've had. Be sure to use each sentence type: simple, compound, and complex.

Name ______________________________

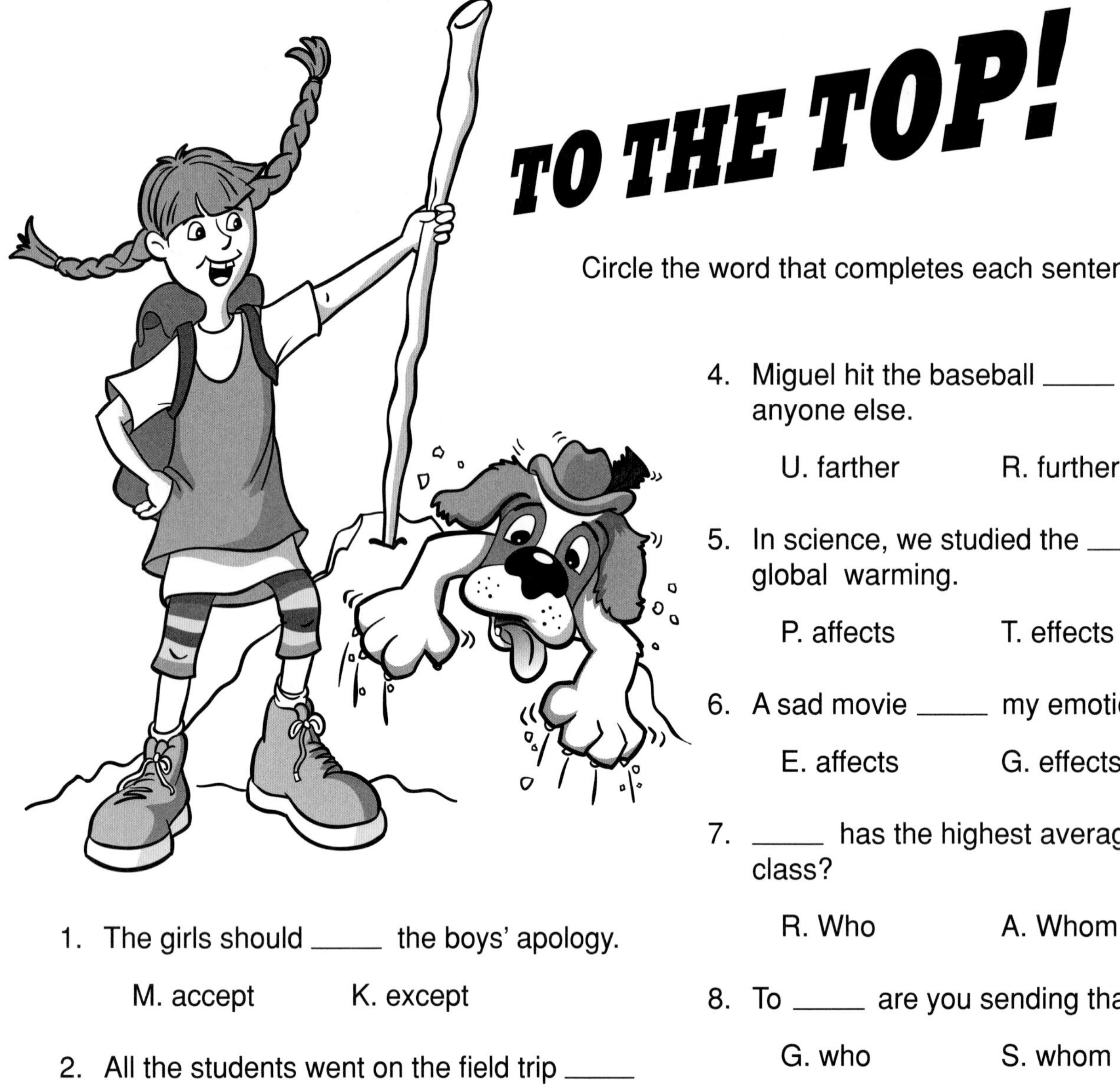

Circle the word that completes each sentence.

1. The girls should _____ the boys' apology.

   M. accept   K. except

2. All the students went on the field trip _____ Mary.

   A. accept   N. except

3. Carrie wants to _____ her study of French.

   C. farther   O. further

4. Miguel hit the baseball _____ than anyone else.

   U. farther   R. further

5. In science, we studied the _____ of global warming.

   P. affects   T. effects

6. A sad movie _____ my emotions.

   E. affects   G. effects

7. _____ has the highest average in the class?

   R. Who   A. Whom

8. To _____ are you sending that email?

   G. who   S. whom

9. Our next-door neighbors keep a close eye on ______ children.

   R. there   I. their

10. Tell the kids to wait _____ by the fence.

    A. there   B. their

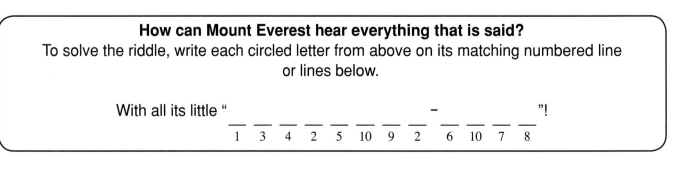

How can Mount Everest hear everything that is said?

To solve the riddle, write each circled letter from above on its matching numbered line or lines below.

With all its little "__ __ __ __ __ __ __ __ - __ __ __ __"!

1 3 4 2 5 10 9 2 6 10 7 8

Note to the teacher: Use with “Simple Switch” on page 68.

Name ________________________________

WHAT ARE YOU THINKING?

 Note to the teacher: Use with "What Are You Thinking?" on page 68.

Language Arts TIPS & TOOLS

Prediction Bookmarks

Prereading, activating prior knowledge

Give each child the bookmark shown, which does more than help the reader keep his place. After the student looks at a book's title and text features, he illustrates one bookmark side with something he thinks will happen in the story. Then he answers on paper the questions on the bookmark's other side.

Melissa Barbay, Devers School, Devers, TX

☆ What do you think this book is about?

☆ Who do you think the main character will be?

☆ What do you think happens in the book?

☆ When and where do you think the book's events will take place?

☆ What purpose do you think the author had for writing this book?

Draw something you think will happen in this book.

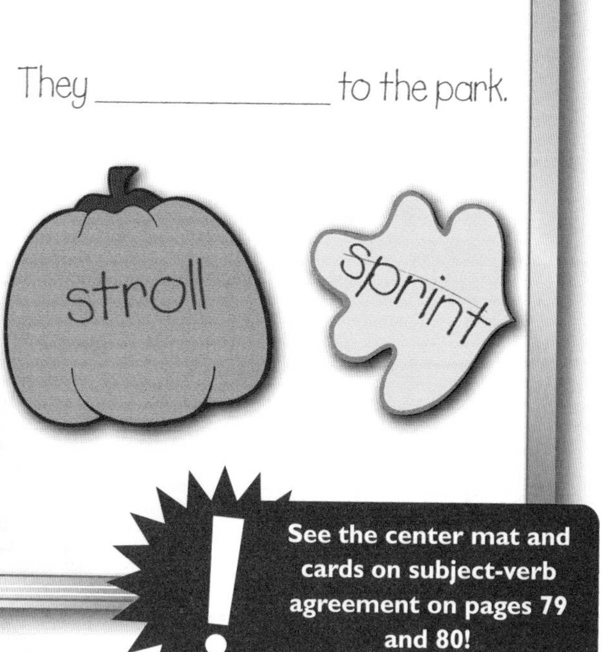

See the center mat and cards on subject-verb agreement on pages 79 and 80!

Act-It-Out Relay

Verbs

Begin this activity by writing on the board a simple cloze sentence. Brainstorm with students vivid action verbs to use in the sentence and list them on the board. Challenge small groups of students to use a thesaurus to list ten more verbs for the sentence. Afterward, label a class supply of seasonal shapes with the best verbs listed. The next day, place half the cutouts atop each of two chairs the same distance from a starting line and have two teams line up behind the line. At your signal, have the first player on each team race to the corresponding chair, select a shape, and return to the finish line performing the action on that shape. The first team to complete the relay wins. After the race, post the cutouts so students can refer to them.

Gretchen Gesell, Palmquist Elementary, Oceanside, CA

In 1773 the British Parliament used ships from the Royal Navy to blockade Boston Harbor.

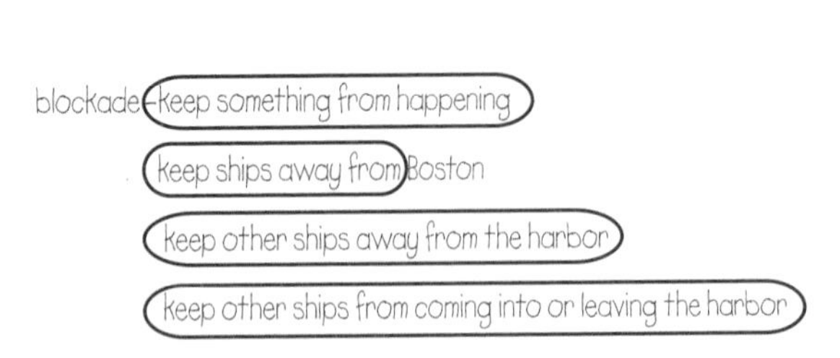

blockade
keep something from happening
keep ships away from Boston
keep other ships away from the harbor
keep other ships from coming into or leaving the harbor

The Meaning's Not a Mystery Anymore!

Vocabulary

To help students better understand key words from a topic currently being studied, read aloud a sentence that includes one of the words. Ask a student what she thinks the word means. Record her response on the board and circle the correct parts of her definition. Continue the process by having two or three more students each modify the definition, keeping each correct part but adding to it. Then have students check a dictionary or glossary to see how close their definition is to the actual meaning. Repeat with other words as time allows.

Diane Marshall, Salem, AL

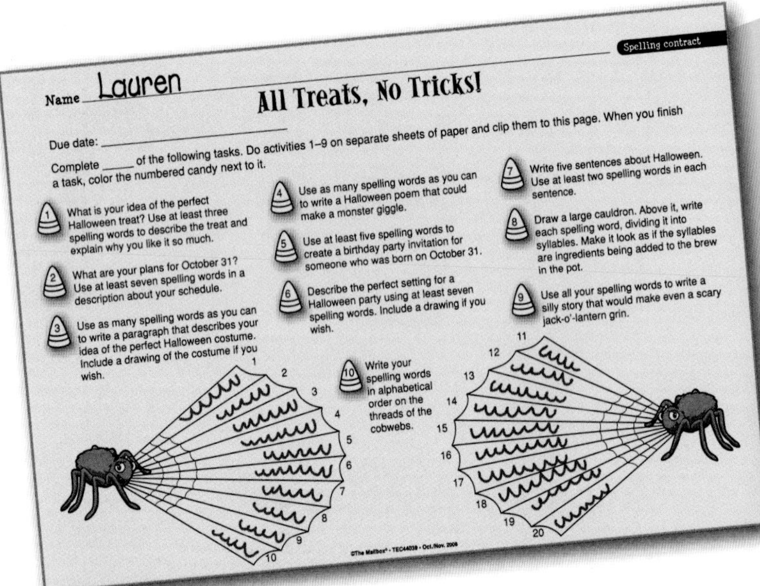

Spelling contract

Name Lauren

All Treats, No Tricks!

Due date: ______

Complete _____ of the following tasks. Do activities 1–9 on separate sheets of paper and clip them to this page. When you finish a task, color the numbered candy next to it.

1. What is your idea of the perfect Halloween treat? Use at least three spelling words to describe the treat and explain why you like it so much.
2. What are your plans for October 31? Use at least seven spelling words in a description about your schedule.
3. Use as many spelling words as you can to write a paragraph that describes your idea of the perfect Halloween costume. Include a drawing of the costume if you wish.
4. Use as many spelling words as you can to write a Halloween poem that could make a monster giggle.
5. Use at least five spelling words to create a birthday party invitation for someone who was born on October 31.
6. Describe the perfect setting for a Halloween party using at least seven spelling words. Include a drawing if you wish.
7. Write five sentences about Halloween. Use at least two spelling words in each sentence.
8. Draw a large cauldron. Above it, write each spelling word, dividing it into syllables. Make it look as if the syllables are ingredients being added to the brew in the pot.
9. Use all your spelling words to write a silly story that would make even a scary jack-o'-lantern grin.
10. Write your spelling words in alphabetical order on the threads of the cobwebs.

All Treats, No Tricks!

Spelling

Motivate students to study their October spelling words with the seasonal contract on page 84. Assign each group or the entire class a due date and the number of tasks you wish them to do. Then let the fun begin!

Julie Alarie, Williston, VT, and Betsy Conlon
Essex, VT

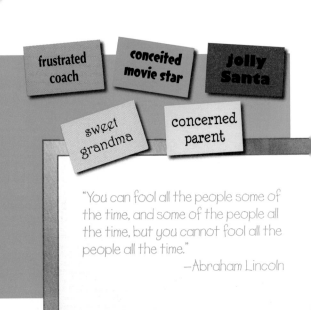

It's How You Say It

Fluency

Use role-playing to help students overcome the fear of reading aloud. Give each child a card labeled with a different character's name. Then write on the board an interesting quote or stanza of poetry. Have students read the text in unison several times before each child reads it in character. If desired, challenge the class to guess the identity of the character being portrayed.

John Hughes, Deerfield Elementary, Cedar Hills, UT

"You can fool all the people some of the time, and some of the people all the time, but you cannot fool all the people all the time."
—Abraham Lincoln

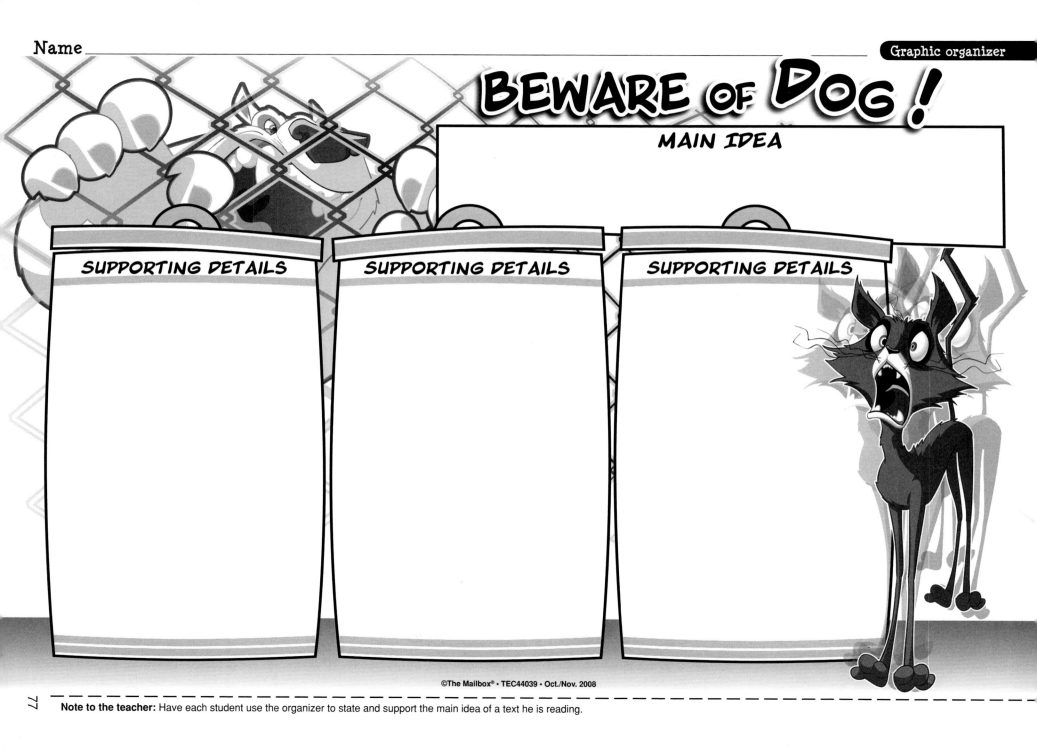

Name ______________________

Beware of Dog!

MAIN IDEA

SUPPORTING DETAILS

SUPPORTING DETAILS

SUPPORTING DETAILS

Note to the teacher: Have each student use the organizer to state and support the main idea of a text he is reading.

Name ____________________

Windows to a Great Read

1. Draw and cut out an old house from a large sheet of construction paper. Make sure the house has six to eight windows and a door. Add details to the house using markers or crayons.

2. Number the windows. Then cut along the center and tops and bottoms of the windows and door so they open as flaps.

3. Somewhere on the house, write your name and the book's title and author.

4. Glue the house onto white paper (but don't glue down the door or window flaps). Color the background to represent a setting from your book.

5. Behind the door flap, write a sentence about your book's plot to reveal the problem or mystery that is solved. Under each window flap, write a different clue related to the plot. Include people, places, and objects in the clues.

Game Cards and Answer Key

Use with "Football Fever" on page 80. Mount on construction paper a copy of the game mat on page 80 and a copy of the cards and answer key below. If desired, laminate the pages before cutting the cards apart.

A He is an amazing athlete. TEC44039	B The team work hard all year. TEC44039	C Bring the football with you. TEC44039
D The coach wants him to tackle the other team's quarterback. TEC44039	E Scores a touchdown for me! TEC44039	F Our team has scored seven points. TEC44039
G They want to join our team. TEC44039	H He am our assistant coach. TEC44039	I Many players tries out for the team. TEC44039
J Our quarterback throws a great pass. TEC44039	K The team's mascot is a mustang horse. TEC44039	L The cheerleaders watches the game from the sidelines. TEC44039
M Fans stand in their seats. TEC44039	N Tickets to our games costs $10 each. TEC44039	O Players must wears helmets on the playing field. TEC44039
P The equipment manager cleans the team's uniforms. TEC44039	Q A sports trainer helps players with injuries. TEC44039	R Our team won the game! TEC44039

Answer Key for "Football Fever"

A. correct
B. works
C. correct
D. correct
E. Score
F. correct
G. correct
H. is
I. try
J. correct
K. correct
L. watch
M. correct
N. cost
O. wear
P. correct
Q. correct
R. correct

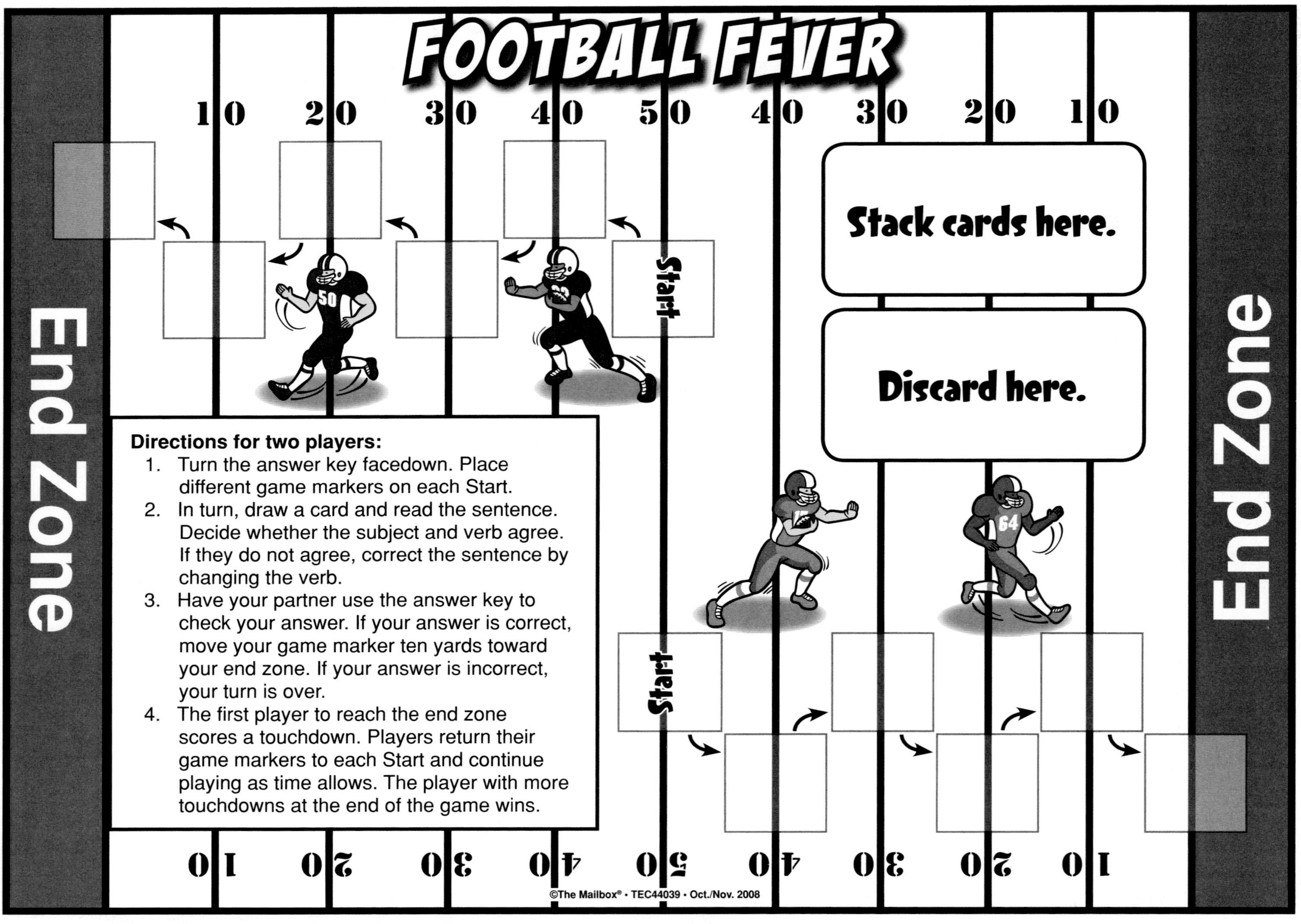

Directions for two players:

1. Turn the answer key facedown. Place different game markers on each Start.
2. In turn, draw a card and read the sentence. Decide whether the subject and verb agree. If they do not agree, correct the sentence by changing the verb.
3. Have your partner use the answer key to check your answer. If your answer is correct, move your game marker ten yards toward your end zone. If your answer is incorrect, your turn is over.
4. The first player to reach the end zone scores a touchdown. Players return their game markers to each Start and continue playing as time allows. The player with more touchdowns at the end of the game wins.

Name ______________________

WORD WEB

A Game for Two Players

Directions:

1. In turn, write a word in the grid, one letter per square. Follow the rules below.
2. If the word is spelled correctly, award points as follows:

   word of six or more letters = 15 points
   five-letter word = 10 points
   four-letter word = 8 points
   three-letter word = 5 points

3. The player with more points after all squares have been used or no more words can be made wins!

Rules

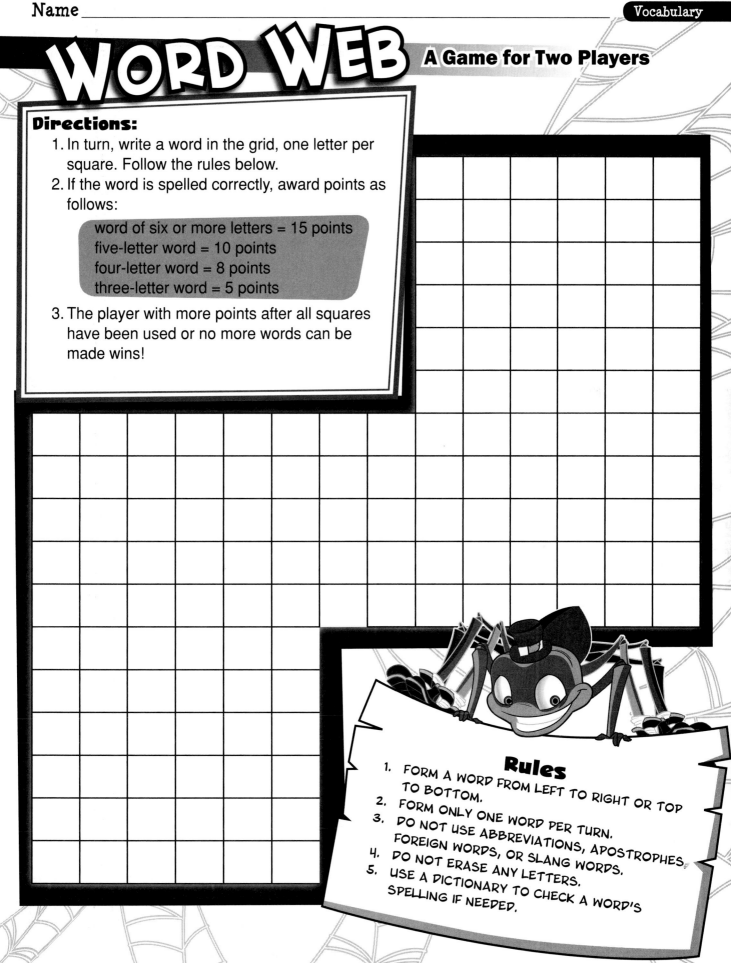

1. FORM A WORD FROM LEFT TO RIGHT OR TOP TO BOTTOM.
2. FORM ONLY ONE WORD PER TURN.
3. DO NOT USE ABBREVIATIONS, APOSTROPHES, FOREIGN WORDS, OR SLANG WORDS.
4. DO NOT ERASE ANY LETTERS.
5. USE A DICTIONARY TO CHECK A WORD'S SPELLING IF NEEDED.

Name ______________________________ Punctuation review

Musical Notes

Decide whether each sentence is punctuated correctly. Then lightly color the musical note in the appropriate column.

	Correct	Incorrect
1. "Renée, are you ready to see the band play?" Mom asked.	D	R
2. Renée answered, "Yes, I've always wanted to see this group in concert"	S	A
3. "We will go to the concert watch the band, and then go get a bite to eat," Dad announced.	K	D
4. "How long do you think the band will play tonight?" Kyle asked Dad.	H	C
5. Mom said, "I just hope the concert isn't too long. I have to get up early in the morning."	A	N
6. Its going to start at 8 PM and should be over by 10 PM" I told everyone.	L	E
7. "We should bring earplugs. I've heard this band is pretty loud," Kyle advised.	N	M
8. "My friends band also is very good. Someday her band wants to put on a concert as well, added Kyle."	T	B

What can you wear on your head to make music?
To solve the riddle, write each colored letter from above on its matching numbered line or lines below.

___ "___ ___ ___ ___ ___ ___ ___ ___"
2 4 6 5 3 8 2 7 1

Rewrite each incorrect sentence from above correctly on the lines below.

Sentence Number

______ ____________________________________

______ ____________________________________

______ ____________________________________

______ ____________________________________

Name ____

HARRY MONSTER'S DILEMMA

Use vivid action verbs to complete the story below.

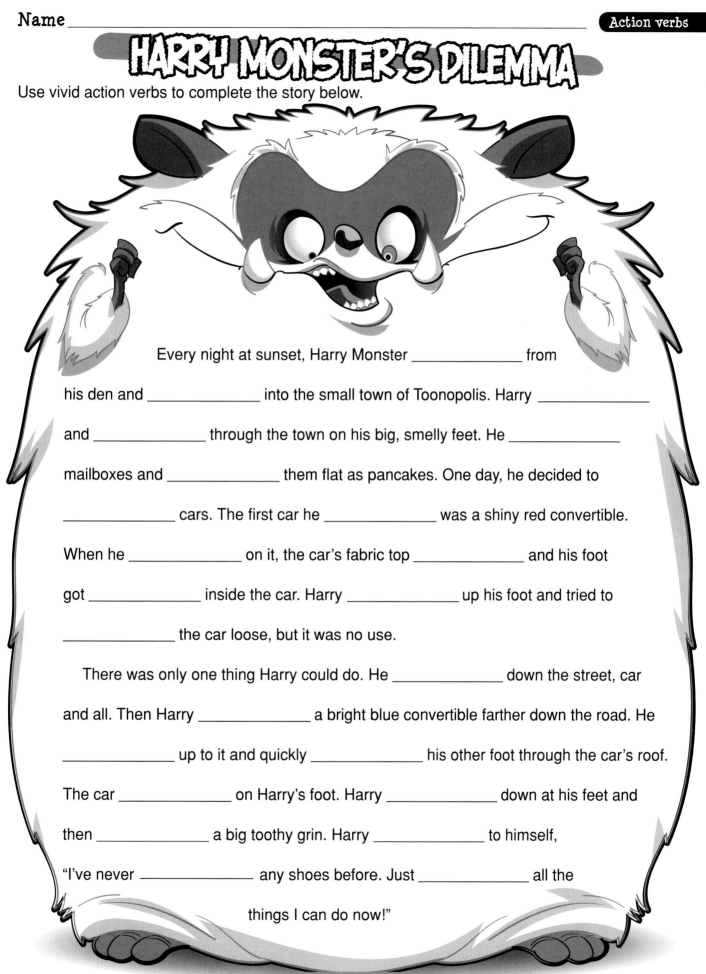

Every night at sunset, Harry Monster ____________ from his den and ____________ into the small town of Toonopolis. Harry ____________ and ____________ through the town on his big, smelly feet. He ____________ mailboxes and ____________ them flat as pancakes. One day, he decided to ____________ cars. The first car he ____________ was a shiny red convertible. When he ____________ on it, the car's fabric top ____________ and his foot got ____________ inside the car. Harry ____________ up his foot and tried to ____________ the car loose, but it was no use.

There was only one thing Harry could do. He ____________ down the street, car and all. Then Harry ____________ a bright blue convertible farther down the road. He ____________ up to it and quickly ____________ his other foot through the car's roof. The car ____________ on Harry's foot. Harry ____________ down at his feet and then ____________ a big toothy grin. Harry ____________ to himself, "I've never ____________ any shoes before. Just ____________ all the things I can do now!"

Name ______________________________

All Treats, No Tricks!

Due date: ______________________

Complete _____ of the following tasks. Do activities 1–9 on separate sheets of paper and clip them to this page. When you finish a task, color the numbered candy next to it.

1. What is your idea of the perfect Halloween treat? Use at least three spelling words to describe the treat and explain why you like it so much.
2. What are your plans for October 31? Use at least seven spelling words in a description about your schedule.
3. Use as many spelling words as you can to write a paragraph that describes your idea of the perfect Halloween costume. Include a drawing of the costume if you wish.
4. Use as many spelling words as you can to write a Halloween poem that could make a monster giggle.
5. Use at least five spelling words to create a birthday party invitation for someone who was born on October 31.
6. Describe the perfect setting for a Halloween party using at least seven spelling words. Include a drawing if you wish.
7. Write five sentences about Halloween. Use at least two spelling words in each sentence.
8. Draw a large cauldron. Above it, write each spelling word, dividing it into syllables. Make it look as if the syllables are ingredients being added to the brew in the pot.
9. Use all your spelling words to write a silly story that would make even a scary jack-o'-lantern grin.
10. Write your spelling words in alphabetical order on the threads of the cobwebs.

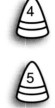

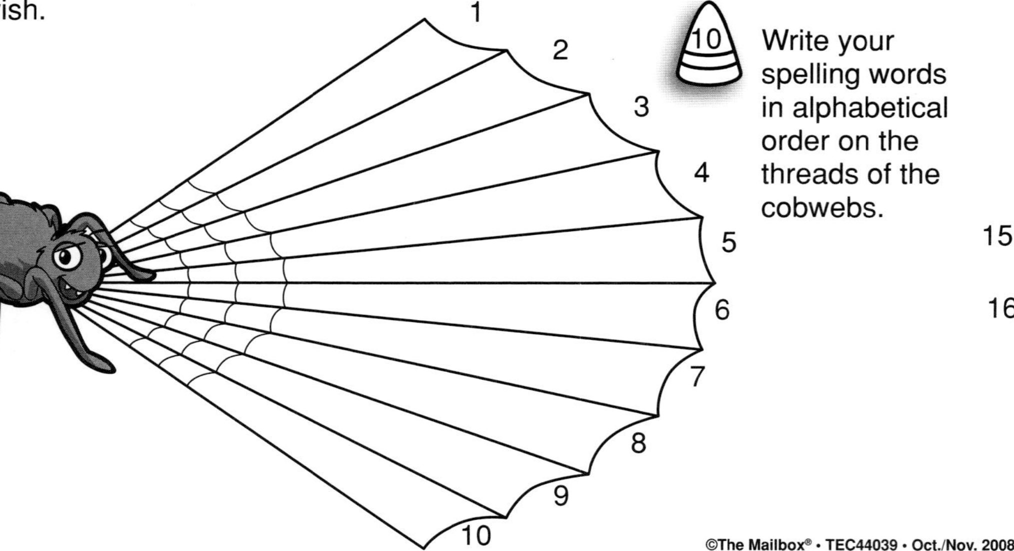

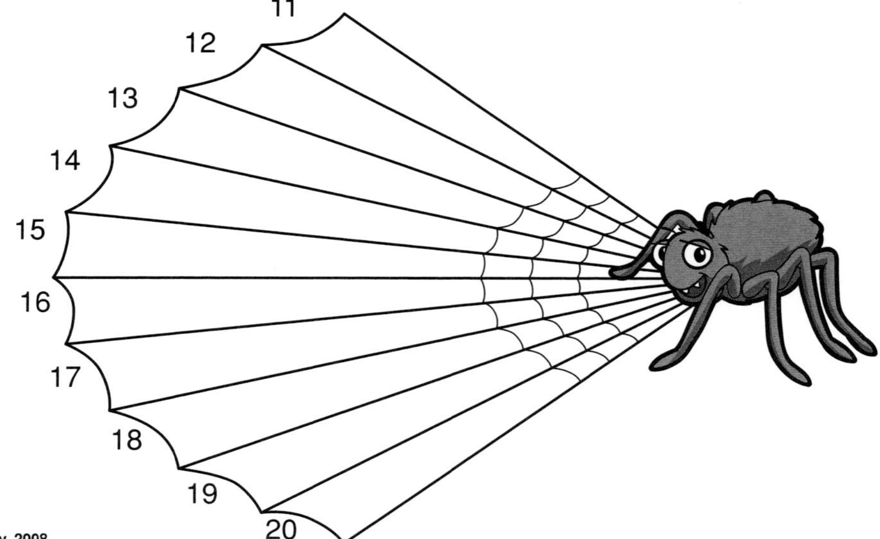

Note to the teacher: Use with "All Treats, No Tricks!" on page 76.

Language Arts Tips & Tools

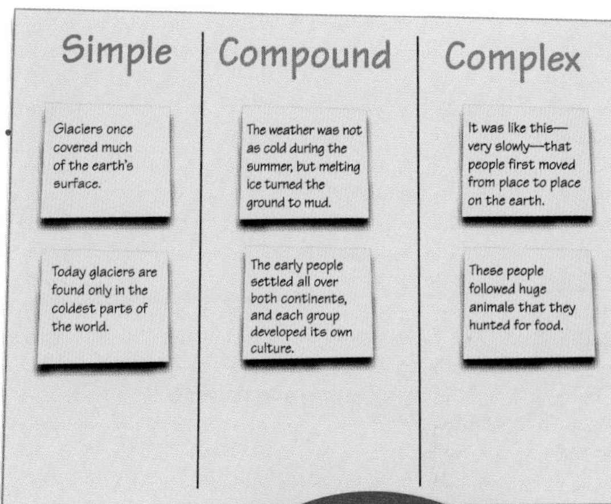

Simple
Compound
Complex
Glaciers once covered much of the earth's surface.
The weather was not as cold during the summer, but melting ice turned the ground to mud.
It was like this—very slowly—that people first moved from place to place on the earth.
Today glaciers are found only in the coldest parts of the world.
The early people settled all over both continents, and each group developed its own culture.
These people followed huge animals that they hunted for food.

Which Is It?

Simple, compound, and complex sentences

Display a poster labeled in three different colors as shown. Next, give each student a grade-appropriate reading passage (fiction or nonfiction) from a magazine or newspaper. As the child reads, instruct him to underline examples of simple, compound, and complex sentences using crayons of the same colors as the poster's labels. Then have him record an example of each sentence type on a separate sticky note and place each note in the appropriate column on the chart. Wrap up the activity by having each child write at least one example of each type of sentence.

Lauren E. Cox, Four Oaks Elementary, Four Oaks, NC

TIP

For further practice, place the chart and sticky notes at a center where students can practice sorting the sentences independently.

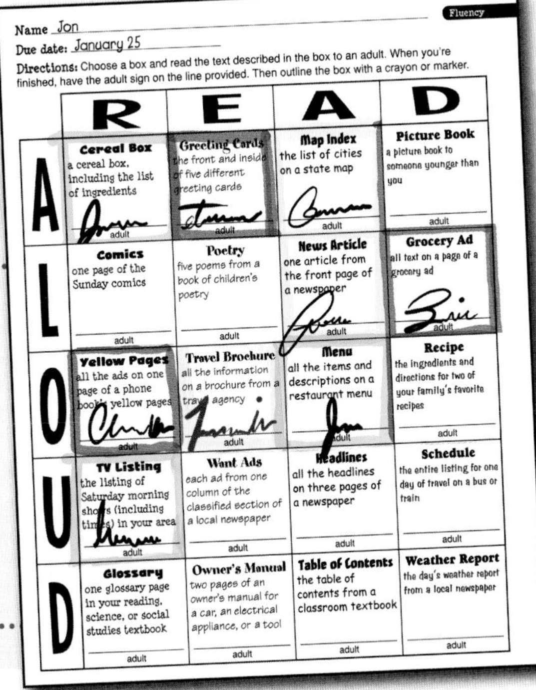

Name Jon — Fluency

Due date: January 25

Directions: Choose a box and read the text described in the box to an adult. When you're finished, have the adult sign on the line provided. Then outline the box with a crayon or marker.

	R	E	A	D
A	**Cereal Box** a cereal box, including the list of ingredients — adult	**Greeting Cards** the front and inside of five different greeting cards — adult	**Map Index** the list of cities on a state map — adult	**Picture Book** a picture book to someone younger than you — adult
L	**Comics** one page of the Sunday comics — adult	**Poetry** five poems from a book of children's poetry — adult	**News Article** one article from the front page of a newspaper — adult	**Grocery Ad** all text on a page of a grocery ad — adult
O	**Yellow Pages** all the ads on one page of a phone book's yellow pages — adult	**Travel Brochure** all the information on a brochure from a travel agency — adult	**Menu** all the items and descriptions on a restaurant menu — adult	**Recipe** the ingredients and directions for two of your family's favorite recipes — adult
U	**TV Listing** the listing of Saturday morning shows (including times) in your area — adult	**Want Ads** each ad from one column of the classified section of a local newspaper — adult	**Headlines** all the headlines on three pages of a newspaper — adult	**Schedule** the entire listing for one day of travel on a bus or train — adult
D	**Glossary** one glossary page in your reading, science, or social studies textbook — adult	**Owner's Manual** two pages of an owner's manual for a car, an electrical appliance, or a tool — adult	**Table of Contents** the table of contents from a classroom textbook — adult	**Weather Report** the day's weather report from a local newspaper — adult

Read It Aloud!

Fluency

Encourage students to do more reading aloud at home by having each child complete a copy of page 90 over several weeks or one grading period. Each time a student reads aloud a selection described in a particular box, have him outline the box with a crayon or marker and obtain the adult listener's signature.

Lori Jensen, Hilton Elementary, Brighton, MI

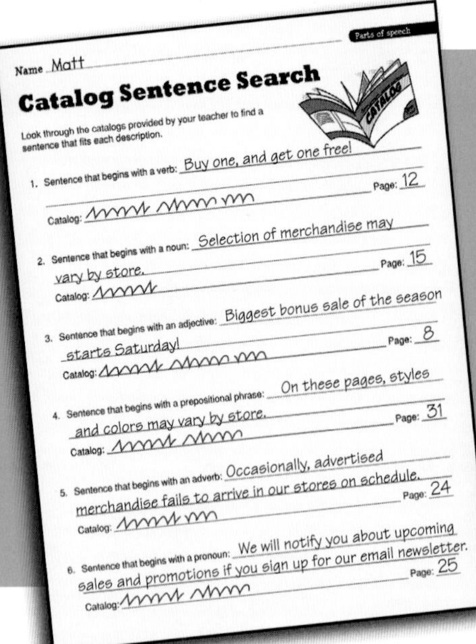
Parts of speech

Name Matt

Catalog Sentence Search

Look through the catalogs provided by your teacher to find a sentence that fits each description.

1. Sentence that begins with a verb: Buy one, and get one free!
Catalog: ________ Page: 12
2. Sentence that begins with a noun: Selection of merchandise may vary by store.
Catalog: ________ Page: 15
3. Sentence that begins with an adjective: Biggest bonus sale of the season starts Saturday!
Catalog: ________ Page: 8
4. Sentence that begins with a prepositional phrase: On these pages, styles and colors may vary by store.
Catalog: ________ Page: 31
5. Sentence that begins with an adverb: Occasionally, advertised merchandise fails to arrive in our stores on schedule.
Catalog: ________ Page: 24
6. Sentence that begins with a pronoun: We will notify you about upcoming sales and promotions if you sign up for our email newsletter.
Catalog: ________ Page: 25

Catalog Sentence Search

Parts of speech

Here's a nifty way to put those leftover shopping catalogs from the holidays to good use. Place the catalogs in a spot that's accessible to students. Then have each child select one or more catalogs to help him complete a copy of page 91 as directed.

Beth Main, Bethune Academy, Haines City, FL

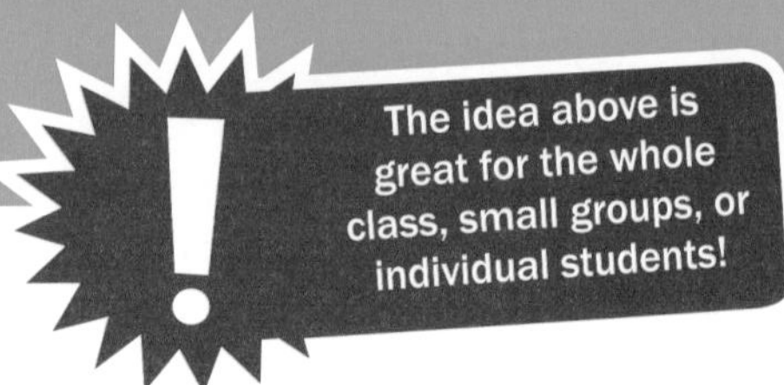

!
The idea above is great for the whole class, small groups, or individual students!

Support the Answers!

Comprehension

Caitlyn

1. Why do Jim and Sarah not have many friends?

Sarah is very quiet and timid, and Jim loses his temper easily.

Clues:
- ________
- ________

Challenge students to search for supportive text clues in an unexpected way. After students read a selection, give each reader a copy of several questions and their answers. Explain that since the questions are already answered, the students' task is to search the passage for clues that lead to each answer. Shifting the focus from finding answers to finding clues makes practicing this important reading skill more fun!

Diana Boykin, DeZavala Elementary, Midland, TX

Recite...Then Write!

Irregular verbs

To begin this relay game, Player 1 from each of two teams goes to the board and writes the present tense form of an irregular verb, such as *go*. Player 2 adds the verb's past and past participle forms and then writes the present tense of another irregular verb, such as *do*, on the next line. Player 3 adds that verb's next two tenses and then writes the present tense of another irregular verb, such as *grow*. The game continues until the first player on each team adds the final two forms of the last irregular verb. Then award each team one point for every correct verb tense. Give an extra point to the first team to finish the round. Play additional rounds until one team reaches a predetermined number of points and wins the match.

Patricia E. Dancho, Apollo-Ridge Middle School, Spring Church, PA

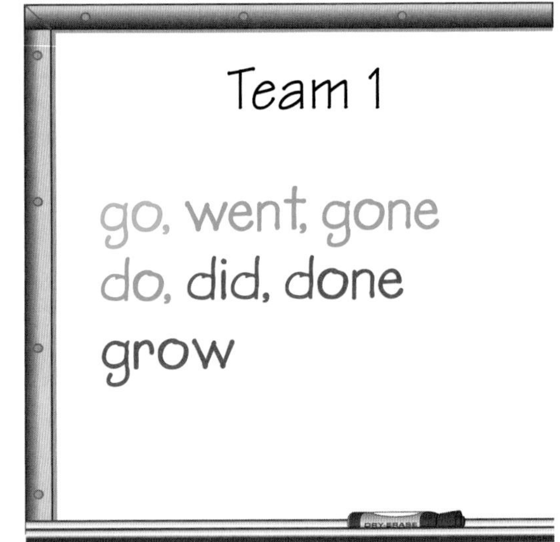

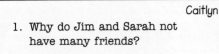

Name ______________________________

Unlock the Information

Before reading, look at the text features in the selection.
Then complete the organizer below.

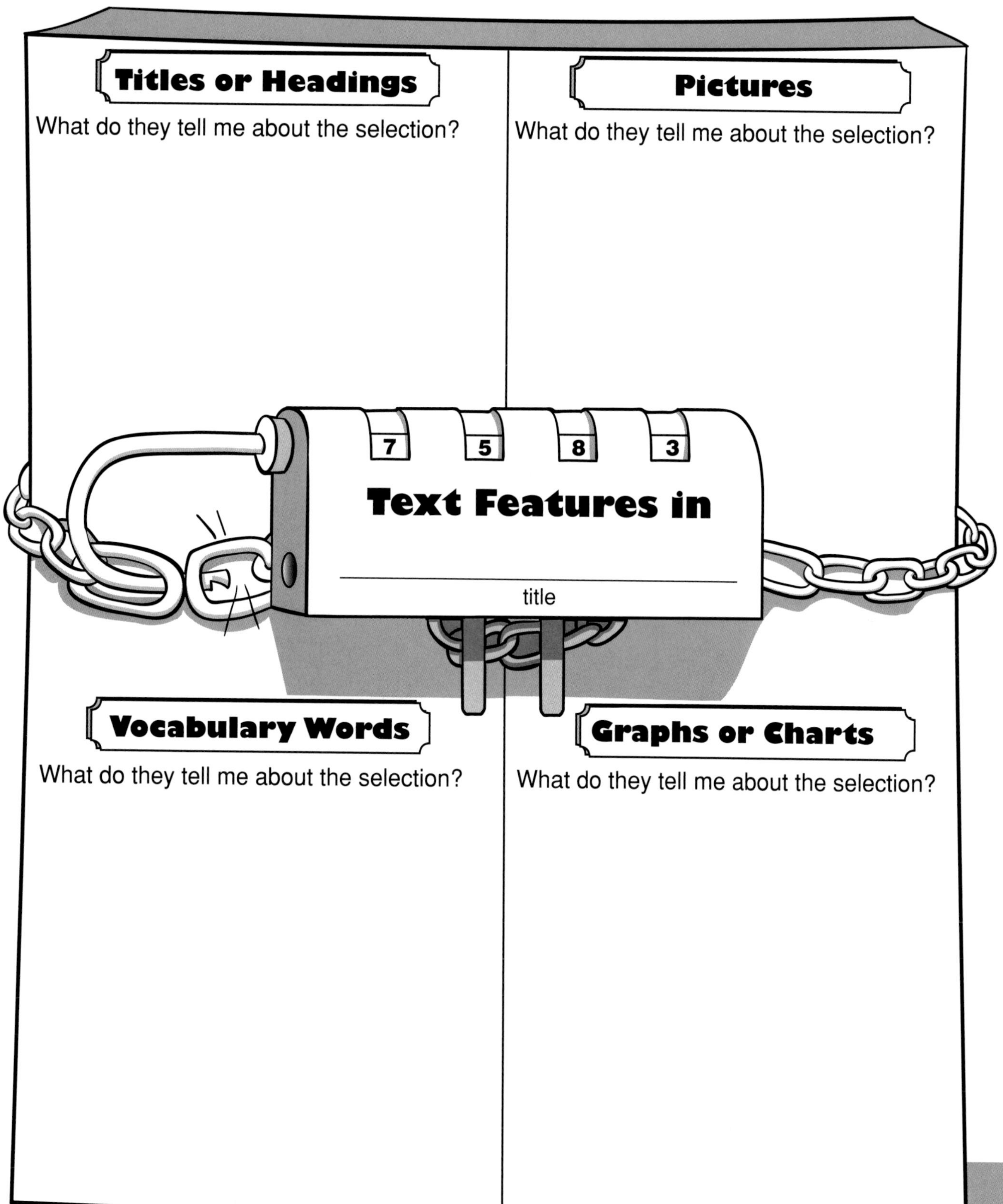

Titles or Headings
What do they tell me about the selection?
Pictures
What do they tell me about the selection?
7
5
8
3
Text Features in
title
Vocabulary Words
What do they tell me about the selection?
Graphs or Charts
What do they tell me about the selection?

Alien Invasion

Use a ruler to draw straight lines that connect each word's dot to its meanings' dots. Match each word to its two different meanings.

1. ball •
2. bank •
3. bark •
4. bat •
5. case •
6. date •
7. fair •
8. fan •
9. hide •
10. yard •

L B
A
C Y H
G U
S X K F T
A E Z R
R
D
I S Y
T
J P I M
D C
O
N
Q K
V

- a box for holding something
- a flying mammal
- a formal dance
- a fruit
- a lawyer's assignment
- a period of time
- a place that holds money
- a place with rides and games
- a round object used in a game
- a short, loud cry of a dog
- a solid stick used in games
- a steep slope of land
- a supporter
- a tough covering of a tree
- a unit of measure
- an animal skin
- an object that creates a breeze
- an outdoor area open to the sky
- honest
- to put out of sight

What has three feet but cannot walk?

To find out, write each uncrossed letter from above in order from left to right and top to bottom on the lines below.

___ ___ ___ ___ ___ ___ ___ ___ ___ ___!

Name ____________________ Adjectives

Hoops!

Label each underlined adjective by the code.

Adjective Code

P = proper adjective: *German, English*
A = article: *a, an, the*
C = common adjective: *big, blue*
D = demonstrative adjective: *this, that, these, those*

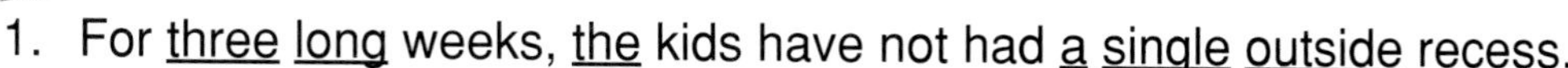

1. For three long weeks, the kids have not had a single outside recess.
2. Bad weather has kept the kids indoors.
3. Today Ms. Brite said her fifth-grade class could play trash-can basketball in the classroom.
4. Her excited students liked that idea.
5. Some of them hurried to move desks out of the way.
6. The Australian student put an empty trash can near the front board.
7. Marty and Kendra used yellow tape to make a free-throw line on the tile floor.

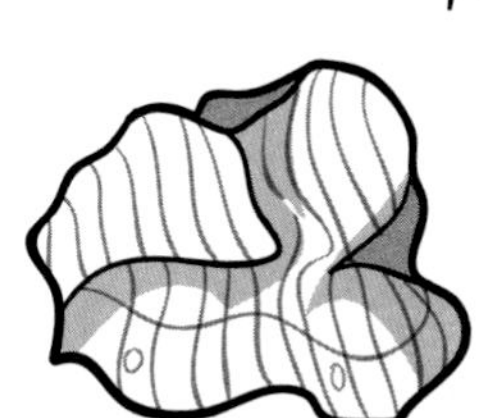

Underline each adjective. Then label each by the code. (Hint: there are 27 adjectives.)

8. The smiling American teacher listed the game rules.
9. The goal was to toss a paper ball into the trash can.
10. Each player would stand behind that free-throw line to toss the ball.
11. Each basket would equal one point for the team.
12. She would keep track of these points on the front board.
13. The eager students quickly formed equal teams.
14. Ms. Brite named each team after those four types of adjectives studied.
15. Then the contest began.

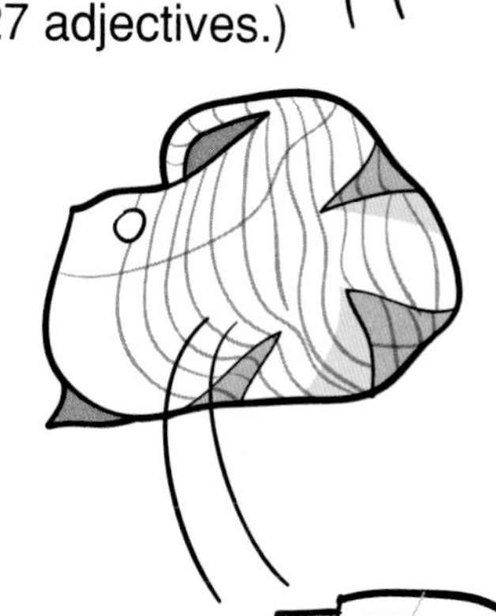

Name ____________________

Due date: ____________________

Directions: Choose a box and read the text described in the box to an adult. When you're finished, have the adult sign on the line provided. Then outline the box with a crayon or marker.

	R	E	A	D
A	**Cereal Box** a cereal box, including the list of ingredients ______ adult	**Greeting Cards** the front and inside of five different greeting cards ______ adult	**Map Index** the list of cities on a state map ______ adult	**Picture Book** a picture book to someone younger than you ______ adult
L	**Comics** one page of the Sunday comics ______ adult	**Poetry** five poems from a book of children's poetry ______ adult	**News Article** one article from the front page of a newspaper ______ adult	**Grocery Ad** all text on a page of a grocery ad ______ adult
O	**Yellow Pages** all the ads on one page of a phone book's yellow pages ______ adult	**Travel Brochure** all the information on a brochure from a travel agency ______ adult	**Menu** all the items and descriptions on a restaurant menu ______ adult	**Recipe** the ingredients and directions for two of your family's favorite recipes ______ adult
U	**TV Listing** the listing of Saturday morning shows (including times) in your area ______ adult	**Want Ads** each ad from one column of the classified section of a local newspaper ______ adult	**Headlines** all the headlines on three pages of a newspaper ______ adult	**Schedule** the entire listing for one day of travel on a bus or train ______ adult
D	**Glossary** one glossary page in your reading, science, or social studies textbook ______ adult	**Owner's Manual** two pages of an owner's manual for a car, an electrical appliance, or a tool ______ adult	**Table of Contents** the table of contents from a classroom textbook ______ adult	**Weather Report** the day's weather report from a local newspaper ______ adult

 Note to the teacher: Use with "Read It Aloud!" on page 85.

Name ______________________________

Catalog Sentence Search

Look through the catalogs provided by your teacher to find a sentence that fits each description.

1. Sentence that begins with a verb: ______________________________

   ____

   Catalog: ______________________________ Page: _____

2. Sentence that begins with a noun: ______________________________

   ____

   Catalog: ______________________________ Page: _____

3. Sentence that begins with an adjective: ______________________________

   ____

   Catalog: ______________________________ Page: _____

4. Sentence that begins with a prepositional phrase: ______________________________

   ____

   Catalog: ______________________________ Page: _____

5. Sentence that begins with an adverb: ______________________________

   ____

   Catalog: ______________________________ Page: _____

6. Sentence that begins with a pronoun: ______________________________

   ____

   Catalog: ______________________________ Page: _____

Note to the teacher: Use with "Catalog Sentence Search" on page 86.

Language Arts TIPS & TOOLS

Get the Scoop

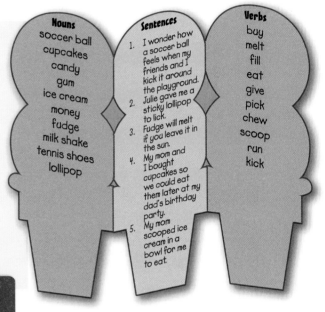

Subject-verb agreement, object pronouns

Begin by having each student list ten nouns and ten verbs on a cutout copy of page 100 as shown. Then have each child use the words to write in the center section five different sentences that include at least one object pronoun. If desired, require two sentences to be complex sentences that also include subject and possessive pronouns. When students have finished writing their sentences, have each child fold her project and decorate it.

Amber Barbee, Wharton, TX

For practice using adjectives and adverbs, check out the activity on page 98!

Nouns
soccer ball
cupcakes
candy
gum
ice cream
money
fudge
milk shake
tennis shoes
lollipop

Sentences
1. I wonder how a soccer ball feels when my friends and I kick it around the playground.
2. Julie gave me a sticky lollipop to lick.
3. Fudge will melt if you leave it in the sun.
4. My mom and I bought cupcakes so we could eat them later at my dad's birthday party.
5. My mom scooped ice cream in a bowl for me to eat.

Verbs
buy
melt
fill
eat
give
pick
chew
scoop
run
kick

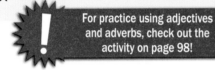

Underline	Quotation Marks
Tuck Everlasting	"...3, 2, 1...Lift Off!"
Charlotte's Web	"How the West Was Won"
The Buffalo Brigade	"The Road Not Taken"
Anthology of Poetry	"Man Survives Car Crash"
Ranger Rick	"The Case of the Missing Masterpiece"

Title Search

Punctuating titles

This small-group scavenger hunt helps students review the proper way to punctuate titles of published works in writing. First, display a textbook, a chapter book, and a poetry anthology. Explain that, in written work, the titles shown on the *outside* of published works should be underlined. Then open each sample, in turn, to a chapter, an article, or a poem. Explain that, in written work, the titles on the *inside* of a published work should be in quotation marks. Then have each small group search published works in the classroom and record at least five examples for each type as shown. For a fun review of various punctuation marks, see page 101.

LaVone Novotny, Marion, OH

High-Flying Vocabulary

Antonyms and synonyms

Give students practice with vocabulary skills by having them make one of these kites. Have each child cut a diamond shape from construction paper and then divide it and program it with the labels shown. Assign him a word to write on his cutout (see the list of suggestions). Then have him use appropriate resources to record a definition, an antonym, and a synonym for his word. After students add details to make their shapes look like kites, display their work on a bulletin board titled "High-Flying Vocabulary."

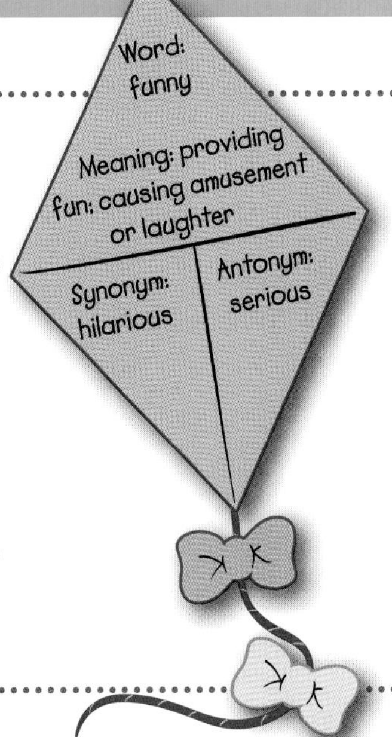

Word: funny
Meaning: providing fun; causing amusement or laughter
Synonym: hilarious
Antonym: serious

Words

beautiful	many
clumsy	new
disgusting	quick
friendly	rare
funny	rough
huge	round
jolly	short
kind	tender
lazy	tired
magnificent	yummy

Hmmm...her sneakers were sopping. I wonder what the word *sopping* means. The sentence right before it says that the grass was wet. If the girl's sneakers touched the wet grass, they probably got wet. *Sopping* must mean "wet."

Thinking Out Loud

Using context clues

Make good use of your read-aloud time by modeling a valuable reading strategy. As you read aloud from a chapter book, pause at appropriate times to think out loud. Refer to an unfamiliar vocabulary word in the passage and model how to use context clues to determine its meaning. After you demonstrate this several times, have each student use her reading text or a library book to practice this strategy with a partner.

Dee Demyan, Atwater, OH

Link by Link

Cause and effect

Read aloud to students a picture book that contains several examples of cause and effect, such as *If You Give a Mouse a Cookie* by Laura Joffe Numeroff. Then give each child seven paper strips in each of two different colors. Instruct him to write a cause on one strip, its effect on a different-colored strip, and then link the strips together to form a chain. With each additional link, he uses his remaining strips to build on his cause-and-effect story.

If you give me a basketball,
I will try to dribble it down the court and score a basket.

Leigh Anne Newsom, Cedar Road Elementary, Chesapeake, VA

Snoozing Away
ZZZZZZ
Differences
Topic One
Differences
Topic Two
Similarities

Name ______________________________

STAMP OF APPROVAL

Check the box after you complete each task.

☐ On the postage stamp pattern below, design a stamp featuring the person you read about. (Include the current postage rate.)

☐ Cut out the stamp and glue it to colorful paper.

☐ On the paper, write a persuasive paragraph explaining why this person should be featured on a postage stamp.

Putting Rosa Parks on a postage stamp is a great idea! She was a brave woman whose actions contributed to the U.S. civil rights movement. Her refusal to give up her bus seat to a white man led to her arrest. That event led to a boycott of the Montgomery, Alabama, bus system by its black citizens. After more than a year-long boycott, segregated seating on the city's bus system was declared unconstitutional by the U.S. Supreme Court. If Rosa Parks hadn't stood up for herself, who knows how long it would have taken for those changes to be made? To show appreciation for her actions, let's feature Rosa Parks on a postage stamp.

Carmen

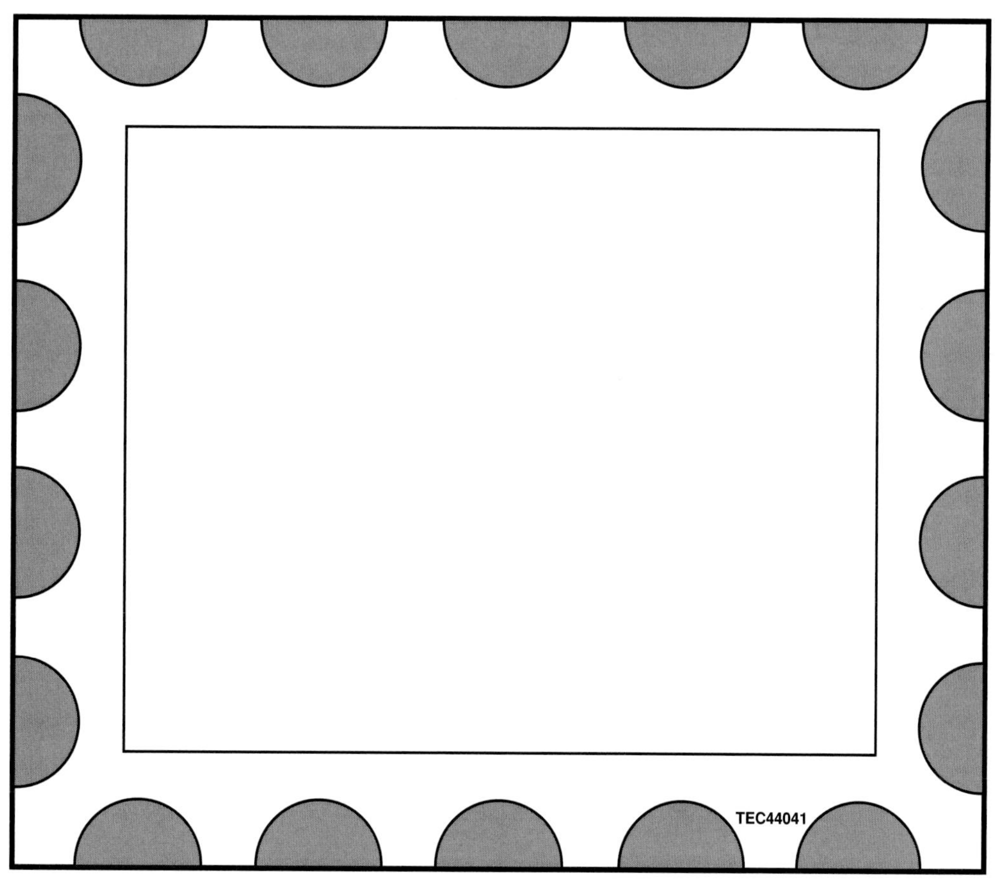

Parts of Speech Cards and Answer Key

Use with "Park the Cars!" on page 97. Mount on construction paper a copy of the game mat on page 97 and a copy of the cards and answer key below. If desired, laminate the pages before cutting the cards apart.

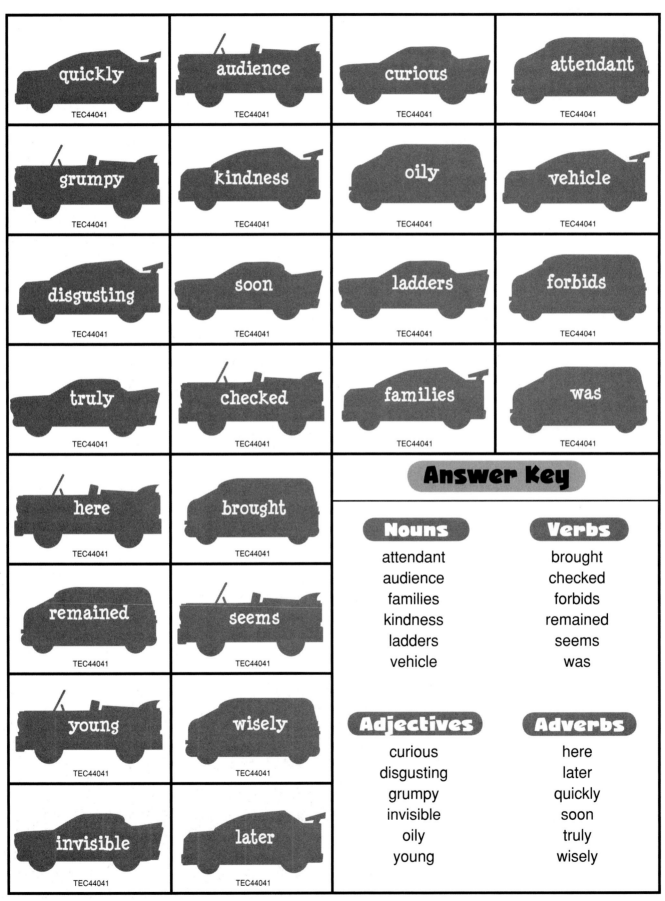

quickly TEC44041	audience TEC44041	curious TEC44041	attendant TEC44041
grumpy TEC44041	kindness TEC44041	oily TEC44041	vehicle TEC44041
disgusting TEC44041	soon TEC44041	ladders TEC44041	forbids TEC44041
truly TEC44041	checked TEC44041	families TEC44041	was TEC44041
here TEC44041	brought TEC44041		
remained TEC44041	seems TEC44041		
young TEC44041	wisely TEC44041		
invisible TEC44041	later TEC44041		

Answer Key

Nouns

attendant
audience
families
kindness
ladders
vehicle

Verbs

brought
checked
forbids
remained
seems
was

Adjectives

curious
disgusting
grumpy
invisible
oily
young

Adverbs

here
later
quickly
soon
truly
wisely

Park the Cars!

Directions for two players:

1. Shuffle the cards and deal 12 cards facedown to each player.
2. Take turns turning over one card at a time. Decide whether the word on your card is a noun, a verb, an adjective, or an adverb. Place the card on the matching parking lot on your game mat.
3. When all the cards have been sorted, use the key to check your answers. Award five points for each correct match.
4. The player with more points wins.

Player 1

Noun Parking Lot

Exit

Verb Parking Lot

Exit

Adjective Parking Lot

Exit

Adverb Parking Lot

Exit

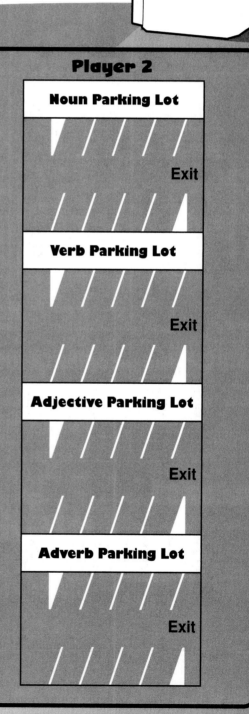

Player 2

Noun Parking Lot

Exit

Verb Parking Lot

Exit

Adjective Parking Lot

Exit

Adverb Parking Lot

Exit

Name ______________________________

S-t-r-e-t-c-h It Out!

Lengthen each sentence by adding adjectives and adverbs. Include phrases if you wish.

1. We watched the man during the jump. ______________________________
2. The sun shone in the sky. ______________________________
3. Birds were in the tree. ______________________________
4. A crowd stood on the bridge. ______________________________
5. Did you see the rocks by the water? ______________________________
6. A butterfly landed on the flower. ______________________________
7. Deer grazed in the field. ______________________________
8. Did squirrels scamper across the trail? ______________________________
9. The creek ran down the hill. ______________________________
10. This was part of the day. ______________________________

Name ____________________

Rumble Through the Jungle

A Game for Two Players

Directions:

1. Choose a path.
2. In turn, roll a die. In the next available space, write a word with the matching prefix or suffix.
   - Roll of 1 = prefix that means "not"
   - Roll of 2 = prefix that means "below"
   - Roll of 3 = prefix that means "again"
   - Roll of 4 = suffix that means "without"
   - Roll of 5 = suffix that means "state, process, or act of"
   - Roll of 6 = suffix that means "one who"
3. Use a dictionary to check the word. If the word is incorrect, erase it.
4. If you erase a word or cannot write a word, your turn is over.
5. The first player to write a word in each space on his or her path wins.

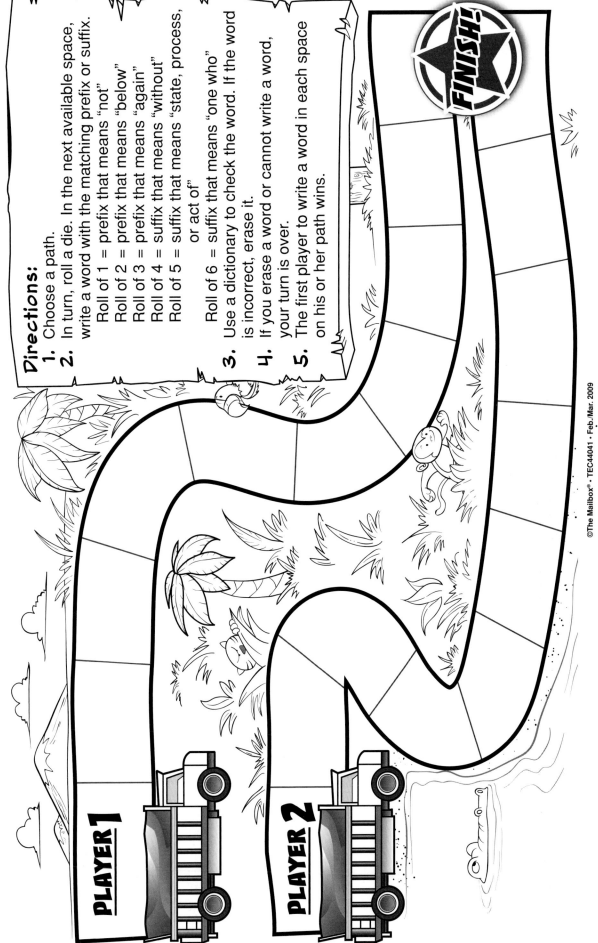

PLAYER 1

PLAYER 2

FINISH!

Ice Cream Pattern

Use with "Get the Scoop" on page 92.

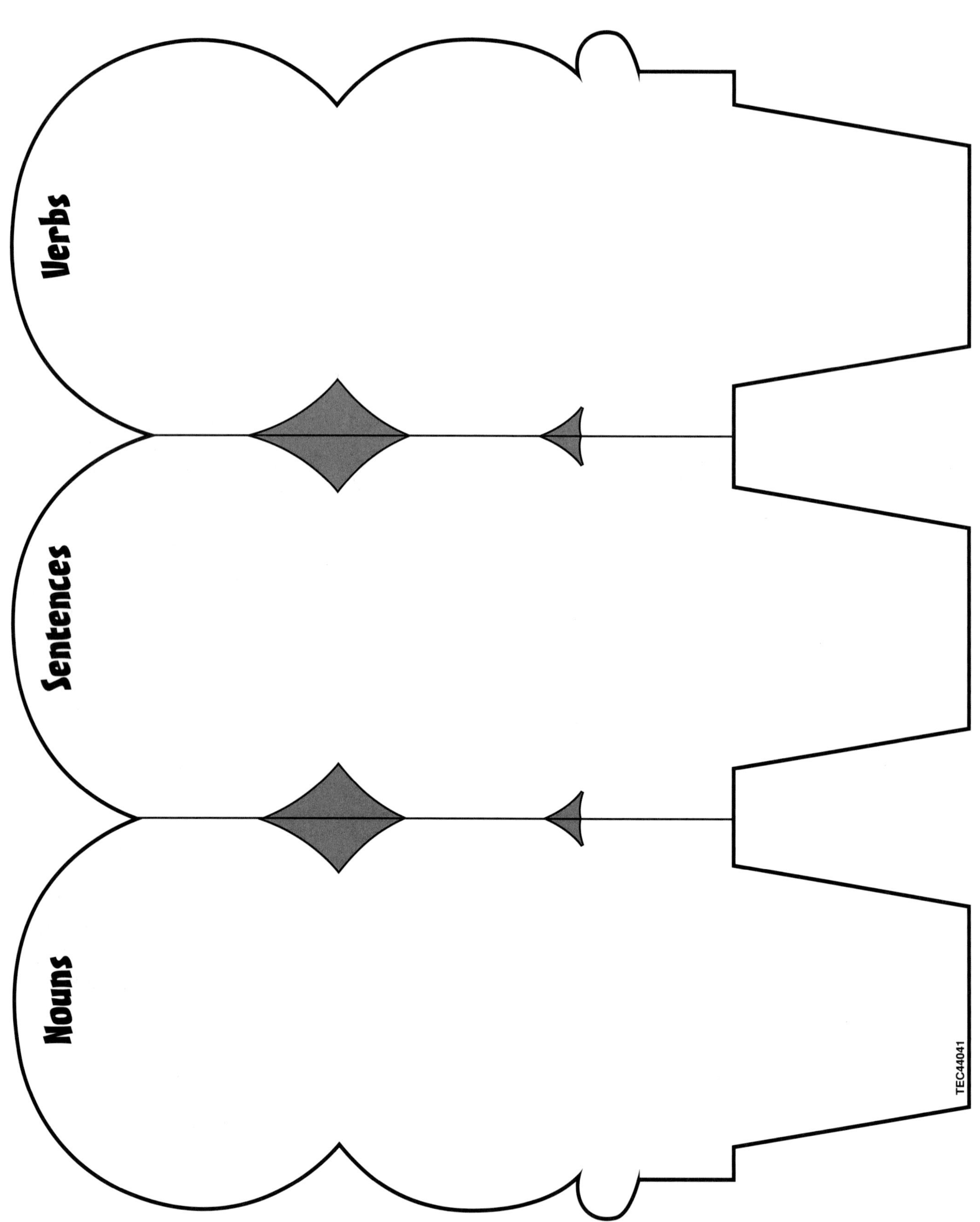

Name ____________________

Karaoke Kate

Punctuate each sentence correctly.

1. Kate was invited to a karaoke birthday party for her friend Chad
2. She was nervous because shed never been to a karaoke party before
3. Why are you nervous her mother asked You sing in front of your friends all the time
4. But Im not sure Ill know the words to the songs well sing Kate said worriedly
5. That wont be a problem Kates mother explained because youll read each songs words from a video screen
6. Oh Kate replied then yes I *do* want to go to Chads party
7. When Kate arrived at the party, her friends were eating chips drinking sodas and talking excitedly
8. Chads mom then set up the karaoke machine and everyone cheered
9. By 800 pm Chad and his guests had each sung two songs
10. Kate performed so well that Chad gave her a nickname Karaoke Kate

Note to the teacher: Use with "Title Search" on page 92.

LANGUAGE ARTS TIPS & TOOLS

"Comma-tition" Relay

Punctuation review

Your students will beg to practice using commas with this relay. Divide students in groups of three or four and line them up in an open space. Supply each group with a large laminated comma or a baton. For each group, place on a chair a set distance away a clipboard holding a copy of game sheet A from page 107 and a pencil. To play, a student runs to the chair, corrects a sentence, runs back to the starting line, and passes the comma to the next player on his team. When all the sentences have been corrected, check the game sheet and award a point for each correctly punctuated sentence. The group with the most points wins. If time allows, repeat play with copies of game sheet B from page 107.

Nicole Hughes, R. F. Bumpus Middle School, Hoover, AL

Helping Heroes

Main verbs and helping verbs

Superheroes need sidekicks just as main verbs sometimes need helping verbs! With this partner activity, students practice identifying and using common helping verbs. To begin, provide each pair with a copy of page 108. Have students cut apart the superhero and sidekick cards. Then have them write a sentence using one superhero card (main verb) and one to three sidekick cards (helping verbs). Any form of the main verb can be used, such as "laughed" or "laughing" for "laugh." Have students write six or more sentences, underlining the helping verbs in blue and the main verbs in red. When all the pairs are finished, have them share their most creative sentences.

Carol Lawrence, Madera, CA

Fooled You!

Vocabulary

Introduce new vocabulary words by playing this fun guessing game. Divide students into small groups and give each student a card labeled with a new word. Have each student make up three definitions for his word and then use a dictionary to write the real definition. The other students in the group try to guess the definition of the word from the four given. Award a point for each successful bluff.

Debbie Price, Truitt Intermediate, Chesapeake, VA

fidget
fidget:
a finger
to move or act restlessly or nervously
to play with
to mess up

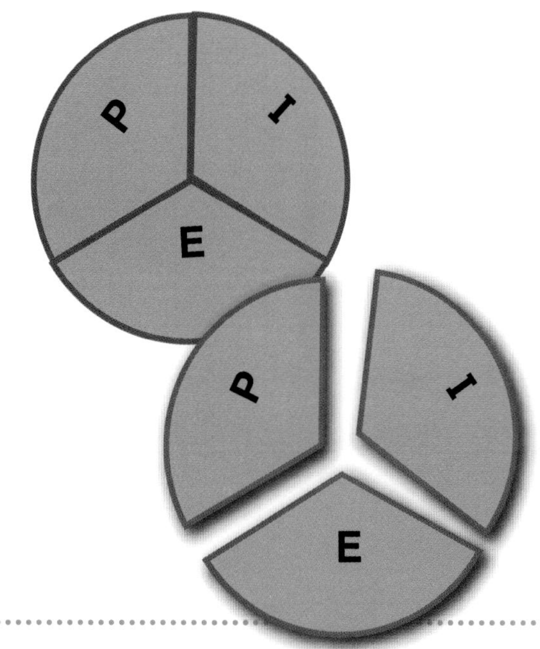

Easy as Pie

Writing a speech

Use this pie-themed idea to assign students the purposes and introductions of their speeches. Divide several six-inch circles into thirds and label each piece with a *P, I,* or *E,* as shown. Make enough circles so each student will have one section. Then place the sections in a large bag. Have each student draw a section from the bag. Then write on the board "Persuade, Inform, or Entertain." Reveal to students that the letters on their slices correspond to the purposes of giving their speeches. Have each student write down his speech's purpose. Then collect the sections and have students choose pieces again. This time write on the board how students will start their speeches: "Personal Story, Interesting Fact, or Effective Visual." Later, after students give their speeches, celebrate by slicing up some real pie!

Colleen Dabney, Williamsburg, VA

Pigs' Perspective

Point of view

Gather familiar picture books to practice first- and third-person points of view. Read aloud a version of the traditional story *The Three Little Pigs.* Have students list pronouns they hear as you read. After reading, compile these pronouns on the board. Then read aloud *The True Story of the 3 Little Pigs* by Jon Scieszka, again asking students to write pronouns they hear. Compare this list to the one already on the board. Ask students which version uses third-person point of view (the traditional version) and which uses first-person point of view *(The True Story of the 3 Little Pigs).* Then use this idea as a PIG (partner, individual, or group) activity to have students compare other books' points of view.

Chrystal Brooks, Helena Elementary, Timberlake, NC

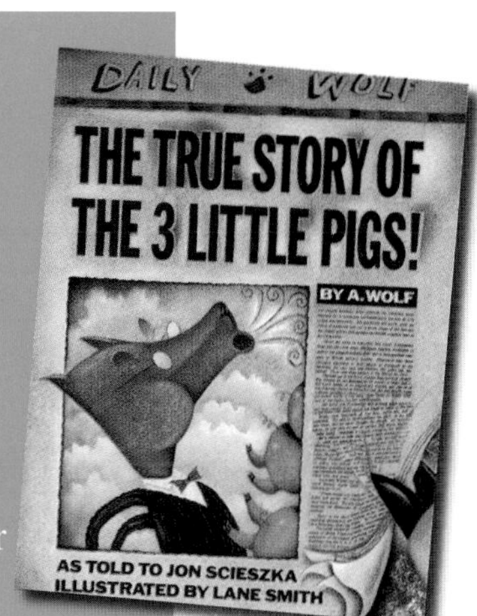

DAILY WOLF
THE TRUE STORY OF THE 3 LITTLE PIGS!
BY A. WOLF
AS TOLD TO JON SCIESZKA
ILLUSTRATED BY LANE SMITH

Name ______________________

It's All in Your Head (and Heart, and...)

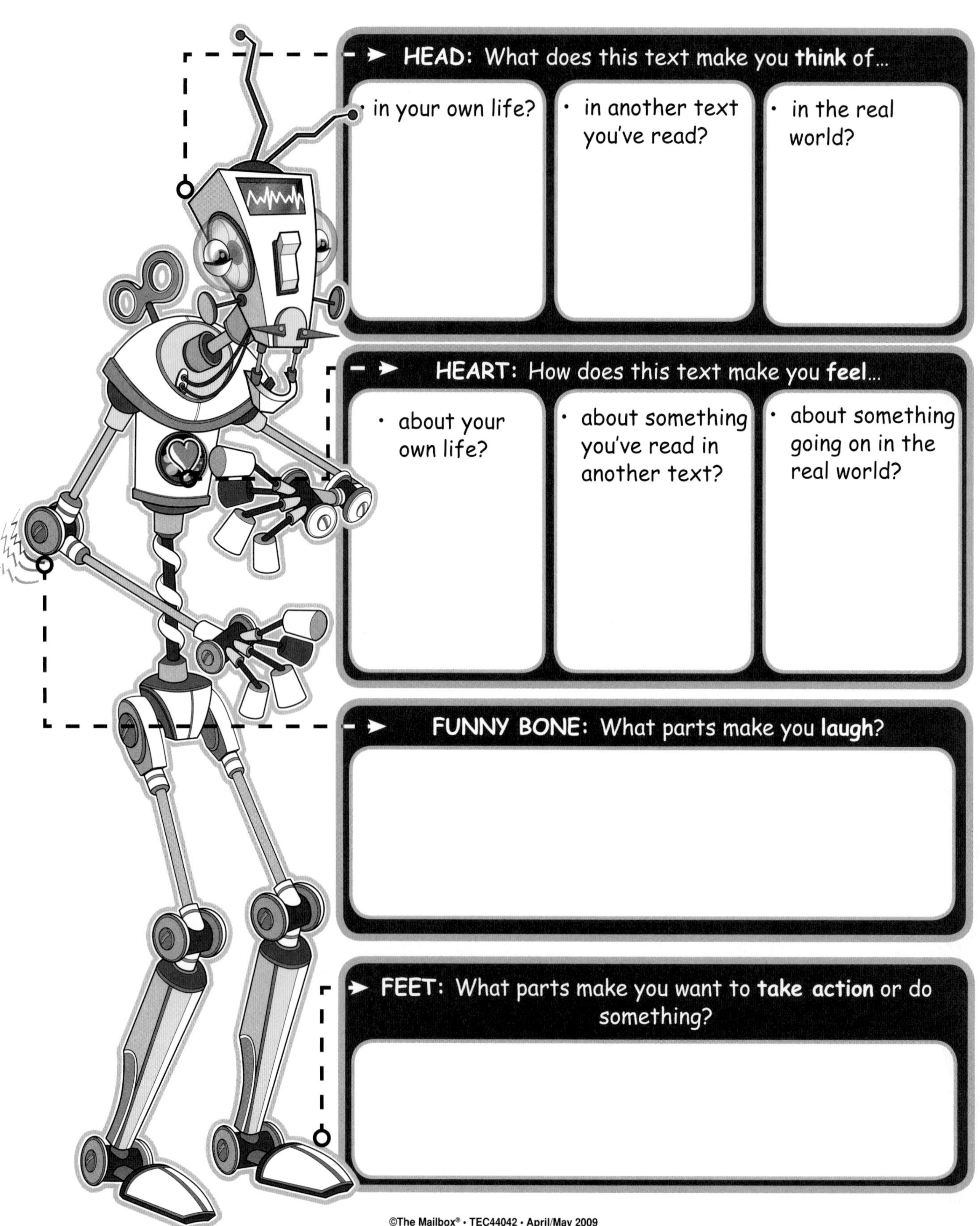

HEAD: What does this text make you think of...
• in your own life?
• in another text you've read?
• in the real world?
HEART: How does this text make you feel...
• about your own life?
• about something you've read in another text?
• about something going on in the real world?
FUNNY BONE: What parts make you laugh?
FEET: What parts make you want to take action or do something?

Note to the teacher: Have each student use the organizer to make text-to-self, text-to-text, and text-to-world connections about a selection he is reading.

Name ____

Supertoastie Saves the Day

Write an appropriate pronoun in each blank.

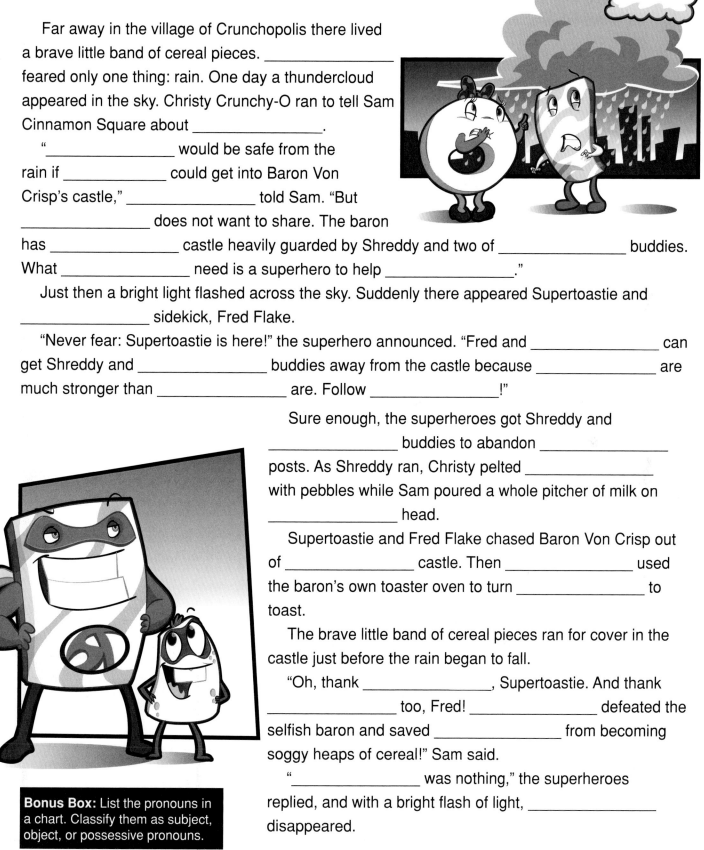

Far away in the village of Crunchopolis there lived a brave little band of cereal pieces. ______________ feared only one thing: rain. One day a thundercloud appeared in the sky. Christy Crunchy-O ran to tell Sam Cinnamon Square about ______________.

"______________ would be safe from the rain if ____________ could get into Baron Von Crisp's castle," ______________ told Sam. "But ______________ does not want to share. The baron has ______________ castle heavily guarded by Shreddy and two of ______________ buddies. What ______________ need is a superhero to help ______________."

Just then a bright light flashed across the sky. Suddenly there appeared Supertoastie and ______________ sidekick, Fred Flake.

"Never fear: Supertoastie is here!" the superhero announced. "Fred and ______________ can get Shreddy and ______________ buddies away from the castle because ______________ are much stronger than ______________ are. Follow ______________!"

Sure enough, the superheroes got Shreddy and ______________ buddies to abandon ______________ posts. As Shreddy ran, Christy pelted ______________ with pebbles while Sam poured a whole pitcher of milk on ______________ head.

Supertoastie and Fred Flake chased Baron Von Crisp out of ______________ castle. Then ______________ used the baron's own toaster oven to turn ______________ to toast.

The brave little band of cereal pieces ran for cover in the castle just before the rain began to fall.

"Oh, thank ______________, Supertoastie. And thank ______________ too, Fred! ______________ defeated the selfish baron and saved ______________ from becoming soggy heaps of cereal!" Sam said.

"______________ was nothing," the superheroes replied, and with a bright flash of light, ______________ disappeared.

Bonus Box: List the pronouns in a chart. Classify them as subject, object, or possessive pronouns.

Name ________________________________

Cover to Cover

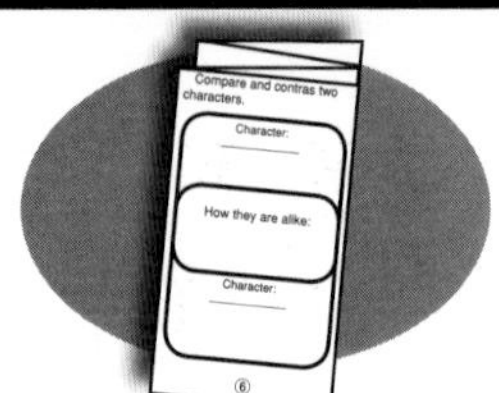

Cut out the pattern below. Fold it in half along the dotted line and then in thirds to make a brochure as shown. Complete each section as directed.

①

Title: ____________

Author: ____________

List and describe the major characters.

____

⑥

Compare and contrast two characters.

Character: ____________

How they are alike:

Character: ____________

⑤

Draw the main character.

②

Explain the plot in your own words.

____

③

Yak, yak, yak!

If you met the main character on the street, what would you talk about?

____

④

Ha, ha, hee, hee! What part is the funniest? ____________

! What part is the most exciting? ____________

What part is the saddest? ____________

 Note to the teacher: Have each student complete this project after reading any fiction selection.

SHEET A

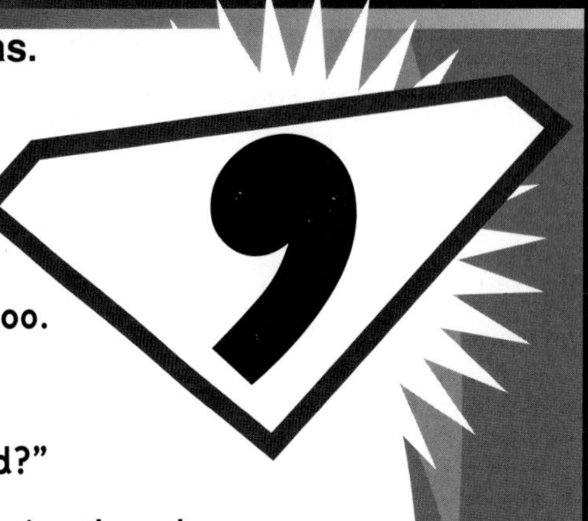

Correct the sentence by adding or marking out commas.

1. Last night I ate steak, mashed potatoes and salad.
2. My littlest dog Carleigh likes to play with her toys.
3. We left for our vacation last year on June, 16.
4. Math is my favorite subject in school but, I like reading too.
5. Have you ever been to Houston Texas?
6. Max asked "Do you know where the game is being played?"
7. When you are learning a new game it takes time to memorize the rules.
8. For homework I had spelling math, social studies and science.
9. My family loves to eat out but we also like to cook dinner at home.
10. When was the last time you saw your friend, Jamal riding his bike?
11. The camping trip will be on Saturday May 23.
12. We are visiting my grandparents in Fort Myers Florida.

SHEET B

Correct the sentence by adding or marking out commas.

1. My new school is located in Roanoke Virginia.
2. Mom sent me to the store to buy, milk bread potato chips, and lunch meat.
3. Lucy, asked "Did you know my favorite ice cream is strawberry?"
4. I was born on September 14 1999.
5. The casserole we ate last night chicken and rice made my stomach hurt.
6. When the weekend finally arrives I, want to play outside.
7. My dad said we had to go to sleep early but, then he changed his mind.
8. When I was little my favorite food was spaghetti.
9. I have saved my allowance since December, 26, 2008.
10. Payton my best friend, had to move to a new state.
11. I thought all our games were over but the last one is actually tomorrow.
12. Patrick Roberto and Cole are my three best friends.

Superhero and Sidekick Cards

Use with "Helping Heroes" on page 102.

Language Arts TIPS & TOOLS

Sweet Punctuation

Reviewing less common punctuation

For this mouthwatering punctuation activity, ask parents to supply candies and small paper cups. Then create a poster like the one shown. Next, have each pair of students write a separate sentence using each punctuation mark. Also give each twosome a sheet of light-colored construction paper, glue, and a cup of mixed candies. Instruct each pair to write its sentences on the paper, leaving extra space around the punctuation. Then have them glue the candies on top of the corresponding punctuation marks. While partners share their sentences with the class, allow students to snack on extra candies.

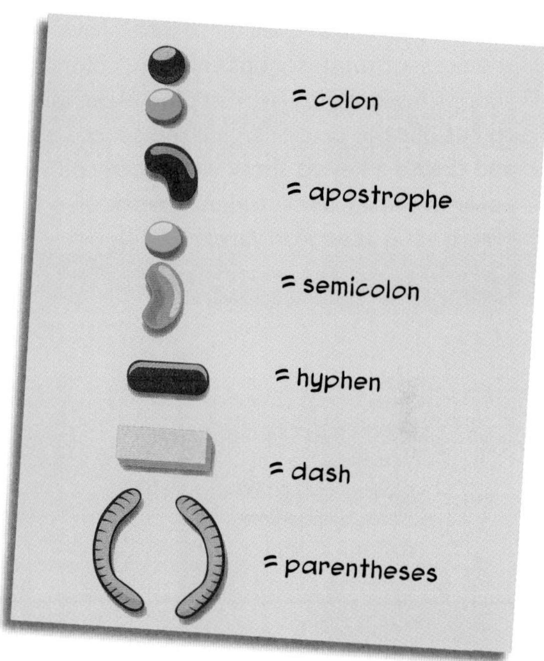

Code

Part of Speech		Value
article	=	$0.01
adjective	=	$0.05
adverb	=	$0.10
noun	=	$0.25
verb	=	$0.50
preposition	=	$0.06
pronoun	=	$0.30
helping verb	=	$0.75

The total value is $1.38.

The old brown dog slept lazily on the sunny back porch.

Valuable Sentences

Parts of speech

Here's a great way to tie math into reviewing parts of speech. Gather real coins or transparent coin manipulatives. (Or make a transparent copy of the coins on page 117 and cut them out.) Also post a code like the one shown. Then write a sentence on the overhead and have students tell you each word's part of speech. As they do, place the appropriate coin or coins above each word. Once all parts of speech have been labeled, have students calculate the sentence's total value. Repeat with additional sentences as time allows.

Terri Moody, North Platte Intermediate, Edgerton, MO

Here's the Scoop!
Irregular verbs

Add flavor to verb practice with this fun activity on past and present tenses of irregular verbs. Give each student a copy of page 118 and a sheet of construction paper. Instruct him to read each verb and decide whether its form is present or past tense. Then have the student color the present tense scoops rainbow colors and the past tense scoops his favorite flavor's color. Next, instruct the student to cut out the patterns, glue the scoops above the cones, and create a key to show what each color represents. For a colorful display, post students' work on a bulletin board titled "Here's the Scoop on Verbs!"

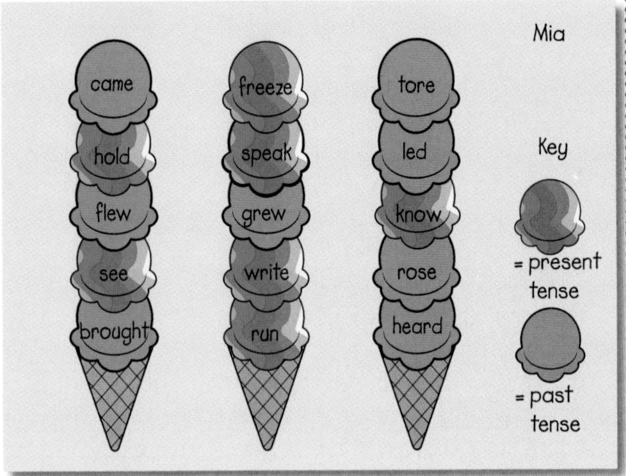

Heather Kime Markland, Springfield, PA

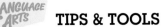

Charlie is a poor boy who finds the last golden ticket to Willie Wonka's chocolate factory.
He takes his Grandpa Joe to the factory where they are given a grand tour.
Mr. Wonka decides to give the factory to Charlie and his family.

One Big Summary
Summarizing

This small-group activity gives students a visual representation of what they read. After students read a story or a book chapter, give each child three sticky notes. Instruct each student to write on each note a one-sentence summary: one for the selection's beginning, one for the middle, and one for the end. Then have one student read his sentences aloud and arrange them vertically in chronological order. If the next student shares a similar idea, have her place her note on top of the first student's note. If not, have her rearrange the order of the existing sticky notes to include her idea. Continue until all students' sticky notes are placed in the vertical column.

Donna Rivarde-Viola, McPherson, KS

A Mango Among Us
Anagrams

Challenge students to create anagrams (words formed by rearranging the letters of other words) and use them in silly sentences. In advance, ask your school librarian to suggest anagram books to use as examples, such as *Elvis Lives! and Other Anagrams* by Jon Agee. Have students write their silly sentences on construction paper cutouts related to their sentences. Once students have shared their sentences with the class, use their sentences for a creative display titled "A Mango Among Us."

Mother's thermos let my soup get cold!
Do not stab the bats!

Jennifer Otter, Oak Ridge, NC

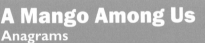

Name ______________________________

Here and There

Complete the organizer to compare where you live to the setting of the selection you are reading.

Where I live:

My story's setting:

How Are They Alike?

How Are They Different?

- Time
- People
- Landforms
- Plants
- Weather/Climate
- Buildings

Game Cards and Answer Key

Use with "Tip Your Hat to Genres!" on page 113. Mount on construction paper a copy of the game mat on page 113 and a copy of the cards and answer key below. If desired, laminate the pages before cutting the cards apart.

1 • suspect • crime TEC44043	**2** • long, long ago • good versus evil TEC44043	**3** • a past time or period • authentic setting TEC44043	**4** • modern, real-world setting • believable characters TEC44043
5 • good wins, evil loses • magic TEC44043	**6** • solving a puzzle • detective TEC44043	**7** • tale that teaches a moral • talking plant, animal, or thing TEC44043	**8** • time travel into the future • technology TEC44043
9 • first person • author's life TEC44043	**10** • outrageous exaggeration • clever hero TEC44043	**11** • origin of universe • supernatural TEC44043	**12** • passed through generations • based on a real person or event TEC44043
13 • aliens • scientific principles TEC44043	**14** • make-believe • brief TEC44043	**15** • text features • factual information TEC44043	**16** • unusual creatures • strange worlds TEC44043
17 • god or goddess • explanation of nature TEC44043	**18** • folktale told as a true story • based on real people or events TEC44043	**19** • exaggeration • hero or heroine TEC44043	**20** • memoir • diary entries TEC44043
21 • specific text structure • factual TEC44043	**22** • mix of fictional and real events • may have real and fictional characters TEC44043	**23** • imaginary • magical powers TEC44043	**24** • believable setting and events • ordinary characters TEC44043

Answer Key for "Tip Your Hat to Genres!"

1. mystery
2. fairy tale
3. historical fiction
4. realistic fiction
5. fairy tale
6. mystery
7. fable
8. science fiction
9. autobiography
10. tall tale
11. myth
12. legend
13. science fiction
14. fable
15. informational
16. fantasy
17. myth
18. legend
19. tall tale
20. autobiography
21. informational
22. historical fiction
23. fantasy or fairy tale
24. realistic fiction

TEC44043

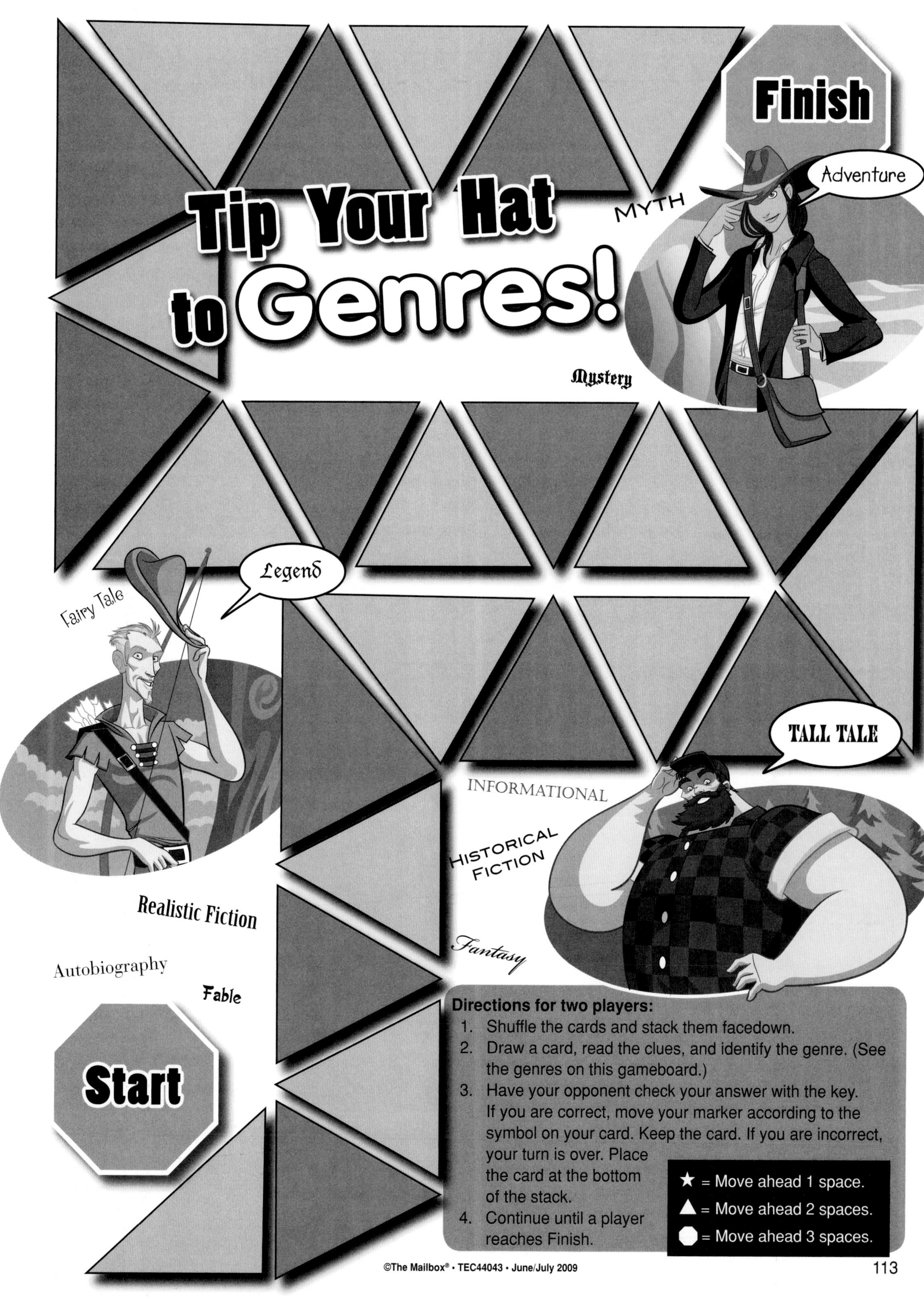

Directions for two players:

1. Shuffle the cards and stack them facedown.
2. Draw a card, read the clues, and identify the genre. (See the genres on this gameboard.)
3. Have your opponent check your answer with the key. If you are correct, move your marker according to the symbol on your card. Keep the card. If you are incorrect, your turn is over. Place the card at the bottom of the stack.
4. Continue until a player reaches Finish.

★ = Move ahead 1 space.
▲ = Move ahead 2 spaces.
⬢ = Move ahead 3 spaces.

Name ____________________

Fishing for the Right Word

Write the correct word for each clue.

1. The prefix of this sea creature's name means "eight." ____________
2. This term is the name given to someone who studies oceans. ____________
3. The name of this ocean means "peaceful." ____________
4. The letters in this word stand for the special gear that helps divers breathe oxygen when under water. ____________
5. This sea creature's head and neck are similar to the land animal for which it was named. ____________
6. This vehicle travels deep in the ocean and has a prefix that means "under" or "below." ____________
7. This word for the area of shore between high tide and low tide levels has a prefix that means "between." ____________
8. The name of this sea animal is a homophone for *muscles.* ____________
9. This star-shaped animal with five arms is also known as a sea star. ____________
10. This one-syllable word names a fearful sea creature whose skeleton is made of cartilage instead of bone. ____________
11. This term identifies a wave's highest point. ____________
12. This phrase refers to the circular movement of water from the earth's surface to the sky and back. ____________

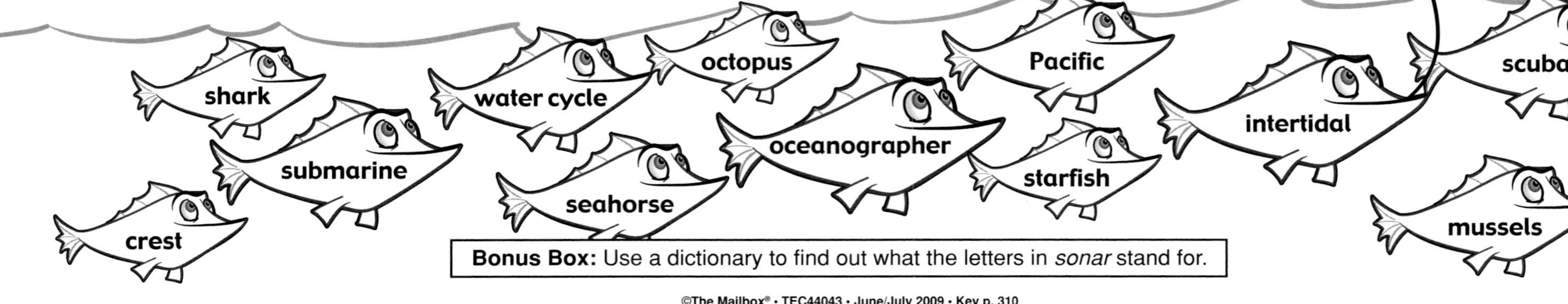

Bonus Box: Use a dictionary to find out what the letters in *sonar* stand for.

Name ______________________________

Yum!

Write three prepositional phrases to tell where each bakery item is in the display.

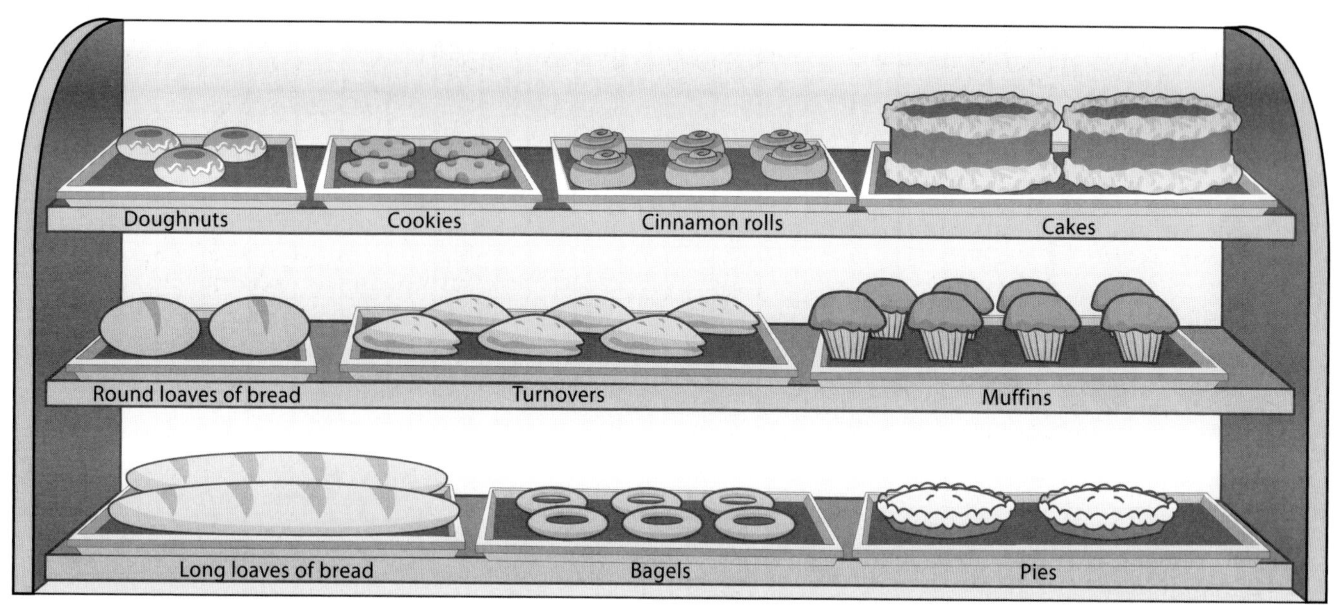

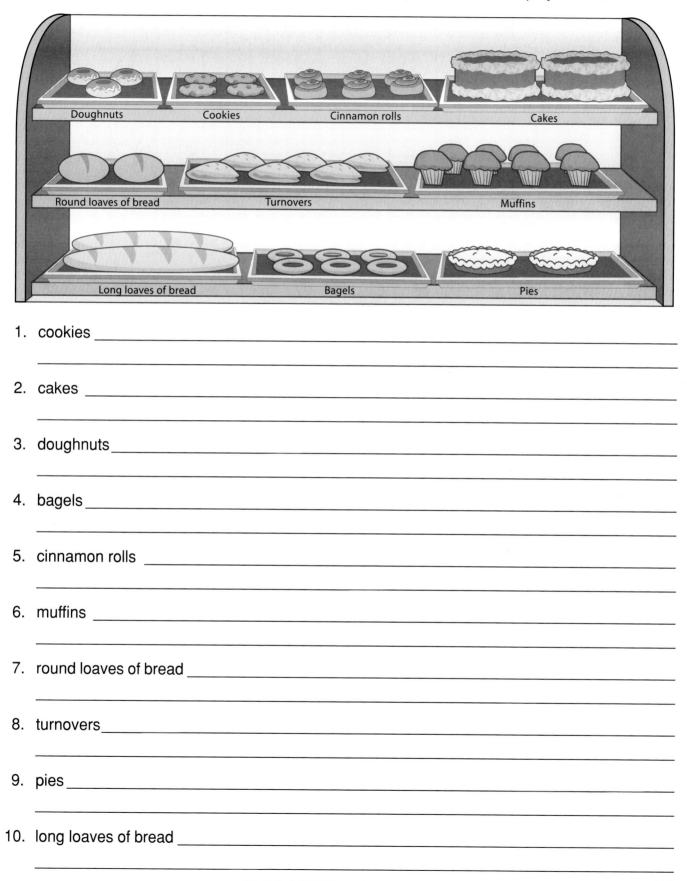

1. cookies ______________________________
2. cakes ______________________________
3. doughnuts ______________________________
4. bagels ______________________________
5. cinnamon rolls ______________________________
6. muffins ______________________________
7. round loaves of bread ______________________________
8. turnovers ______________________________
9. pies ______________________________
10. long loaves of bread ______________________________

Names____

Wimpy Word Wipeout

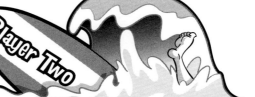

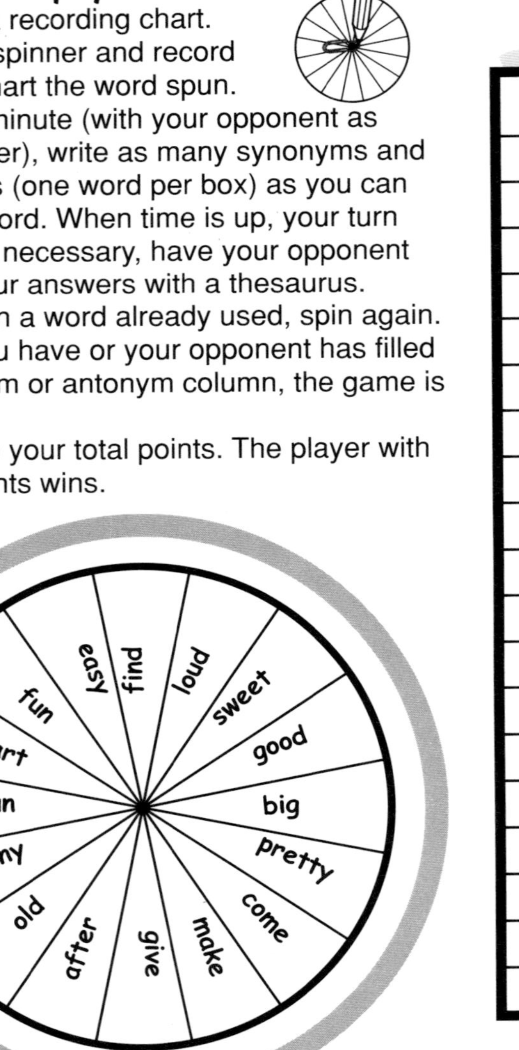

Wimpy Word	Synonyms (1 point each)	Antonyms (2 points each)
Points		
Total Points		

Directions for two players:

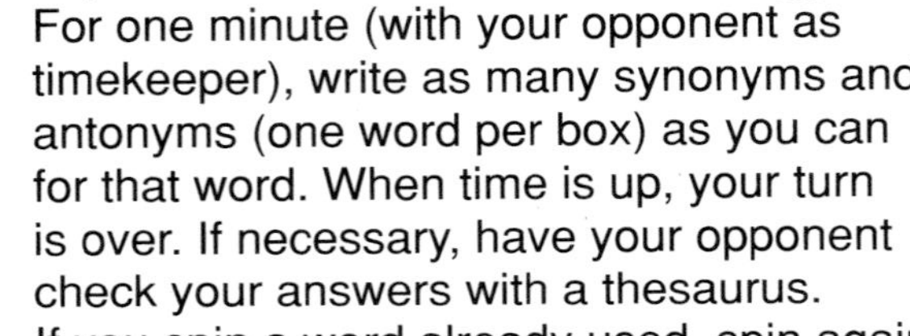

1. Choose a recording chart.
2. Spin the spinner and record in your chart the word spun.
3. For one minute (with your opponent as timekeeper), write as many synonyms and antonyms (one word per box) as you can for that word. When time is up, your turn is over. If necessary, have your opponent check your answers with a thesaurus.
4. If you spin a word already used, spin again.
5. When you have or your opponent has filled a synonym or antonym column, the game is over.
6. Calculate your total points. The player with more points wins.

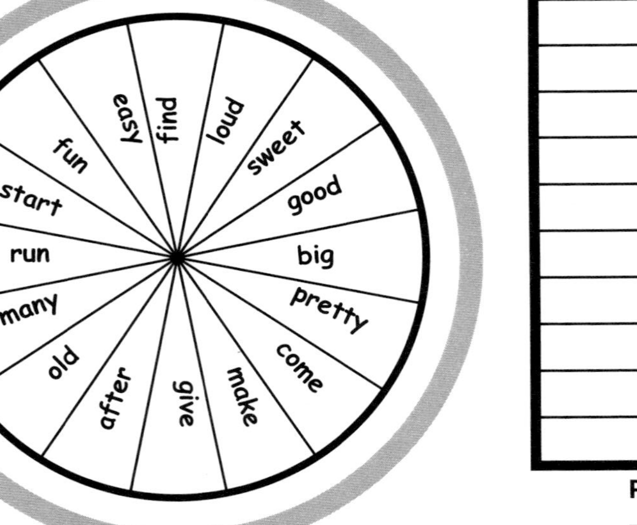

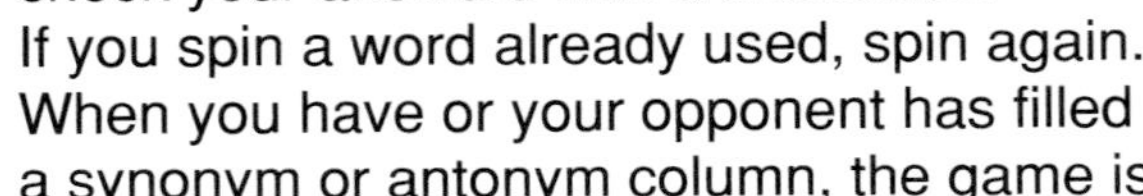

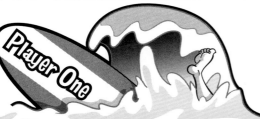

Wimpy Word	Synonyms (1 point each)	Antonyms (2 points each)
Points		
Total Points		

Coin Patterns

Use with "Valuable Sentences" on page 109.

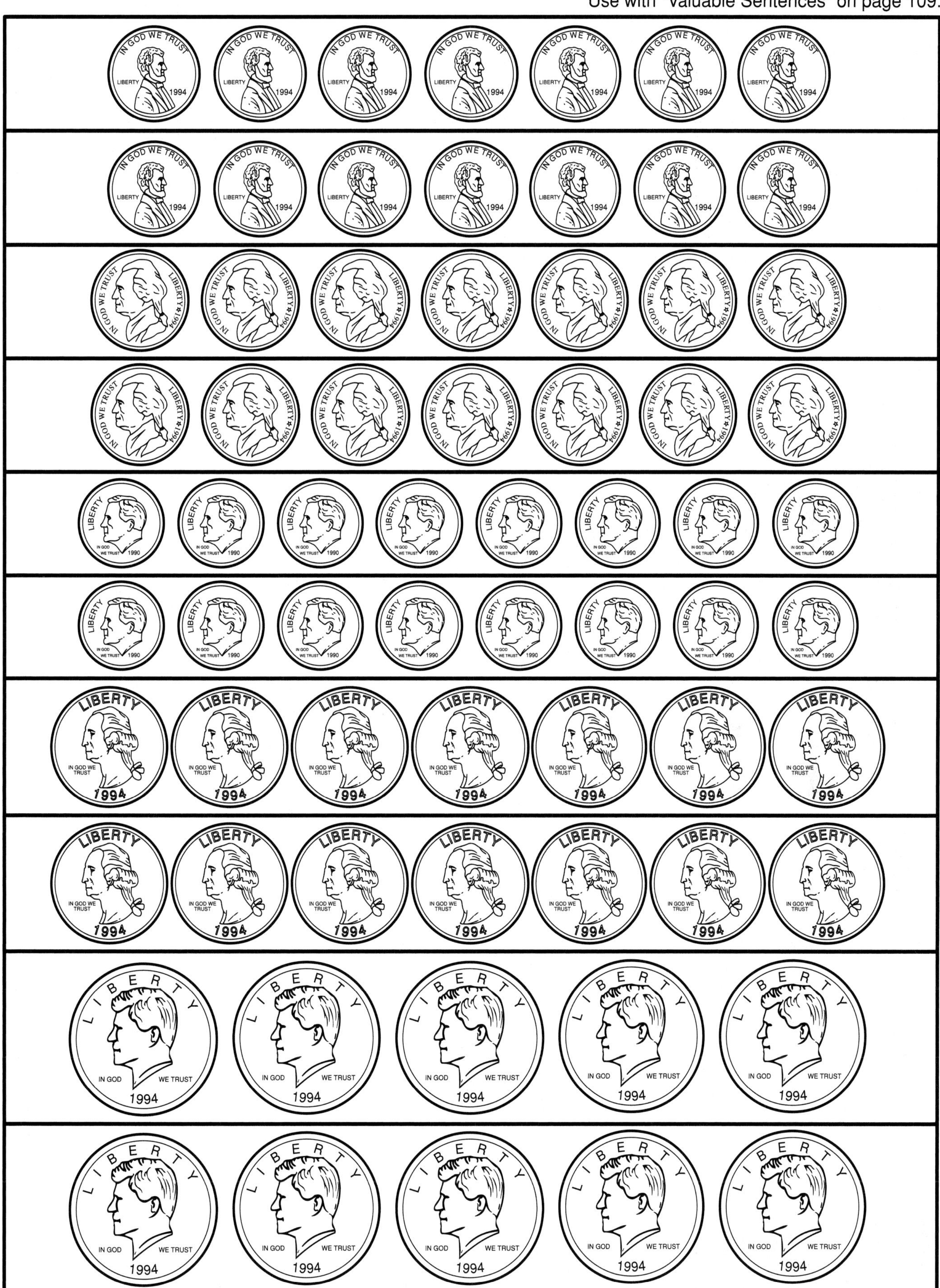

Scoop and Cone Patterns

Use with "Here's the Scoop!" on page 110.

BRAIN BOOSTERS

Brain Booster 1

List the nine state names that include the letter sequence *an.*

TEC44038

Brain Booster 2

Think of an object. Write its name in the first blank.

________ is similar to ________ because...
object

TEC44038

Next, fill in the second blank with one of the words below. Then see how many endings you can list for the sentence starter.

mold **ice** **a cell phone** **a kitchen sink**

Brain Booster 3

The answer is "bubble gum." What are all the questions you can think of that have this answer?

TEC44038

Brain Booster 4

What three homophones can each be spelled using only the letters *b, e, u,* or *y*? Hint: No word has more than three letters.

TEC44038

What three homophones can each be spelled using only the letters *a, e, i, p,* or *r*? Hint: Each word has only four letters.

Brain Booster 5

What famous fairy-tale titles are abbreviated in the list below?
Hint: Each letter begins a different word in the title.

TEC44038

a. SW and the SD
b. G and the TB
c. LRRH
d. H and G
e. The TBGG

Brain Booster 6

Use your knowledge of prefixes to come up with a definition for each nonsense word below.

TEC44038

- circummalling
- trisandwich
- quadraplate

Brain Booster 7

What four-letter word can you add to the beginning or end of each word below to make a familiar compound word?

TEC44038

slide
farm
mark
home

Brain Booster 8

What real compound words could be substituted for the made-up compound words below?

TEC44038

a. bloomcontainer
b. clatterreptile
c. housetoil
d. piecedocument

Note to the teacher: Give each student a copy of this page (or one card at a time) to work on during free time.

Brain Booster 1

Write a different word from the word bank in each blank.

a. a _________ meal
b. the _________ Office
c. the Bermuda _________
d. an ice _________
e. the food _________
f. a baseball _________
g. a four-_________ engine
h. the _________ building

Word Bank	
cube	Pentagon
cylinder	pyramid
diamond	square
Oval	Triangle

TEC44039

Brain Booster 2

Rearrange the boldfaced words so that the paragraph makes sense.

In a **gift** call, Graham learns that his **mom** is bringing the **toaster** a **family** when he returns from a **dad** trip. But the **business** is so bad, Graham can't understand what the gift is. He tells his **connection** that his dad is bringing a poster. When his dad arrived, he'd brought them a **phone.**

TEC44039

Brain Booster 3

Complete this magic word square by writing a word for each clue. The words going down and across are the same.

1. at daylight
2. pain
3. an exclamation of delight
4. to lack something useful

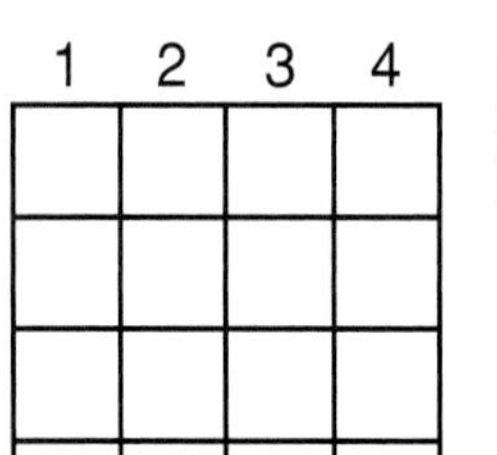

TEC44039

Brain Booster 4

Identify the two antonyms that are woven together. Do not change the order of any letters.

p s o r o l b u t l e i o m n

TEC44039

Brain Booster 5

Start with *board.* Remove one letter at a time to form a new word, rearranging the letters, if needed, until only *o* remains.

board

___ ___ ___ ___

___ ___ ___

___ ___

o

TEC44039

Brain Booster 6

A *spoonerism* is a word or phrase in which letters or syllables are switched. For example, *Go and shake a tower* for *Go and take a shower.* Rewrite each sentence as a spoonerism. Hint: They don't have to make sense.

a. This is our first meal in the new house.
b. Do we need rice for dinner?
c. Don't wake the bear!
d. You shouldn't take sides.

TEC44039

Brain Booster 7

What familiar sayings are illustrated?

a.

SHE HAS

iii
iii

b.

SEARCHING

AND

SEARCHING

TEC44039

Brain Booster 8

Use the numbers to spell the names of six different animals.

a. 2833256
b. 7268437
c. 7322625
d. 2433824
e. 6286787
f. 2855364

TEC44039

Note to the teacher: Give each student a copy of this page (or one card at a time) to work on during free time.

BRAIN BOOSTERS

Brain Booster 1

Write six number words that each have exactly six letters.

? ? ? ? ? ?

TEC44040

Brain Booster 2

Complete each proverb with the name of a different animal or animals.

a. You can't teach an old _____ new tricks.
b. The early _____ catches the _____.
c. Don't count your _____ until they're hatched.
d. When the _____ is away, the _____ will play.
e. You can lead a _____ to water, but you can't make it drink.

TEC44040

Brain Booster 3

Use your knowledge of prefixes to identify each fear below.

a. photophobia = fear of _______________
b. thermophobia = fear of _______________
c. zoophobia = fear of _______________
d. bibliophobia = fear of _______________
e. graphophobia = fear of _______________

TEC44040

Brain Booster 4

What two color words are homophones (words such as *way* and *weigh* or *so* and *sew*)? Use each color word with its homophone in a different sentence.

TEC44040

Brain Booster 5

Write seven personal pronouns that can be spelled using only the letters in *weights*. Include possessive pronouns.

TEC44040

Brain Booster 6

Copy this paragraph. Circle four more hidden fruits and vegetables.

Watch five foods magically ap(pear)! Line up each one carefully. When you're finished, clap, please. I'll be waiting around the corner near a spot at our favorite snack shop.

TEC44040

Brain Booster 7

What four-letter word completes each set of idioms?

a. _____ it easy, _____ care, _____ charge
b. _____ up to someone, _____ into, _____ after
c. _____ out, _____ over a new leaf, _____ a cold shoulder
d. _____ the rug out from under, _____ the wool over your eyes, _____ your leg

TEC44040

Brain Booster 8

Start with *left*. Change one letter at a time to spell *hand*.

LEFT

_ _ _ _

_ _ _ _

_ _ _ _

HAND

TEC44040

Note to the teacher: Give each student a copy of this page (or one card at a time) to work on during free time.

BRAIN BOOSTERS

Brain Booster 1

If you list the 50 U.S. states in alphabetical order, which two states come first? Which state is last?

TEC44041

Brain Booster 2

Spell at least six four-letter words using the letters of this word from left to right.

TEC44041

importance

Brain Booster 3

Find at least four nouns in this paragraph that can also be used as verbs. Then find four verbs that can also be used as nouns.

TEC44041

Do you have time to prepare a bowl of chopped fruit? If so, please cut up some apples, peaches, and pears. I'll make the other snacks. We can watch TV as we work. I cannot bear the thought of not having any food for our guests!

Brain Booster 4

Many contractions end in *n't,* such as the ones shown. Write at least ten contractions that **don't** end in *n't.*

TEC44041

can't **won't** **shouldn't**

Brain Booster 5

Find and correct the eight mispelled words in this paragraph. This task will seperate the good spellers from the great spellers. Your likly to find some of the errors very quickly. You will probalby need to check each differnt line and word. It dosen't matter which words you find first. No doubt the eigth word will be the hardest to find!

TEC44041

Brain Booster 6

Add one letter to each word below to spell the name of an animal. Add the letter to the beginning, middle, or end of the word. For example, *hose* + *r* = *horse.*

TEC44041

a. came
b. muse
c. sea
d. oat
e. hale
f. badge
g. easel
h. hark

Brain Booster 7

Use the clues below to identify the mystery word.

TEC44041

a. It has nine letters and three syllables.
b. Some of its synonyms are *excellent, marvelous,* and *sensational.*
c. Its last letter is *l.*

Brain Booster 8

Think of three related words that rhyme with the words in each group below. For example, related rhyming words for *toffee, knee, silk* would be *coffee, tea, milk.*

TEC44041

a. dive, tricks, heaven
b. life, cork, tune
c. slack, fight, tray

Note to the teacher: Give each student a copy of this page (or one card at a time) to work on during free time.

Brain Booster 1

Rearrange the letters in each phrase to spell the two-word name of a common food. For example, *pale pipe* = *apple pie.*

A. adapt as loot
B. rice pea jug
C. open zappier zip

TEC44042

Brain Booster 2

The answer is "Be kind to your feet." What are all the questions you can think of that have this answer?

TEC44042

Brain Booster 3

What action verbs could you type using only the left-hand keys on a keyboard?

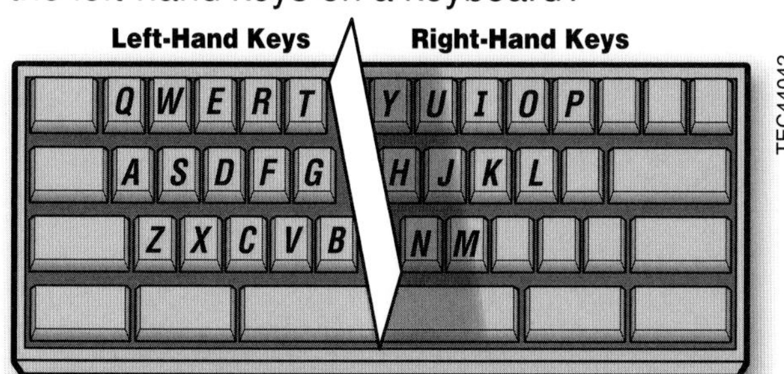

TEC44042

Brain Booster 4

How would a dentist, a plumber, and a cook each finish this sentence?

Today at work, I did the most embarrassing thing ever when I...

TEC44042

Brain Booster 5

Six U.S. states are spelled with one set of double letters. Three are spelled with more than one set of double letters. List the states in each group.

One set of double letters: ? ? ? ? ? ?

More than one set of double letters: ? ? ?

TEC44042

Brain Booster 6

Which month comes next in this sequence?

April, August, December, February, __?__

TEC44042

Brain Booster 7

How many words can you list that both begin and end with this letter?

TEC44042

Brain Booster 8

Use only the letters in *grapefruit* to spell a word for each clue.

A. the pointed end of an object ___ ___ ___
B. artificial grass ___ ___ ___ ___
C. to complain with grumbling ___ ___ ___ ___ ___
D. a person who robs at sea ___ ___ ___ ___ ___ ___
E. mental or physical exhaustion ___ ___ ___ ___ ___ ___ ___

TEC44042

Note to the teacher: Give each student a copy of this page (or one card at a time) to work on during free time.

Brain Booster 1

Spell the plural form of these nouns.

A. moose
B. crisis
C. teaspoonful
D. brother-in-law
E. oboe

TEC44043

Brain Booster 2

Unscramble this joke and its answer.

Q: chicken the basketball the cross Why court did?

A: calling It fowls the referee heard.

TEC44043

Brain Booster 3

Use a color word from the box to form a familiar word, phrase, or name.

green	yellow
pink	Purple
red	blue

A. _______ jacket
B. _______ Heart
C. _______ print
D. _______ thumb
E. _______ slip
F. _______ carpet

Can you form four more words, phrases, or names that include the color words above?

TEC44043

Brain Booster 4

Famous and *bulky* are both synonyms for *great*. List at least seven more.

?, ?, ?, ?, ?, ?, and ?

TEC44043

Brain Booster 5

Lakes and streams are bodies of water. What are other words for bodies of water?

TEC44043

Brain Booster 6

List at least ten words that each contains the name of a different animal.

beet bowling

TEC44043

Brain Booster 7

These occupations all end with the letter *r*. How many occupations can you list that do not end with *r?*

doctor
banker
engineer
farmer

TEC44043

Brain Booster 8

Find the state capital that is spelled using the letters in each person's name.

A. Tommy Goren
B. Carmen Oats
C. Honest Carl

TEC44043

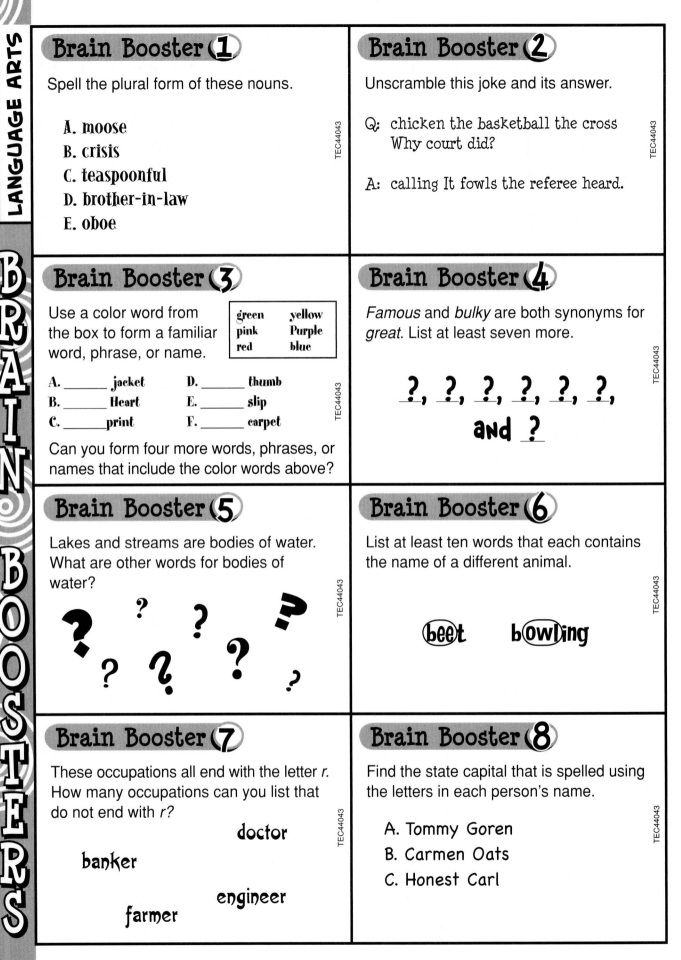

Note to the teacher: Give each student a copy of this page (or one card at a time) to work on during free time.

Cut out a copy of the cards to use as center or free-time activities.

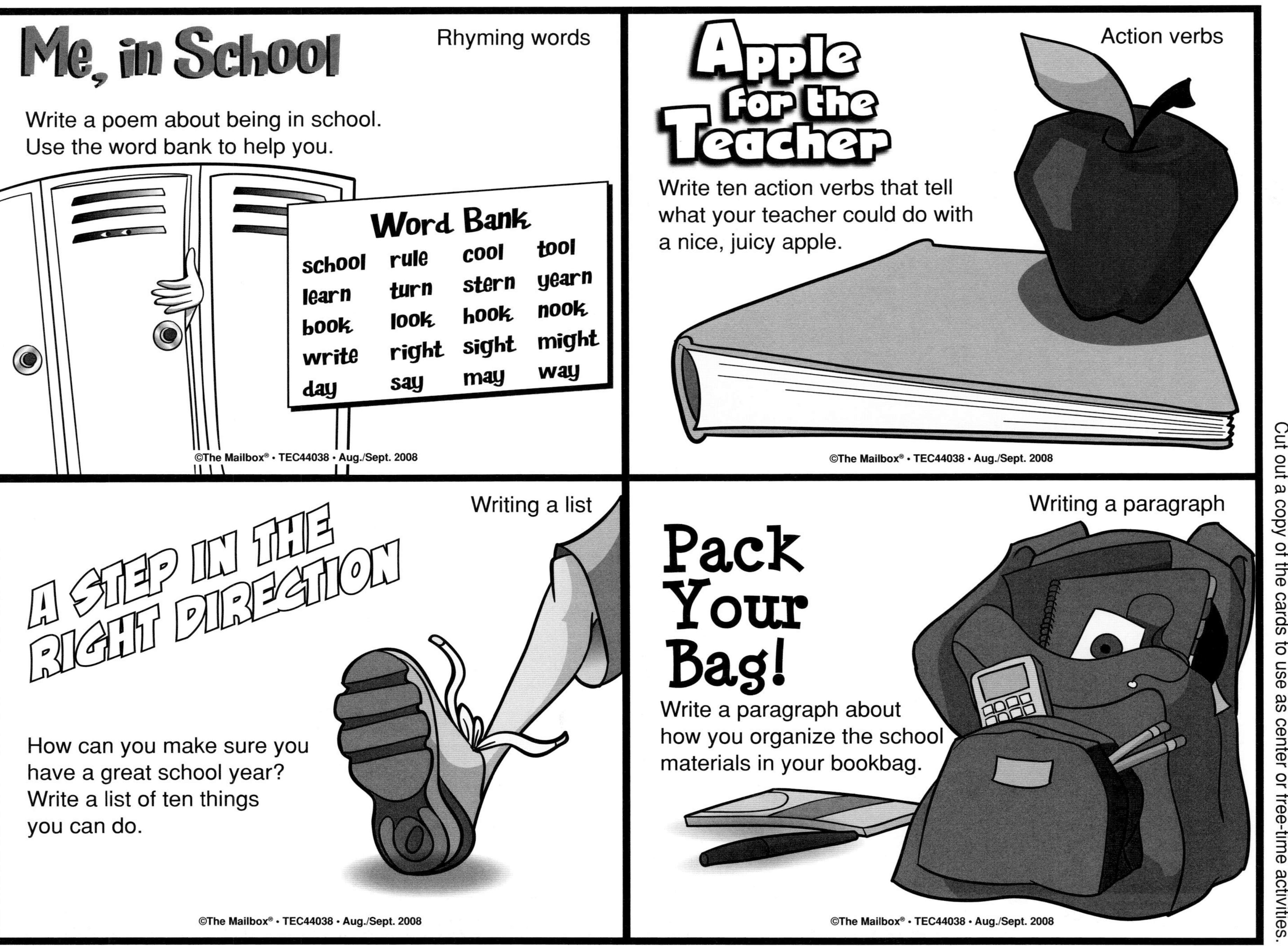

Me, in School

Rhyming words

Write a poem about being in school.
Use the word bank to help you.

Word Bank
school rule cool tool
learn turn stern yearn
book look hook nook
write right sight might
day say may way

Apple for the Teacher

Action verbs

Write ten action verbs that tell what your teacher could do with a nice, juicy apple.

A Step in the Right Direction

Writing a list

How can you make sure you have a great school year? Write a list of ten things you can do.

Pack Your Bag!

Writing a paragraph

Write a paragraph about how you organize the school materials in your bookbag.

Language Arts Activity Cards

Cut out a copy of the cards to use as center or free-time activities.

Proper nouns

Nuts About Nouns

Write two or more proper nouns for each common noun. Then write two sentences that each include three or more proper nouns from your list.

Synonyms

Now Accepting Trade-Ins

Write five strong adjectives that could take the place of each overused word.

Story sequence

What's This?

Write a sentence about what you think is happening in the picture.

Write a sentence about what might have happened before what is shown in the picture.

Then write a sentence about what might happen next.

If you wish, use your sentences to write a story about the alien.

Five Ws

Just Rolling Along

Answer each question to tell what you think is happening in the picture.

1. Who?
2. What?
3. When?
4. Where?
5. Why?

If you wish, use your answers to write a story!

Language Arts Activity Cards

Cut out a copy of the cards to use as center or free-time activities.

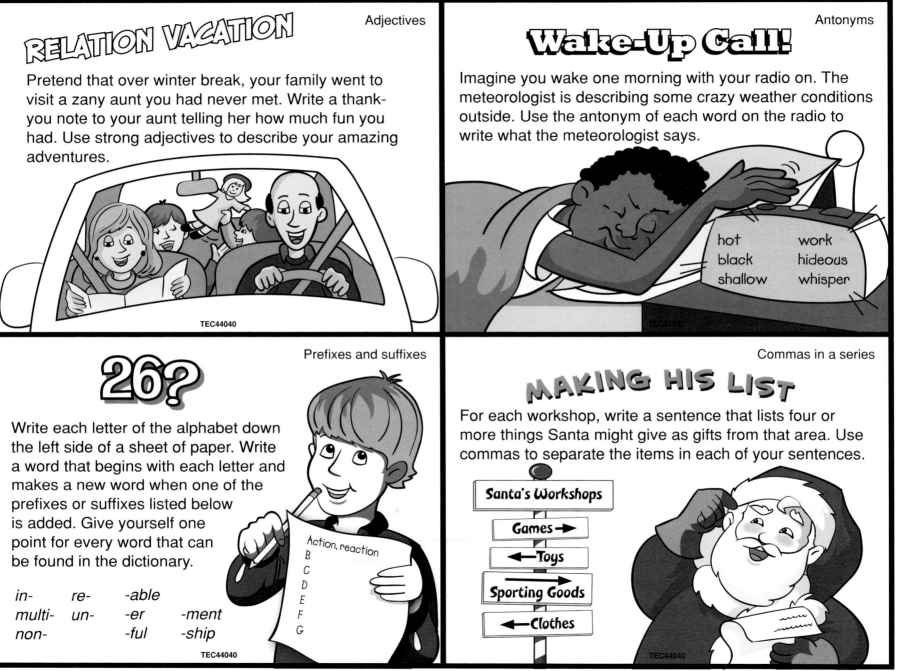

RELATION VACATION

Adjectives

Pretend that over winter break, your family went to visit a zany aunt you had never met. Write a thank-you note to your aunt telling her how much fun you had. Use strong adjectives to describe your amazing adventures.

TEC44040

Wake-Up Call!

Antonyms

Imagine you wake one morning with your radio on. The meteorologist is describing some crazy weather conditions outside. Use the antonym of each word on the radio to write what the meteorologist says.

hot
black
shallow
work
hideous
whisper

TEC44040

26?

Prefixes and suffixes

Write each letter of the alphabet down the left side of a sheet of paper. Write a word that begins with each letter and makes a new word when one of the prefixes or suffixes listed below is added. Give yourself one point for every word that can be found in the dictionary.

in-	*re-*	*-able*	
multi-	*un-*	*-er*	*-ment*
non-		*-ful*	*-ship*

Action, reaction
B
C
D
E
F
G

TEC44040

MAKING HIS LIST

Commas in a series

For each workshop, write a sentence that lists four or more things Santa might give as gifts from that area. Use commas to separate the items in each of your sentences.

TEC44040

Language Arts Activity Cards

Cut out a copy of the cards to use as center or free-time activities.

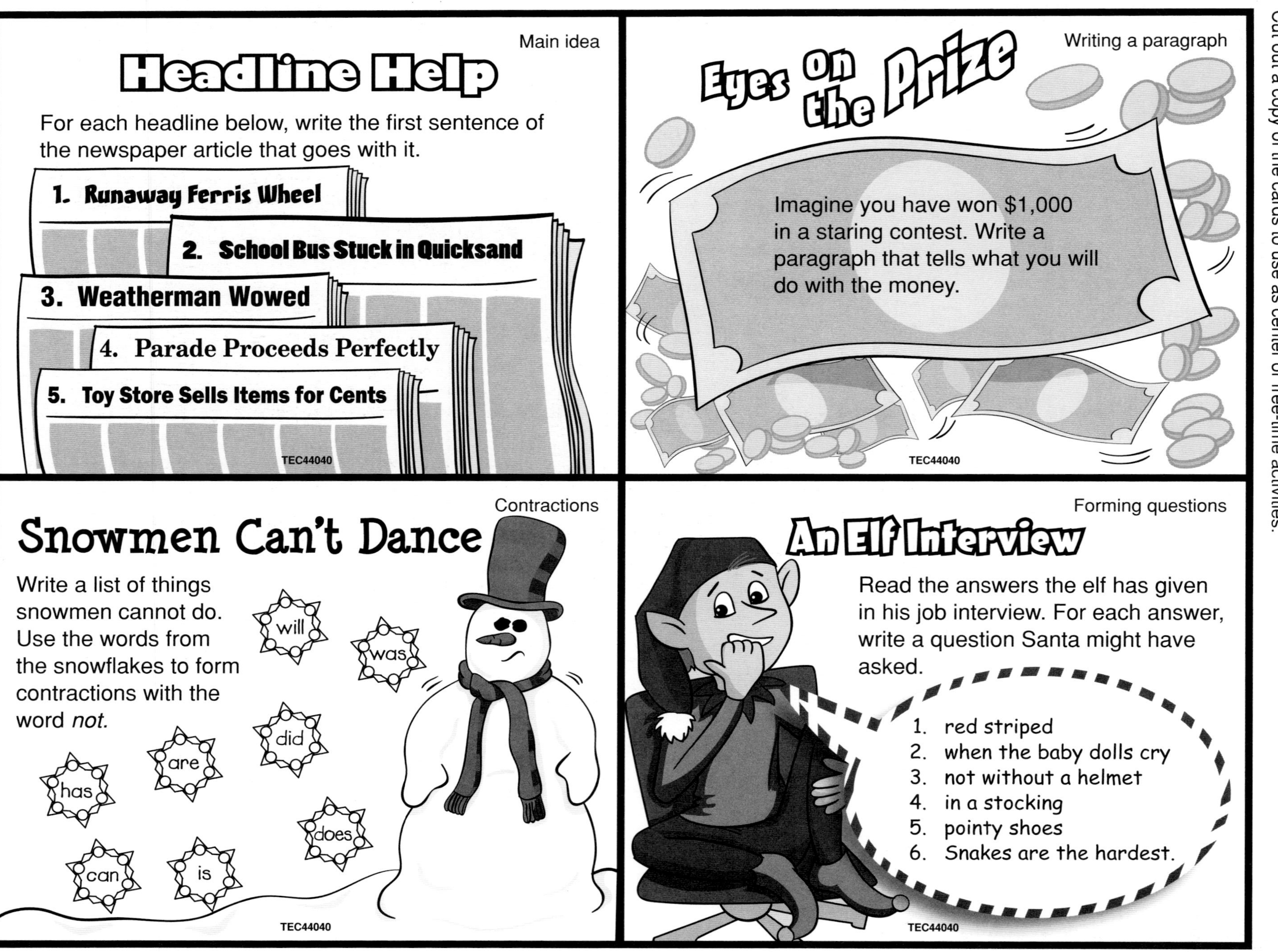

Main idea

Headline Help

For each headline below, write the first sentence of the newspaper article that goes with it.

1. Runaway Ferris Wheel
2. School Bus Stuck in Quicksand
3. Weatherman Wowed
4. Parade Proceeds Perfectly
5. Toy Store Sells Items for Cents

TEC44040

Writing a paragraph

Eyes on the Prize

Imagine you have won $1,000 in a staring contest. Write a paragraph that tells what you will do with the money.

TEC44040

Contractions

Snowmen Can't Dance

Write a list of things snowmen cannot do. Use the words from the snowflakes to form contractions with the word *not*.

TEC44040

Forming questions

An Elf Interview

Read the answers the elf has given in his job interview. For each answer, write a question Santa might have asked.

1. red striped
2. when the baby dolls cry
3. not without a helmet
4. in a stocking
5. pointy shoes
6. Snakes are the hardest.

TEC44040

Cut out a copy of the cards to use as center or free-time activities.

Combining verb phrases
Staying Busy
Complete each short phrase to make a list of things you can do after school.
Then combine two or more of the phrases in one sentence.
Write five different sentences in all.
After school I eat a snack, go to soccer practice, and do my homework.
To-Do List
eat a...
do my...
go to...
talk with...
walk to...
clean my...
take a...
meet my...
play with...
listen to...
TEC44042
Prepositions
Tree Glee
Prepositions
about
against
alongside
around
before
below
beside
between
during
inside
near
on
under
up
with
Write ten sentences about things that could make a tree happy.
Include a preposition in each sentence.
Use the word bank to help you.
TEC44042
Homophones
Toad Towed
Write five silly sentences. Use a different homophone pair below in each sentence.
Everyone guessed that the frog was the reason the guest got upset at the restaurant.
guessed, guest
rows, rose
steel, steal
thrown, throne
sight, cite
TEC44042
Prefixes and suffixes
Toss 'Em!
Unchangeable!
Use the prefixes, suffixes, and base words to form as many words as you can.
Then write two sentences. Include two or more of the words you built in each sentence.
-tion
-er
mis-
-ment
-less
re-
pre-
sent
amuse
un-
-able
change
punish
generate
TEC44042

Language Arts Activity Cards

Cut out a copy of the cards to use as center or free-time activities.

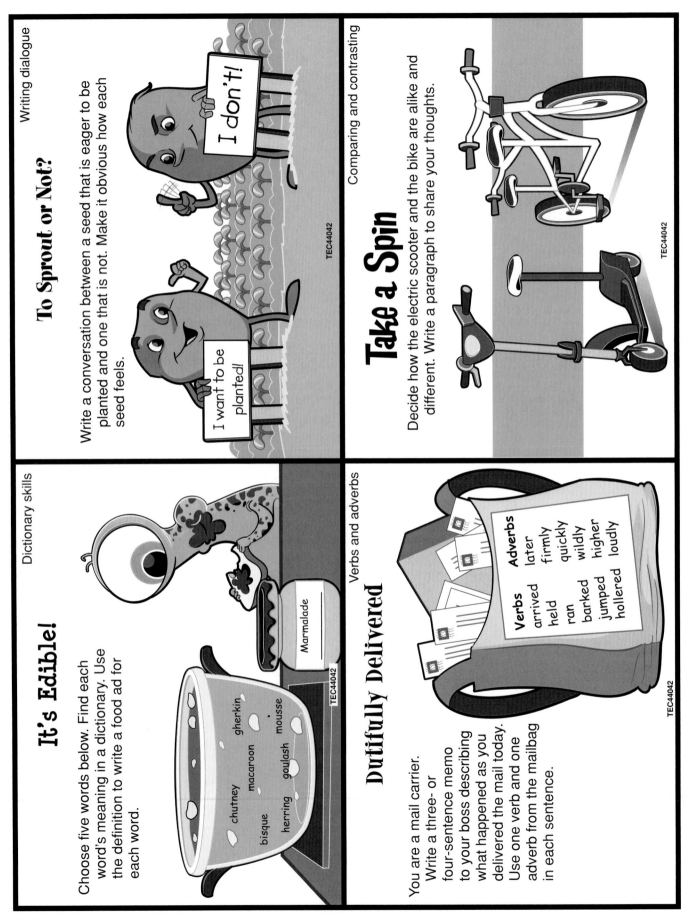

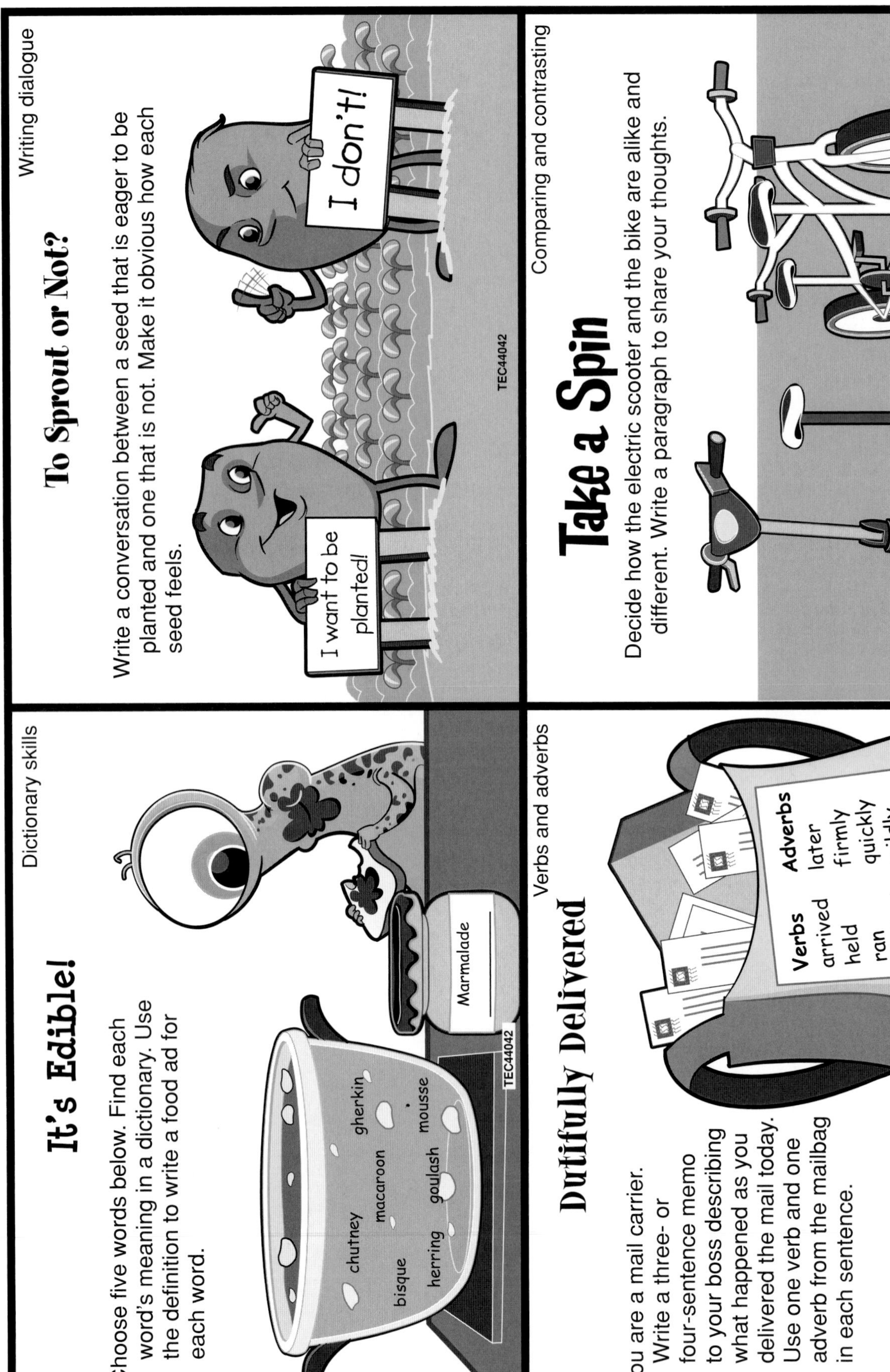

Writing dialogue
To Sprout or Not?
Write a conversation between a seed that is eager to be planted and one that is not. Make it obvious how each seed feels.
I want to be planted!
I don't!
TEC44042
Comparing and contrasting
Take a Spin
Decide how the electric scooter and the bike are alike and different. Write a paragraph to share your thoughts.
TEC44042
Dictionary skills
It's Edible!
Choose five words below. Find each word's meaning in a dictionary. Use the definition to write a food ad for each word.
chutney
macaroon
gherkin
bisque
herring
goulash
mousse
Marmalade
TEC44042
Verbs and adverbs
Dutifully Delivered
You are a mail carrier. Write a three- or four-sentence memo to your boss describing what happened as you delivered the mail today. Use one verb and one adverb from the mailbag in each sentence.
Verbs
arrived
held
ran
barked
jumped
hollered
Adverbs
later
firmly
quickly
wildly
higher
loudly
TEC44042

Writing

WRITE NOW!

Let's Make a Model!

Writing a paragraph

To introduce or review good paragraph structure, have a student sit in an open area and make a statement (topic sentence) such as the one shown. Next, have three more students sit behind student A and state reasons that support his statement (supporting detail sentences). If desired, have pairs of students sit behind each of those three students to offer corresponding examples (additional detail sentences). Then select a final student to sit behind the last row and recap what the participants said (concluding sentence).

Jacquelyn Patterson, Murfreesboro, TN

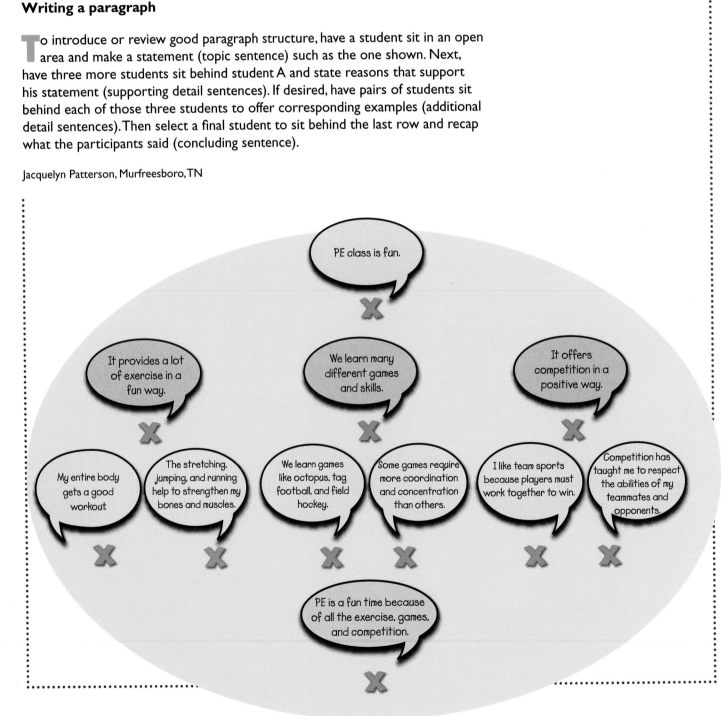

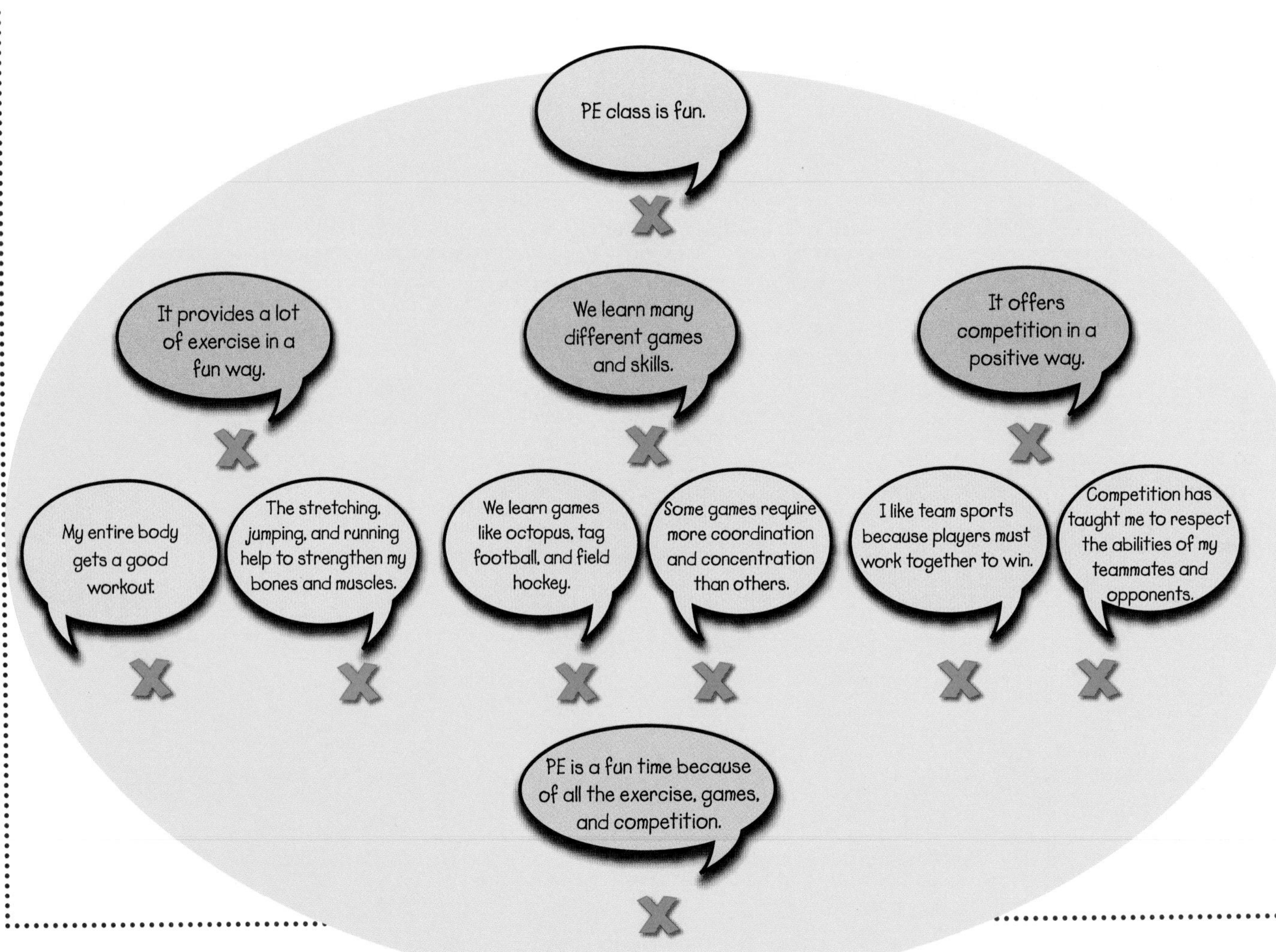

Write It Right

Editing

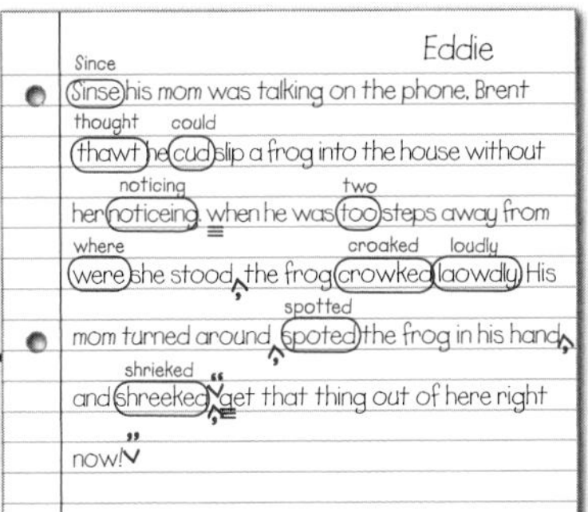

Since his mom was talking on the phone, Brent thought he could slip a frog into the house without her noticing. When he was two steps away from where she stood, the frog croaked loudly. His mom turned around, spotted the frog in his hand, and shrieked, "Get that thing out of here right now!"
Eddie

Use an unexpected technique—dictation—to sharpen students' editing skills. Make a transparency of a paragraph from a recently read story. Without displaying the transparency, read the paragraph aloud one phrase at a time. As you do, have each child write the dictated words on his paper until he has recorded the entire paragraph. Then have the student work with a partner to correct his spelling, punctuation, and capitalization errors. When students are finished, display the transparency so each child can compare his edited work with the original paragraph. Invite students to share whether your voice inflection revealed where to use specific punctuation marks.

Jewell Flint-Stewart, Ellsworth, ME

Fix-It Station

Fragments and run-on sentences

For this nifty center, make a copy of page 135 and cut apart the cards. A child selects a card, identifies whether the group of words on the card is a run-on sentence or a fragment, and decides what repair to make. She then writes the correction on her paper, continuing until she has made corrections for all ten cards.

Lauren E. Cox, Four Oaks Elementary, Four Oaks, NC

A File and a Folder

Management tip

To set up an efficient system for managing writing assignments—one that frees you and your students to focus on the writing process itself—try this tip. For each student, label a hanging file folder and a pocket folder with the student's name. Students keep all work in progress, from prewriting to final draft, in their pocket folders. Store the pocket folders alphabetically in a plastic basket when not in use. When the pocket folders become overcrowded, have students move all work no longer in process to their hanging files. If you need writing samples to establish a student's progress, just pull them from the files.

Alana Green, Deer Park Elementary, Deer Park, TX

Name ____________________

New Trend, Inc.

A major company wants you to design a hot new bookbag for kids your age. You decide to write a proposal for your idea.

Introduction

Why are you writing?

How can you grab the company's attention?

Description

What will the new bookbag look like?

Conclusion

What is the most important feature of the new bookbag?

Write your proposal for the new bookbag. Get the company's attention and be as descriptive as possible.

Fragment and Run-on Sentence Cards

Use with "Fix-It Station" on page 133.

1

All the way from Idaho to visit.

TEC44038

2

Why are you buying a new backpack yours looks great.

TEC44038

3

Who played that cool song on the keyboard I do not know him.

TEC44038

4

The girl from Ohio.

TEC44038

5

Get their new car?

TEC44038

6

Looking for my jacket when I saw yours.

TEC44038

7

A week from this Saturday.

TEC44038

Is his first soccer game.

TEC44038

To try out next year but practice a lot first.

TEC44038

I want to win a trophy. As a skateboarder.

TEC44038

WRITE NOW!

Buffalo-Skin Stories

Writing a *pourquoi* tale

Asking why comes naturally to kids in any culture. Brainstorm with students naturally occurring things in the world that Native Americans might have wondered about—for example, why the opossum's tail is bare or why a rabbit's tail is short. Record the topics on the board and have each child pick one to write about. Next, have him tear the edges of a sheet of light brown construction paper to make it look like an animal hide. Then have him write his final draft on the hide and add colorful illustrations. If desired, have students crumple the hides to make them more authentic looking.

Shauna Harris, Bainbridge Island, WA

If I Were a...

Writing poetry

Generate a bumper crop of poems by first brainstorming with students several objects associated with the current month or season. Have each child write a poem about one of the objects using the format shown and then copy the final version onto a cutout of the object.

Renee Cooperman
Kenmore Town of Tonawanda School District, Kenmore, NY

If I were a...
I would taste...
I would be full of...
I would like to...
I'd want...

If I were a...
I would...
I would wish...
I would love...
I would listen for...
I would...

If I were a pumpkin,
I would taste sweet.
I would be full of seeds.
I would like to be carved.
I'd want to sit in your front window and glow.

If I were a pumpkin,
I would greet trick-or-treaters.
I would wish for fall to last longer.
I would love to smile brightly.
I would listen for kids asking for treats.
I would watch kids pick me from a pumpkin patch.

Kelly

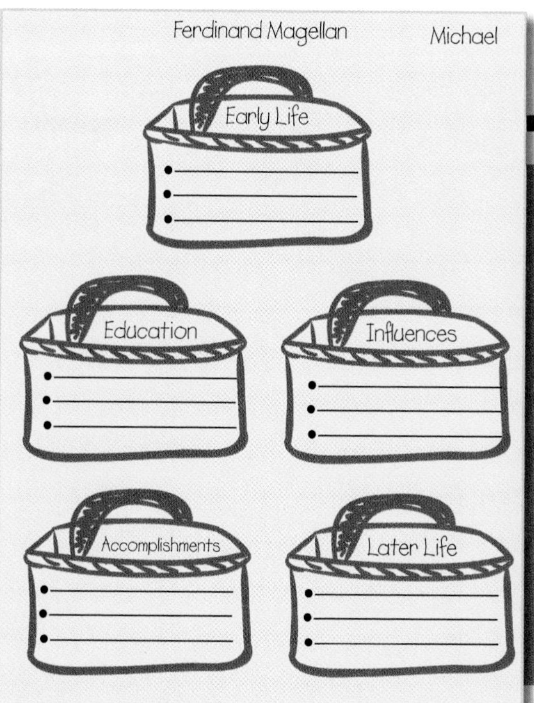

Fact Farming

Notetaking, report writing

Help students harvest bushels of facts to use in writing reports about famous people. Assign each child a different person to research; then instruct him to draw and label five baskets on his paper as shown. As he looks for facts that fit each category, have him decide whether he should "harvest" each fact (record it on his organizer). Once he has several interesting facts in each basket, have him use them to write a five-paragraph report about his person.

Farrah Milby, Weddington Hills Elementary, Concord, NC

Reel In the Reader!

Writing introductory sentences

To give students practice with writing interesting hooks, label several same-color fish cutouts with the same boring introductory sentence. Repeat the process, using a different color and sentence each time, until the number of cutouts equals the total number of students and the number of colors equals the desired number of student groups. Then randomly distribute the fish. Have students group themselves by fish color and, within each group, brainstorm at least five ways to change the sentence on their fish into an exciting hook. Provide time for groups to share their hooks with the class.

There are three reasons we should have recess.

We're going to my grandparents' house for Thanksgiving.

Katie Kolowski, Bolin School, East Peoria, IL

Weigh the Facts!

Persuasive/argumentative writing

This small-group activity helps students argue both sides of an issue. Assign each group a different question like one of those shown. Instruct each group's members to record the question on a copy of page 140 and then list supportive reasons for each side. When the group has recorded at least three reasons in each column, have each group member decide which side of the argument she feels is stronger. Then have her use the listed reasons to write an essay advocating that stance.

Teri Nielsen, Tracey's Elementary, Tracys Landing, MD

Questions

Should soda machines be allowed in schools?
Should kids be allowed to have cell phones at school?
Should boys and girls be in separate classrooms?
Should text messaging be taught in school?
Should parents put a limit on how much time their children spend watching TV?
Should kids be allowed to get credit cards?
Should movie theaters show more animated movies than live-action movies?
Should people pay a fee for each book they check out of a library?
Should the cafeteria serve pizza every day?

Name ______________________________

Here I Go!

You are the first leaf to fall from a tree that is losing its leaves.

2 Plan

Beginning
How do you feel about being the first leaf to drop?

What does it feel like when the tree first turns you loose?

Middle
How does it feel to fall through the air?

What's happening around you?

End
How does it feel when you land on the ground?

How do you feel about never being attached to a tree again?

Write about your experience of falling from the tree. Tell what your journey was like.

Name ____________________

R.E.S.P.E.C.T. Your Writing!

Is your writing ready for someone to read? Check each box below to be sure.

Did you…

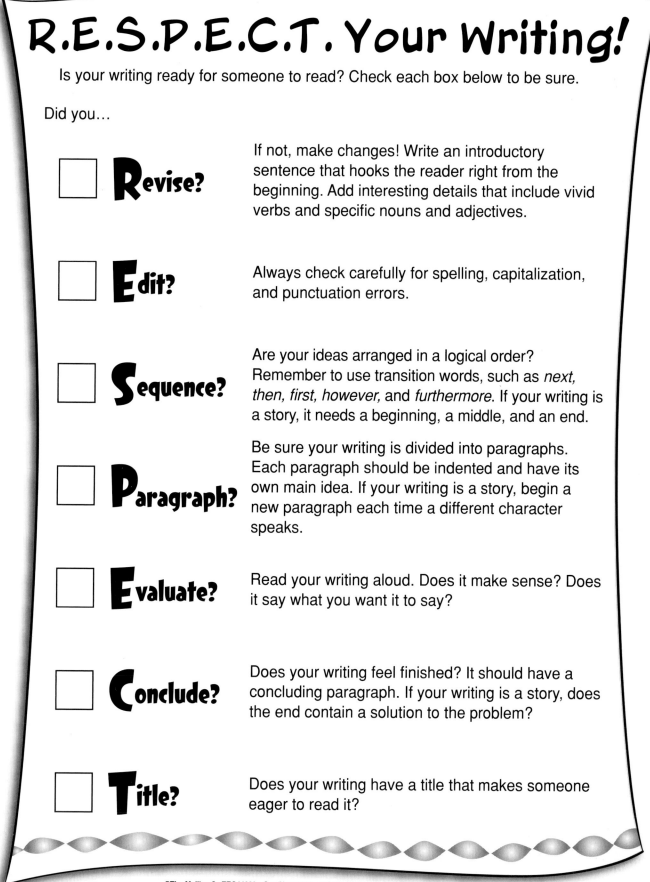

☐ **Revise?** If not, make changes! Write an introductory sentence that hooks the reader right from the beginning. Add interesting details that include vivid verbs and specific nouns and adjectives.

☐ **Edit?** Always check carefully for spelling, capitalization, and punctuation errors.

☐ 

Are your ideas arranged in a logical order? Remember to use transition words, such as *next, then, first, however,* and *furthermore*. If your writing is a story, it needs a beginning, a middle, and an end.

☐ 

Be sure your writing is divided into paragraphs. Each paragraph should be indented and have its own main idea. If your writing is a story, begin a new paragraph each time a different character speaks.

☐ 

Read your writing aloud. Does it make sense? Does it say what you want it to say?

☐ 

Does your writing feel finished? It should have a concluding paragraph. If your writing is a story, does the end contain a solution to the problem?

☐ 

Does your writing have a title that makes someone eager to read it?

Note to the teacher: Have each student keep a copy of this page in his writing folder as a reference. Or have him attach a copy of the page to each final draft he completes.

Names ____________________

TAKE A STAND!

Question: ____________________

____

____

____

YOU BET!	NO WAY!

Note to the teacher: Use with "Weigh the Facts!" on page 137.

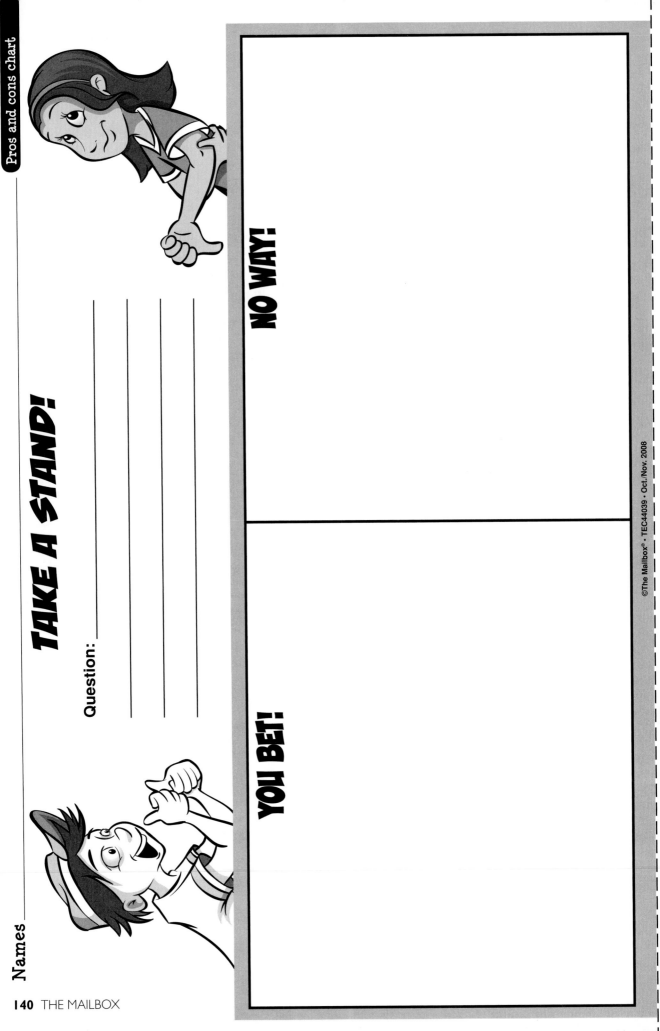

WRITE NOW!

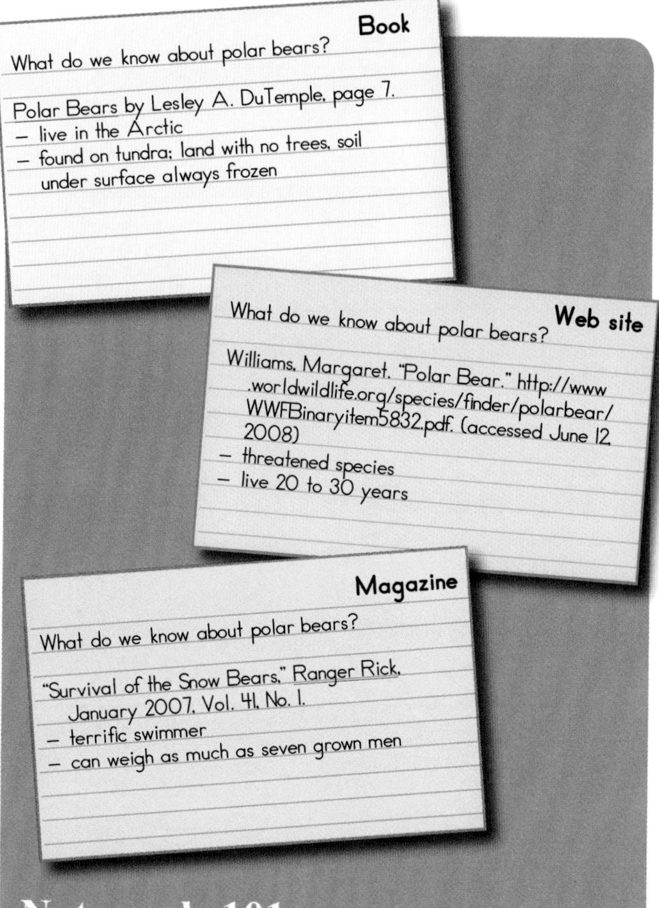

Book
What do we know about polar bears?
Polar Bears by Lesley A. DuTemple, page 7.
– live in the Arctic
– found on tundra; land with no trees, soil under surface always frozen
What do we know about polar bears?
Web site
Williams, Margaret. "Polar Bear." http://www.worldwildlife.org/species/finder/polarbear/WWFBinaryitem5832.pdf. (accessed June 12, 2008)
– threatened species
– live 20 to 30 years
Magazine
What do we know about polar bears?
"Survival of the Snow Bears," Ranger Rick, January 2007, Vol. 41, No. 1.
– terrific swimmer
– can weigh as much as seven grown men

Notecards 101
Notetaking

Prepare students for report writing by showing them how to set up and add notes from different sources to notecards. On a transparency, model how to summarize in your own words a source's details and facts. Emphasize using key words and phrases instead of complete sentences. Also include a quote, using quotation marks around the exact text, so students will know to copy information word-for-word only when they want to quote directly. Have students copy your examples onto index cards to keep in their writing folders as references.

adapted from an idea by Pat Dancho
Apollo-Ridge Middle School
Spring Church, PA

Roll a Story!
Prewriting, story elements

Here's a perfect way to interest kids in writing. Have each child write the five questions below, skipping a line between each one. To answer the questions, give each group of students a pair of dice and a copy of page 145. Instruct each member of the group, in turn, to roll the dice and record the words that correspond to the number rolled. Once all the questions are answered, each student is ready to write his story.

Maxine Gaul
Spalding Catholic School
Alton, IA

Peyton

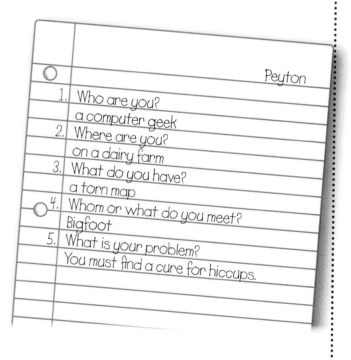

1. Who are you?
   a computer geek
2. Where are you?
   on a dairy farm
3. What do you have?
   a torn map
4. Whom or what do you meet?
   Bigfoot
5. What is your problem?
   You must find a cure for hiccups.

Convince Your Parents!

Persuasive letter

Students will need little encouragement to complete this writing activity. Have each child write a persuasive letter to his parents explaining why they should buy him that big-ticket item he desperately wants for Christmas. Instruct him to include information about where the item can be purchased and why he deserves this gift, such as he is respectful and obedient, helps around the house, or is on the honor roll. Parents may appreciate your putting an educational spin on the "I want" fever that distracts most students before the holidays! Repeat the activity later on by having students focus on birthday gifts they want to receive.

Kelly Gray, Rochester Middle School, Rochester, NH

Flesh Out the Framework!

Paragraph writing

To help writers nail down good paragraph structure, display a guide similar to the one at the right. Use it to model a sample paragraph on the board. Then have each writer follow the guide to write a paragraph about a topic of her choice or one she selects from the list shown.

Debbie Berris, Poinciana Day School, West Palm Beach, FL

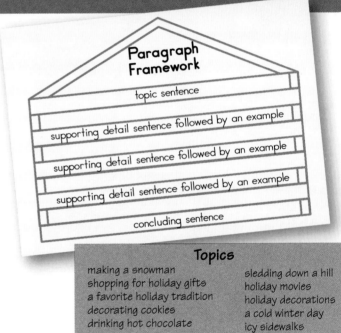

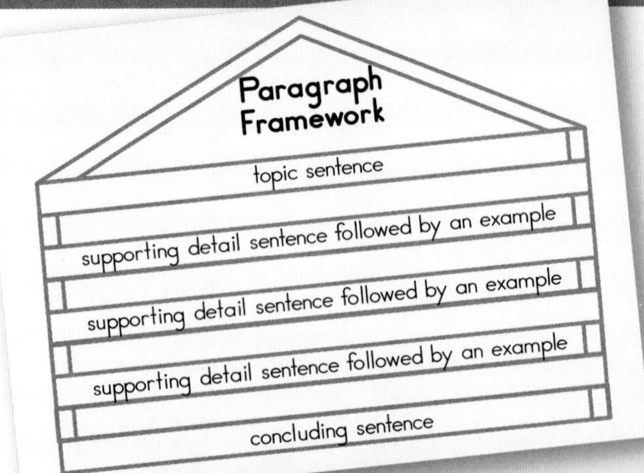

Paragraph Framework
topic sentence
supporting detail sentence followed by an example
supporting detail sentence followed by an example
supporting detail sentence followed by an example
concluding sentence

Topics

- making a snowman
- shopping for holiday gifts
- a favorite holiday tradition
- decorating cookies
- drinking hot chocolate
- sledding down a hill
- holiday movies
- holiday decorations
- a cold winter day
- icy sidewalks

When the bowl of ice cream crashed to the floor, I nearly jumped out of my skin!

Editors and Actors

Peer editing

To keep editing from being a lonely, dull task, make it fun and dramatic! Once each writer's story or poem is ready to be edited, make a copy of it for the author to give to a classmate of his choice. Instruct the author to read his written piece aloud slowly and with great expression as an actor would. Direct his partner to follow along on the copy, listening carefully and adding or changing punctuation where the actor's voice indicates. When a writer reads his own work aloud, he unfailingly shows with his voice where punctuation marks are needed. Partners then switch roles so the actor can become an editor.

Jewell Flint-Stewart, Ellsworth, ME

Name ______________________________

What a Find!

1 Prompt

While exploring your grandmother's attic, you find a box of photos you have never seen before. It contains a photo of your grandmother wearing the most ridiculous outfit you have ever seen.

2 Plan

What type of hat is on your grandmother's head?

What type of shirt or coat is she wearing?

What type of skirt or pants does she have on?

What kind of shoes are on her feet?

What other accessories does she have?

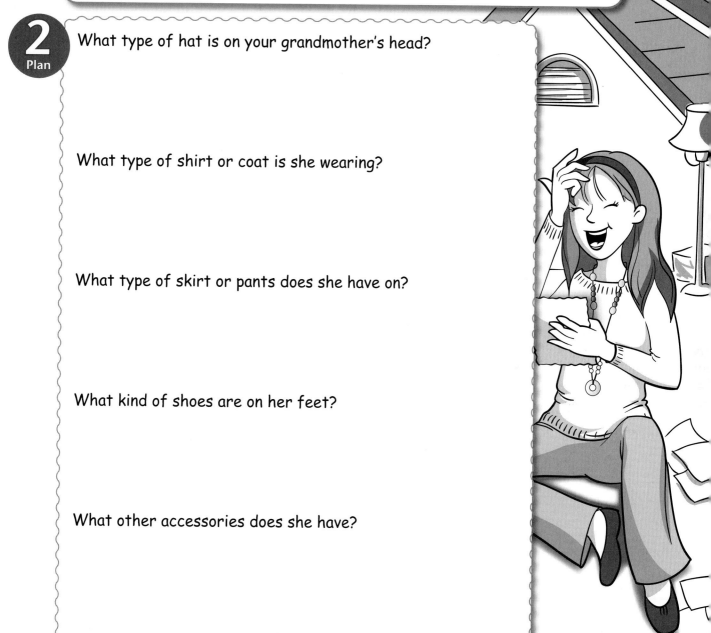

3 Write

Write a newspaper article that could appear with this photo of your grandmother. Explain in detail how she is dressed. Organize the article by what your grandmother is wearing in order from head to toe.

Name ____________________

Jake's Jokes

Edit the jokes using the symbols in the box. Rewrite the jokes correctly on another sheet of paper.

Editing Symbols	
Symbol	Meaning
¶	Start a new paragraph.
◯	Correct the spelling.
℘	Delete or remove.
⁀‿	Close the gap.
^	Add a letter or word.
#	Make a space.
∼	Reverse the order of letters or words.
^,	Insert a comma.
⊙	Insert a period.
^'	Insert an apostrophe.
^" ^"	Insert quotation marks.
≡	Make the letter a capital.
/	Make the letter lowercase.

Jake Jokester, Comedy Writer

Mr. Cox: "Excuse me waiter, is there spaghetti on the menu?"

Waiter: "No, sir, I wiped it off"

"Doctor, doctor! I think, I'm a dog!" exclaimed the patient.

"Well, come and sit on the sofa so we can about talk your problem," the Doctor replied.

The patient answered, "But Im not allowed on the sofa!"

A band class was just getting under way when a large insect flu into th room. The music students, eager to play there shiny new instruments tried to ignore the buzzing intruder. Eventually, one student, Greg could stand it no more. He rolled up his music book and swatted the insect. Then he stomped on it to ensure it's fate.

"Was it a bee? " another student asked.

"No," Greg replied. "Bee flat.

A student asked her teacher whether a person should be punished for something she hadn't done.

"No," replied the

teacher "of course not!"

Good, said the girl "Because I didn't do my homework."

Names ____________________

ROLL A STORY!

WHO ARE YOU?

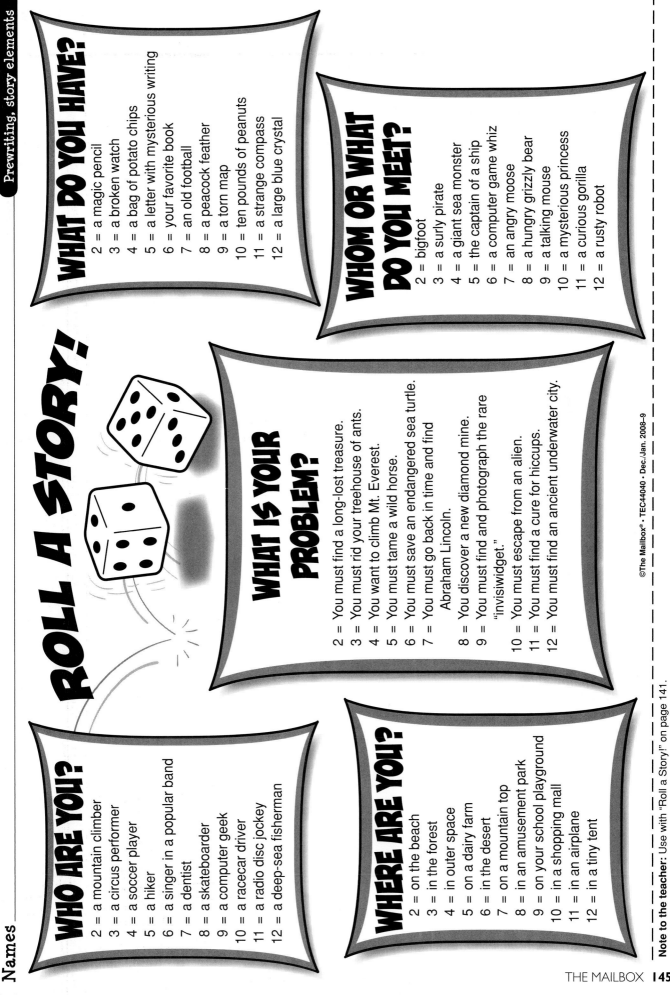

2 = a mountain climber
3 = a circus performer
4 = a soccer player
5 = a hiker
6 = a singer in a popular band
7 = a dentist
8 = a skateboarder
9 = a computer geek
10 = a racecar driver
11 = a radio disc jockey
12 = a deep-sea fisherman

WHERE ARE YOU?

2 = on the beach
3 = in the forest
4 = in outer space
5 = on a dairy farm
6 = in the desert
7 = on a mountain top
8 = in an amusement park
9 = on your school playground
10 = in a shopping mall
11 = in an airplane
12 = in a tiny tent

WHAT IS YOUR PROBLEM?

2 = You must find a long-lost treasure.
3 = You must rid your treehouse of ants.
4 = You want to climb Mt. Everest.
5 = You must tame a wild horse.
6 = You must save an endangered sea turtle.
7 = You must go back in time and find Abraham Lincoln.
8 = You discover a new diamond mine.
9 = You must find and photograph the rare "invisiwidget."
10 = You must escape from an alien.
11 = You must find a cure for hiccups.
12 = You must find an ancient underwater city.

WHAT DO YOU HAVE?

2 = a magic pencil
3 = a broken watch
4 = a bag of potato chips
5 = a letter with mysterious writing
6 = your favorite book
7 = an old football
8 = a peacock feather
9 = a torn map
10 = ten pounds of peanuts
11 = a strange compass
12 = a large blue crystal

WHOM OR WHAT DO YOU MEET?

2 = bigfoot
3 = a surly pirate
4 = a giant sea monster
5 = the captain of a ship
6 = a computer game whiz
7 = an angry moose
8 = a hungry grizzly bear
9 = a talking mouse
10 = a mysterious princess
11 = a curious gorilla
12 = a rusty robot

Note to the teacher: Use with "Roll a Story!" on page 141.

WRITE NOW!

Broad	Specific
visiting Grandma	helping Grandma bake cookies
trip to an amusement park	riding the new roller coaster
sports	scoring the winning goal in a game
last weekend	breakfast with Dad on Saturday
trip to the lake	catching my first fish
playing outside	riding my bike on a new trail

Narrowing Narratives

Choosing a topic

To help students focus on a smaller element of a broad writing topic, list on the board broad topics, such as those above. For each broad topic, have students brainstorm ideas that are more specific. Record students' suggestions on the board. Then have each child write a personal narrative about one of the more specific ideas, telling what happened at the beginning, middle, and end, as well as what she thought and felt during the experience. Not only will your students find the narrative easier to write, but their writing skills are sure to improve.

Debbie Berris, Poinciana Day School
West Palm Beach, FL

Putting It in Order

Organizing paragraphs

For this partner activity, have each twosome cut apart the sentence strips on a copy of page 150. Instruct the duo to order the sentences to form five sensible paragraphs, setting aside any sentences that contain irrelevant information. Then have the partners copy the paragraphs onto a sheet of paper. As each twosome reads its essay aloud, discuss any differences in the work that's shared.

Jacquelyn Patterson, Murfreesboro, TN

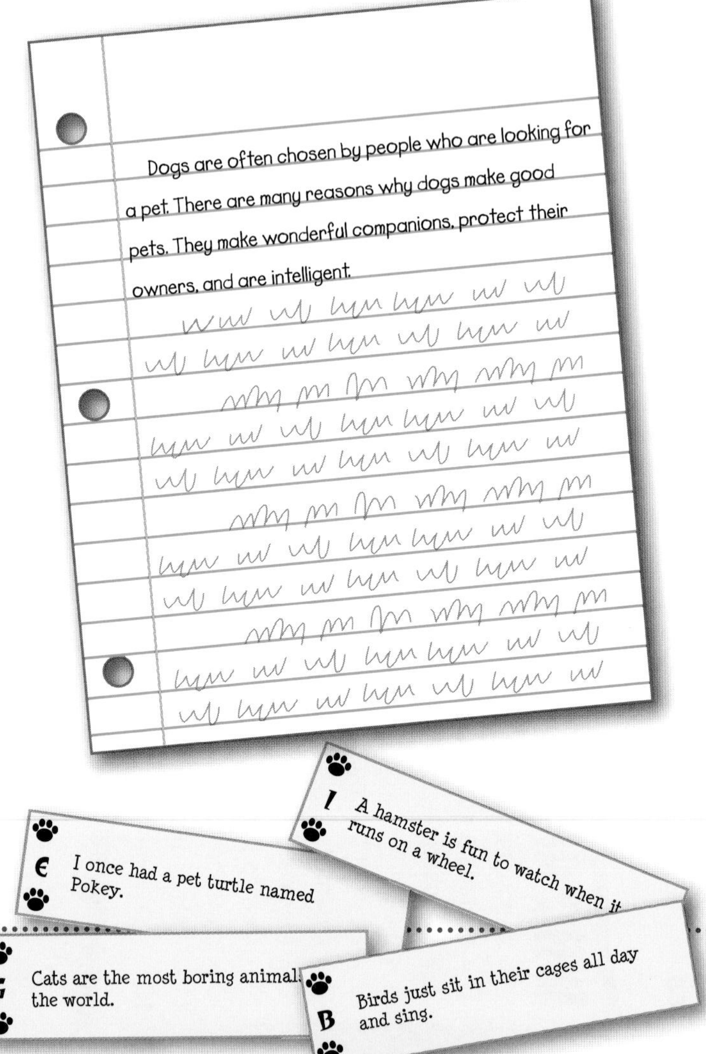

Dogs are often chosen by people who are looking for a pet. There are many reasons why dogs make good pets. They make wonderful companions, protect their owners, and are intelligent.
I A hamster is fun to watch when it runs on a wheel.
E I once had a pet turtle named Pokey.
G Cats are the most boring animal the world.
B Birds just sit in their cages all day and sing.

Tasty Treats
Writing a descriptive paragraph

Cook up mouthwatering descriptions by having each child use construction paper scraps to create and label a simple model of his favorite food. Instruct him to attach a piece of paper to the bottom of his model. Have students pass their food items around the room until every child has listed a different word on each paper to describe each food. Then have him use the words listed by his classmates to write a descriptive paragraph about the food.

Farrah Milby, Weddington Hills Elementary, Concord, NC

fried chicken
crunchy
crispy
delicious
delectable
tender
moist
lip-smacking

Man! I am so excited I can hardly stand it! Saturday I'm getting a new mountain bike. I don't know if I will be able to wait that long! I don't even think I'll be able to sleep until then because the bike is really awesome!

From the Heart
Writing with a personal voice

Begin by having each student cut out a magazine picture of a person or an animal that has a very distinctive facial expression. Have the child mount the picture on colorful paper and attach a large speech bubble cutout. Then he writes on the cutout a passionate paragraph expressing the subject's feelings and emotions.

Nikki Kunkel, Seth Paine Elementary, Lake Zurich, IL

Get the Job Done
Peer editing

Involve all students in the peer-editing process by assigning three or four students to each role shown. Explain that, for the activity, each expert should focus only on her assigned skill when she edits a classmate's paper. When a student finishes a writing assignment, direct her to have her rough draft edited by each type of expert before doing her final draft.

Brooke Beverly, Dudley Elementary, Dudley, MA

Editing Experts
- Capitalization Captain
- Mechanics Master
- Spelling Supporter
- Paragraph Protector
- Introduction Inspector
- Conclusion Coach
- Punctuation Pilot
- Content Chief

Name ______________________________

Gym Shoe Mix-Up

1 Prompt You have been asked to write a story about gym class for the school newspaper. Your story begins, "I always thought gym shoes were supposed to be worn on your feet, not..."

2 Plan

Introduction

Who:

When:

Where:

Rising Action

Event 1:

Event 2:

Climax

Event 3:

Falling Action

Event 4:

Conclusion

How it ends:

3 Write Write an interesting story for the school newspaper that includes all the events from above.

Name ______________________________

A President's Life

Cut out each detail and glue it in the organizer in logical order. Use the completed outline to write an expository essay on another sheet of paper. Remember to include an introduction and a conclusion.

Abraham Lincoln

I. Early Childhood

A.

B. 

C.

II. Adult Life

A.

B. 

C. 

D.

III. 

A.

B.

C.

D.

Borrowed neighbors' books to learn	Had four sons	Worked to reunite the nation after the Civil War
Life as President	Born on February 12, 1809, in Hardin County, Kentucky	Was the 16th president of the United States
Was assassinated on April 14, 1865	Moved with his parents from Kentucky to Indiana	Married Mary Todd
Issued the Emancipation Procla-mation to free the slaves	Studied law and became a lawyer	Became interested in politics

Sentence Strips

Use with "Putting It in Order" on page 146.

A Dogs are often chosen by people who are looking for a pet.	**K** They can also be taught to search for bombs or illegal substances.
B Birds just sit in their cages all day and sing.	**L** Some dogs are even trained to help disabled people, such as guiding someone who is blind.
C There are many reasons why dogs make good pets.	**M** They offer their owners companionship and protection, plus they can be trained to assist with important tasks.
D They can also be fun playmates for people of all ages.	**N** They make wonderful companions, protect their owners, and are intelligent.
E I once had a pet turtle named Pokey.	**O** Dogs are great companions because they are loyal, loving, and friendly.
F Many families with children look for these traits in a pet.	**P** In addition to making good companions, dogs can also protect their owners.
G Cats are the most boring animals in the world.	**Q** Dogs sometimes even protect homes from burglars when the family is away.
H Not only do these animals make great companions and keep their owners safe, but dogs are smart too.	**R** They can bark to ward off an intruder or warn the family of danger.
I A hamster is fun to watch when it runs on a wheel.	**S** Overall, dogs make great pets.
J They can learn to do tricks like sitting and fetching.	**T** For these reasons, dogs are an awesome pet choice.

WRITE NOW!

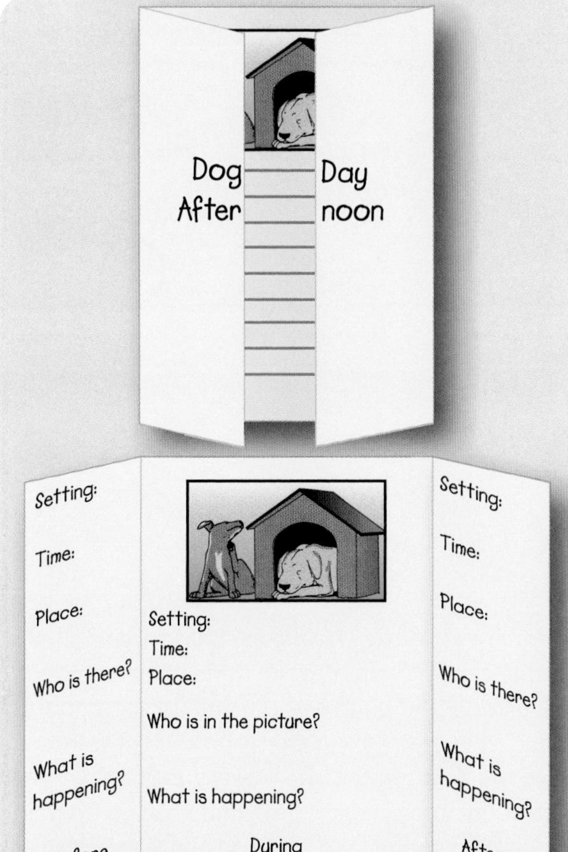

Before, During, and After

Narrative writing

Help students plan and write stories with this simple organizer. Each child trifolds a large sheet of light-colored construction paper and labels each section as shown. In the middle section, he glues a picture from a magazine and writes a brief description of what is happening in the picture. He completes the remainder of the organizer with information about what happened before and after the picture was taken. Finally, the child writes his story's title on the outside of the organizer and writes the complete story on another sheet of paper.

MaryLouise Alu Curto
Newgrange School
Mercerville, NJ

Watercolor Poetry

Writing sensory poems

To begin, have each student pick a color other than white, gray, or black. Have him complete a copy of the graphic organizer on page 155, using his senses to list items he associates with his color. Next, direct the student to use the information to write a poem about his color on unlined paper. Finally, have him paint different objects from his poem around the page, using the color he chose. Post the completed poems to make a colorful display!

Jean Swarat
McKinley Elementary
Fresno, CA

Blue
Blue is the color of blueberry pie,
A blue jay's feathers, and the bright noon sky.
Blue is the color of ocean scenes,
Picasso's art and my favorite jeans.

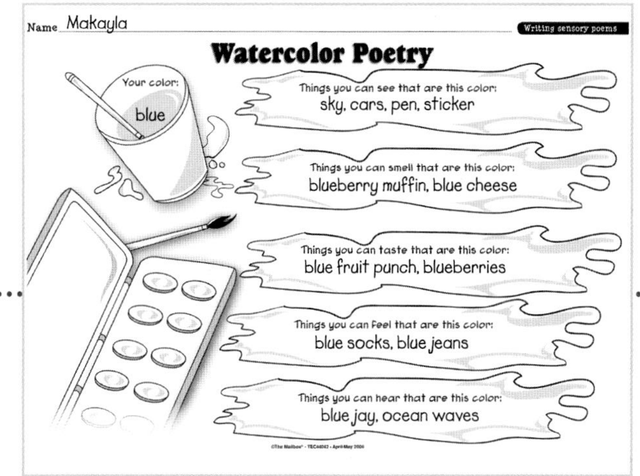

Name Makayla
Writing sensory poems
Watercolor Poetry
Your color:
blue
Things you can see that are this color:
sky, cars, pen, sticker
Things you can smell that are this color:
blueberry muffin, blue cheese
Things you can taste that are this color:
blue fruit punch, blueberries
Things you can feel that are this color:
blue socks, blue jeans
Things you can hear that are this color:
blue jay, ocean waves

Road Atlas Writing

Writing a friendly letter and directions

In advance, tear out for each student one state map from an old road atlas. The student imagines she lives in one city on her map. She then selects a second city on her map in which a pretend friend lives. Next, the student writes a letter to her friend telling of fun things to do in and around her city, such as visiting a nearby lake or hiking in a local state park. In her letter she also includes directions to get from her friend's city to her city. If desired, encourage students to include cardinal and intermediate directions, interstate highway numbers, travel distances using the map scale, and the approximate travel time.

Karen Schilling, Summerfield Elementary, Shreveport, LA

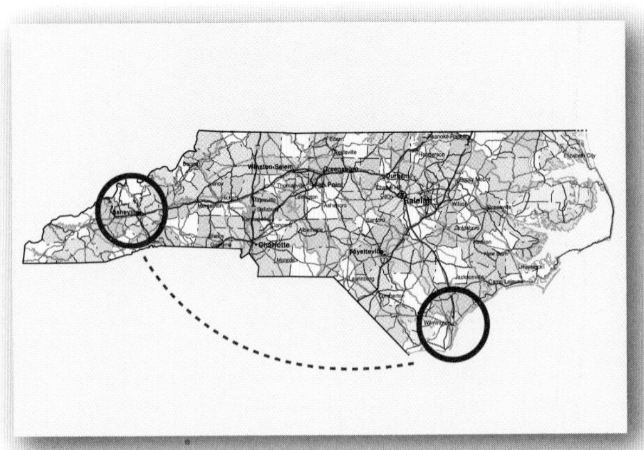

One Sip at a Time

Organizing details

Using a permanent marker, have each student pair label a disposable cup with the title or topic of an essay. On a sheet of paper, have the duo research and list facts about the topic. Next, have the pair cut each fact on its list into a strip and place the strips in the cup. Have the duo then pull the strips out of the cup one at a time and arrange them in logical order. Instruct the pair to place any unrelated or redundant strips back in the cup. Finally, have the partners use the ordered strips to write their essay.

Kim Minafo, Apex, NC

The Key

Editing and revising

Key
Topic sentence: red font
Details: underlined in green
Elaboration: italics
Conclusion: blue font

After students have rough drafts, help them improve each paragraph while meeting technology standards at the same time. To begin, have each child type his essay on a computer. For each paragraph, have him identify the main idea, supporting details, elaboration, and conclusion using the key shown. Then have the student add more specific vocabulary and transition words and delete any extra information.

Carol Horta, John J. Ahern Middle School, Foxborough, MA

Summer is definitely my favorite time of year. <u>First of all, I like the warm temperatures</u>. *It's more fun to wear sandals than heavy snow boots.* <u>Also, my family always goes to Lake Sun to swim, boat, fish, and hike</u>. *I look forward to leaping off the diving board and staying underwater as long as I can hold my breath.* <u>The fresh fruits and vegetables</u>, *especially berries and tomatoes,* <u>make summer dining better than winter meals</u>. *Canned and frozen veggies just can't compete with fresh, out-of-the-garden food.* I look forward to summer every year because there just isn't a better season!

Name ____________________

TV Troubles

1
Prompt

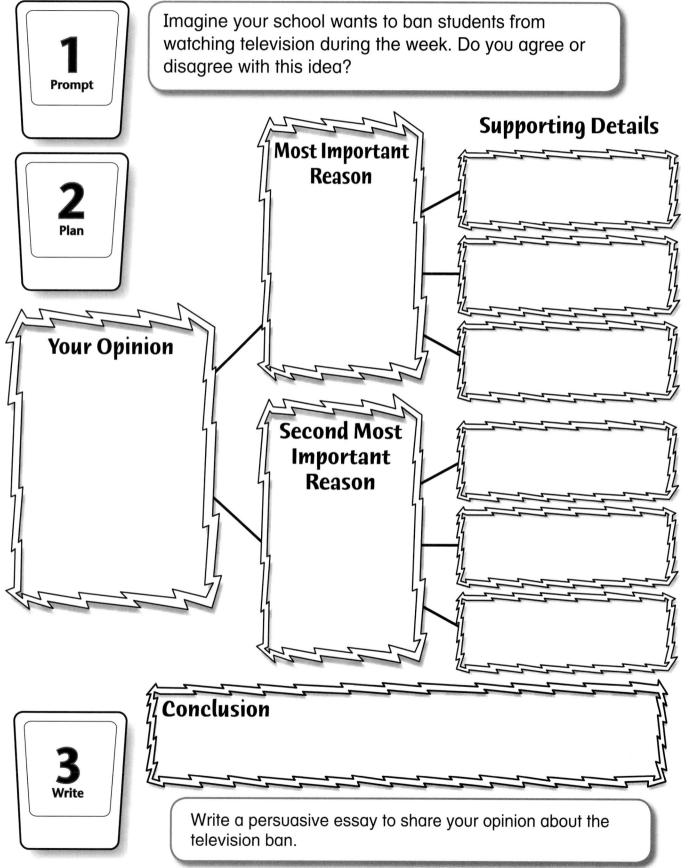

Imagine your school wants to ban students from watching television during the week. Do you agree or disagree with this idea?

2
Plan

Your Opinion

Most Important Reason

Second Most Important Reason

Supporting Details

Conclusion

3
Write

Write a persuasive essay to share your opinion about the television ban.

Story Element Cards

Make a copy of this page for each student. Have the student cut out the cards on the solid lines and hole-punch where indicated. Then have the student fold the cards in half with the text facing out and place them on a binder ring for easy reference when writing essays or reading stories.

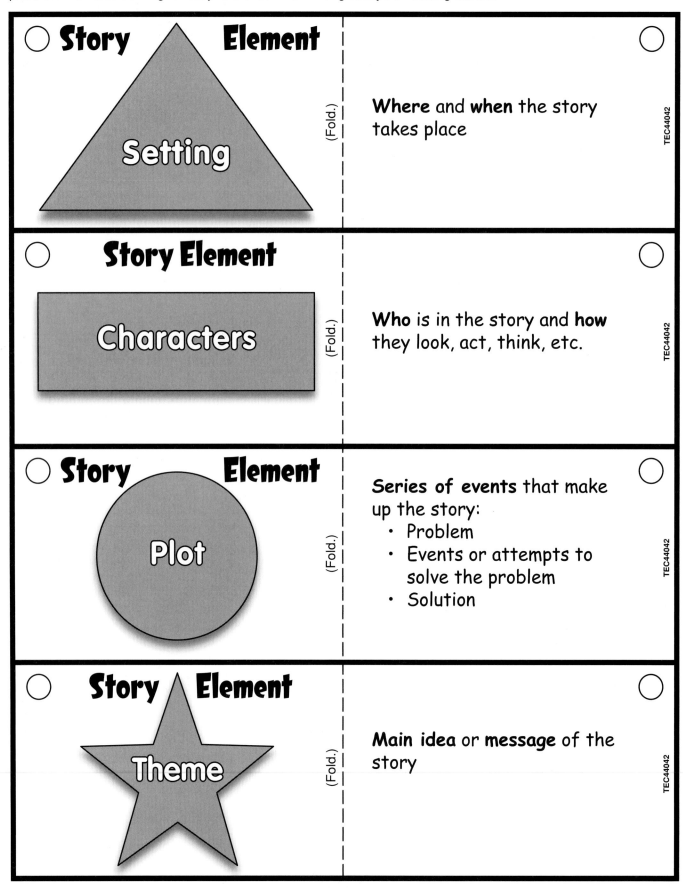

Story Element

Setting

(Fold.)

Where and **when** the story takes place

TEC44042

Story Element

Characters

(Fold.)

Who is in the story and **how** they look, act, think, etc.

TEC44042

Story Element

Plot

(Fold.)

Series of events that make up the story:

- Problem
- Events or attempts to solve the problem
- Solution

TEC44042

Story Element

Theme

(Fold.)

Main idea or **message** of the story

TEC44042

Name ____________________

Watercolor Poetry

Your color:

Things you can see that are this color:

Things you can smell that are this color:

Things you can taste that are this color:

Things you can feel that are this color:

Things you can hear that are this color:

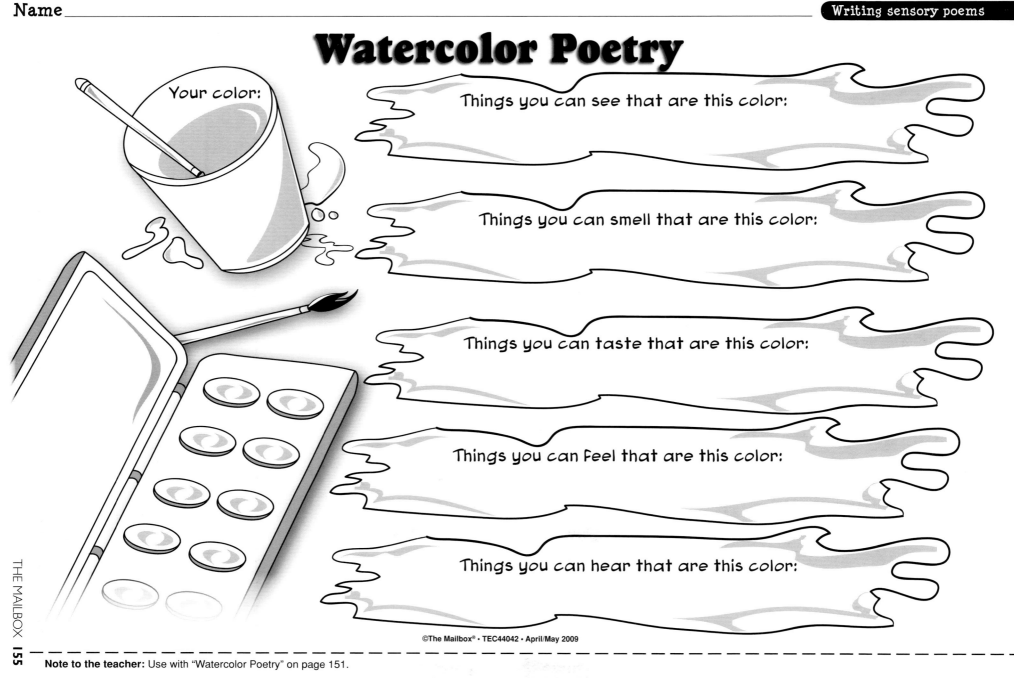

Note to the teacher: Use with "Watercolor Poetry" on page 151.

WRITE NOW!

Planning Blankets
Prewriting

Give your students a chance to brainstorm on a blanket! Purchase at a discount store one inexpensive plastic tablecloth for every eight to 12 students. Cut each tablecloth in half to make two blankets. Next, divide the class into groups of four to six students. Give each group a blanket, several wipe-off markers, and a card labeled with one of the writing topics shown. Instruct each group to use its markers on the blanket to create a web for its topic. Have each group member copy the web onto paper to use as a reference for his writing. When students have finished writing, have them reconvene on their blankets (which have been wiped clean) to share their finished products with their group.

Kim Minafo, Apex, NC

Writing Topics

- What is your favorite pair of summer shoes? Why?
- Tell about your favorite day at school this year.
- How do you feel about school next year? Why?
- Try to convince your parents to let you do something this summer.
- What advice do you have for next year's class?
- If you could invent a new high-tech gadget, what would it be and why?

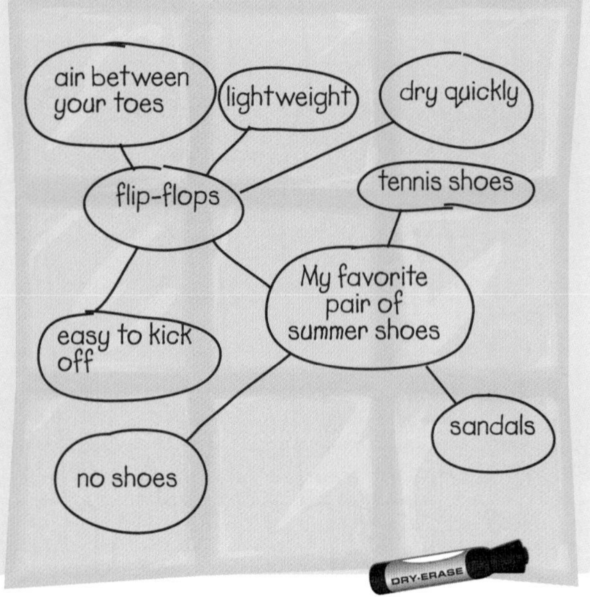

Picture Motivators
Researching and writing a report

Take your students and a digital camera on a nature walk around school grounds to capture motivating research topics. Instruct students to look for interesting occurrences on your walk, such as a butterfly perched on a flower or a spiderweb hanging in a tree. Once a student locates an interesting scene, take a picture of it. After the walk, print a picture for each student. Then instruct each student to create a research question based on her picture. Have her research the answer to her question and write a report to share with the class. If desired, post reports with the pictures on a display titled "Look What We Found!"

Sheri Belk, Buist Academy, Charleston, SC

Add a Line
Narrative writing

Use this class writing activity to demonstrate the importance of staying on topic. Arrange students' desks in a large circle. Post a story beginning, such as the first sentence at the right, and have each student copy it on his paper. Then instruct him to write the story's second sentence. After two minutes, have students pass their papers to the right and have that student add the third sentence. Continue passing papers every two minutes until each paper returns to its original owner. Then allow students to share their stories. Be prepared to laugh!

Heather Colbert, West Lee Learning Center, Wytheville, VA

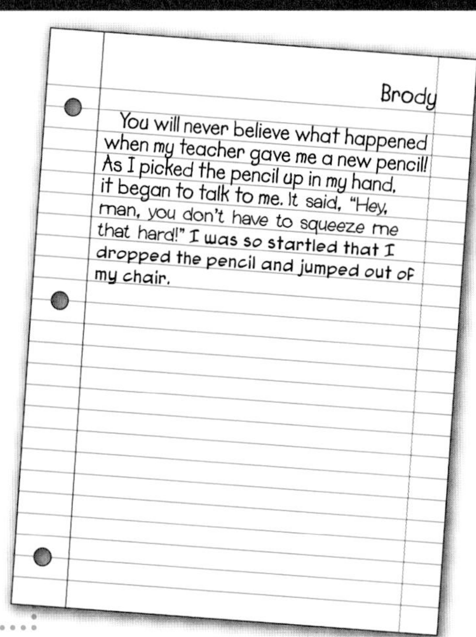

Brody
You will never believe what happened when my teacher gave me a new pencil! As I picked the pencil up in my hand, it began to talk to me. It said, "Hey, man, you don't have to squeeze me that hard!" I was so startled that I dropped the pencil and jumped out of my chair.

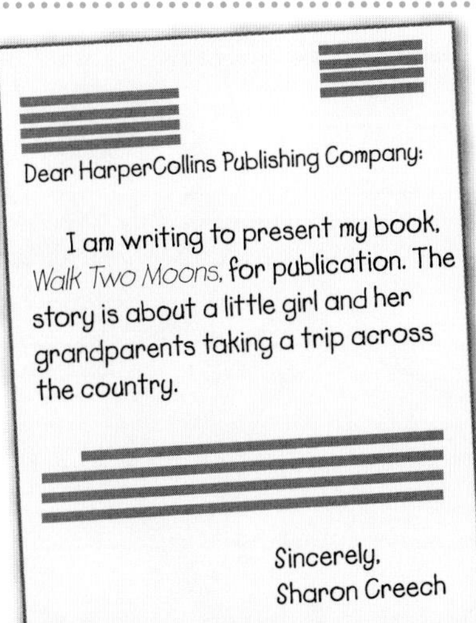

Dear HarperCollins Publishing Company:

I am writing to present my book, *Walk Two Moons*, for publication. The story is about a little girl and her grandparents taking a trip across the country.

Sincerely,
Sharon Creech

Please Publish!
Book report, persuasive writing

Use this activity as a fun twist to writing book reports! After students read a book, have them pretend they are the author trying to get the book published. Instruct each student to write a letter to the book's publisher to convince him or her to publish it. Instruct students to include in their letters a summary of the book as well as reasons why it should be published.

Christy Davis, Keswick Christian School, St. Petersburg, FL

Research the Easy Way
Organizing research

Help students organize their research information into a three-paragraph report in just a few simple steps. After each student chooses a research topic, give her 20 white index cards and six colorful ones. Ask the student to find from multiple sources 20 important facts about her topic and then summarize each fact in one sentence on a white card. Give each child a copy of page 160 to use as a guide for citing sources on the backs of her cards. After she completes her white cards, direct her to sort the 20 sentences by topic, identify the three groups with the most cards, and write a main idea sentence for each group on a separate colorful card. Next, have her reread each of the three stacks of cards, beginning with the main idea card, and write a concluding sentence for each main idea on another colorful card. Finally, have each student use her three organized stacks of cards to write a three-paragraph report on her topic.

Deanna Casebeer, Bolivar, MO

The Pony Express riders had very important jobs.

Many of these lightweight riders were teenagers.

They carried mail from Missouri to California in ten days or less.

Their salaries ranged from $100 to $150 per month.

These young men risked their lives to deliver the mail.

Name ______________________________

A Wild Ride

1 Prompt

Imagine that your log ride has taken an unexpected turn. The log car has left the track and is now flying you to the future.

2 Plan

① Introduction
② Rising Action
③ Climax
④ Falling Action
⑤ Conclusion

1. Who are your story's main characters? ______________________________

   Where does the story take place? ______________________________

2. What problems or conflicts do the characters face? ______________________________

3. What is the turning point in the story? ______________________________

4. What events happen because of the turning point? ______________________________

5. How does the story end? ______________________________

3 Write

Use the information above to write a story about your wild ride from beginning to end.

Name ______________________________

Pet Puzzle

1. Cut out the puzzle pieces.
2. Select the pieces with the most important details about caring for pets.
3. Put those pieces together to form a picture.
4. Glue your pet puzzle to the bottom of another sheet of paper as shown.
5. In the space above your puzzle, use the details to write an informative paragraph about pets.

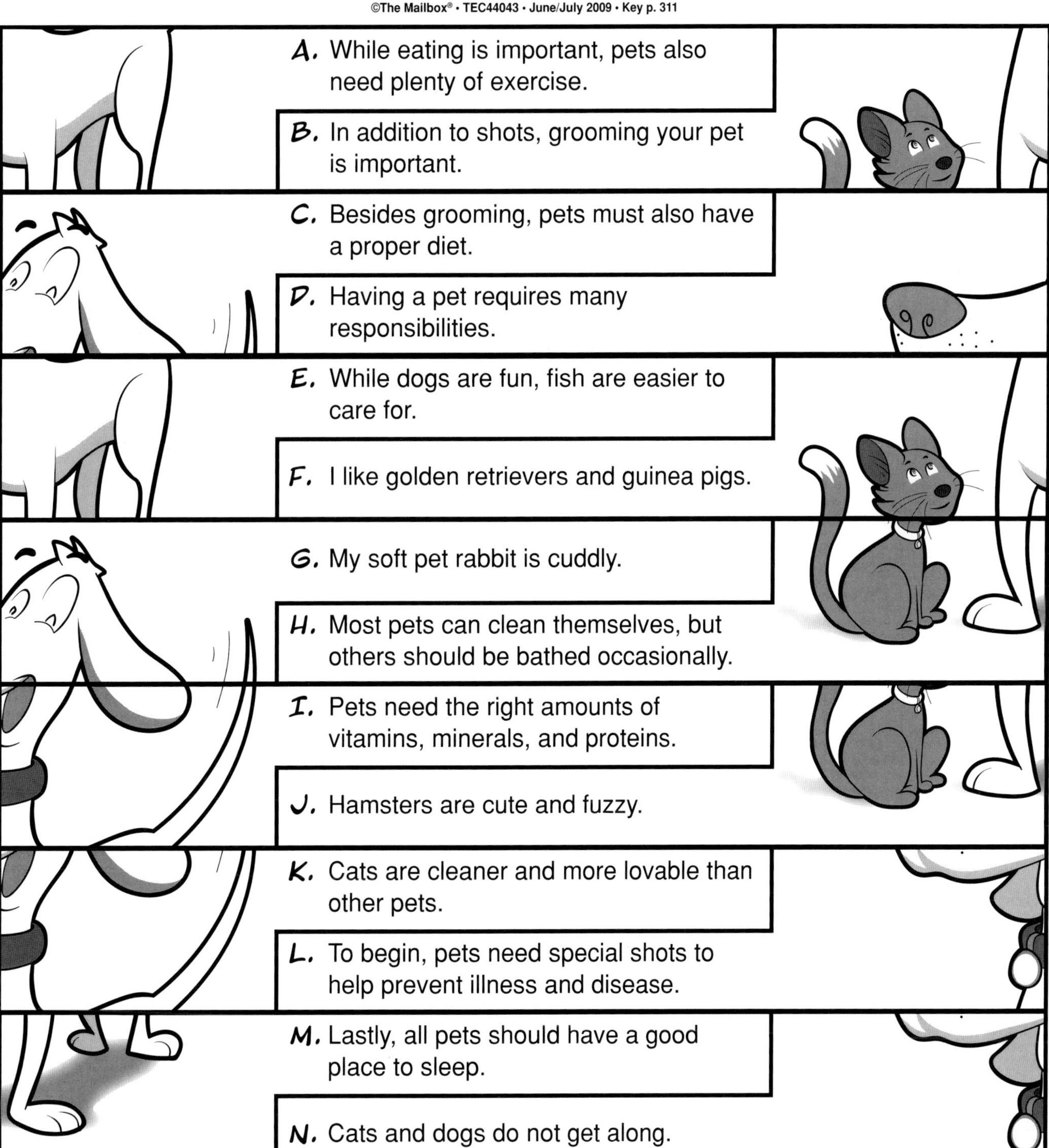

A. While eating is important, pets also need plenty of exercise.
B. In addition to shots, grooming your pet is important.
C. Besides grooming, pets must also have a proper diet.
D. Having a pet requires many responsibilities.
E. While dogs are fun, fish are easier to care for.
F. I like golden retrievers and guinea pigs.
G. My soft pet rabbit is cuddly.
H. Most pets can clean themselves, but others should be bathed occasionally.
I. Pets need the right amounts of vitamins, minerals, and proteins.
J. Hamsters are cute and fuzzy.
K. Cats are cleaner and more lovable than other pets.
L. To begin, pets need special shots to help prevent illness and disease.
M. Lastly, all pets should have a good place to sleep.
N. Cats and dogs do not get along.

Name ____________

Citing Sources

To prepare a bibliography, use the examples below. If a reference's author is not given, begin your listing with the title. If any information given in the examples is not available, skip it and list the information that is.

Book: Author (last name first). Title (underlined). Place of publication: publisher's name, copyright date.

Redmond, Ian. The Elephant Book. Cambridge, MA: Candlewick Press, 2001.

Encyclopedia: Author (last name first). "Article title." Title of the encyclopedia (underlined). Year.

"Elephant." The World Book Encyclopedia. 1996.

Online reference: Author or editor (last name first). "Article title." Source (underlined). Year. Electronic address or URL. Date of access (day, month, year).

Moss, Cynthia. "Elephant." World Book Online Reference Center. 2006. worldbookonline.com. 13 November 2008.

Internet: Author or editor (last name first). "Article title." Source (underlined). Electronic address or URL. Date of access (day, month, year).

Jones, Judy. "Elephant Beginnings." The Elephant Sanctuary. http://www.elephants.com/begin.htm.20 November 2008.

Newspaper: Author (last name first). "Article title." Title of newspaper (underlined) date (day, month, year), section: page number.

Kaufman, Marc. "Increased Demand for Ivory Threatens Elephant Survival." The Washington Post 27 February 2007, A: 10.

Magazine: Author (last name first). "Article title." Title of magazine (underlined) date (day, month, year): article's page numbers.

Cohn, Jeffrey P. "Do Elephants Belong in Zoos?" Bioscience September 2006: 714–717.

CD-ROM or DVD: Author or editor (last name first). Title (underlined). Electronic medium (CD-ROM or DVD). Version. Place of publication: publisher, date of publication (day, month, year).

Nature: Echo of the Elephants. DVD. English. Chicago, IL: Questar, 30 August 2005.

Interview: Name of person interviewed (last name first). Type of interview (personal, telephone). Date of interview (day, month, year).

Hawkins, Marjorie. Personal interview. 15 November 2008.

Note to the teacher: Use with "Research the Easy Way" on page 157. Or give each student a copy of the guide to keep in his writing folder as a reference when he writes a report.

Writing Prompts

Name

August	September
☐ How would you feel if your parent got a new job and you had to move to another state the week before school started?	☐ September 5 is Be Late for Something Day. Which do you think is worse: being late or being early? Explain.
☐ If you could skip a grade in school, would you? Why or why not?	☐ September is Chicken Month. Describe something you know you're too chicken to ever do.
☐ Which is better: having three snow days you must make up at the end of the school year *or* having no snow days and getting out earlier for summer vacation? Explain.	☐ Describe what your life would be like if you could only see in black and white.
☐ Write a letter to your teacher explaining why it won't be necessary to assign you any homework this year.	☐ September is National Courtesy Month. When someone is rude to you, how do you handle it?
☐ The third week in August is Friendship Week. List five ways you can be a good friend to your classmates this year.	☐ September is the ninth month. List nine reasons why you are going to have a great school year.
☐ Explain why you would or would not like to be on a reality television show.	☐ World Gratitude Day is September 21. Write about a time when you were grateful for another person or for something that happened to you.
☐ You've closed your eyes briefly. When you open them, you're in a classroom you've never seen before with a teacher and classmates you don't know. What do you do?	☐ *Fall* is also known as *autumn*. What nicknames are you also known by? How did you get these nicknames?
☐ If your new teacher asks, "How would you describe yourself as a student?" what will be your answer?	☐ Leaves begin to change color in the fall. In what ways have you changed since last September?
☐ Some schools start in August, while others wait until early September. Which starting time is better? Why?	☐ Write about a day when your class's substitute teacher walks in—and it's your mom or dad!
☐ August is Admit You're Happy Month. Describe three things you are happy about today.	☐ Write your opinion about this statement: Fall is more fun than winter.

Note to the teacher: Have each student staple a copy of this page in his writing journal. Or cut copies in half and distribute only one month's prompts at a time to students. When a student uses a prompt, he checks it off in the box.

Writing Prompts

Name

October	November
☐ October is Children's Magazine Month. What's your favorite magazine? Why?	☐ Daylight Saving Time ends the first Sunday in November. This means that people will turn their clocks back an hour. What will you do during the extra hour you'll have on that day?
☐ Pretend you are a spider spinning a web. Describe the web's shape.	☐ If you had a chance to do something over again in order to get it right, what would you do over? Explain.
☐ Some people believe that wolves howl more during a full moon (they really don't). If you heard a wolf howl, would you feel scared? Explain why or why not.	☐ If someone offered you half of their favorite sandwich but it looked like something you wouldn't like, what would you do?
☐ Fire Prevention Week is in October. What would you do if you caught a young child playing with matches?	☐ Would you like to be the person responsible for making sure votes are counted correctly for the general election? Why or why not?
☐ Apple butter is a thick brown jam made by cooking apples with sugar and spices. Would you eat some of it on toast? Why or why not?	☐ Describe something nice you could do for someone today that would bring a smile to that person's face.
☐ Christopher Columbus sailed across the Atlantic Ocean in 1492 trying to reach India. He did not know when or whether he would ever get there. Would you have been brave enough to sail with him? Explain.	☐ National Geography Awareness Week is in November. Pretend that an alien asks you why humans use maps. What will you say?
☐ If your parent asked you to describe the perfect school lunch, what would you say?	☐ Which would you rather do: work some type of puzzle or play a board game? Why?
☐ Explain how you could help a friend who complains a lot become someone who is more thankful and appreciative.	☐ When you're chatting with someone and there's an awkward moment when neither of you can think of anything to say, what do you usually do? Why?
☐ October 16 is Dictionary Day. Invent three new words you'd like to add to the dictionary. Include their meanings.	☐ Do you prefer eating a home-cooked meal at Thanksgiving or going to a restaurant? Why?
☐ National Knock-Knock Day is October 31. Do you like knock-knock jokes? Why or why not?	☐ If turkeys could reason the way humans do, what would they think about being the most sought-after animal for Thanksgiving?

Note to the teacher: Have each student staple a copy of this page in his writing journal. Or cut copies in half and distribute only one month's prompts at a time to students. When a student uses a prompt, he checks it off in the box.

Writing Prompts

Name

December	January
☐ As soon as you get to school, you realize you left the notecards for a presentation you're giving today on the kitchen table. What will you do?	☐ What is your opinion of New Year's resolutions? Why do you feel this way?
☐ Write a letter to your teacher describing the holiday gift you would give her if money were no object.	☐ What do you most hope to achieve in the coming year? Tell how you plan to reach this goal.
☐ You've just opened a gift that has a receipt attached to it with a date 30 years in the future. Explain what the gift is and what you'll do with it.	☐ Explain how you would feel if you got stuck in time on the best day of your life. What if this happened on the worst day of your life?
☐ A holiday event you'd planned to attend has just been canceled because of the weather. What will you now do instead?	☐ Which would you rather be: a pair of mittens or a pair of gloves? Why?
☐ Santa has lost his list! Help him out by listing at least ten people and two things you think each person would like to receive.	☐ Do you believe that a pet should be treated as if it were human? Give your reasons.
☐ Do you believe good things come in small packages? Why or why not?	☐ Write a thank-you note to someone who did something special for you that didn't cost any money.
☐ A person who just sneezed into his hand now wants to shake hands with you. What will you do?	☐ You are about to microwave a bag of popcorn when you hear a small voice asking you to stop. Write about what happens next and whether you ever pop the popcorn.
☐ It's Christmas Eve and your best friend is not speaking to you. What will you do with the gift you'd planned to deliver to your buddy today?	☐ Pretend you have an unusual hobby. Explain how you'll describe this offbeat pastime to a friend.
☐ Some people prefer to live where winters are harsh. Others enjoy milder climates. Which type of winter do you prefer: harsh or mild? Explain.	☐ You overhear your cousin say he's meeting friends to sled across a frozen pond. Ice and snow have been thawing in your town for several days. What will you do?
☐ Pretend you are a snowflake that has just fallen on a sidewalk. You hear a scraping sound and realize that the sidewalk is being shoveled. Describe your feelings.	☐ Pretend you are a flower bulb trapped beneath winter snow. Write a conversation that might take place between you and the snow.

Note to the teacher: Have each student staple a copy of this page in his writing journal. Or cut copies in half and distribute only one month's prompts at a time to students. When a student uses a prompt, he checks it off in the box.

Writing Prompts

Name

February	March
☐ On February 2 a groundhog predicts the number of winter days left until spring. What other animals could warn us of each changing season? Explain why each animal is the best choice.	☐ The first week in March is Celebrate Your Name Week! In honor of the week, describe what life would be like if everyone had the same name.
☐ "Don't cry over spilt milk" is a proverb meaning "don't worry about mistakes you cannot change." Tell about a time when you followed these words of wisdom.	☐ Your mom is spring-cleaning. She wants to give away your lucky T-shirt. What will you say to convince her not to give it away?
☐ Abraham Lincoln was born on February 12, 1809. He once said, "Whatever you are, be a good one." What do you think he meant?	☐ Alexander Graham Bell, the inventor of the telephone, was born on March 3, 1847. Imagine you can call anyone in the world. Who will you call, and what will you say to him or her?
☐ Tell about a time when you should have kept quiet but didn't.	☐ In the Northern Hemisphere, spring begins in March. List 20 things you would like to do outside once the weather gets warmer.
☐ Valentine's Day is a day to celebrate love. Some people give cards and candy. How do you show someone that you care about him or her?	☐ March is National Umbrella Month. Write a poem thanking the umbrella for all it does for mankind.
☐ Think about all the grouchy people in the world. Make a list of ten activities they can do to turn their frowns upside down.	☐ Pretend you just found in your grandmother's backyard a ring she lost ten years ago. Explain why you think it took so long to find this ring.
☐ Imagine your parents have finally agreed to let you have the pet of your dreams. What kind of pet is it, and how will you take care of it?	☐ March is National Frozen Food Month. How would your life change if you did not have frozen food to reheat at a moment's notice?
☐ February is National Cherry Month. To recognize this tasty fruit's seed-filled center, write a brief story about a day you once had that was the pits.	☐ March 22 is International Goof-Off Day. What would you do if you could just goof off for one whole day?
☐ American Heart Month is celebrated in February. Write an essay about a typical day from the point of view of your heart.	☐ March 26 is Make Up Your Own Holiday Day. What holiday would you create, and how would you celebrate this day?
☐ On February 18, 1930, Pluto was discovered as the ninth planet. In 2006, astronomers reclassified it as a dwarf planet. If you discovered a new planet, what would you call it? Explain.	☐ A famous saying states, "If March comes in like a lion, it will go out like a lamb." Compare and contrast two of your favorite animals.

Note to the teacher: Have each student staple a copy of this page in his writing journal. Or cut copies in half and distribute only one month's prompts at a time to students. When a student uses a prompt, he checks it off in the box.

Writing Prompts

Name

April	May
☐ Imagine that as an April Fools' Day joke, you set all the clocks in your house an hour early. Describe the kind of day your family members would have. Tell how it would affect them at work, school, and home.	☐ May is National Smile Month. What makes you smile? List ten things that make you smile from ear to ear.
☐ It is fun to enjoy the great outdoors during April, but you must be careful. Write a list of tips telling a younger child how to stay injury free this spring.	☐ Imagine staring into the sky at night. What do you think about? Maybe you imagine UFOs, space travel, or aliens? Describe your thoughts.
☐ Which do you prefer: outdoor sports or indoor sports? Explain.	☐ You have been given $100 to buy a Mother's Day gift. Write about your shopping trip to find the perfect present.
☐ Juan Ponce de Leon searched for a spring called the Fountain of Youth. Tell whether you think it is better to be young or old. Explain.	☐ May 15 is Bike to Work Day. Explain how to ride a two-wheel bicycle.
☐ Relax and breathe deeply! April is Stress Awareness Month. Think about what causes stress in your life. Make a list of ten ways to lower your stress level.	☐ May is National Moving Month. Pretend you and your family are moving to another state and that you can only take your clothes and three other items. What three things will you take and why?
☐ Write a letter thanking your school librarian for all he or she does for the students in your school.	☐ Pretend that your family is going on a trip, but this is not a trip you can take in your car. Tell about your plans for travel. Be sure to include where you will go, why you are going, and how you will get there.
☐ April is Mathematics Awareness Month. Write two math word problems about yourself or a friend. Give the problems to another student to solve.	☐ Memorial Day is a day to remember those who died fighting for our country. Think of someone who is a hero to you. Describe a monument that you would build to remember him or her. Tell why he or she is a hero.
☐ April showers bring May flowers, but what else do they bring? Write a short story titled "April Showers Bring…"	☐ Time to plan for summer! Write an advertisement telling travelers why they should plan a trip to your town. List the greatest places to visit and tell them about all the fun they will have if they come.
☐ In April we celebrate Earth Day. Design five bumper stickers that will convince the litterbugs in our world to change their habits.	☐ Write a poem titled "Hooray for May!" In your poem, include at least three words that rhyme with *May.*
☐ Arbor Day is a day in April set aside to honor and plant trees. Imagine you have just won a fabulous tree house. Describe the perfect, shaded getaway in the treetops.	☐ May is a time for picnics, barbecues, and cookouts. Describe your idea of the perfect outdoor event. Think about the menu, the guests, and the games you'd play.

Note to the teacher: Have each student staple a copy of this page in his writing journal. Or cut copies in half and distribute only one month's prompts at a time to students. When a student uses a prompt, he checks it off in the box.

Writing Prompts

Name

June	July
☐ During a summer hike, you discover a never-before-seen insect with strange and unusual habits. Describe the bug's quirky antics.	☐ What is your favorite part about celebrating the Fourth of July: the tastes, the smells, the sounds, or the sights? Explain.
☐ Think of a summer job you would like to have. Explain what you could say during your interview to show that you are the best person for the job.	☐ Describe an outfit that would help you stay extra cool this summer.
☐ Benjamin Franklin once wrote, "Early to bed and early to rise makes a man healthy, wealthy, and wise." Do you agree with Mr. Franklin? Why or why not?	☐ July is National Ice Cream Month. Describe a new ice cream dessert that you just invented. Don't forget to give it a special name.
☐ Describe the most exciting amusement park ride you have ever experienced.	☐ Imagine you will go to another state or country this summer to help others in need. Where will you go? Who will you help? Explain.
☐ Pretend you are spending two weeks at summer camp. Write a letter to your parents begging them to either bring you home now or let you stay an extra week.	☐ On July 20, 1969, Neil Armstrong became the first man to walk on the moon. Describe what it might be like to be as weightless as Neil Armstrong was on the moon.
☐ Rip Van Winkle slept for 20 years before waking up to find his world changed. Imagine you slept through the entire summer *and* the next school year. Describe your first day back at school after waking up.	☐ Compare your favorite insect to your least favorite insect.
☐ Describe a new flag to represent the United States today. Include a symbol that represents what you believe is the most valuable part about living in the United States.	☐ List at least six one-day trips you and your family could take this summer instead of going on a longer vacation.
☐ Which would you rather do: surf in the ocean, ride an all-terrain vehicle in the mountains, or spend $500 at the mall of your choice? Explain.	☐ What are you now allowed to do during the summer that you weren't allowed to do when you were younger?
☐ Imagine you are a television reporter covering a watermelon seed–spitting contest. Describe the exciting details of this fun event.	☐ If you could change one thing about your favorite sport to make it more exciting, what would it be? Explain.
☐ June is Adopt-a-Cat Month. Write a paragraph convincing someone to adopt a cat from your local animal shelter.	☐ Which would you rather do during the summer: stay up as late as you want or receive $5 more in allowance each week? Explain your choice.

Note to the teacher: Have each student staple a copy of this page in his writing journal. Or cut copies in half and distribute only one month's prompts at a time to students. When a student uses a prompt, he checks it off in the box.

Math

Build the largest number.

9, 8 7 6, 5 4 3. 2 1 0

Build a Number
Place value

To prepare for this fun team game, place in a bag 20 cards numbered from 0 to 9 (two cards per number). Divide students into three teams.

To play:

1. Have the first player of each team draw lines on the board for the place values being reviewed. Announce whether the object of the game is to build the largest number or the smallest number.
2. Draw a card and announce the number. Have Player 1 on each team write the number on one of his team's lines.
3. Repeat Step 2 until all the lines are filled. Then have students determine the winning number. Award three points to the winning team, two points to the second-place team, and one point to the third-place team.
4. Continue play until every student has had a turn at the board. The team with the most points at the end of the game wins.

Angel David, South Grant Elementary
Dry Prong, LA

Faster Than Ever
Place value, addition, and subtraction

This activity reinforces place value and helps students find sums and differences quickly. Give each child a copy of page 173 and explain how to navigate the chart as shown. Next, have each student cut out the chart and markers and place a marker on a number, such as 43. To add 18 to 43, the student moves her marker down one row to 53 and then right eight boxes to 61, as shown. To subtract, she reverses the steps, placing the marker on 61, moving up one row to 51, and then moving left eight boxes to 43. For sums over 100, as with 77 + 42, students place one marker on 77 and move it down two rows to 97. They place the second marker on 7, move it down one more row to 17 (total move of four rows), and then move it right two boxes to 19. To find the sum, they add 100 to 19.

Evelyn Harris, Oakland Elementary, Greenwood, SC

Tips for Navigating the Number Chart

Columns = Tens
Rows = Ones
Addition = Down (tens) and right (ones)
Subtraction = Up (tens) and left (ones)

1	2	3	4	5	6	7	8	9	10
11	12	13	14	15	16	17	18	19	20
21	22	23	24	25	26	27	28	29	30
31	32	33	34	35	36	37	38	39	40
41	42	43	44	45	46	47	48	49	50
51	52	53	54	55	56	57	58	59	60
Chart Marker	62	63	64	65	66	67	68	69	70
71	72	73	74	75	76	77	78	79	80
81	82	83	84	85	86	87	88	89	90
91	92	93	94	95	96	97	98	99	100

43 plus 18 is 61.

$$\begin{array}{r} 5 = 40 \\ +2 = +16 \\ 8 \times 7 = 56 \end{array}$$

Break Down the Facts

Multiplication

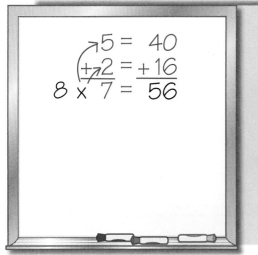

Here's a way to help students who've not yet memorized their multiplication facts. Write a fact in equation form, rewriting the second factor as addends above it, as shown. Then demonstrate how to multiply the first factor by each addend and then add to obtain the answer. Guide students to see that it's to their advantage to pick addends that are easiest to multiply—such as 1, 2, 5, and 10—and that they may want to reverse the factors' order to find a better addend pair to multiply.

Susan Raybuck, Rebecca Creek Elementary, Spring Branch, TX

Roll the Die!

Adding and subtracting multidigit numbers

Begin this fun review by giving each pair of students a calculator, a die, and two copies of a recording sheet from page 174 (for whole-number or decimal practice). Have players follow these steps. For more practice, see page 170.

1. In turn, roll the die. Write the number in any box of problem A on your recording sheet. Aim to form a problem with a larger sum than your partner's.
2. Repeat Step 1 until all boxes in problem A are filled. Then solve the problem. Have your partner use the calculator to check your work. If your sum is larger than your partner's sum, circle the problem on your recording sheet.
3. Repeat Steps 1 and 2 for problem B. This time, try to form a problem with a smaller difference than your partner's.
4. Continue with problems C and D. The winner is the player with more circled problems.

Vickie Robertson, Meadow Green Elementary, Whittier, CA

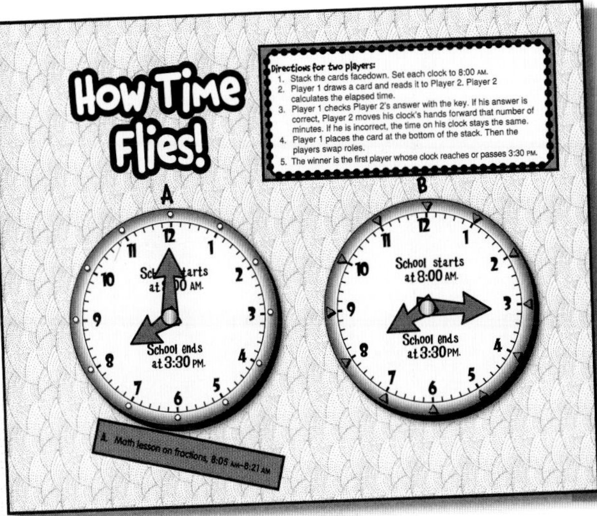

How Time Flies!

Elapsed time

To prepare the game on pages 175 and 176, copy on construction paper the cards, clock hands, and answer key on page 175 and the mat on page 176. If desired, laminate page 175 before cutting out the pieces. Use a brad to attach clock hands to each clock on the mat. Then have students follow the directions on the mat.

Jennifer Otter, Oak Ridge, NC

What's Missing?

Write the missing numbers.

1\.

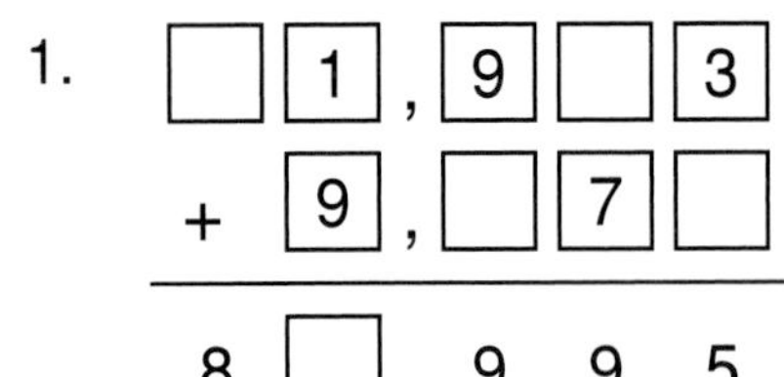

2\.

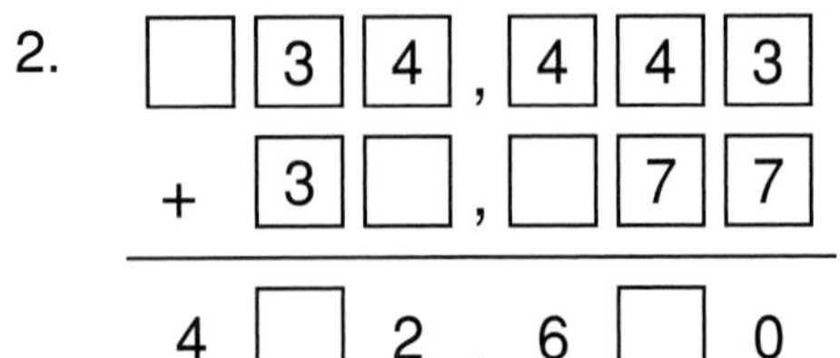

3\.

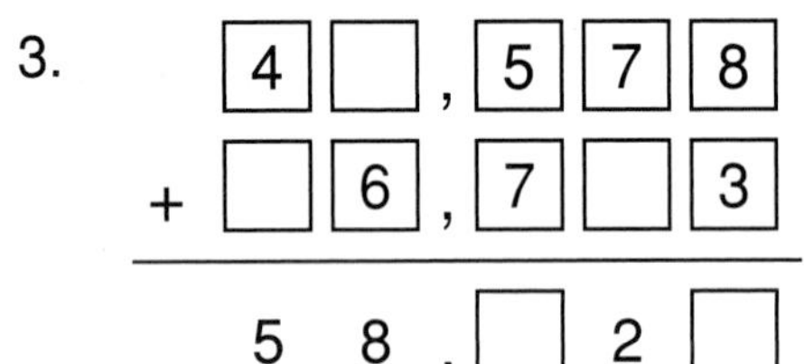

4\.

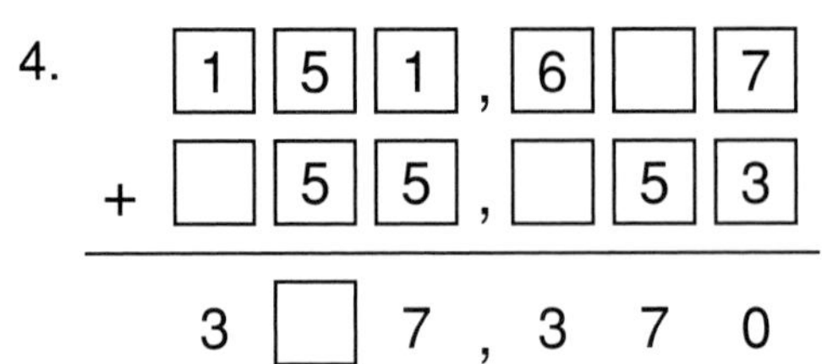

5\.

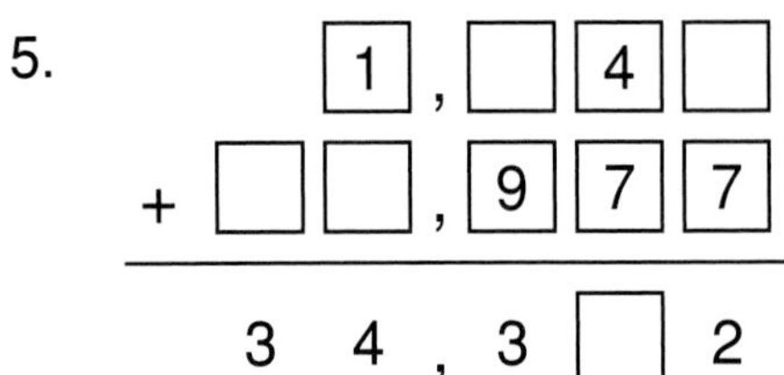

6\.

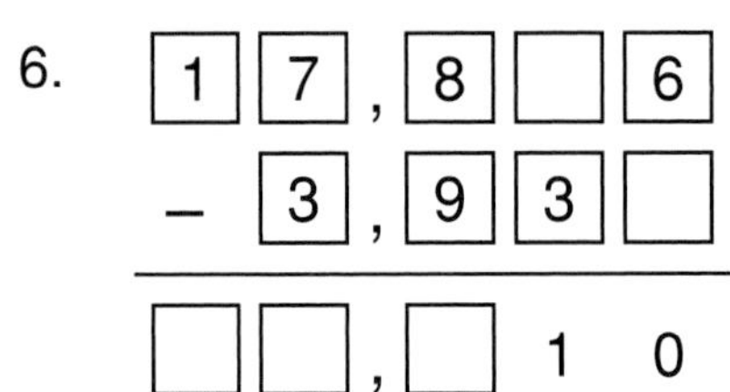

7\.

```
  7 3 □ , 7 5 3
−     2 , □ 2 4
---------------
  □ □ 7 , 7 □ □
```

8\.

```
  □ □ 8 , 6 □ 8
−   3 □ , □ 7 □
---------------
  4 7 6 , 3 3 5
```

9\.

```
  3 0 0 , 0 □ □
−   4 4 , □ 4 5
---------------
  2 □ 5 , 6 5 5
```

10\.

```
  8 0 0 , □ 4 □
− □ 1 8 , 4 8 4
---------------
  4 8 2 , 2 5 9
```

Name ____________________

Canine Conversions

Complete the chart.

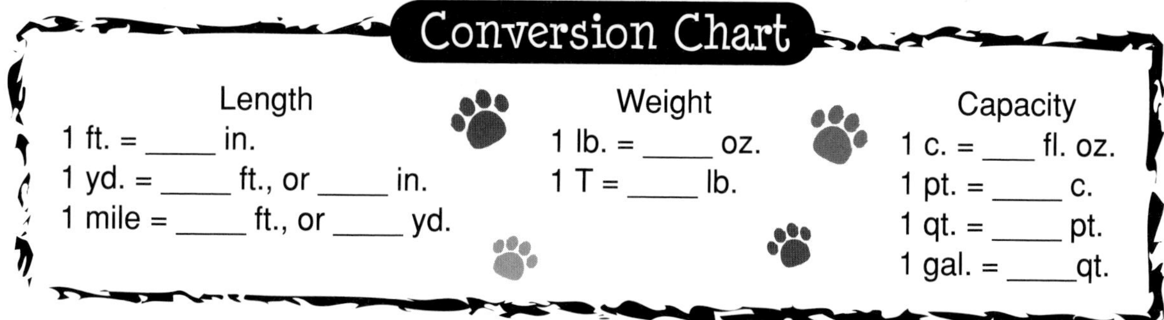

Conversion Chart
Length
1 ft. = _____ in.
1 yd. = _____ ft., or _____ in.
1 mile = _____ ft., or _____ yd.
Weight
1 lb. = _____ oz.
1 T = _____ lb.
Capacity
1 c. = _____ fl. oz.
1 pt. = _____ c.
1 qt. = _____ pt.
1 gal. = _____qt.

Use the chart above and the clues below to match each dog to its correct water bowl, leash, and weight. Draw a pawprint in each box that is true. Make an X in each box that is false.

1. Waldo's leash is 60 inches long.
2. Linus's leash is not a foot shorter than Waldo's.
3. Waldo weighs two more pounds than Baxter and two pounds less than Linus.
4. Amos's weight is a multiple of 10.
5. Waldo's dish has the largest capacity.
6. Linus's dish holds more than Baxter's but less than Amos's.
7. Amos's dish holds 5 pints.
8. The dog with the smallest capacity water dish has the longest leash.

		Waldo	Amos	Baxter	Linus
Leash Length	2 yd.				
	5 ft.				
	48 in.				
	$3\frac{1}{2}$ ft.				
Dogs' Weights	160 oz.				
	$\frac{1}{20}$ T				
	8 lb.				
	192 oz.				
Water Bowl Capacity	3 qt.				
	$\frac{1}{2}$ gal.				
	3 pt.				
	10 c.				

9. What is the combined length of all the dogs' leashes in feet? __________

10. What is the combined weight of all the dogs in ounces? __________

11. What is the combined capacity of all the dogs' water dishes in cups? __________

Name ____________________

Special Delivery

A Game for Two Players

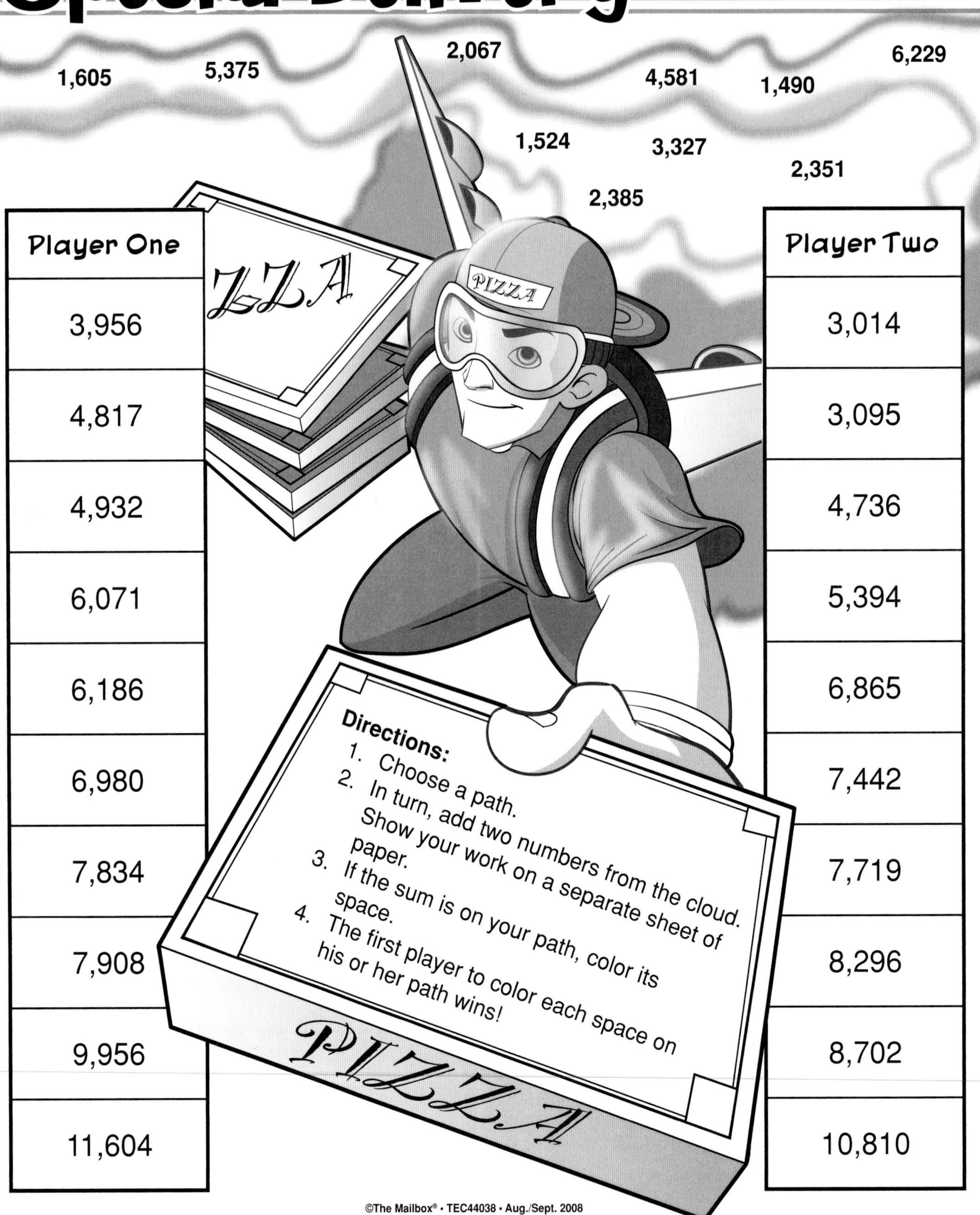

1,605 5,375 2,067 4,581 1,490 6,229 1,524 3,327 2,351 2,385

Player One
3,956
4,817
4,932
6,071
6,186
6,980
7,834
7,908
9,956
11,604

Player Two
3,014
3,095
4,736
5,394
6,865
7,442
7,719
8,296
8,702
10,810

Directions:

1. Choose a path.
2. In turn, add two numbers from the cloud. Show your work on a separate sheet of paper.
3. If the sum is on your path, color its space.
4. The first player to color each space on his or her path wins!

Note to the teacher: Each student pair needs a copy of the page. Each player needs a crayon or colored pencil and a sheet of paper on which to show his work.

Hundred Chart and Markers

Use with "Faster Than Ever" on page 168.

1	2	3	4	5	6	7	8	9	10
11	12	13	14	15	16	17	18	19	20
21	22	23	24	25	26	27	28	29	30
31	32	33	34	35	36	37	38	39	40
41	42	43	44	45	46	47	48	49	50
51	52	53	54	55	56	57	58	59	60
61	62	63	64	65	66	67	68	69	70
71	72	73	74	75	76	77	78	79	80
81	82	83	84	85	86	87	88	89	90
91	92	93	94	95	96	97	98	99	100

TEC44038

Name ______________________

Roll the Die!

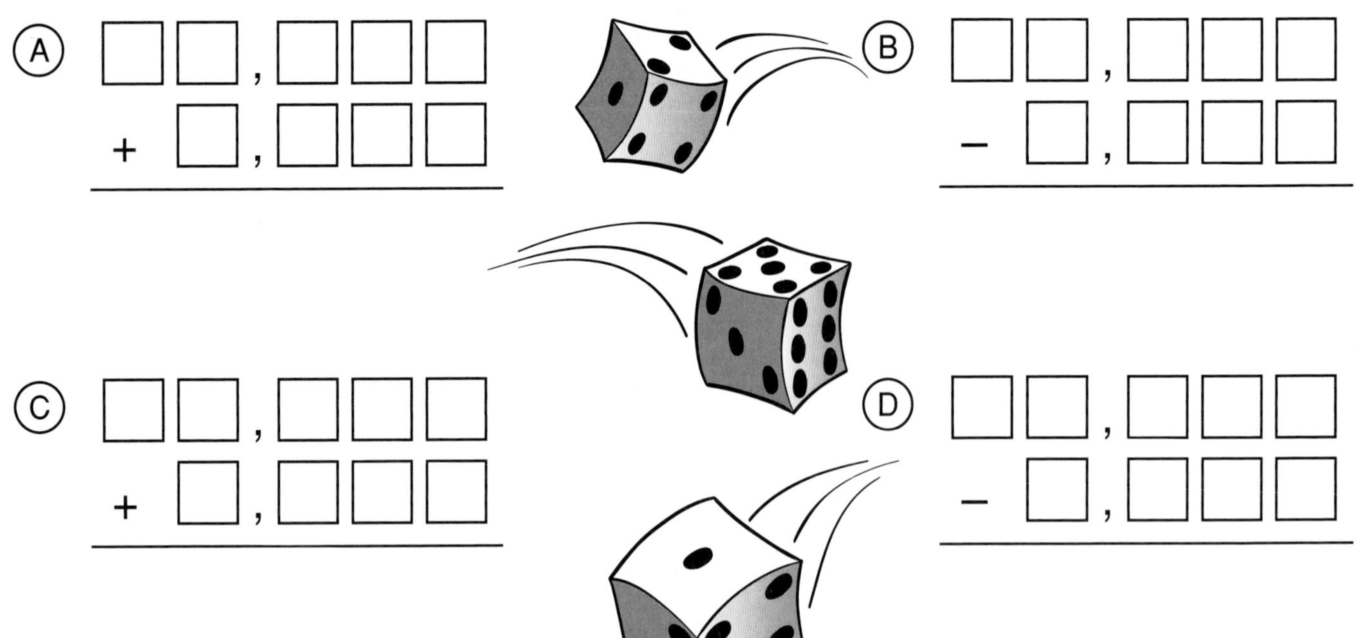

Name ______________________

Roll the Die!

 Note to the teacher: Use with "Roll the Die!" on page 169.

Use with "How Time Flies!" on page 169.

A. Math lesson on fractions, 8:05 AM–8:21 AM TEC44038	**L.** Recess, 11:49 AM–12:07 PM TEC44038
B. Math test, 8:21 AM–8:57 AM TEC44038	**M.** Silent reading, 12:07 PM–12:26 PM TEC44038
C. Math center, 8:57 AM–9:20 AM TEC44038	**N.** Read-aloud, 12:26 PM–12:45 PM TEC44038
D. Math game, 9:20 AM–9:30 AM TEC44038	**O.** Play practice, 12:45 PM–1:12 PM TEC44038
E. School assembly, 9:30 AM–10:05 AM TEC44038	**P.** Journal writing, 1:12 PM–1:32 PM TEC44038
F. Spelling practice, 10:05 AM–10:17 AM TEC44038	**Q.** Class speaker, 1:32 PM–1:46 PM TEC44038
G. Grammar lesson, 10:17 AM–10:30 AM TEC44038	**R.** P.E., 1:46 PM–2:15 PM TEC44038
H. Group project, 10:30 AM–10:52 AM TEC44038	**S.** Research in library, 2:15 PM–2:32 PM TEC44038
I. Check language arts homework, 10:52 AM–11:00 AM TEC44038	**T.** Science vocabulary, 2:32 PM–2:45 PM TEC44038
J. Library, 11:00 AM–11:15 AM TEC44038	**U.** Science experiment, 2:45 PM–2:58 PM TEC44038
K. Lunch, 11:15 AM–11:49 AM TEC44038	**V.** Science project, 2:58 PM–3:12PM TEC44038
	W. End-of-day sharing, 3:12 PM–3:30 PM TEC44038

Answer Key

A. 16 min.	I. 8 min.	Q. 14 min.
B. 36 min.	J. 15 min.	R. 29 min.
C. 23 min.	K. 34 min.	S. 17 min.
D. 10 min.	L. 18 min.	T. 13 min.
E. 35 min.	M. 19 min.	U. 13 min.
F. 12 min.	N. 19 min.	V. 14 min.
G. 13 min.	O. 27 min.	W. 18 min.
H. 22 min.	P. 20 min.	

TEC44038

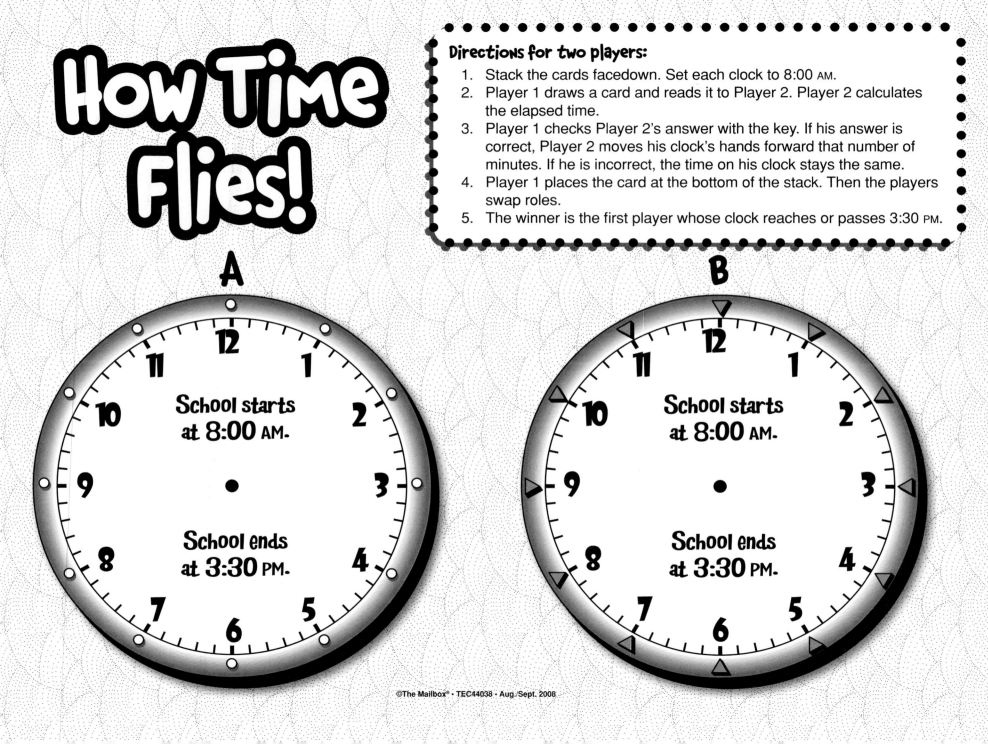

How Time Flies!

Directions for two players:

1. Stack the cards facedown. Set each clock to 8:00 AM.
2. Player 1 draws a card and reads it to Player 2. Player 2 calculates the elapsed time.
3. Player 1 checks Player 2's answer with the key. If his answer is correct, Player 2 moves his clock's hands forward that number of minutes. If he is incorrect, the time on his clock stays the same.
4. Player 1 places the card at the bottom of the stack. Then the players swap roles.
5. The winner is the first player whose clock reaches or passes 3:30 PM.

A

School starts at 8:00 AM.

School ends at 3:30 PM.

B

School starts
at 8:00 AM.
School ends
at 3:30 PM.

MATH TIPS + TOOLS

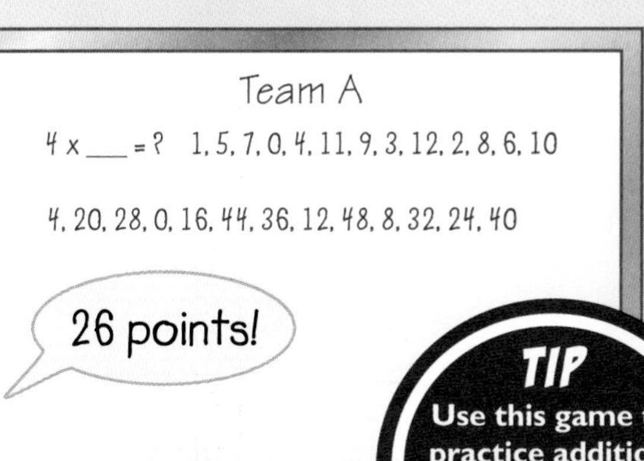

Team A
4 x ___ = ?   1, 5, 7, 0, 4, 11, 9, 3, 12, 2, 8, 6, 10
4, 20, 28, 0, 16, 44, 36, 12, 48, 8, 32, 24, 40
26 points!

TIP
Use this game to practice addition, subtraction, and division facts too!

Math Football
Multiplication facts

For this fun two-team game, divide a board into two sections. During the game, spectators awaiting a turn at the board participate by recording the products on paper so they can referee (check the answers) after each play!

To play:

1. Player 1 from each team goes to his assigned board section and lists the numbers 0 through 12 as you call them out in random order.
2. Beside the list, each player writes the play that you (the quarterback) announce: a number between 1 and 12 followed by the symbols shown. The two players then turn away from the board.
3. When you yell "Hike," the players face the board again and multiply the announced number by each listed number.
4. The first player to record all the products and turn around again earns two points for each correct answer. The other player earns one point per correct answer.
5. Continue until every student has had a turn at the board. The team with more points wins.

Libby Sluder, Taylor Hicks School, Prescott, AZ

What's My Rule?
Patterns, relations, and functions

To strengthen students' algebra skills, display a laminated table as shown (minus the numbers and labels) and a laminated hundred chart. Each week, post a question above the display. Then use a wipeoff marker to add appropriate headers to the table and a list of numbers in its left column. Have each child record the question, headers, and numbers on a copy of a recording sheet from page 179 and then complete the table's right column. After a few minutes, ask one child at a time to record one of his answers on the laminated table. Once the right column is filled in, verify the answers and circle them on the hundred chart. Have students do the same on their papers. Ask students to identify the pattern the numbers represent and state it as a rule. Then add the rule to the display while each child writes it on his paper.

Deborah Bettes, Alta Mesa Elementary, Redding, CA

How many legs are on eight spiders?

Number of Spiders	Number of Legs
1	8
2	16
3	24
4	32
5	40
6	48
7	56
8	64
9	72
10	80

1	2	3	4	5	6	7	8	9	10
11	12	13	14	15	16	17	18	19	20
21	22	23	24	25	26	27	28	29	30
31	32	33	34	35	36	37	38	39	40
41	42	43	44	45	46	47	48	49	50
51	52	53	54	55	56	57	58	59	60
61	62	63	64	65	66	67	68	69	70
71	72	73	74	75	76	77	78	79	80
81	82	83	84	85	86	87	88	89	90
91	92	93	94	95	96	97	98	99	100

Rule: Add 8.

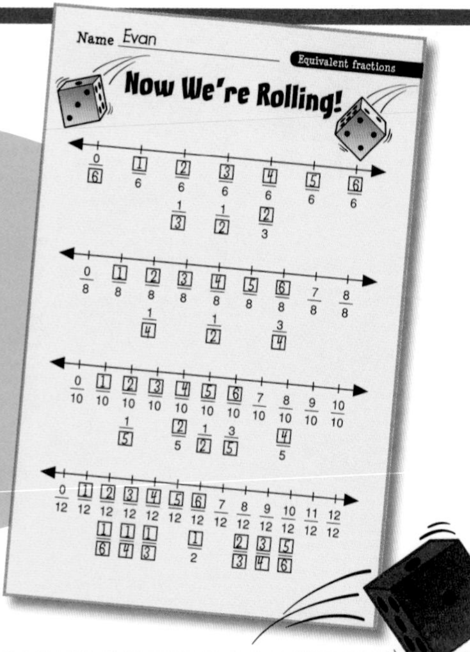

Now We're Rolling!

Equivalent fractions

Give each pair of students a copy of the game mats from page 180 and a die. Have each partner, in turn, roll the die and record the number rolled as the numerator or denominator of as many fractions on his number lines as he can. If the number rolled is one he does not need, he records nothing and his turn is over. The first student to label all his number lines correctly wins.

Vickie Robertson, Meadow Green Elementary, Whittier, CA

The Lineup

Ordering numbers

Have each student label an index card with a whole number, mixed decimal, or fraction. Choose six students to stand in line with their cards so the numbers are ordered from least to greatest. Next, ask one student at a time to join the line, positioning herself correctly, until all students are lined up. Then challenge students to rearrange themselves so their numbers are ordered from greatest to least. Finally, have small groups of students order their cards from least to greatest. To check, have the groups line up one at a time. Then have the class signal thumbs-up or thumbs-down to show whether the lineup is correct. For more practice, see page 181.

Vickie Robertson

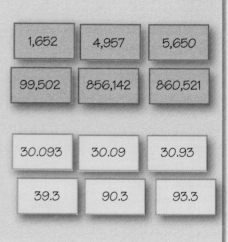

1,652 | 4,957 | 5,650
99,502 | 856,142 | 860,521

30.093 | 30.09 | 30.93
39.3 | 90.3 | 93.3

Shuffleboard Math

Computation

Use this whole-class activity with whole numbers, decimals, or fractions. Write a series of problems—from easiest to most challenging—across the board, ending about 12 inches from its right edge. Then select a student to slide the eraser from right to left down the tray. Everyone solves the problem above the stopped eraser. After checking students' work, replace the problem with a new one of equal or greater difficulty, and select a different child to slide the eraser! See page 182 for more practice.

Vickie Robertson

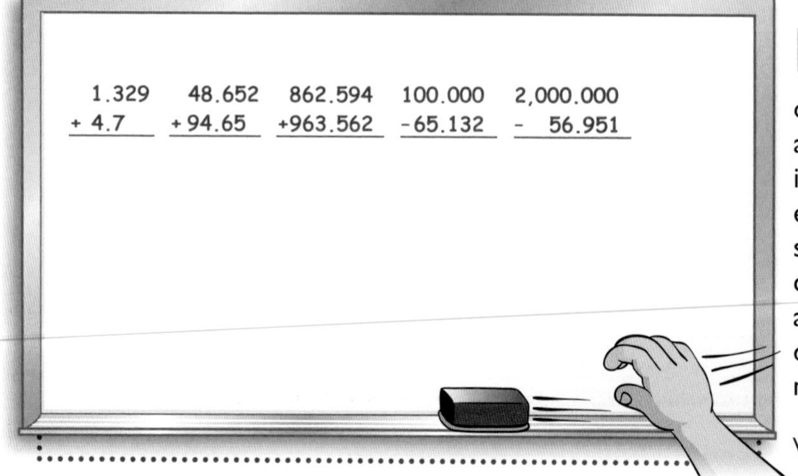

Name ________________ **Recording sheet**

What's the Rule?

Question: ______________________________

Rule: ______________________________

1	2	3	4	5	6	7	8	9	10
11	12	13	14	15	16	17	18	19	20
21	22	23	24	25	26	27	28	29	30
31	32	33	34	35	36	37	38	39	40
41	42	43	44	45	46	47	48	49	50
51	52	53	54	55	56	57	58	59	60
61	62	63	64	65	66	67	68	69	70
71	72	73	74	75	76	77	78	79	80
81	82	83	84	85	86	87	88	89	90
91	92	93	94	95	96	97	98	99	100

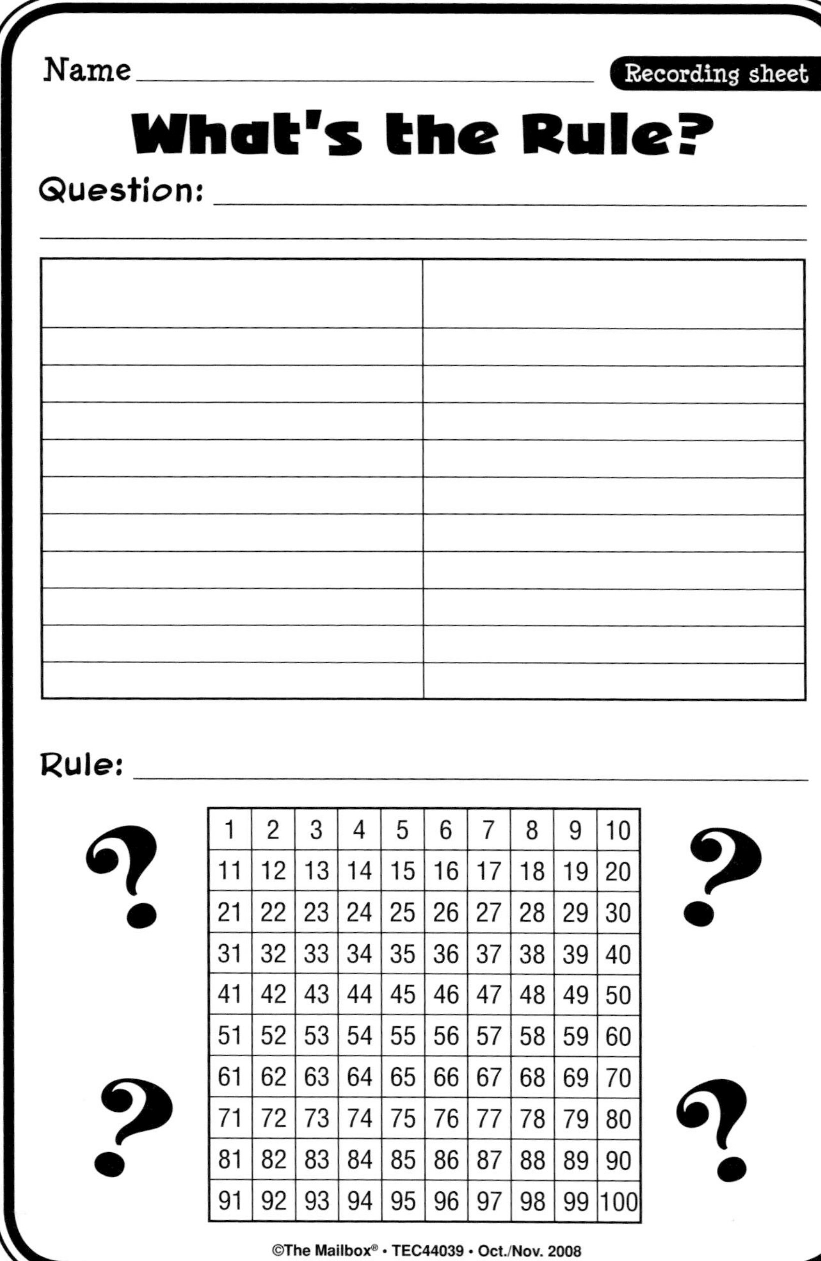

Name ________________ Recording sheet

What's the Rule?

Question: ______________________________

Rule: ______________________________

1	2	3	4	5	6	7	8	9	10
11	12	13	14	15	16	17	18	19	20
21	22	23	24	25	26	27	28	29	30
31	32	33	34	35	36	37	38	39	40
41	42	43	44	45	46	47	48	49	50
51	52	53	54	55	56	57	58	59	60
61	62	63	64	65	66	67	68	69	70
71	72	73	74	75	76	77	78	79	80
81	82	83	84	85	86	87	88	89	90
91	92	93	94	95	96	97	98	99	100

©The Mailbox® • TEC44039 • Oct./Nov. 2008

Note to the teacher: Use with "What's My Rule?" on page 177.

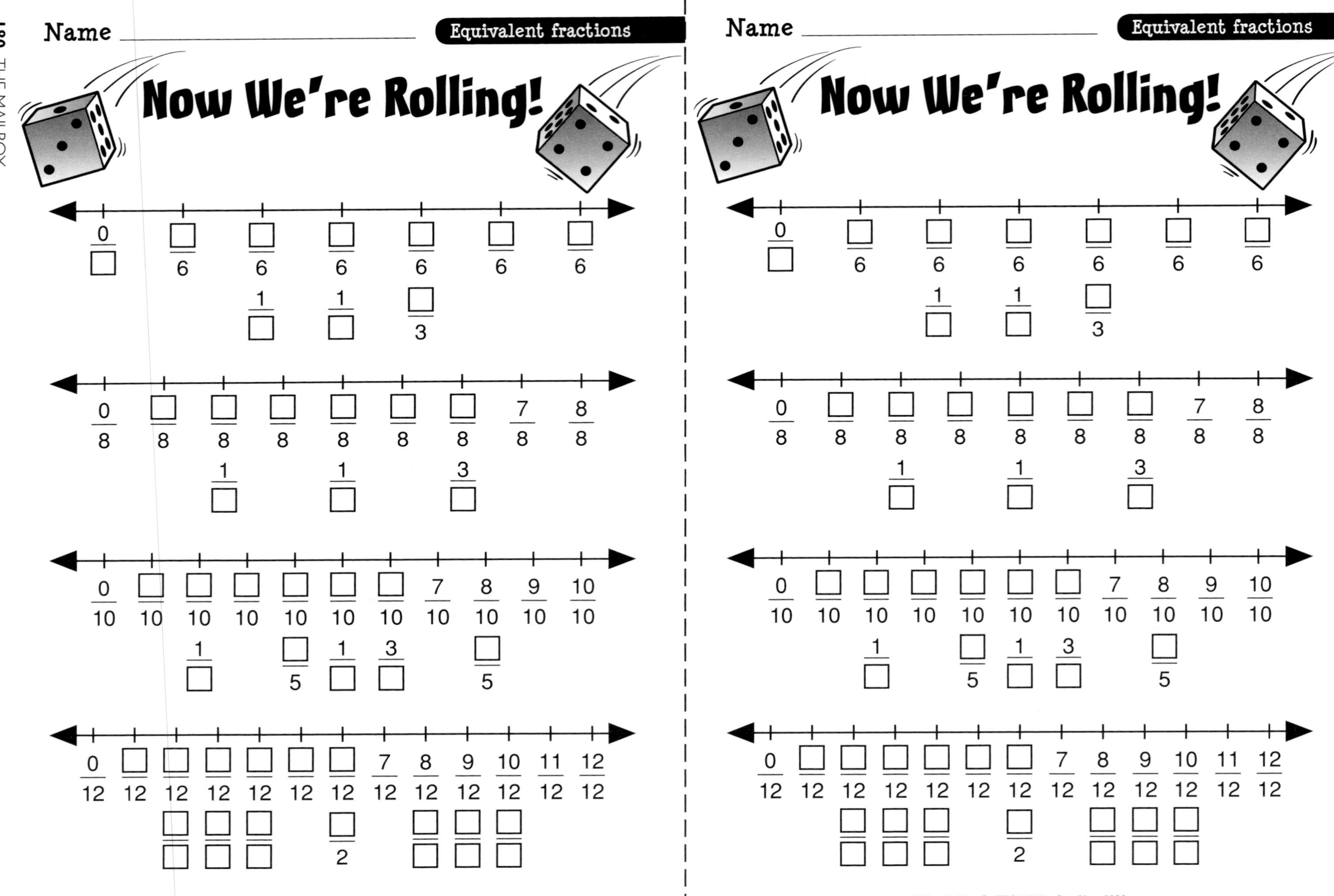

Note to the teacher: Use with "Now We're Rolling!" on page 178.

Name ____________________

Order in the Court!

Write each set of numbers in order from least to greatest.

1. 562,142; 56,421; 504,142; 54,642

   ____ G ____ K ____ H ____ J

2. 999,998; 99,989; 98,988; 98,998

   ____ V ____ E ____ S ____ Q

3. 504,142; 241,504; 241,540; 524,041

   ____ N ____ E ____ Y ____ D

4. 876,542; 76,452; 867,542; 854,762

   ____ T ____ N ____ G ____ E

5. 210,602; 602,012; 201,206; 206,210

   ____ C ____ U ____ T ____ B

6. 387,652; 38,652; 36,652; 378,652

   ____ P ____ O ____ E ____ V

7. 499,998; 499,989; 498,998; 498,889

   ____ N ____ B ____ T ____ N

8. 667,654; 665,445; 676,777; 56,677

   ____ R ____ A ____ G ____ C

9. 700,001; 70,001; 71,001; 710,001

   ____ D ____ E ____ S ____ K

10. 188,881; 181,818; 188,188; 181,188

    ____ T ____ Y ____ F ____ S

When is an English teacher like a judge?

To answer the question, write each letter from above on its matching numbered line below.

When she hands out lon____ (54,642) ____ (99,989) ____ (241,540) ____ (854,762) ____ (210,602) ____ (378,652) ____ (498,889) ____ (676,777) ____ (71,001) ____ (188,881)!

Note to the teacher: Use with "The Lineup" on page 178.

Name ____________________ **Decimals**

Shuffle Right Along!

Start at the bottom.

For each board, add or subtract, using the number at Start and the bottom number in the left column. Write the answer in the bottom box at the right.

Next, use the first and second numbers in the left column to add or subtract and then the second and third numbers, recording your answers and continuing until you reach the top.

+ 0.78	
+ 16.307	
+ 504.186	
+ 6.7	
+ 789.07	
+ 2.9	
+ 78.05	
+ 31.09	
+ 658.2	666.11
+ 7.91	92.08
84.17 **Start**	

– 0.04	
– 0.05	
– 0.07	
– 78.2	
– 89	
– 189.09	
– 356.23	
– 1,687.05	
– 2,210.75	
– 3,027.208	1,979.266
5,006.474 **Start**	

 Note to the teacher: Use with “Shuffleboard Math” on page 178.

MATH TIPS + TOOLS

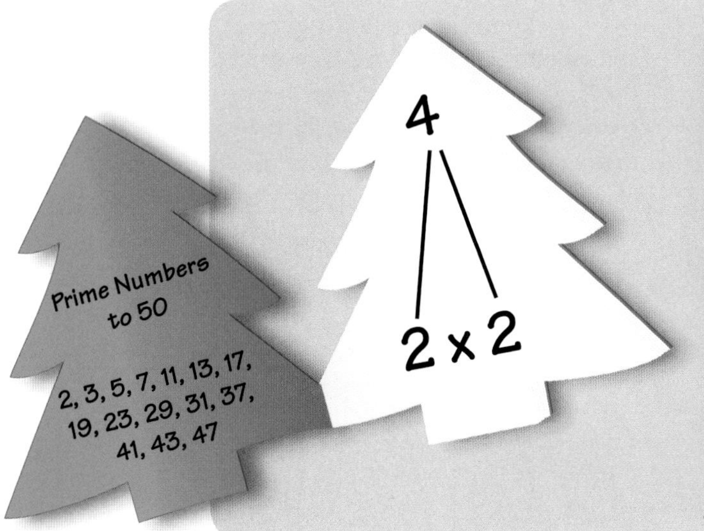

A Factor Forest

Prime factors to 50

Give each student a copy of page 190 and have her follow the directions to make a tree-shaped booklet. Afterward, discuss with students the difference between prime and composite numbers. Point out that 0 and 1 are neither prime nor composite. Next, have students determine the prime numbers to 50 and list them on the booklet's inside front cover. Then have each child draw factor trees on the booklet's pages and on each side of the back cover to show the prime factors of the 34 composite numbers to 50.

Jennifer Otter, Oak Ridge, NC

Search for Sides!

Parallel and perpendicular sides

Review with students that a polygon with one set of perpendicular sides has one right angle, a polygon with two sets of perpendicular sides has two right angles, and so on. Next, have each pair of students label two sheets of construction paper as shown. Also give each duo two copies of page 191. Instruct the partners to cut apart one set of cards and sort them by section on the perpendicular-sides sheet. Before gluing the cards in place, have students check the cards' placement, as needed, by tracing the figures' perpendicular sides with colored pencils. Partners then use the second copy of page 191 to complete the parallel-sides sheet.

Jennifer Otter

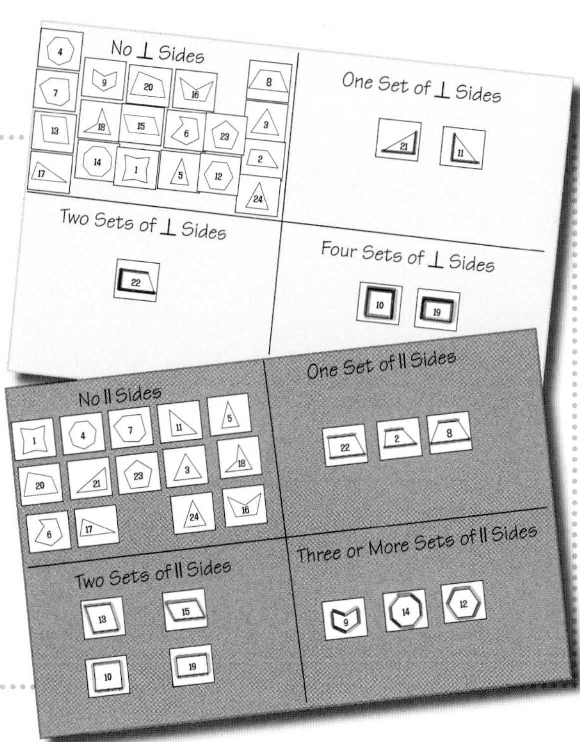

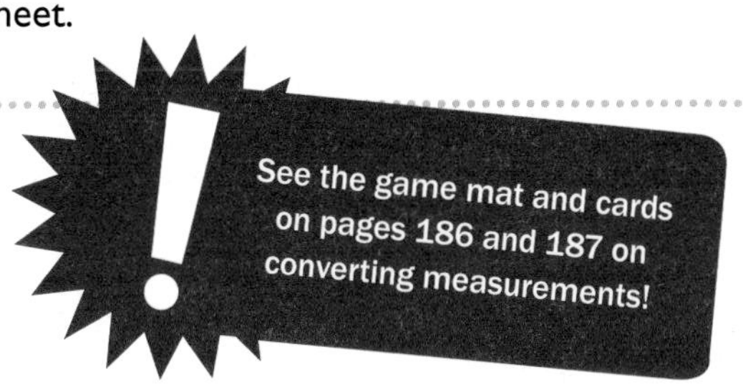
See the game mat and cards on pages 186 and 187 on converting measurements!

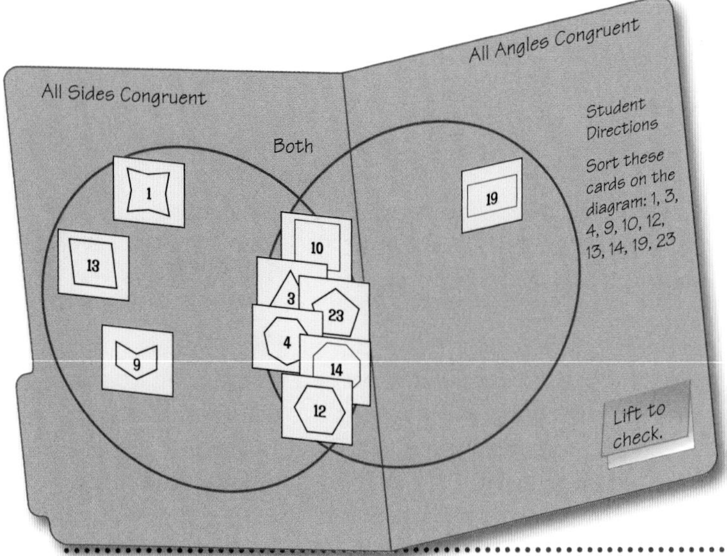

Sort These, Please!

Polygon attributes

Make this self-checking center by drawing a Venn diagram inside an open file folder and labeling it as shown. Copy and cut out the cards on page 191. Cut a flap in the lower right corner of the folder and write the solution to the sorting task on the back of the flap. Then place the specified cards inside the folder. After the student sorts the cards, she lifts the flap to check her answers.

Jennifer Otter, Oak Ridge, NC

Partners vs. Partners

Simplifying fractions

To prepare for this game, each group of four students labels each of 20 index cards with a different number from the box. The foursome then shuffles its cards and stacks them facedown. Next, the group divides into two pairs of partners. Each player draws a card, combines it with his partner's card to make a proper fraction, and writes the fraction in simplest form. The duos check each other's work and award a point for each correct fraction. Then they return the cards to the pile to be reshuffled. Play continues until one team earns ten points.

Jennifer Otter

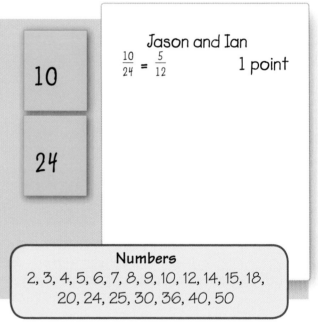

10

24

Jason and Ian

$\frac{10}{24} = \frac{5}{12}$ 1 point

Numbers

2, 3, 4, 5, 6, 7, 8, 9, 10, 12, 14, 15, 18, 20, 24, 25, 30, 36, 40, 50

Of the people in the photo,
• 1/6 of the group is wearing glasses
• 3/6, or 1/2, is wearing a cap
• 6/6, or the whole group, is smiling and has brown hair
• 1/6 has freckles
• 2/6, or 1/3, is wearing something green
• 1/6 is pointing at something
Evan

Fraction Folks

Parts of a group

Have each student cut out a magazine picture of a group that includes at least four people. Instruct the student to tape the picture to construction paper and then add descriptors that use fractions, similar to the ones shown. Allow time for students to share their work with the class.

Leigh Anne Newsom, Cedar Road Elementary, Chesapeake, VA

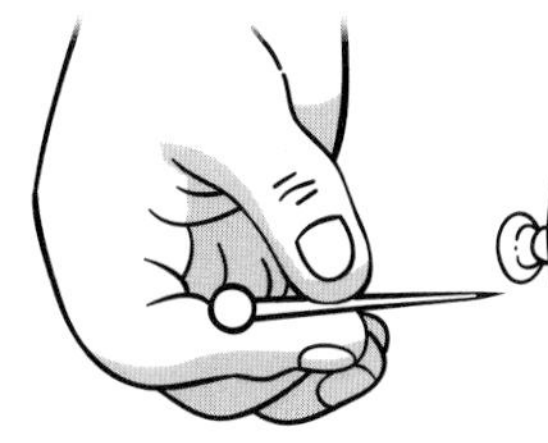

Balloon Buster

A Game for Two Players

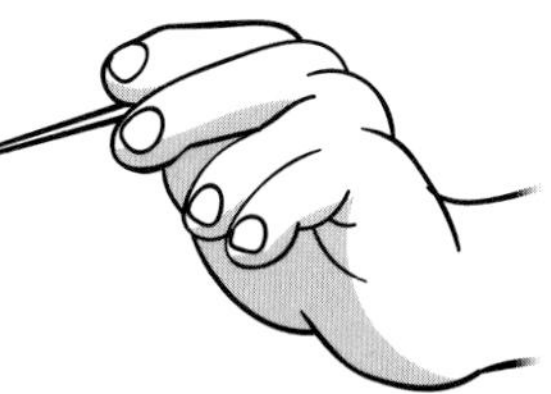

Directions:

1. Write the measurements from below in random order on the balloons.
2. Choose a crayon or colored pencil that's a different color from your opponent's.
3. In turn, select a clue and find the balloon with the matching measurement. Your opponent checks your answer with the key. If you are correct, color the balloon. Then ✓ the box. If you are incorrect, your turn is over.
4. The first player to color four balloons (horizontally, vertically, or diagonally) or who has more colored balloons when all the clues have been used wins.

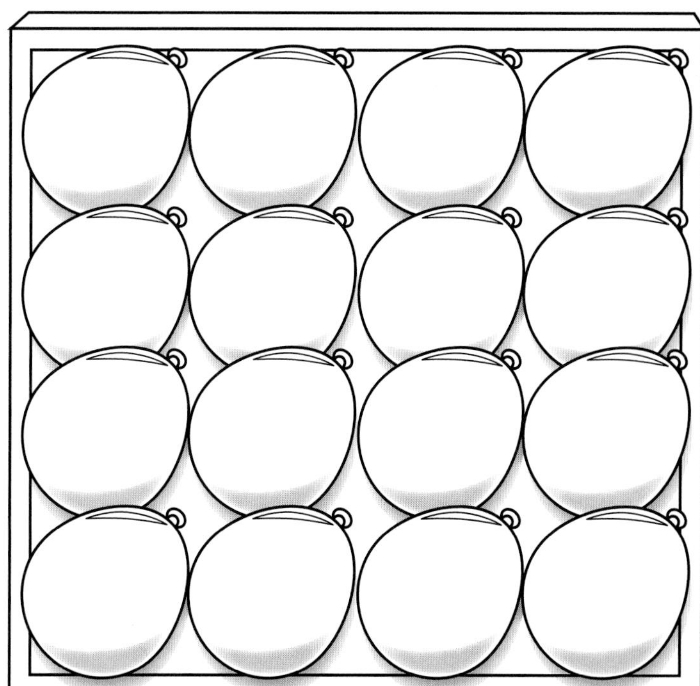

Measurements to Use

22°	91°	89°	80°
105°	170°	45°	180°
96°	2°	14°	1°
179°	90°	99°	21°

Clues

- ☐ acute angle divisible by 11
- ☐ even and prime acute angle
- ☐ right angle
- ☐ acute angle divisible by 3 and 7
- ☐ half the measure of a right angle
- ☐ largest whole-number acute angle
- ☐ 10° less than a straight angle
- ☐ 15° more than a right angle
- ☐ twice the measure of a right angle
- ☐ smallest whole-number acute angle
- ☐ obtuse angle divisible by 11
- ☐ smallest whole-number obtuse angle
- ☐ 5° more than the smallest obtuse angle
- ☐ acute angle that is a multiple of 7 but not of 3
- ☐ 10° less than a right angle
- ☐ largest whole-number obtuse angle

Note to the teacher: Each student pair needs one copy of the page and one copy of the key on page 311. Each player needs a crayon or colored pencil (two different colors).

Game Cards and Answer Key

Use with "Tip the Scales!" on page 187. Mount on construction paper a copy of the game mat on page 187 and a copy of the cards and answer key below. If desired, laminate the pages before cutting the cards apart.

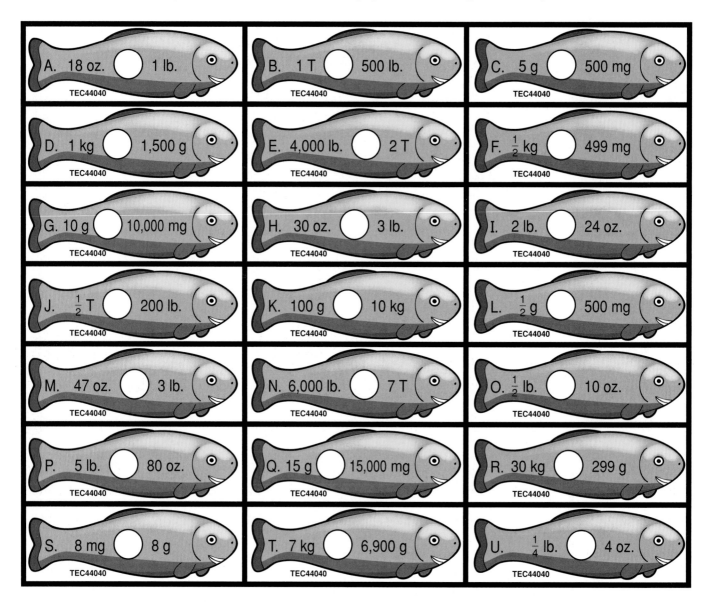

A. 18 oz. ◯ 1 lb. TEC44040	B. 1 T ◯ 500 lb. TEC44040	C. 5 g ◯ 500 mg TEC44040
D. 1 kg ◯ 1,500 g TEC44040	E. 4,000 lb. ◯ 2 T TEC44040	F. $\frac{1}{2}$ kg ◯ 499 mg TEC44040
G. 10 g ◯ 10,000 mg TEC44040	H. 30 oz. ◯ 3 lb. TEC44040	I. 2 lb. ◯ 24 oz. TEC44040
J. $\frac{1}{2}$ T ◯ 200 lb. TEC44040	K. 100 g ◯ 10 kg TEC44040	L. $\frac{1}{2}$ g ◯ 500 mg TEC44040
M. 47 oz. ◯ 3 lb. TEC44040	N. 6,000 lb. ◯ 7 T TEC44040	O. $\frac{1}{2}$ lb. ◯ 10 oz. TEC44040
P. 5 lb. ◯ 80 oz. TEC44040	Q. 15 g ◯ 15,000 mg TEC44040	R. 30 kg ◯ 299 g TEC44040
S. 8 mg ◯ 8 g TEC44040	T. 7 kg ◯ 6,900 g TEC44040	U. $\frac{1}{4}$ lb. ◯ 4 oz. TEC44040

Answer Key

A. 18 oz. > 1 lb.
B. 1 T > 500 lb.
C. 5 g > 500 mg
D. 1 kg < 1,500 g
E. 4,000 lb. = 2 T
F. $\frac{1}{2}$ kg > 499 mg
G. 10 g = 10,000 mg

H. 30 oz. < 3 lb.
I. 2 lb. > 24 oz.
J. $\frac{1}{2}$ T > 200 lb.
K. 100 g < 10 kg
L. $\frac{1}{2}$ g = 500 mg
M. 47 oz. < 3 lb.
N. 6,000 lb. < 7 T

O. $\frac{1}{2}$ lb. < 10 oz.
P. 5 lb. = 80 oz.
Q. 15 g = 15,000 mg
R. 30 kg > 299 g
S. 8 mg < 8 g
T. 7 kg > 6,900 g
U. $\frac{1}{4}$ lb. = 4 oz.

TEC44040

Tip the Scales!

Directions for two players:

1. Stack the cards facedown.
2. Player 1 draws a card and tells Player 2 whether the first measurement is greater than, less than, or equal to the second.
3. Player 2 checks the key. If the answer is correct, Player 1 places the card on his side of the scale. If he is incorrect, he places the card at the bottom of the stack. Then the players swap roles.
4. The winner is the player with more cards when all cards have been won.

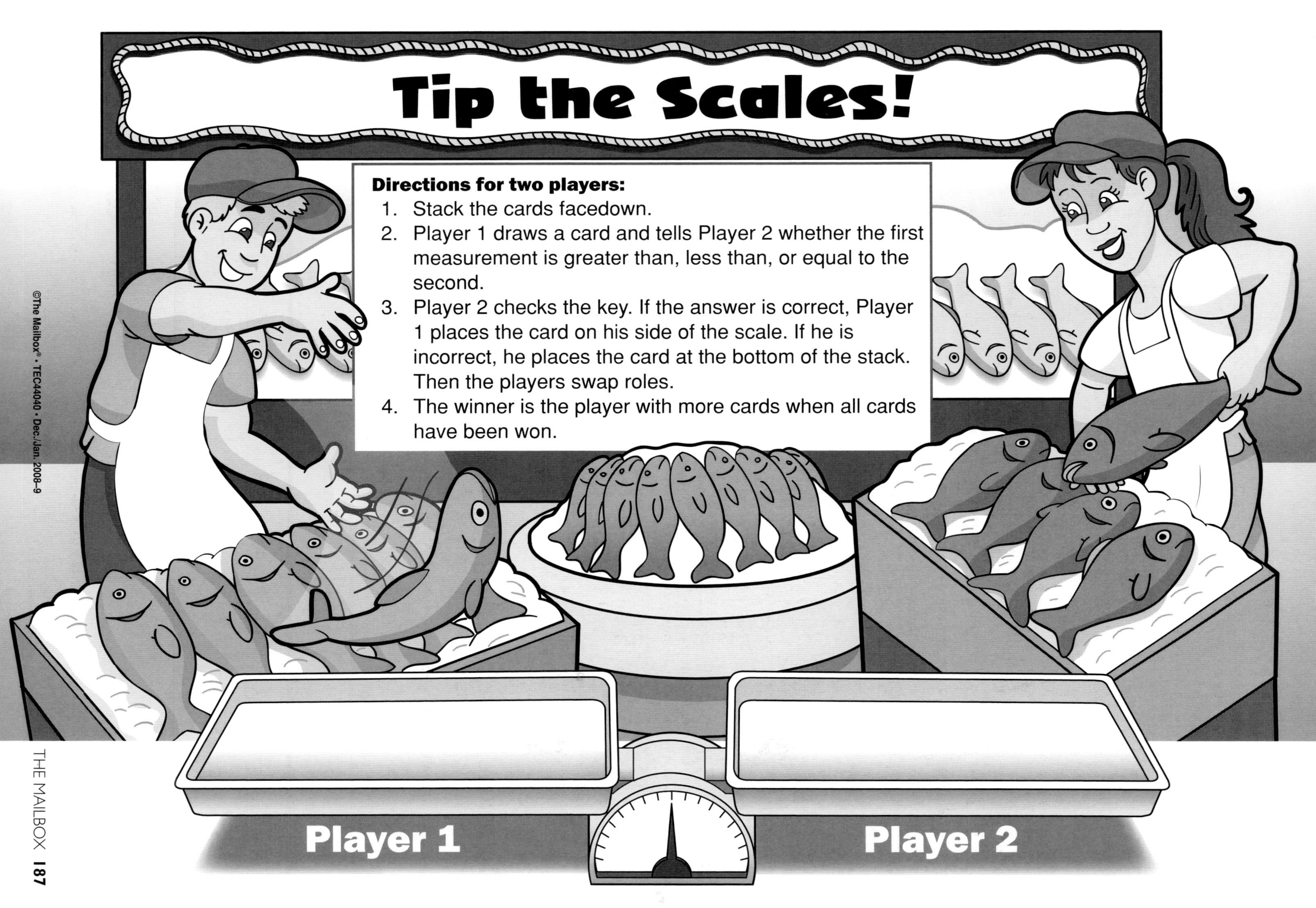

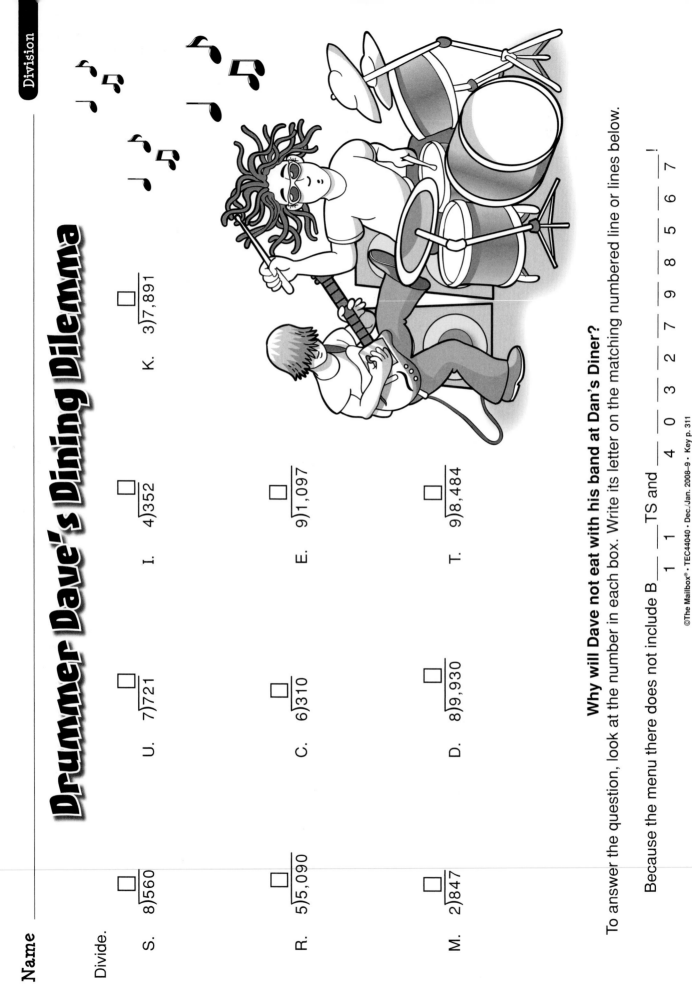

Name ______________________________

Drummer Dave's Dining Dilemma

Divide.

S. $8\overline{)560}$	U. $7\overline{)721}$	I. $4\overline{)352}$	K. $3\overline{)7,891}$
R. $5\overline{)5,090}$	C. $6\overline{)310}$	E. $9\overline{)1,097}$	
M. $2\overline{)847}$	D. $8\overline{)9,930}$	T. $9\overline{)8,484}$	

Why will Dave not eat with his band at Dan's Diner?

To answer the question, look at the number in each box. Write its letter on the matching numbered line or lines below.

Because the menu there does not include B___ ___TS and ___ ___ ___ ___ ___ ___ ___ ___ ___ ___!

1 1 4 0 3 2 7 9 8 5 6 7

 Key p. 311

Name ____________________

Stack It High!

Multiply. Show your work on another sheet of paper. Then record the product and color each sandwich layer to match the corresponding answer.

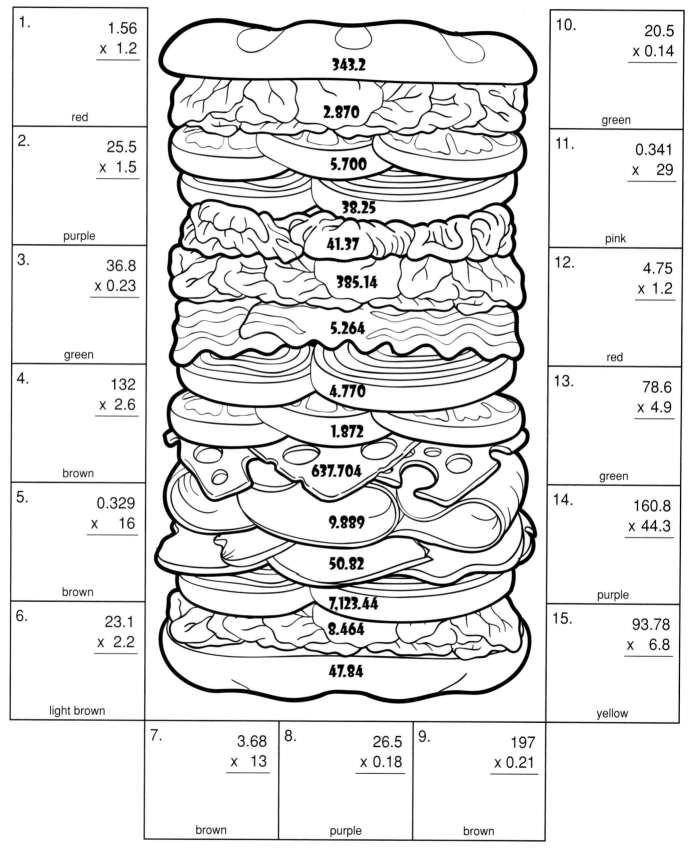

1. 1.56 x 1.2 — red
2. 25.5 x 1.5 — purple
3. 36.8 x 0.23 — green
4. 132 x 2.6 — brown
5. 0.329 x 16 — brown
6. 23.1 x 2.2 — light brown 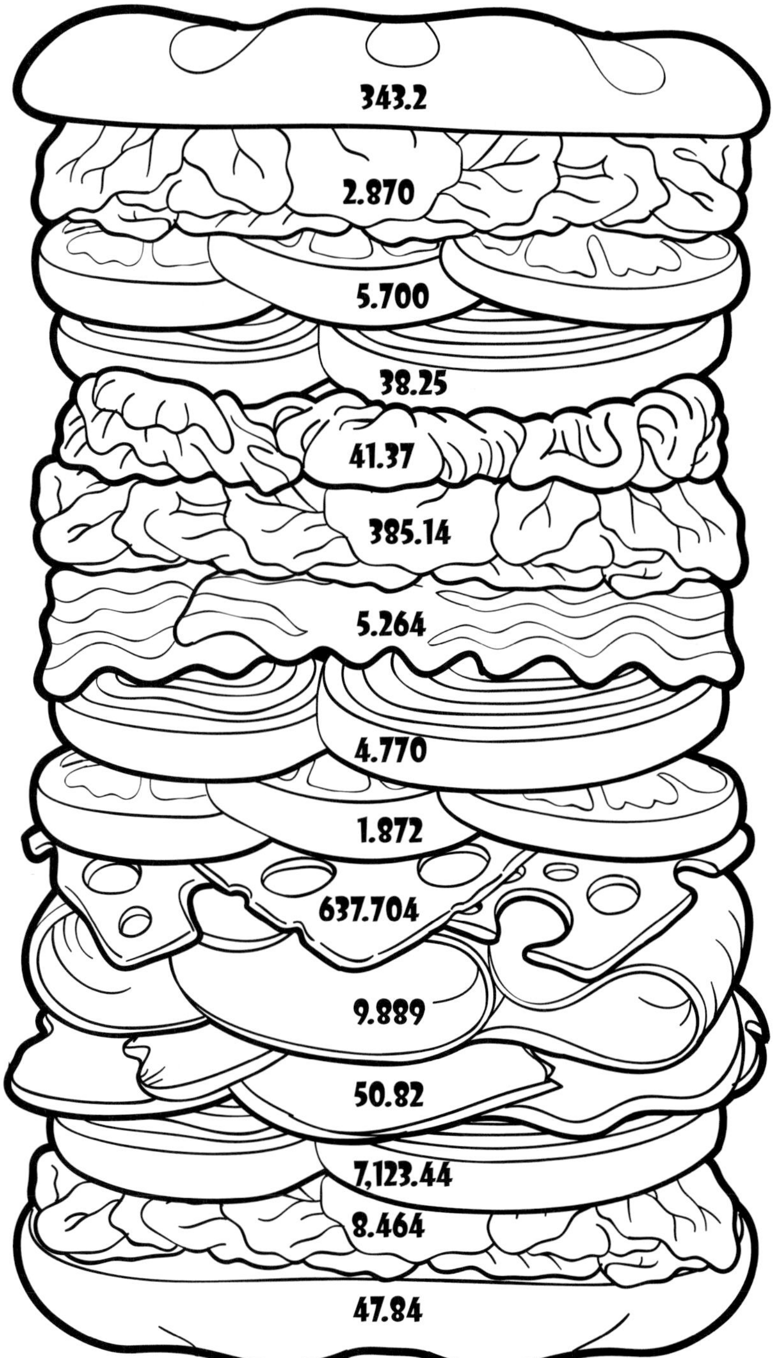
7. 3.68 x 13 — brown
8. 26.5 x 0.18 — purple
9. 197 x 0.21 — brown
10. 20.5 x 0.14 — green
11. 0.341 x 29 — pink
12. 4.75 x 1.2 — red
13. 78.6 x 4.9 — green
14. 160.8 x 44.3 — purple
15. 93.78 x 6.8 — yellow

343.2

2.870

5.700

38.25

41.37

385.14

5.264

4.770

1.872

637.704

9.889

50.82

7,123.44

8.464

47.84

Name ____________________ **Prime factorization, following directions**

A Factor Forest

Materials:
4 sheets of white copy paper, half sheet of green construction paper, scissors, stapler

Directions:

1. Cut out the pattern below.
2. Stack your four sheets of white paper. Fold the stack in half twice. Fold your green paper in half to make a booklet cover.

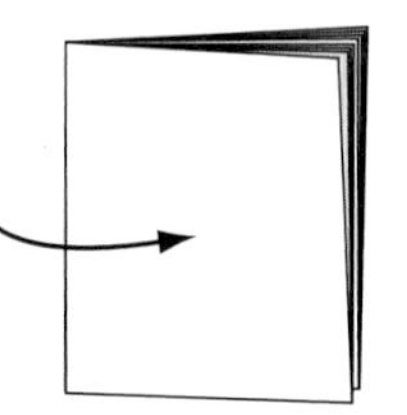

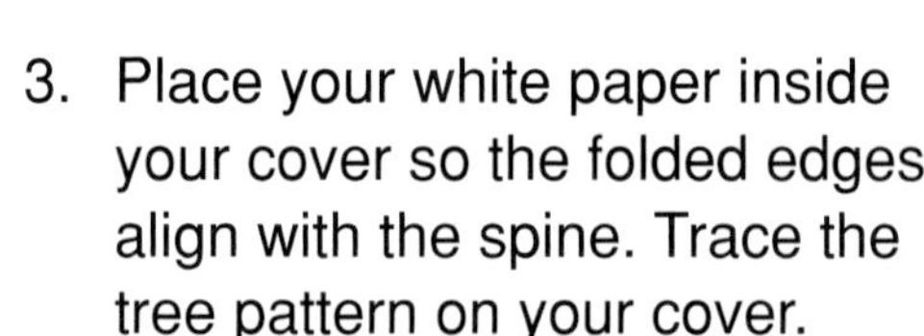

3. Place your white paper inside your cover so the folded edges align with the spine. Trace the tree pattern on your cover.

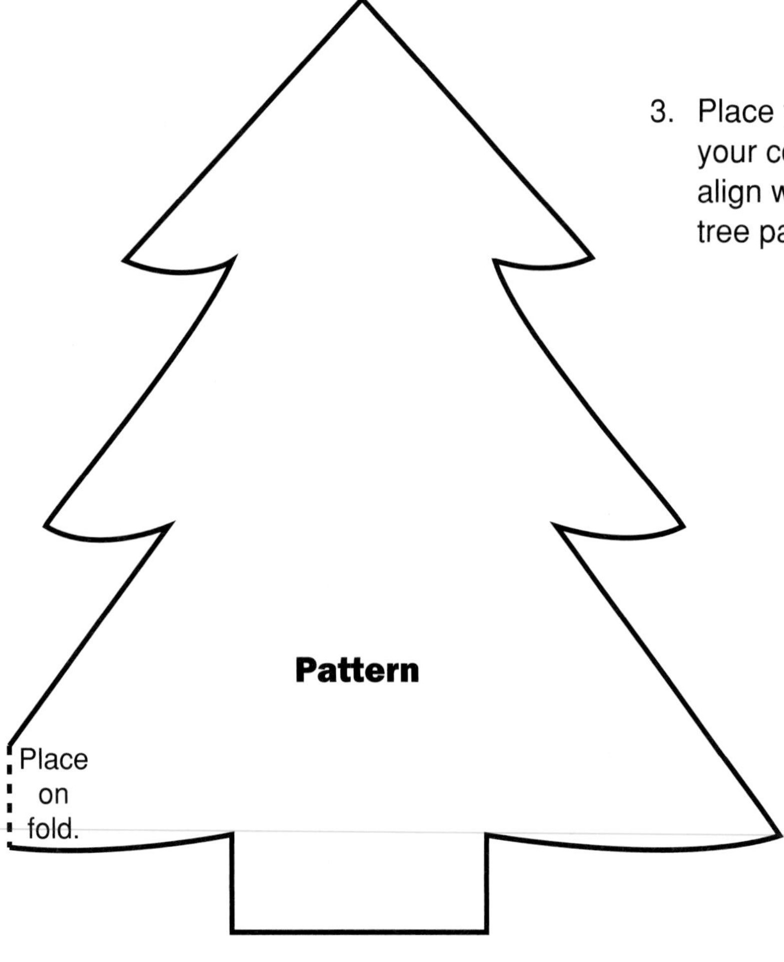

4. Cut out your booklet and staple it at the fold. If it is hard for you to cut through all the layers, cut through two folded sheets at a time and then assemble the booklet.
5. Title your booklet "A Factor Forest."
6. Write your name on your booklet.
7. Follow your teacher's instructions to finish your booklet's pages.

 Note to the teacher: Use with "A Factor Forest" on page 183.

Polygon Cards

Use with "Search for Sides!" on page 183 and "Sort These, Please!" on page 184.

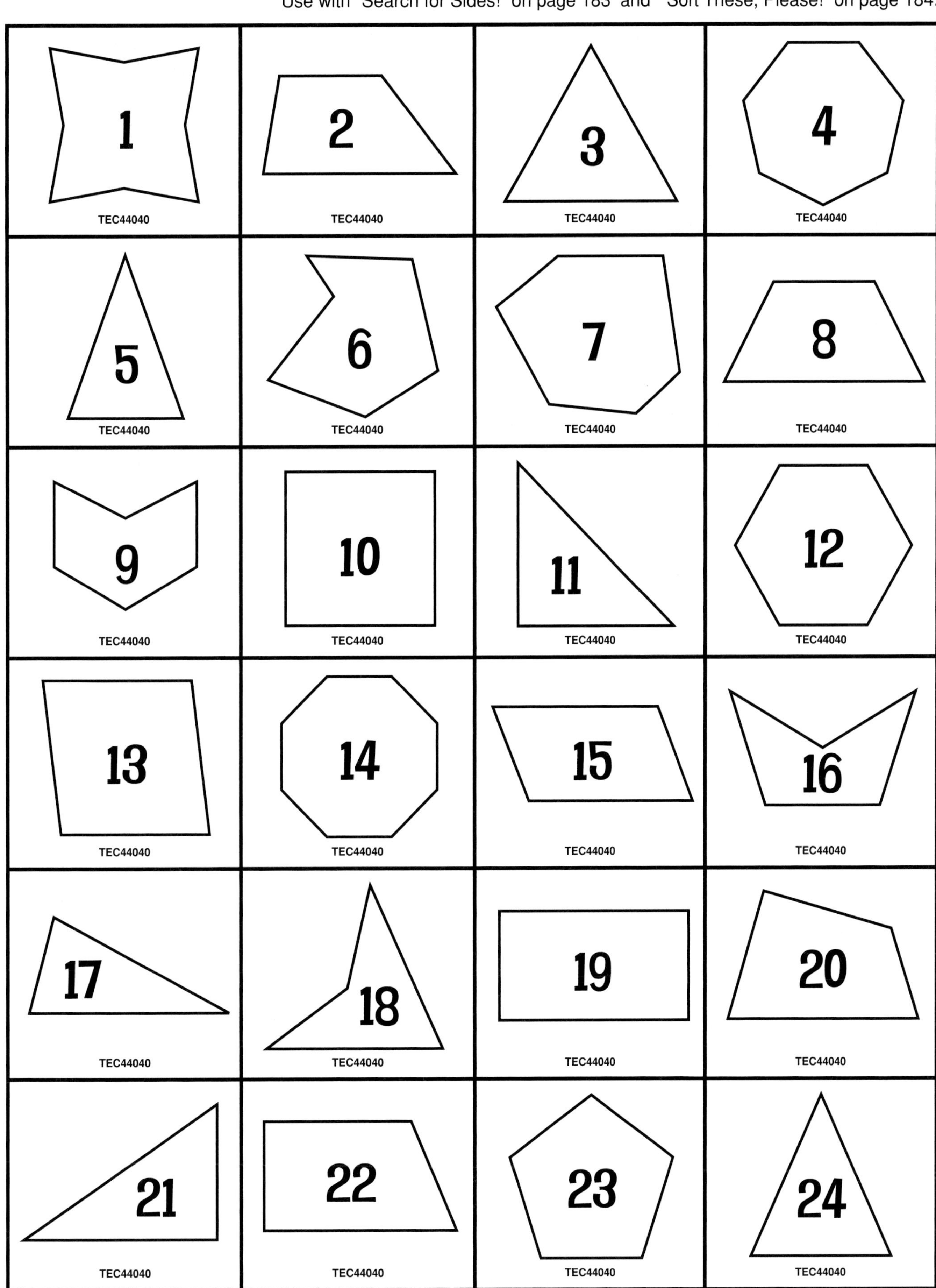

MATH TIPS + TOOLS

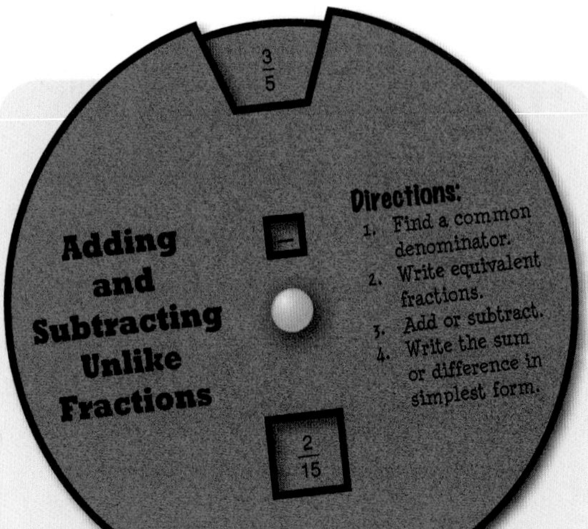
Adding and Subtracting Unlike Fractions
Directions:
1. Find a common denominator.
2. Write equivalent fractions.
3. Add or subtract.
4. Write the sum or difference in simplest form.
Aden
$\frac{3}{5} - \frac{2}{15} =$
$\frac{9}{15} - \frac{2}{15} = \frac{7}{15}$

Take a Spin!

Adding and subtracting unlike fractions

For this fun practice activity, have each student cut out the patterns and answer key from a copy of page 196 and assemble the wheel with a brad as shown above. Next, have the student rotate his wheel to create ten different problems. Then have him solve the problems and check his work with the key.

Vickie Robertson, Meadow Green Elementary
Whittier, CA

Mental Math Sticks

Problem solving

This easy-to-adapt time filler is a perfect way for students to practice mental math. Label both sides of several craft sticks with problems like the ones below, writing a problem at one end of the stick and its answer at the other. Store the sticks in a container. When you need to fill some time, remove a stick and slowly read one of its problems aloud. Have students perform the operations in the order called out, not by the standard order of operations. Let the first student who answers correctly have the honor of pulling out the next stick!

Karen Hall, S. S. Dixon Intermediate, Pace, FL

MENTAL MATH
5 x 6 – 10 ÷ 4 5
250 + 150 ÷ 4 – 75 x 5 125

Let's Shoot Some Hoops!

Ratios

Students will love this team review because it gets them out of their seats! Place a trash can on the floor five steps away from a strip of masking tape. Have a child from each team stand behind the tape, in turn, and toss five small balls (or wads of paper) into the container. Have the player then write a ratio on his row of his team's chart to express the number of "baskets" made in his five attempts. When everyone has had a turn, play two more rounds, moving the tape back one step after each round. Then have each player write a final ratio to represent his success for all three rounds. If desired, have students calculate their shooting percentages or order their final ratios from greatest to least or least to greatest.

Deborah Lamb, Butler Elementary, Savannah, GA

Team 1's Baskets				
Player	Five Steps Away	Six Steps Away	Seven Steps Away	Total
Colin	$\frac{2}{5}$	$\frac{2}{5}$	$\frac{1}{5}$	$\frac{5}{15}$, or $\frac{1}{3}$
Amber	$\frac{3}{5}$	$\frac{4}{5}$	$\frac{3}{5}$	$\frac{10}{15}$, or $\frac{2}{3}$
Sara	$\frac{2}{5}$	$\frac{2}{5}$	$\frac{2}{5}$	6, or $\frac{2}{5}$
Todd	$\frac{4}{5}$	$\frac{4}{5}$	$\frac{3}{5}$	$\frac{11}{15}$

Stats Lineup

Mean, median, mode, and range

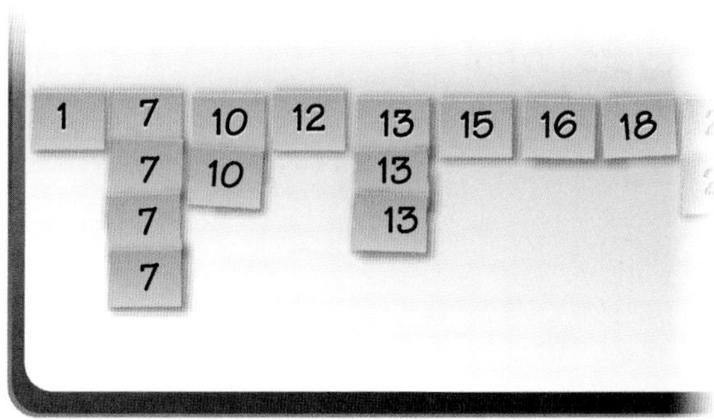

To clarify the meaning of mean, median, mode, and range, have each child write her favorite number from 1 to 100 on a sticky note and affix it in numerical order to a whiteboard. If there are duplicates of any number, have students attach those notes to one another in a column. After the class identifies the mode and range, have two students start at opposite ends of the whiteboard and move toward each other one number at a time to identify the median. Discuss any outliers (numbers much smaller or larger than the main group). Then conclude the activity by working together to find the mean.

Terry Healy, Marlatt Elementary, Manhattan, KS

A Matter of Degrees

Relating angle measurements and fractional parts of a circle

Begin this hands-on activity by having each child color circle A on a copy of page 197 and then cut out all the circles. Review with students that there are 360 degrees in a circle. Next, have students fit circles A and B together to show that ⅓ of the circle (120 degrees) is uncolored and ⅔ (240 degrees) is colored. In turn, have students use circle A with each remaining circle in a similar way to represent different angle measurements and their fractional equivalents. Once students are comfortable with the manipulatives, have them use the tools to solve problems, such as finding the number of degrees in ¾ of a circle *(270 degrees)* or ⅚ of a circle *(300 degrees)*.

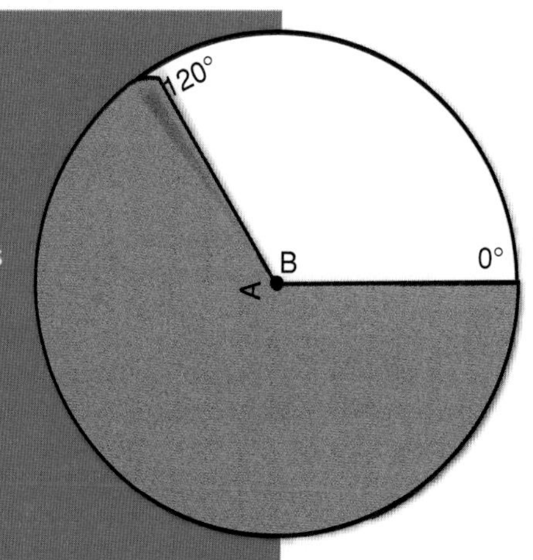

Jeanette Griggs, Swartz Creek, MI

Name ____________________

All Fenced In!

Solve. Show your work on the back of this page.

1. Farmer Green planted green beans in a square garden. If one side of the garden measures 4 yards, what is its perimeter? ________ Its area? ________

2. Farmer Smith's watermelon patch is pentagon-shaped with sides measuring 5 feet, 5 feet, 6 feet, 6 feet, and 8 feet. What is its perimeter? ________

3. Farmer Jones planted his corn in a rectangular garden. One side is 6 feet long. The other side is 10 feet long. What is its perimeter? ________ Its area? ________

4. Farmer Johnson's pigpen measures 7 yards by 11 yards. What is its perimeter? ________ Its area? ________

5. This sketch shows the rose garden belonging to Farmer Davis's wife. If the garden's perimeter is 34 feet, what are the two missing measurements? ________

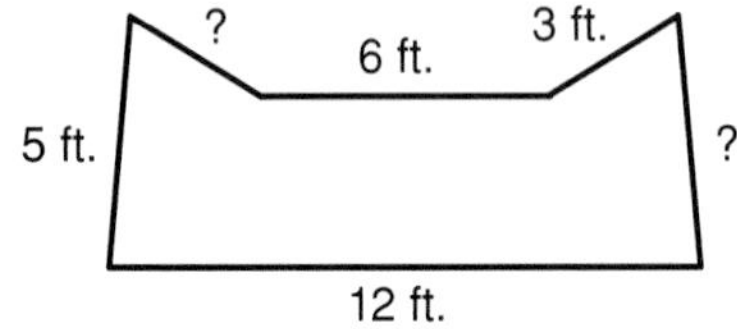

6. Farmer Jackson drew this sketch of his chicken yard. What is its perimeter? ________

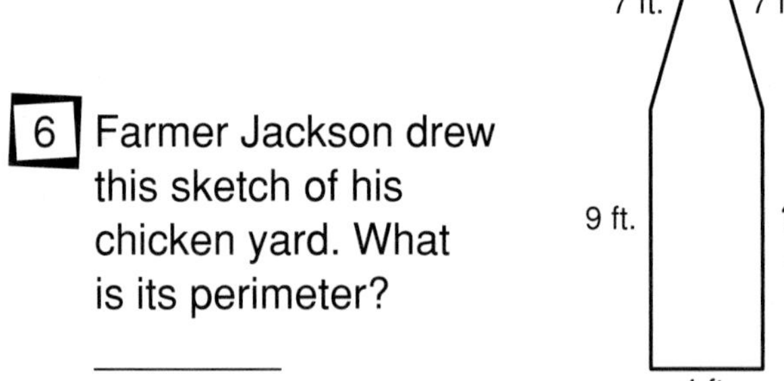

7. Farmer Marshall fenced in a pasture for his ostriches. Based on this diagram, how much fencing did he buy? ________

5 ft.
6 ft.
1 ft.
5 ft.
4 ft.
7 ft.
5 ft.

8. Farmer Gray is increasing the length and width of his rectangular cow pasture by 12 yards each. If its current size is 12 yards by 10 yards, what will its new perimeter be? ________ Its new area? ________

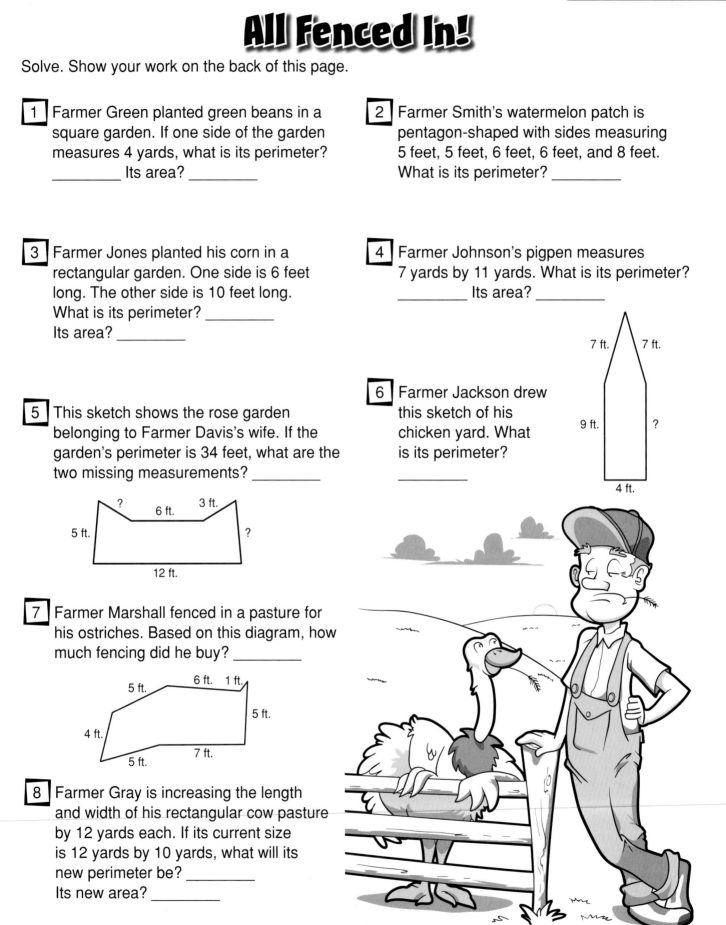

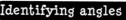

Name ______________________

Wading and Watching

Lightly color the circles by the code to identify each angle.

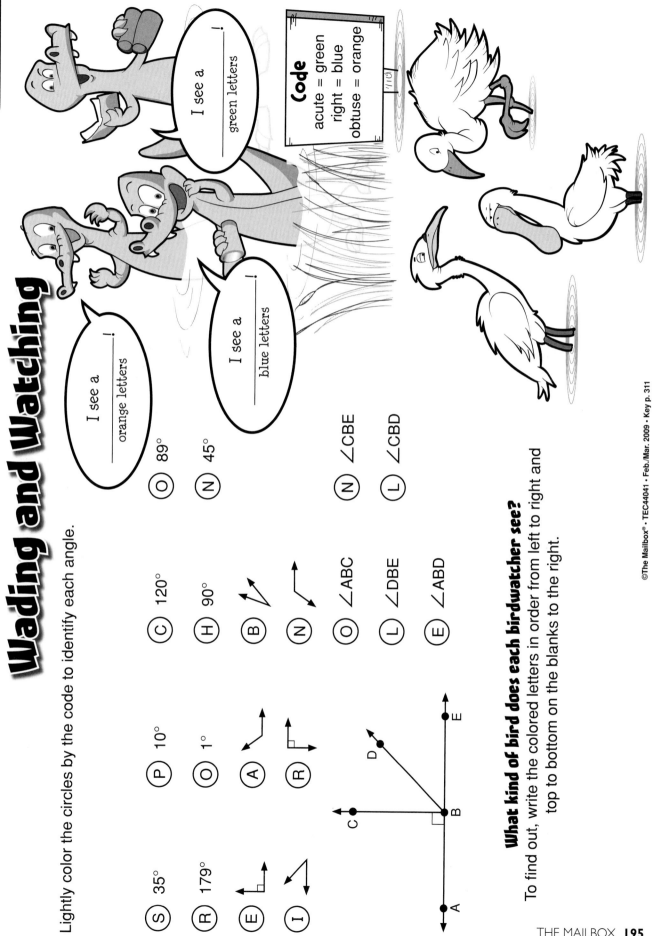

(S) 35°	(P) 10°	(C) 120°	(O) 89°
(R) 179°	(O) 1°	(H) 90°	(N) 45°
(E) [angle]	(A) [angle]	(B) [angle]	
(I) [angle]	(R) [angle]	(N) [angle]	
[diagram: A, B, C, D, E]		(O) ∠ABC	(N) ∠CBE
		(L) ∠DBE	(L) ∠CBD
		(E) ∠ABD	

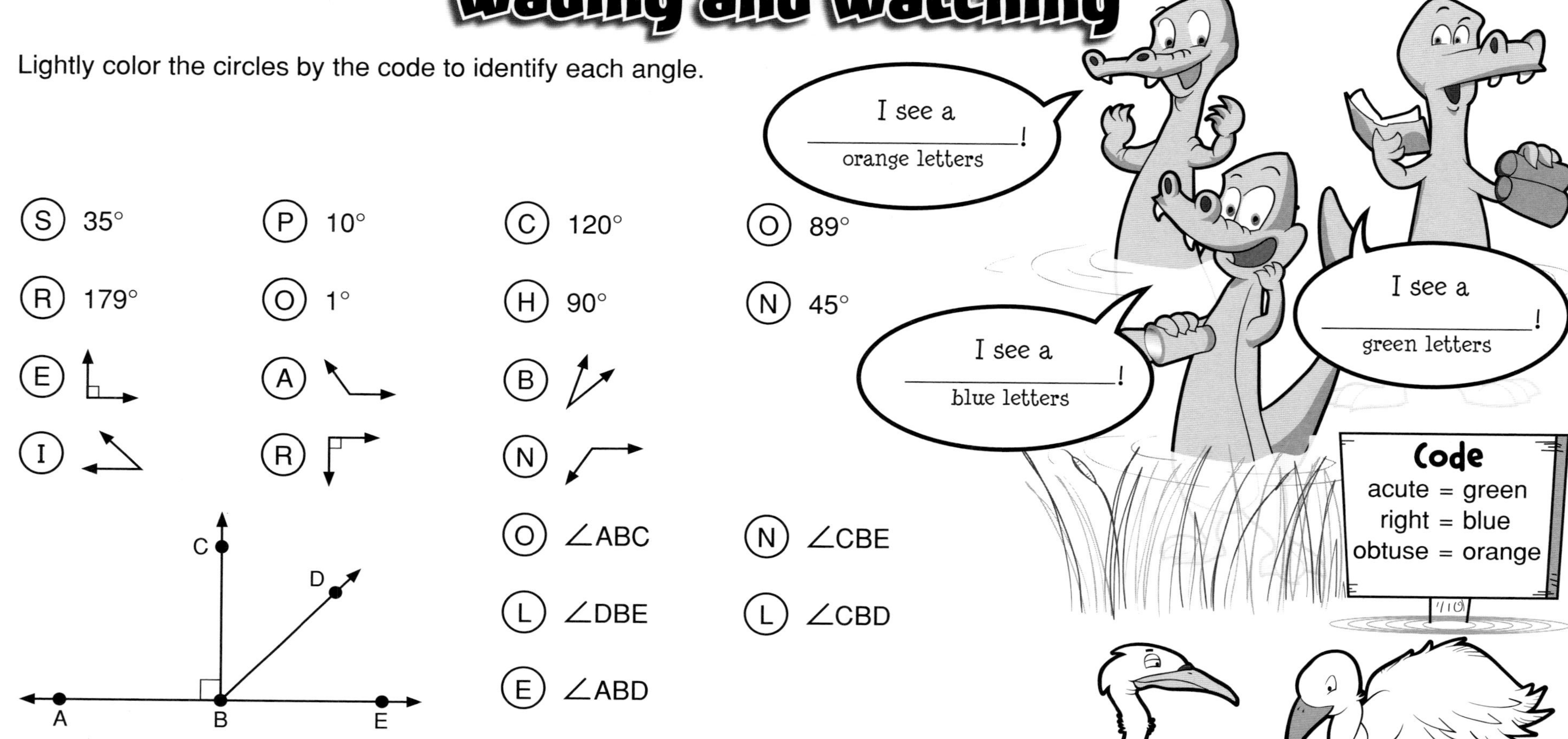
I see a ______________! orange letters
I see a ______________! blue letters
I see a ______________! green letters
Code
acute = green
right = blue
obtuse = orange

What kind of bird does each birdwatcher see?
To find out, write the colored letters in order from left to right and top to bottom on the blanks to the right.

Wheel Patterns and Answer Key

Use with "Take a Spin!" on page 192.

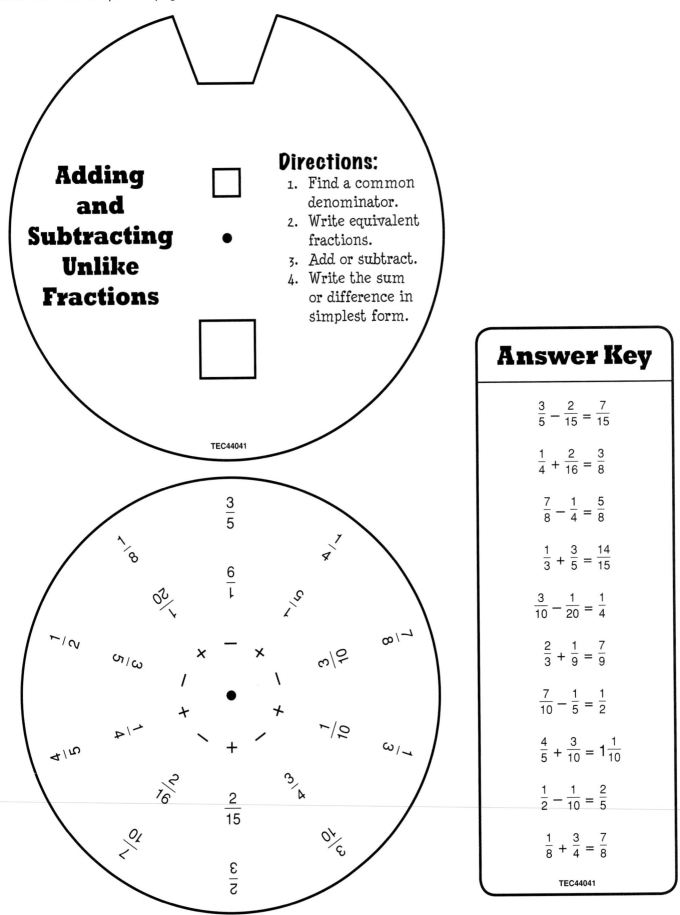

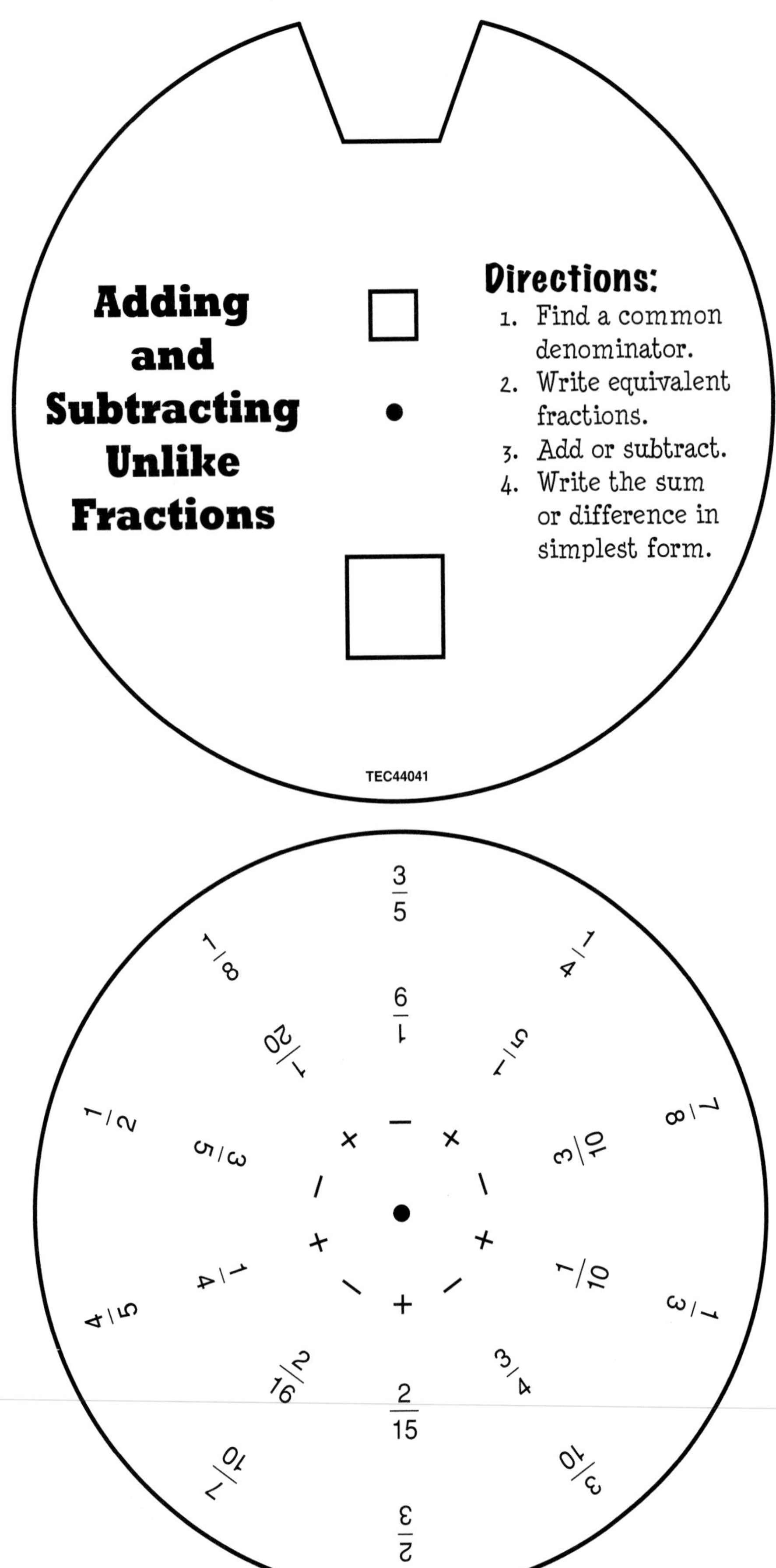

Adding
and
Subtracting
Unlike
Fractions
Directions:
1. Find a common denominator.
2. Write equivalent fractions.
3. Add or subtract.
4. Write the sum or difference in simplest form.
TEC44041

Answer Key

$\frac{3}{5} - \frac{2}{15} = \frac{7}{15}$

$\frac{1}{4} + \frac{2}{16} = \frac{3}{8}$

$\frac{7}{8} - \frac{1}{4} = \frac{5}{8}$

$\frac{1}{3} + \frac{3}{5} = \frac{14}{15}$

$\frac{3}{10} - \frac{1}{20} = \frac{1}{4}$

$\frac{2}{3} + \frac{1}{9} = \frac{7}{9}$

$\frac{7}{10} - \frac{1}{5} = \frac{1}{2}$

$\frac{4}{5} + \frac{3}{10} = 1\frac{1}{10}$

$\frac{1}{2} - \frac{1}{10} = \frac{2}{5}$

$\frac{1}{8} + \frac{3}{4} = \frac{7}{8}$

TEC44041

Circle Patterns

Use with "A Matter of Degrees" on page 193.

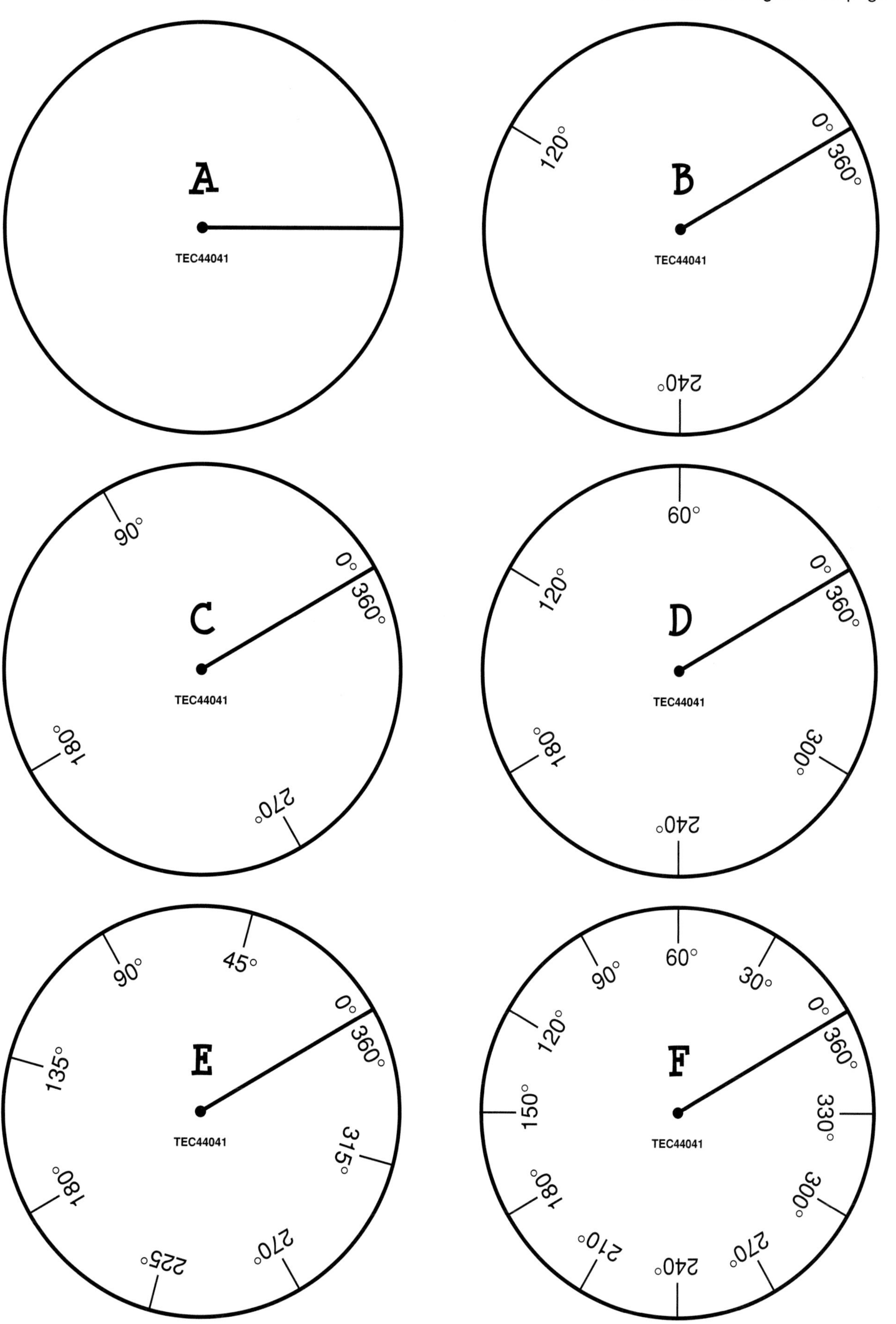

MATH TIPS + TOOLS

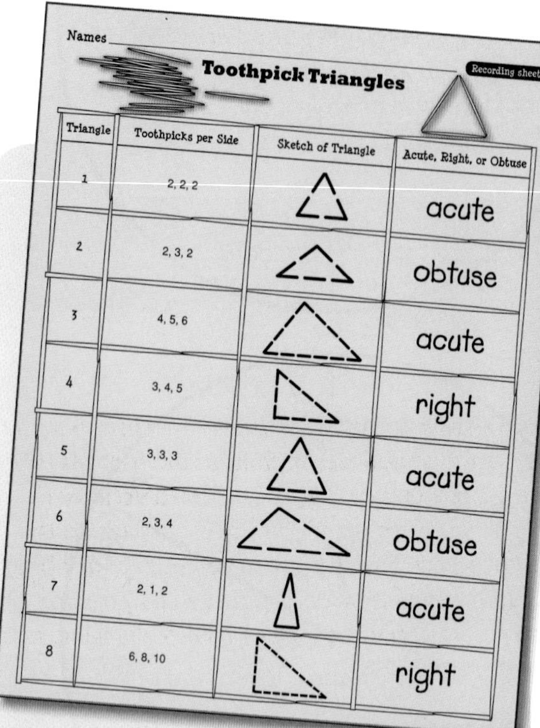

Names

Toothpick Triangles

Recording sheet

Triangle	Toothpicks per Side	Sketch of Triangle	Acute, Right, or Obtuse
1	2, 2, 2		acute
2	2, 3, 2		obtuse
3	4, 5, 6		acute
4	3, 4, 5		right
5	3, 3, 3		acute
6	2, 3, 4		obtuse
7	2, 1, 2		acute
8	6, 8, 10		right

Toothpick Triangles

Acute, right, and obtuse triangles

This fun-to-do activity is perfect for partners. At a center, place copies of the recording sheet from page 205 and a small resealable plastic bag filled with 24 toothpicks. Have the partners use the number of toothpicks specified on the recording sheet to form each triangle. Then have them complete the page as shown.

Jennifer Otter, Oak Ridge, NC

Funny-Paper Fractions

Addition, subtraction, multiplication, and division

For a clever way to practice basic operations with fractions, have students bring in comics sections from Sunday newspapers until you have one for each pair of students. Instruct the partners to cut out eight pictures that each show one or more characters. Next, have the duo arrange its cutouts to form four proper fractions and glue them to construction paper to create two different problems that practice the skills you want to reinforce. After the partners solve their problems on the back of their paper, check their work. Then have duos swap papers and instruct each student to solve the problems on his own paper. Continue until each student solves ten problems.

Jennifer Otter

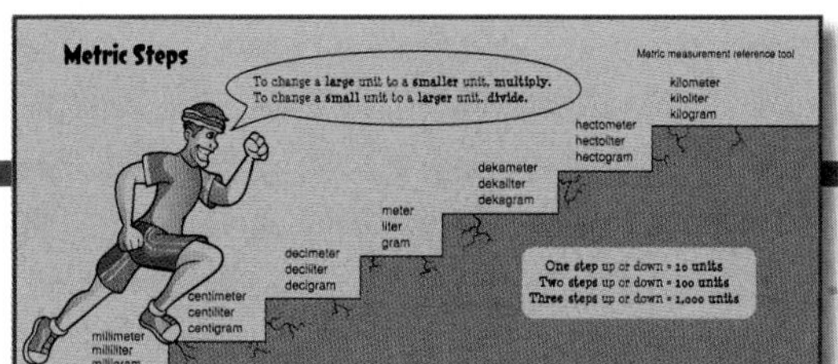
Metric Steps
Metric measurement reference tool
To change a large unit to a smaller unit, multiply.
To change a small unit to a larger unit, divide.
kilometer
kiloliter
kilogram
hectometer
hectoliter
hectogram
dekameter
dekaliter
dekagram
meter
liter
gram
decimeter
deciliter
decigram
centimeter
centiliter
centigram
millimeter
milliliter
milligram
One step up or down = 10 units
Two steps up or down = 100 units
Three steps up or down = 1,000 units

MATH

Metric Steps

Comparing and converting metric units

To help students better understand the metric system and the base-ten system upon which it is built, give each child a copy of the metric measurement reference tool on page 206. (White out any units your students do not use before making copies.) Explain that the steps represent the metric units from smallest (bottom step) to largest (top step). The basic units of length, capacity, and weight are on the middle step. After discussing the diagram, have students practice using it to solve problems, such as converting five decimeters to millimeters *(500 millimeters)* and converting 600 decimeters to meters *(60 meters).*

Maxine Gaul, Spalding Catholic School, Alton, IA

$2\frac{3}{4}$ $2\frac{5}{6}$
Two and five-sixths is greater.

The Jury Is Out!

Fractions, decimals, and mixed numbers

Begin this adaptable game for two teams by having the first player from Team A write on the whiteboard a number of the type you announce. Then have the first player on Team B write either a greater or smaller number, according to your instructions. If Team B's player is correct, have Team A's player sit in his team's jury box (a space to the left of the whiteboard). If Team B's player is incorrect, have her sit in her team's jury box (to the right of the whiteboard). Continue until one team has 12 jurors in its jury box or time runs out. The team with fewer jurors wins. To make the game more challenging, have students write problems instead of single numbers.

Vickie Robertson, Meadow Green Elementary, Whittier, CA

The Battle Is On!

Integers

−5 < 7

Want a new way for students to practice comparing positive and negative numbers? Have each student assemble a number line using the strips from page 206. Then give each duo a deck of cards with which to play this version of War.

Directions for two players:

1. Deal all the cards (including jokers) facedown so each player has a stack.
2. Turn your top card faceup at the same time as your opponent.
3. Write on your paper the number values of the faceup cards. Draw a circle between the numbers. Then compare the two numbers using the following rules:
   - Red cards = negative numbers
   - Black cards = positive numbers
   - For face card number values: jack = 11, queen = 12, king = 13, joker = 0, and ace = 1
4. Solve the problem as quickly as you can, using your number line for help. The first player to solve the problem correctly wins both faceup cards.
5. Continue until all cards have been captured. The player who captures more cards wins.

TIP
Use this game to practice adding and subtracting integers also.

Barbara Starck, St. Matthias School, Milwaukee, WI

Names ____________________

Come and Get It!

A Game for Two Players

Directions:

1. Choose a crayon or colored pencil that is a different color than your partner's.
2. In turn, multiply any two fractions from the stick of butter. Show your work on your paper, writing your answer in simplest form.
3. Find your answer on the corn cob and color its kernel. If your answer is not on the corn cob or the kernel has already been colored, your turn is over.
4. Play for a set amount of time or until all kernels have been colored. The player with more colored kernels wins.

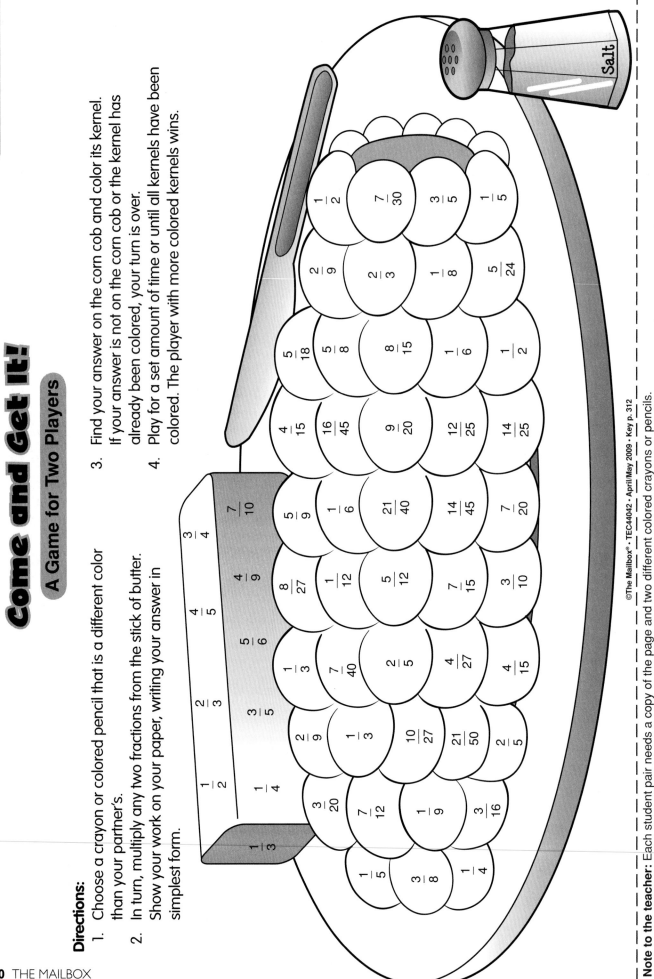

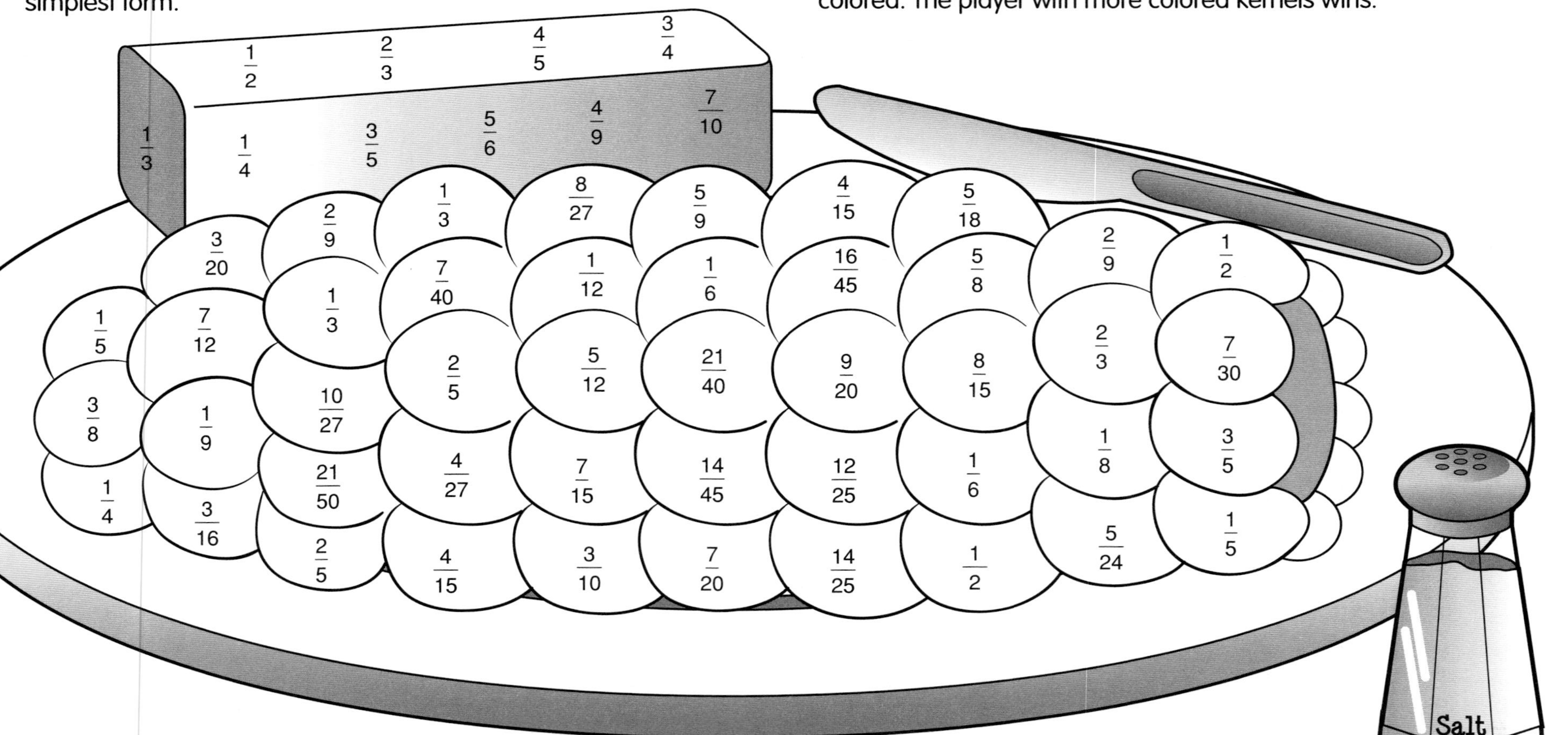

Note to the teacher: Each student pair needs a copy of the page and two different colored crayons or pencils.

Game Cards and Answer Key

Use with "Space Spies" on page 202. Each player needs a supply of small game markers that are a different color than his opponent's. Mount on construction paper a copy of the game mat on page 202 and a copy of the cards and answer key below. If desired, laminate the pages before cutting the cards apart.

A $20 \div (5 \times 4) = b$	B $(7 \times 7) - d = 47$	C $81 \div (9 \times 3) = s$
D $r = (30 \div 2) - 11$	E $p = 100 \div (4 \times 5)$	F $(24 \div 8) + m = 9$
G $6(s + 1) = 48$	H $g = (22 + 10) \div 4$	I $n \times 12 = 108$
J $120 \div (2 \times 6) = t$	K $99 \div w = 9$	L $14 - w = 6 \div 3$
M $19 - m = 2 + 4$	N $28 \div q = 10 \div 5$	O $(4 + 2) \times 5 = c \times 2$
P $(2 \times 2) \times (4 + 0) = y$	Q $(30 + 4) \div 2 = v$	R $(81 \div 9) \times (12 \div 6) = z$
S $20 - n = 30 \div 30$	T $e = 320 \div 16$	U $105 \div 5 = d$
V $(6 + 5) \times 2 = r$	W $x = 30 - (14 \div 2)$	X $4 \times 3 \times 2 = x$
Y $(10 \times 10) \div 4 = x$	Z $2 \times (9 + 4) = y$	AA $39 - (144 \div 12) = y$
BB $y = 7 \times (5 - 1)$	CC $(60 - 2) \div 2 = k$	DD $j = (8 \times 5) - 10$
EE $(60 + 2) \div 2 = k$	FF $(8 \times 8) \div 2 = s$	GG $(6 + 5) \times 3 = f$
HH $100 - (11 \times 6) = y$	II $f = (7 \times 10) \div 2$	JJ $(2 + 2) \times 9 = q$
KK $c = (9 \times 8) - (33 + 2)$	LL $(8 \times 6) - (2 \times 5) = u$	MM $x = 16 + 23$
NN $(11 \times 4) - 2^2 = p$	OO $h = 50 - (18 \div 2)$	PP $2 \times 3 \times 7 = m$
QQ $n = (8 \times 6) - 5$	RR $(8 \times 11) \div 2 = q$	SS $x = (2 + 3) \times 9$

Answer Key for "Space Spies"

A. 1
B. 2
C. 3
D. 4
E. 5
F. 6
G. 7
H. 8
I. 9

J. 10
K. 11
L. 12
M. 13
N. 14
O. 15
P. 16
Q. 17
R. 18

S. 19
T. 20
U. 21
V. 22
W. 23
X. 24
Y. 25
Z. 26
AA. 27

BB. 28
CC. 29
DD. 30
EE. 31
FF. 32
GG. 33
HH. 34
II. 35
JJ. 36

KK. 37
LL. 38
MM. 39
NN. 40
OO. 41
PP. 42
QQ. 43
RR. 44
SS. 45

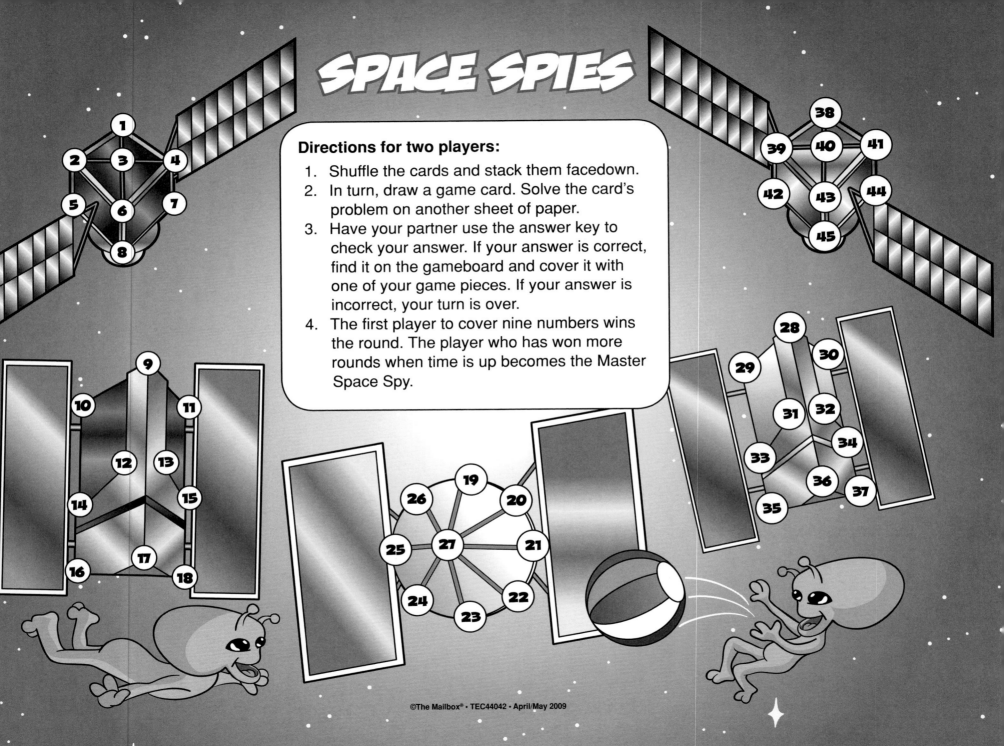

SPACE SPIES

Directions for two players:

1. Shuffle the cards and stack them facedown.
2. In turn, draw a game card. Solve the card's problem on another sheet of paper.
3. Have your partner use the answer key to check your answer. If your answer is correct, find it on the gameboard and cover it with one of your game pieces. If your answer is incorrect, your turn is over.
4. The first player to cover nine numbers wins the round. The player who has won more rounds when time is up becomes the Master Space Spy.

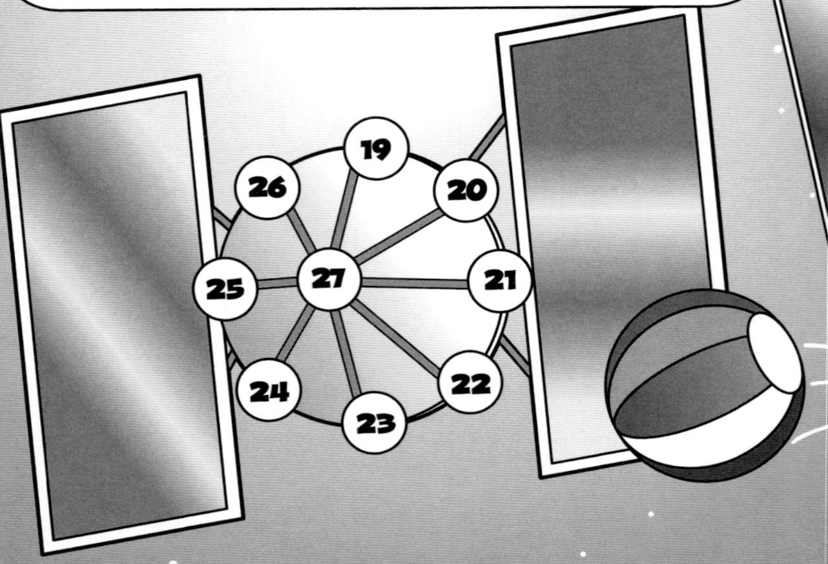

Name ____________________ Geometry, probability

Gem Dandies

Color the gems according to their labels. Then answer the questions. Write your answers in simplest form.

What is the probability of choosing a gem

A. whose shape is a hexagonal prism? ________

B. that is not pink? ________

C. whose shape is a hexagonal prism or triangular pyramid? ________

D. that is yellow and is not a hexagonal prism? ________

E. that is not green? ________

F. whose shape is a cone? ________

G. whose shape is a cylinder? ________

H. that is not purple? ________

I. that is pink or purple? ________

J. that is not yellow or green? ________

K. that is pink, yellow, or purple? ________

L. whose shape is a cube? ________

M. that has a circular base? ________

N. that is orange? ________

O. whose shape is not a hexagonal prism or a cone? ________

yellow
green
pink
yellow
purple
pink
purple
pink
yellow
orange

Note to the teacher: Each student will need crayons or colored pencils to complete this page.

Name ____________________

All the King's Crowns

Write in simplest form an equivalent decimal and fraction for each percent.

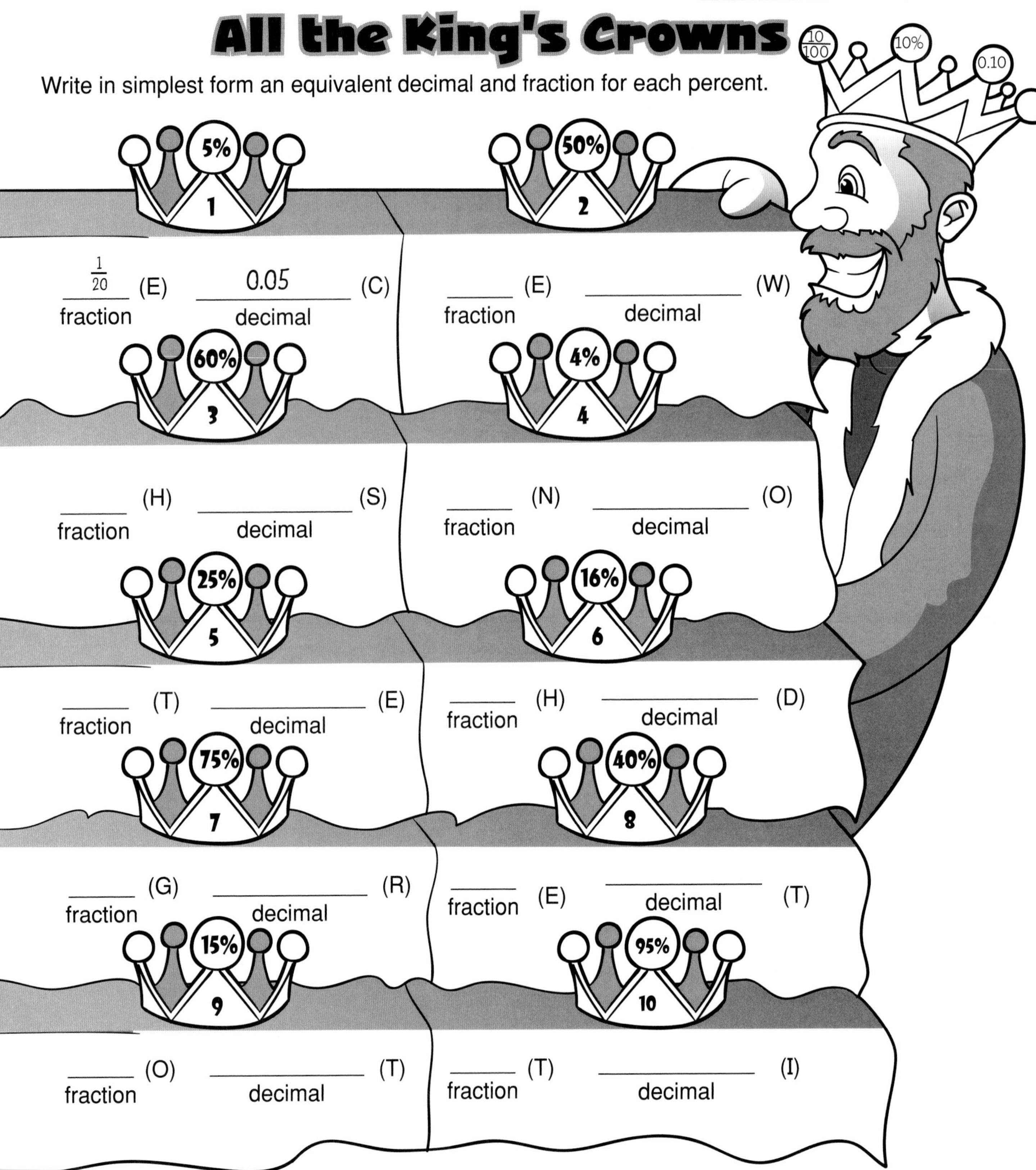

Why did the king go to the dentist?

To find out, write each letter from above on its matching numbered line below.

$\frac{1}{4}$ 0.04 $\frac{3}{4}$ $\frac{1}{20}$ 0.4 $\frac{4}{25}$ 0.95 0.6   0.15 0.25 $\frac{1}{2}$ $\frac{19}{20}$ $\frac{3}{5}$ 0.05 0.75 $\frac{3}{20}$ 0.5 $\frac{1}{25}$ $\frac{2}{5}$ 0.16 !

Names ____ Recording sheet

Toothpick Triangles

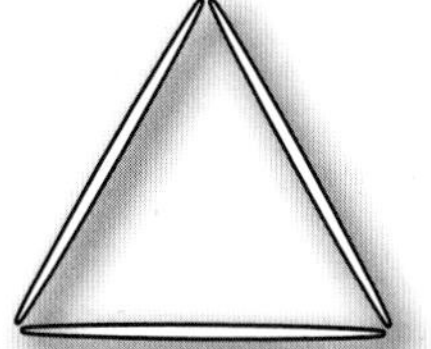

Triangle	Toothpicks per Side	Sketch of Triangle	Acute, Right, or Obtuse?
1	2, 2, 2		
2	2, 3, 2		
3	4, 5, 6		
4	3, 4, 5		
5	3, 3, 3		
6	2, 3, 4		
7	2, 1, 2		
8	6, 8, 10		

Note to the teacher: Use with "Toothpick Triangles" on page 198.

Number Line Strips

Use with "The Battle Is On!" on page 199.

Metric Steps

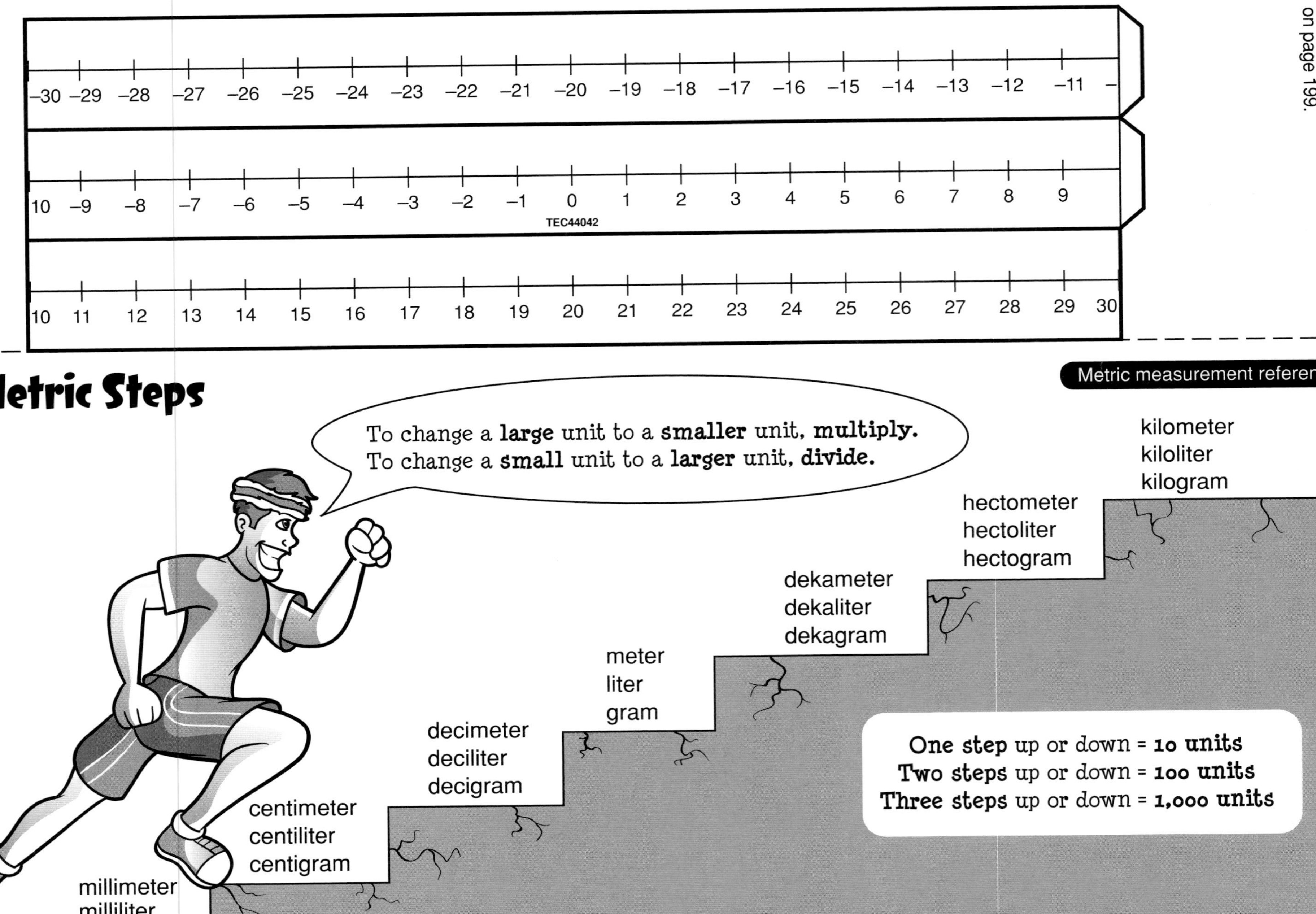

Note to the teacher: Use with "Metric Steps" on page 199.

MATH TIPS + TOOLS

Always, Sometimes, or Never

Congruency

Give each student pair a copy of the top half of page 211, three sheets of construction paper, scissors, glue, and a marker. Have the partners cut apart the cards and title each piece of construction paper "Sometimes Congruent," "Always Congruent," or "Never Congruent." Instruct each pair to divide each paper into two columns and then read each card and answer its question by gluing the card in the left column of the appropriate paper. In the right column, have the partners draw an example that supports their answer. On the "Sometimes Congruent" paper, have students draw two examples: one for when the statement is true and one for when it is false.

Jennifer Otter, Oak Ridge, NC

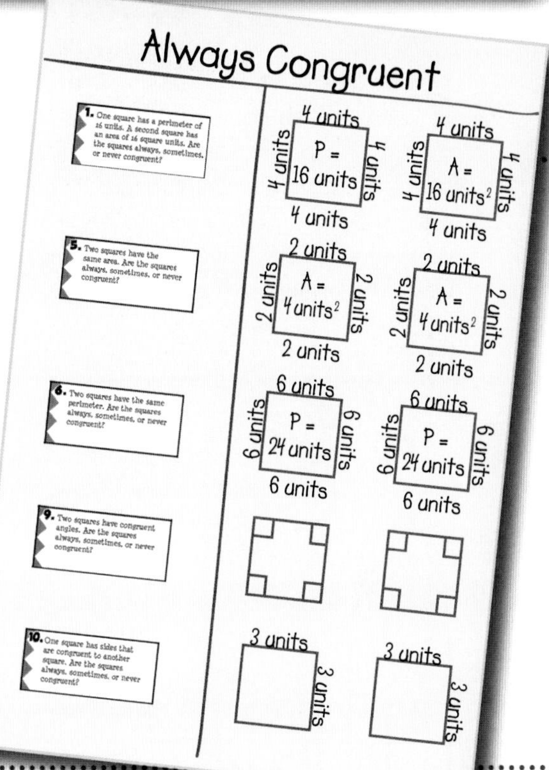

Fraction and Decimal War

Converting fractions to decimals

For this fun game, provide each group of four students with a copy of the bottom half of page 211. Have the students cut apart the cards and spread them out facedown. To play, each student selects a card, adds the two fractions, and converts the sum to a decimal. The group checks the answers with the key. The player with the highest sum wins a point for that round. The players then set the used cards aside and select new cards. The game continues until all cards have been played. The player with the most points at the end of the game wins. If time allows, let players play again, but this time stipulate that the object is to have the lowest sum each round.

My decimal is larger! That's a point for me!
$\frac{3}{5} = \frac{6}{10}$
$+ \frac{7}{10} = \frac{7}{10}$
$\frac{13}{10} = 1\frac{3}{10} = 1.3$
$\frac{3}{5} + \frac{7}{10}$

Fraction Pickup

Adding fractions

Put a twist on this classic partner game by labeling 24 craft sticks with common fractions and displaying a point chart like the one shown. To play, one student gently drops all the fraction sticks on the table. She chooses two sticks from the pile and adds the fractions on her paper to determine her points. Player two then takes a turn. The game continues until all 24 sticks have been used. The player with more points wins.

Jennifer Otter, Oak Ridge, NC

Sum	Points
$0 < \text{sum} \leq \frac{1}{2}$	1
$\frac{1}{2} < \text{sum} < 1$	2
sum = 1	4
sum > 1	3

TIP
This game is easy to adapt for other operations with fractions.

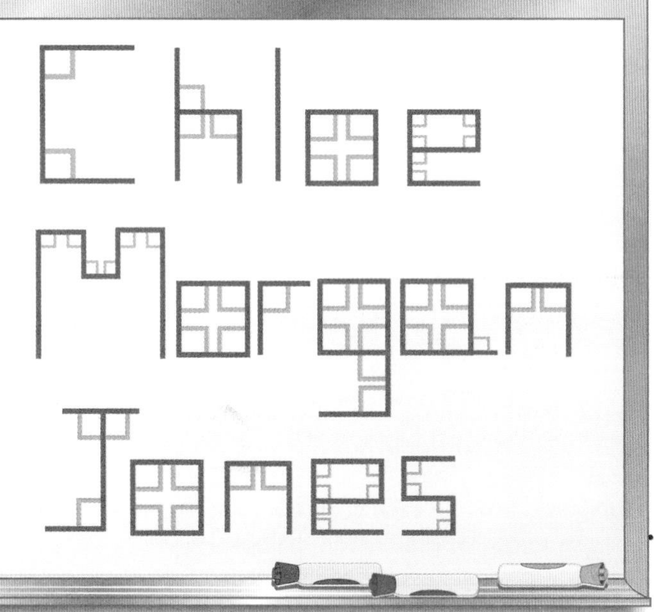

Name Your Angles

Right angles

On the board or overhead, write a person's first, middle, and last name using only line segments and right angles as shown. Ask students to help you identify the right angles in each letter. Mark each right angle with a square. Then have each child write his full name in the same way, marking all right angles. If time allows, ask students to count the number of right angles in their names. Then write the data on the board and have students find the average number of right angles in their names.

Teresa Campbell, Clark-Pleasant Middle School, Whiteland, IN

Temperature Rules!

Temperature conversions

Help students understand the relationship between Celsius and Fahrenheit temperatures by giving each child a copy of the thermometer chart on page 212. Have students use the tool to solve problems involving temperature, such as the following:

- Which is colder: 35°F or 10°C?
- If the temperature is 98°F, what is the temperature in Celsius?
- How much colder is 20°C than 80°F?

As a follow-up, have kids make up similar problems, swap with partners, and solve each other's problems.

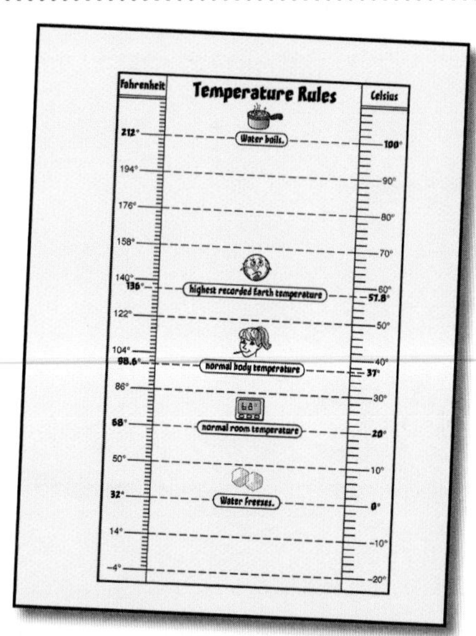

Name ____ **Number patterns**

The Beat Goes On!

Write the missing numbers in the grid on each drum.

1

19		25	
13	16	19	
7		13	16
1	4	7	10

2

51		61	66
	48	53	
35			50
27		37	
	24		34
	16	21	
3	8		18

3

	15			27		
8		16				
	9	13				
2			14	18		

4. Describe the rules for each drum's number pattern.

Drum 1: ____

Drum 2: ____

Drum 3: ____

Name ____________________

Patching Potholes

Cut out the shapes below.
Fit the specified shapes in each square.
Glue the shapes in place.

1. 4 large triangles and 2 large squares

2. 8 small triangles, 4 medium squares, and 4 small squares

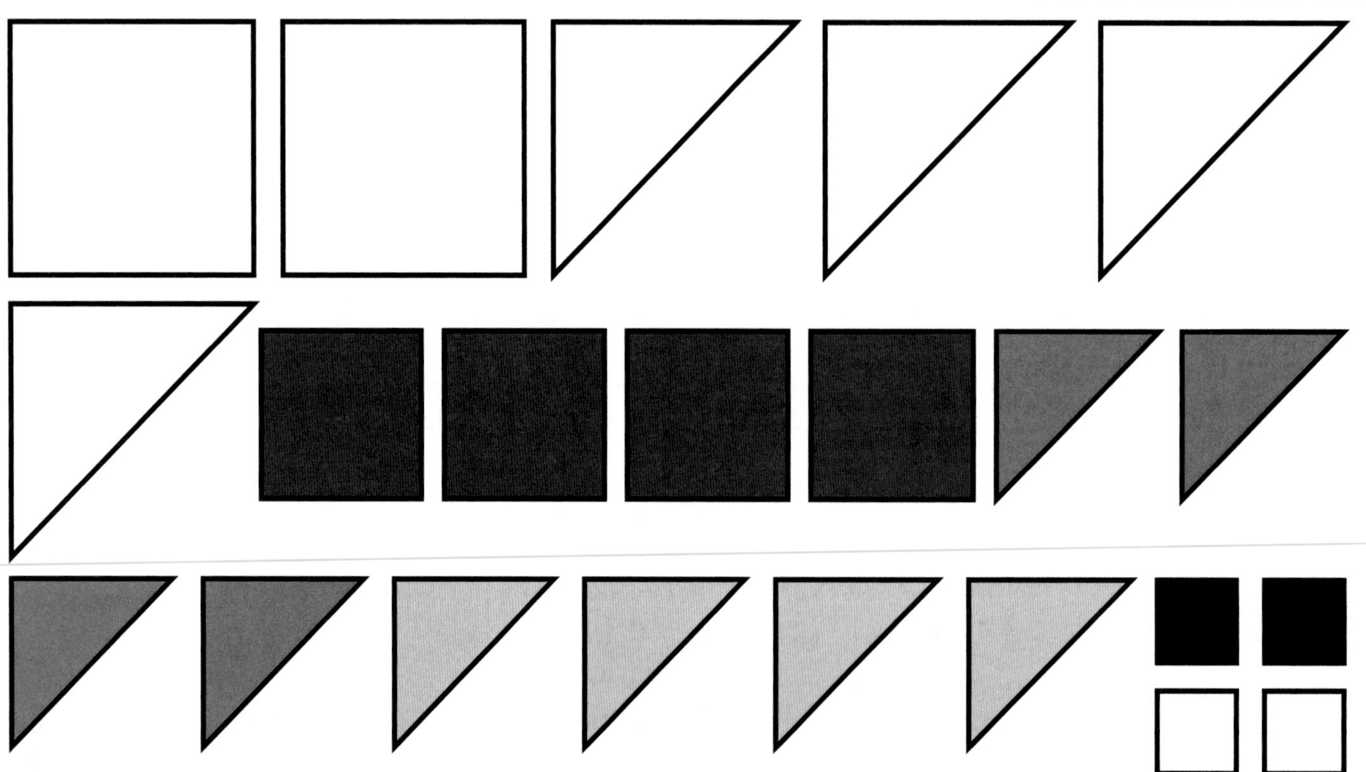

 Note to the teacher: For an extra challenge, have students try to fit the shapes to make a symmetrical design.

Congruency Cards

Use with "Always, Sometimes, or Never" on page 207.

1. One square has a perimeter of 16 units. A second square has an area of 16 square units. Are the squares always, sometimes, or never congruent? TEC44043	**2.** One triangle is obtuse. A second triangle is isosceles. Are the triangles always, sometimes, or never congruent?	**3.** Two rectangles have the same perimeter. Are the rectangles always, sometimes, or never congruent?
4. Two rectangles have the same area. Are the rectangles always, sometimes, or never congruent?	**5.** Two squares have the same area. Are the squares always, sometimes, or never congruent?	**6.** Two squares have the same perimeter. Are the squares always, sometimes, or never congruent?
7. Two equilateral triangles have different perimeters. Are the triangles always, sometimes, or never congruent?	**8.** One square has an area of 36 square units. Another square has a perimeter of 36 units. Are the squares always, sometimes, or never congruent?	**9.** Two squares have congruent angles. Are the squares always, sometimes, or never congruent?
10. One square has sides that are congruent to another square. Are the squares always, sometimes, or never congruent?	**11.** One rectangle has a perimeter of 20 units. A second rectangle has a perimeter of 24 units. Are the rectangles always, sometimes, or never congruent?	**12.** One triangle is a right triangle. A second triangle is an acute triangle. Are the triangles always, sometimes, or never congruent?

Fraction Cards and Answer Key

Use with "Fraction and Decimal War" on page 207.

A $\frac{1}{6} + \frac{2}{6}$	**B** $\frac{2}{25} + \frac{2}{100}$	**C** $\frac{1}{12} + \frac{2}{12}$	**D** $\frac{24}{40} + \frac{2}{10}$	**E** $\frac{6}{8} + \frac{1}{2}$
F $\frac{15}{16} + \frac{13}{16}$	**G** $\frac{1}{2} + \frac{9}{10}$	**H** $\frac{2}{20} + \frac{1}{5}$	**I** $\frac{8}{10} + \frac{3}{10}$	**J** $\frac{14}{50} + \frac{16}{50}$
K $\frac{2}{3} + \frac{5}{6}$	**L** $\frac{6}{30} + \frac{3}{30}$	**M** $\frac{3}{5} + \frac{7}{10}$	**N** $\frac{10}{24} + \frac{8}{24}$	**O** $\frac{6}{20} + \frac{1}{10}$
P $\frac{11}{20} + \frac{7}{20}$	**Q** $\frac{9}{18} + \frac{18}{36}$	**R** $\frac{20}{60} + \frac{22}{60}$	**S** $\frac{4}{5} + \frac{9}{10}$	**T** $\frac{1}{6} + \frac{1}{30}$

Answer Key

A. $\frac{1}{2} = 0.5$
B. $\frac{1}{10} = 0.1$
C. $\frac{1}{4} = 0.25$
D. $\frac{4}{5} = 0.8$
E. $1\frac{1}{4} = 1.25$
F. $1\frac{3}{4} = 1.75$
G. $1\frac{2}{5} = 1.4$
H. $\frac{3}{10} = 0.3$
I. $1\frac{1}{10} = 1.1$
J. $\frac{3}{5} = 0.6$
K. $1\frac{1}{2} = 1.5$
L. $\frac{3}{10} = 0.3$
M. $1\frac{3}{10} = 1.3$
N. $\frac{3}{4} = 0.75$
O. $\frac{2}{5} = 0.4$
P. $\frac{9}{10} = 0.9$
Q. 1
R. $\frac{7}{10} = 0.7$
S. $1\frac{7}{10} = 1.7$
T. $\frac{1}{5} = 0.2$

TEC44043

Thermometer Chart

Use with "Temperature Rules!" on page 208.

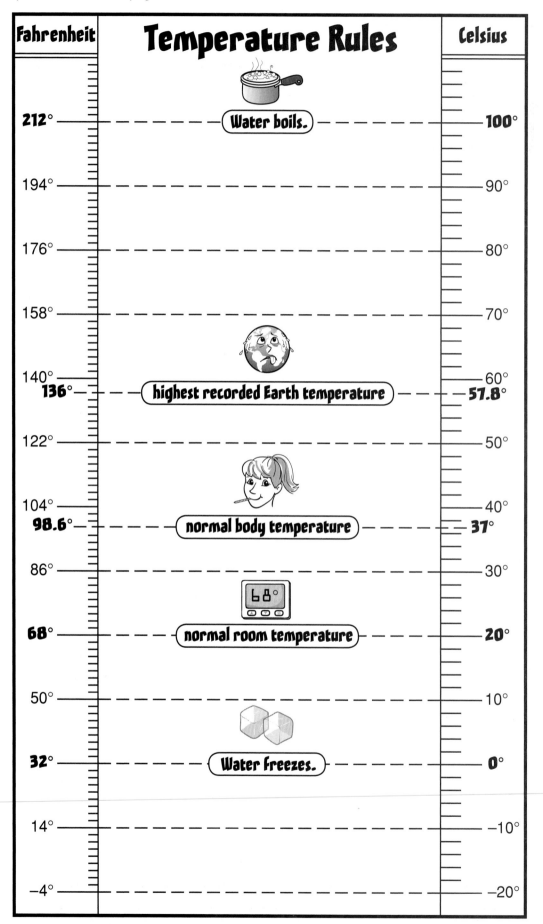

Fahrenheit	Temperature Rules	Celsius
212°	Water boils.	**100°**
194°		90°
176°		80°
158°		70°
140°		60°
136°	highest recorded Earth temperature	**57.8°**
122°		50°
104°		40°
98.6°	normal body temperature	**37°**
86°		30°
68°	normal room temperature	**20°**
50°		10°
32°	Water freezes.	**0°**
14°		–10°
–4°		–20°

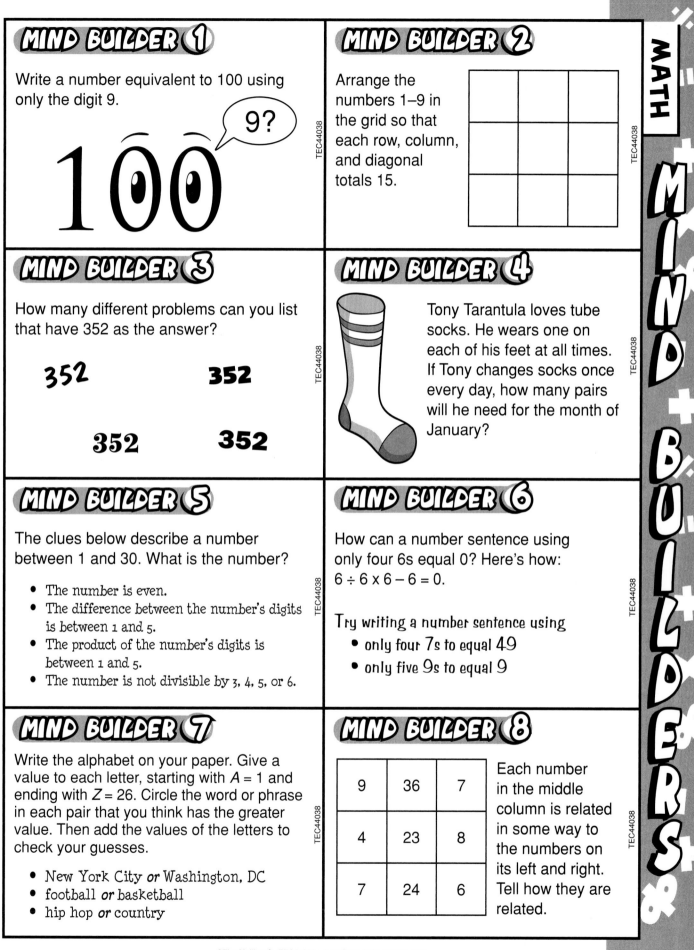

MATH MIND BUILDERS

MIND BUILDER 1

Write a number equivalent to 100 using only the digit 9.

9?

100

TEC44038

MIND BUILDER 2

Arrange the numbers 1–9 in the grid so that each row, column, and diagonal totals 15.

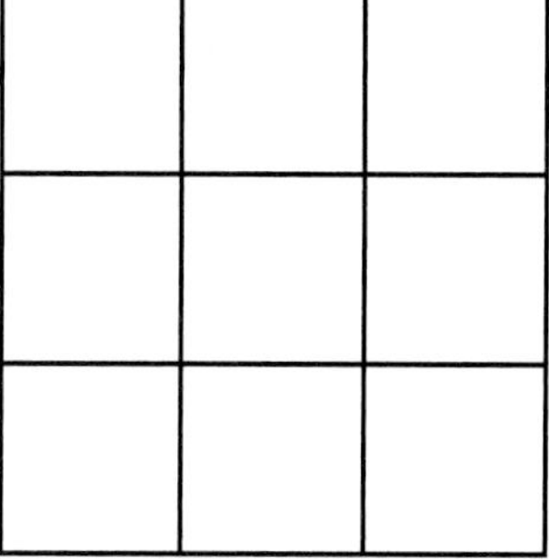

TEC44038

MIND BUILDER 3

How many different problems can you list that have 352 as the answer?

352 352

352 352

TEC44038

MIND BUILDER 4

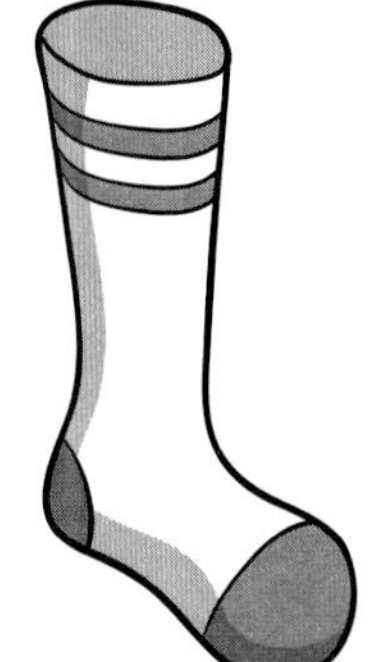

Tony Tarantula loves tube socks. He wears one on each of his feet at all times. If Tony changes socks once every day, how many pairs will he need for the month of January?

TEC44038

MIND BUILDER 5

The clues below describe a number between 1 and 30. What is the number?

- The number is even.
- The difference between the number's digits is between 1 and 5.
- The product of the number's digits is between 1 and 5.
- The number is not divisible by 3, 4, 5, or 6.

TEC44038

MIND BUILDER 6

How can a number sentence using only four 6s equal 0? Here's how:
6 ÷ 6 x 6 – 6 = 0.

Try writing a number sentence using

- only four 7s to equal 49
- only five 9s to equal 9

TEC44038

MIND BUILDER 7

Write the alphabet on your paper. Give a value to each letter, starting with *A* = 1 and ending with *Z* = 26. Circle the word or phrase in each pair that you think has the greater value. Then add the values of the letters to check your guesses.

- New York City *or* Washington, DC
- football *or* basketball
- hip hop *or* country

TEC44038

MIND BUILDER 8

9	36	7
4	23	8
7	24	6

Each number in the middle column is related in some way to the numbers on its left and right. Tell how they are related.

TEC44038

Note to the teacher: Give each student a copy of this page (or one card at a time) to work on during free time. Have them solve the problems on their own papers.

MATH

MIND BUILDERS

MIND BUILDER 1

Complete the grid with numbers that make a path of nine consecutive numbers through the grid. Draw arrows to show the path.

	19 →	20
	23	

TEC44039

MIND BUILDER 2

Each number 0–8 has been placed above or below the bar for a reason. Where should 9 be written: above or below the line? Why?

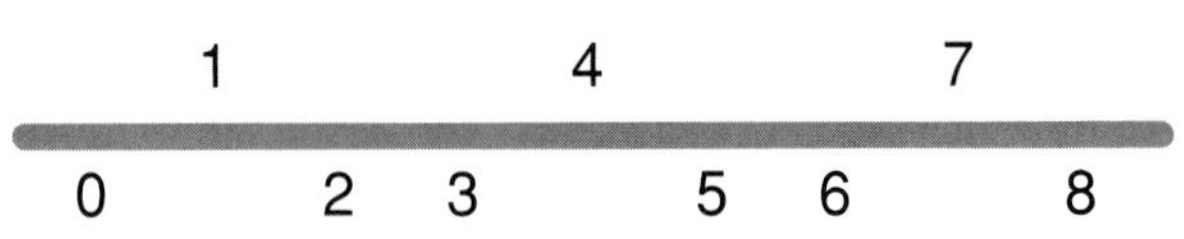

TEC44039

MIND BUILDER 3

Draw the next figure in the pattern. What is the pattern?

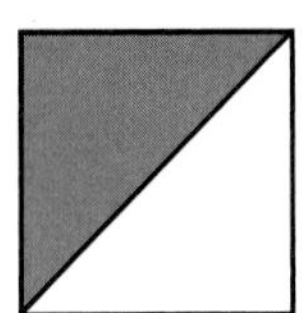
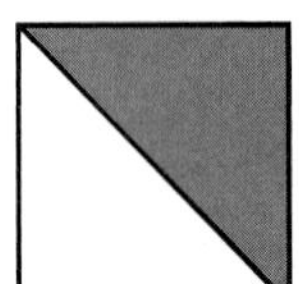
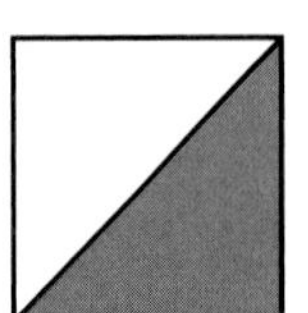
?

TEC44039

MIND BUILDER 4

The first set of scales balance. How many *Y*s will make the second set balance?

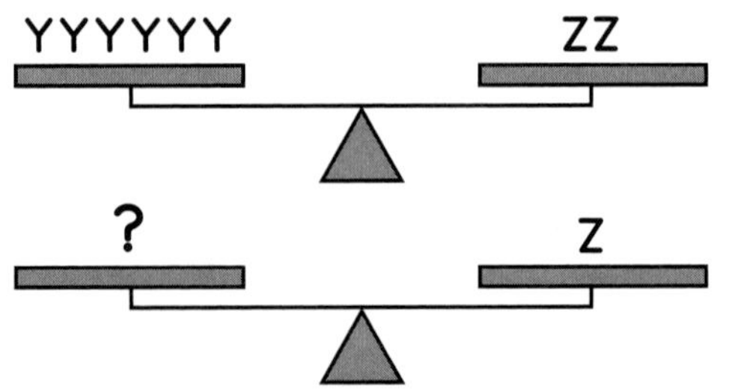

TEC44039

MIND BUILDER 5

Solve the problems. Write each answer as a roman numeral.

a. CLX + DXIX = ?
b. MDCCXLIV – DCCCVI = ?
c. CDIV x IX = ?
d. MMI ÷ III = ?

TEC44039

MIND BUILDER 6

Draw lines to divide the dog into six sections that each have the sum of 17.

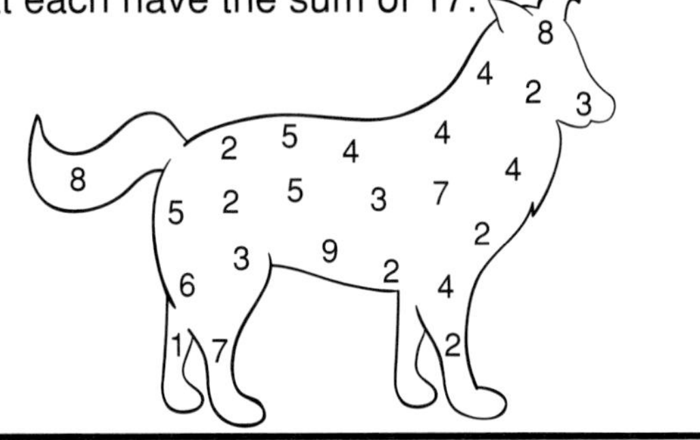

TEC44039

MIND BUILDER 7

The numbers in column D are related in some way to those in columns A, B, and C. What number should replace the question mark? Explain how the numbers are related.

A	B	C	D
6	4	3	8
4	9	6	6
12	5	10	6
7	8	4	?

TEC44039

MIND BUILDER 8

The numbers on each wedge of this dartboard have the same sum. The numbers on each ring also have the same sum. The same number should replace the six question marks. What is that number?

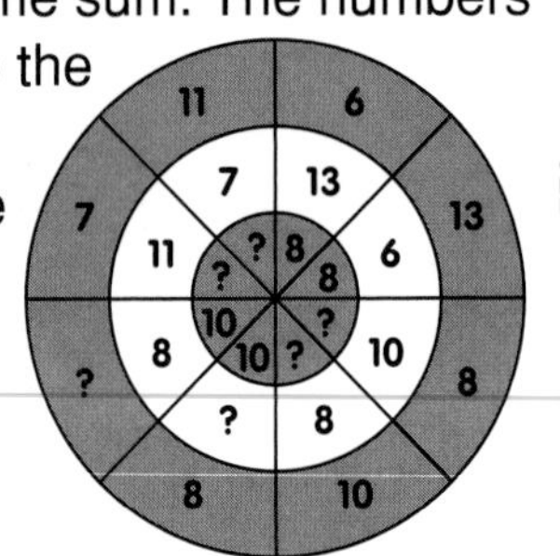

TEC44039

Note to the teacher: Give each student a copy of this page (or one card at a time) to work on during free time. Have the student solve the problems on a separate sheet of paper.

MIND BUILDER 1

Sort the numbers below into two groups that each have the same sum.

42 70 16 6 109 17 36

TEC44040

MIND BUILDER 2

How many ways can you make $1.00 with exactly 7 coins?

TEC44040

MIND BUILDER 3

The answer is 2%. List five possible questions.

TEC44040

MIND BUILDER 4

Wendy's bottle cap collection doubles every month. If she has 200 bottle caps in April, in what month did she have 50 bottle caps?

TEC44040

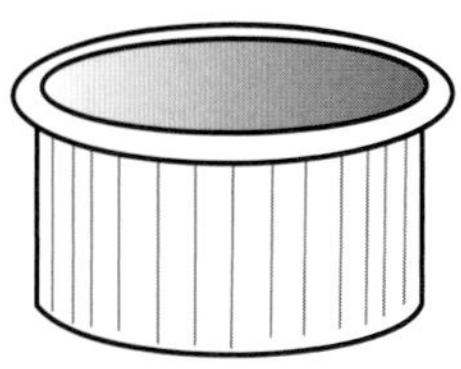

MIND BUILDER 5

On a clock, 11 + 2 = 1. Solve the clock math problems below.

a. 12 + 3 = ?

b. 6 + 6 = ?

c. 7 + 7 = ?

d. 10 + 5 = ?

TEC44040

MIND BUILDER 6

Use the digits *2, 3, 4,* and *7* to complete the problem below. Can you find *two* solutions?

TEC44040

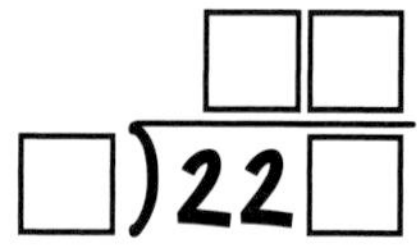

MIND BUILDER 7

How many triangles are in the figure below?

TEC44040

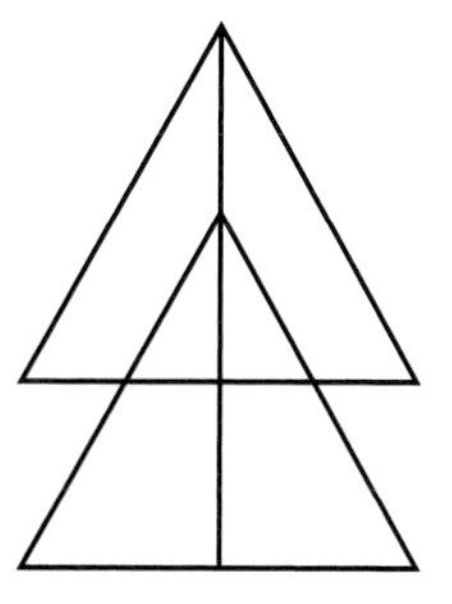

MIND BUILDER 8

Name an item that matches each measurement below.

a. about 5 inches

b. about 5 feet

c. about 5 yards

TEC44040

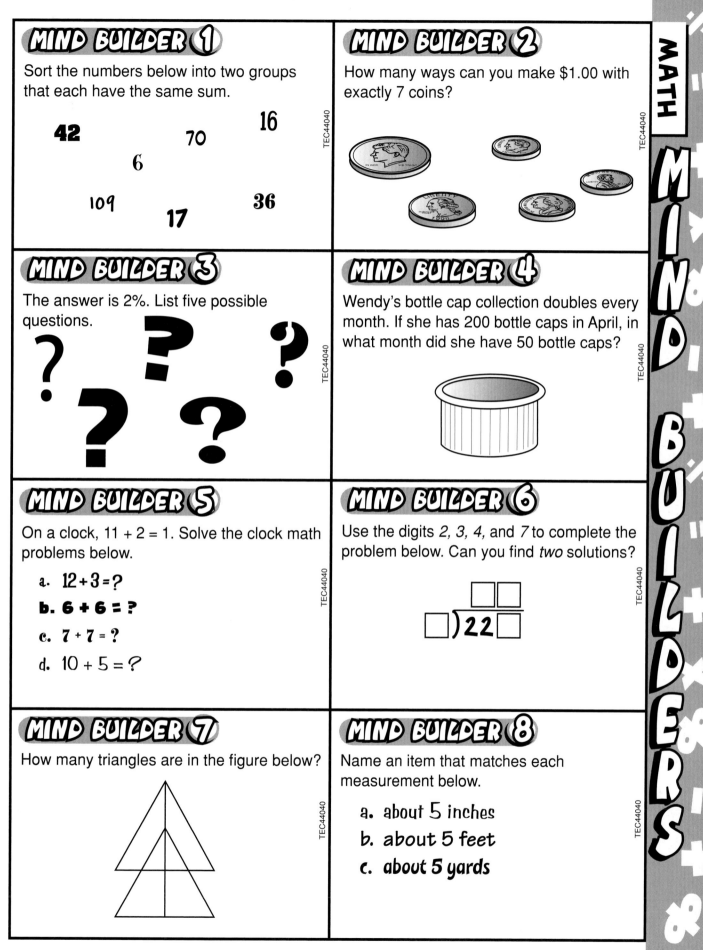

Note to the teacher: Give each student a copy of this page (or one card at a time) to work on during free time. Have the student solve the problems on a separate sheet of paper.

MATH

MIND BUILDERS

MIND BUILDER 1

If March 1 falls on a Monday, on what day of the week does April 1 fall?

Thursday? Monday? Tuesday? Wednesday? Saturday? Sunday? Friday?

TEC44041

MIND BUILDER 2

For each statement below, figure out what the letters stand for. For example, 12 = I in a F would be 12 inches in a foot.

a. 52 = W in a Y
b. 60 = S in a M
c. 16 = O in a P
d. 100 = C in a M
e. 2,000 = P in a T
f. 4 = Q in a G

TEC44041

MIND BUILDER 3

Name three factors of 12 whose sum is 11.

? + ? + ? = 11

TEC44041

MIND BUILDER 4

Which item will cost the least?

a. a $10 game at 25% off
b. a $16 CD at 50% off
c. an $18 T-shirt at 60% off

TEC44041

MIND BUILDER 5

Sort each number below into one of the three categories. (Hint: There are three numbers in each category.)

a. multiples of 9
b. odd numbers
c. three numbers whose sum is 30

3 6 9 11 15 18 21 27 45

TEC44041

MIND BUILDER 6

If this shape were dipped into a bucket of red paint, how many faces would be red?

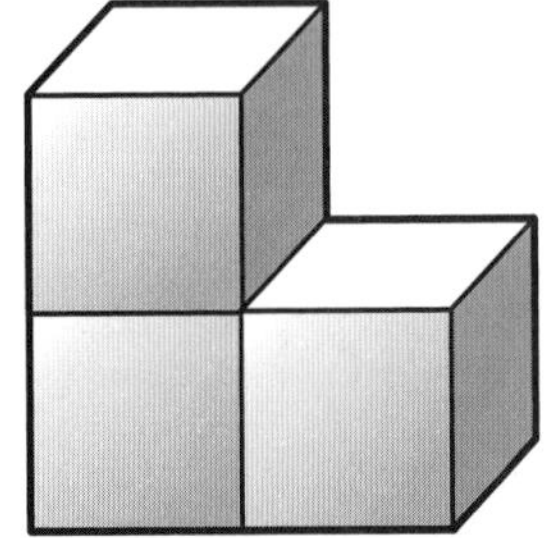

TEC44041

MIND BUILDER 7

If it takes 8 people 3 days to dig a ditch that is 1,000 feet long, how long will it take 4 people to dig a ditch that is 500 feet long?

TEC44041

MIND BUILDER 8

One beep equals three bops, and one bop equals two bams.

a. How many bams are in four bops?
b. How many bams are in four beeps?
c. How many beeps are in 30 bams?

TEC44041

Note to the teacher: Give each student a copy of this page (or one card at a time) to work on during free time. Have the student solve the problems on a separate sheet of paper.

MIND BUILDERS

MIND BUILDER 1

Kara walks 9 blocks to school. Each block is 65 feet long. How many yards does Kara walk each day to and from school?

TEC44042

MIND BUILDER 2

This is 1 square.

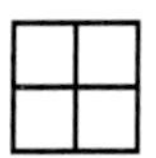

This grid has 5 squares.

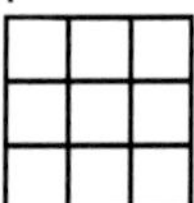

How many squares are in this grid?

TEC44042

MIND BUILDER 3

How many factors of this number are odd numbers?

120

TEC44042

MIND BUILDER 4

Rearrange the digits in this problem so the sum is 1,000.

$176 + 923$

Can you find *both* solutions?

TEC44042

MIND BUILDER 5

You've decided to play a trick on your brother. When he goes to bed at 9:30 PM, you turn his clock ahead 2 hours. Your brother sleeps for 9 hours. What time does the clock say when he wakes? What time is it really?

TEC44042

MIND BUILDER 6

If you have 7 pairs of socks and exactly 2 pairs have holes, 10 socks have no holes. In this situation, 7 pairs – 2 pairs = 10 socks, not 5.

Describe a situation that could represent this equation.

$$3 - 2 \neq 1$$

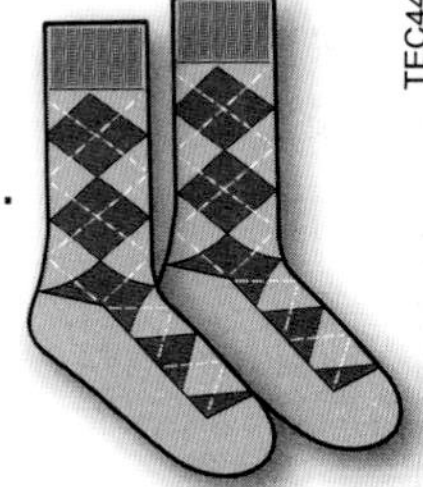

TEC44042

MIND BUILDER 7

These are Zinkles.

These are not Zinkles.

Which of these are Zinkles?

How do you know?

TEC44042

MIND BUILDER 8

Scott bought 6 dozen doughnuts for a party. He and each of his 8 guests ate 3 doughnuts apiece. How many dozen doughnuts were left at the end of Scott's party?

TEC44042

Note to the teacher: Give each student a copy of this page (or one card at a time) to work on during free time. Have the student solve the problems on a separate sheet of paper.

MATH

MIND BUILDERS

MIND BUILDER 1

If odd numbers are grapes and even numbers are pineapples, which fruit is the answer for each problem?

A. grapes + grapes = ?

B. grapes + pineapple = ?

C. grapes x pineapple = ?

TEC44043

MIND BUILDER 2

On what date is the 100th day of 2009?
On what date is the 200th day of 2009?

TEC44043

MIND BUILDER 3

Your birthday is in June. If your friend closes his eyes and randomly points to a date on a June calendar, what are the chances of that date being

A. your birthday?
B. an even numbered day?
C. a Sunday?

TEC44043

MIND BUILDER 4

Three friends played a game and totaled the points. Kyle had $\frac{2}{3}$ of the points. Kelsie had $\frac{1}{4}$ of the points, and Keith had $\frac{1}{9}$ of the points. Is this possible? Explain your answer.

TEC44043

MIND BUILDER 5

Add ( ), +, –, x, and/or ÷ to make each equation correct.

A. 3 15 9 = 18

B. 6 10 12 = 5

C. 13 5 12 6 = 16

TEC44043

MIND BUILDER 6

On Mars, 45 + 91 = 19, 134 + 267 = 23, and 236 + 99 = 29. Using Martian math, what is the sum of these numbers?

$$\begin{array}{r} 654 \\ +\ 218 \\ \hline \end{array}$$

TEC44043

MIND BUILDER 7

Four turtles are in a race. Myrtle is 4 inches ahead of Bertle. Gertle is 8 inches ahead of Nurtle, who is 6 inches behind Myrtle. From first place to last place, in what order are the turtles?

TEC44043

MIND BUILDER 8

These are the sums of some consecutive numbers squared.

$3^2 + 4^2 = 25$

$6^2 + 7^2 = 85$

$8^2 + 9^2 = 145$

What two consecutive numbers squared have a sum of 365?

TEC44043

Note to the teacher: Give each student a copy of this page (or one card at a time) to work on during free time. Have the student solve the problems on a separate sheet of paper.

Copy and cut out the cards to use as center or free-time activities.

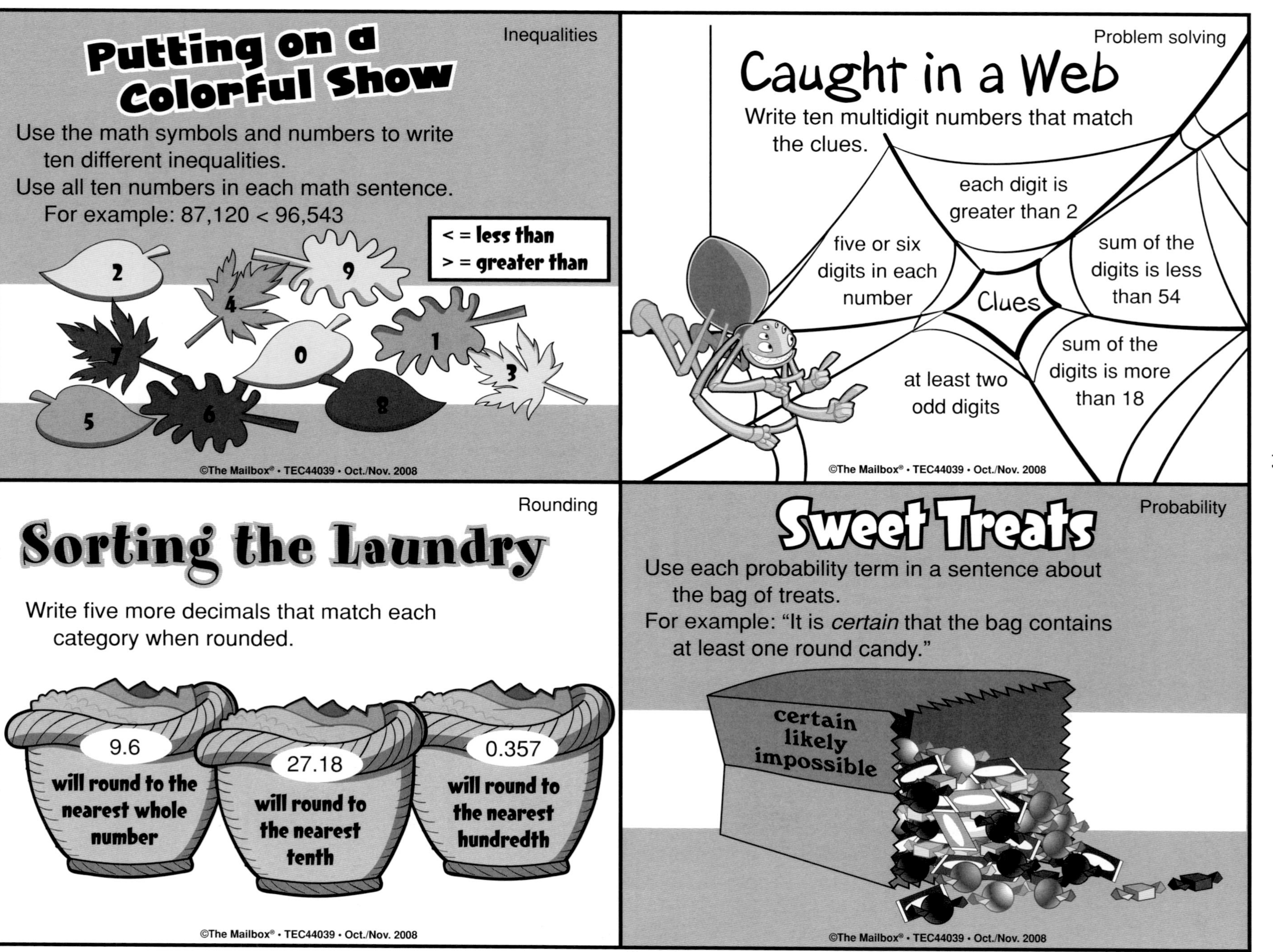

Inequalities
Putting on a Colorful Show
Use the math symbols and numbers to write ten different inequalities.
Use all ten numbers in each math sentence.
For example: 87,120 < 96,543
< = less than
> = greater than
2
9
4
7
0
1
3
5
6
8
©The Mailbox® • TEC44039 • Oct./Nov. 2008
Problem solving
Caught in a Web
Write ten multidigit numbers that match the clues.
Clues
each digit is greater than 2
five or six digits in each number
sum of the digits is less than 54
at least two odd digits
sum of the digits is more than 18
©The Mailbox® • TEC44039 • Oct./Nov. 2008
Rounding
Sorting the Laundry
Write five more decimals that match each category when rounded.
9.6
will round to the nearest whole number
27.18
will round to the nearest tenth
0.357
will round to the nearest hundredth
©The Mailbox® • TEC44039 • Oct./Nov. 2008
Probability
Sweet Treats
Use each probability term in a sentence about the bag of treats.
For example: "It is *certain* that the bag contains at least one round candy."
certain
likely
impossible
©The Mailbox® • TEC44039 • Oct./Nov. 2008

Math Activity Cards

Copy and cut out the cards to use as center or free-time activities.

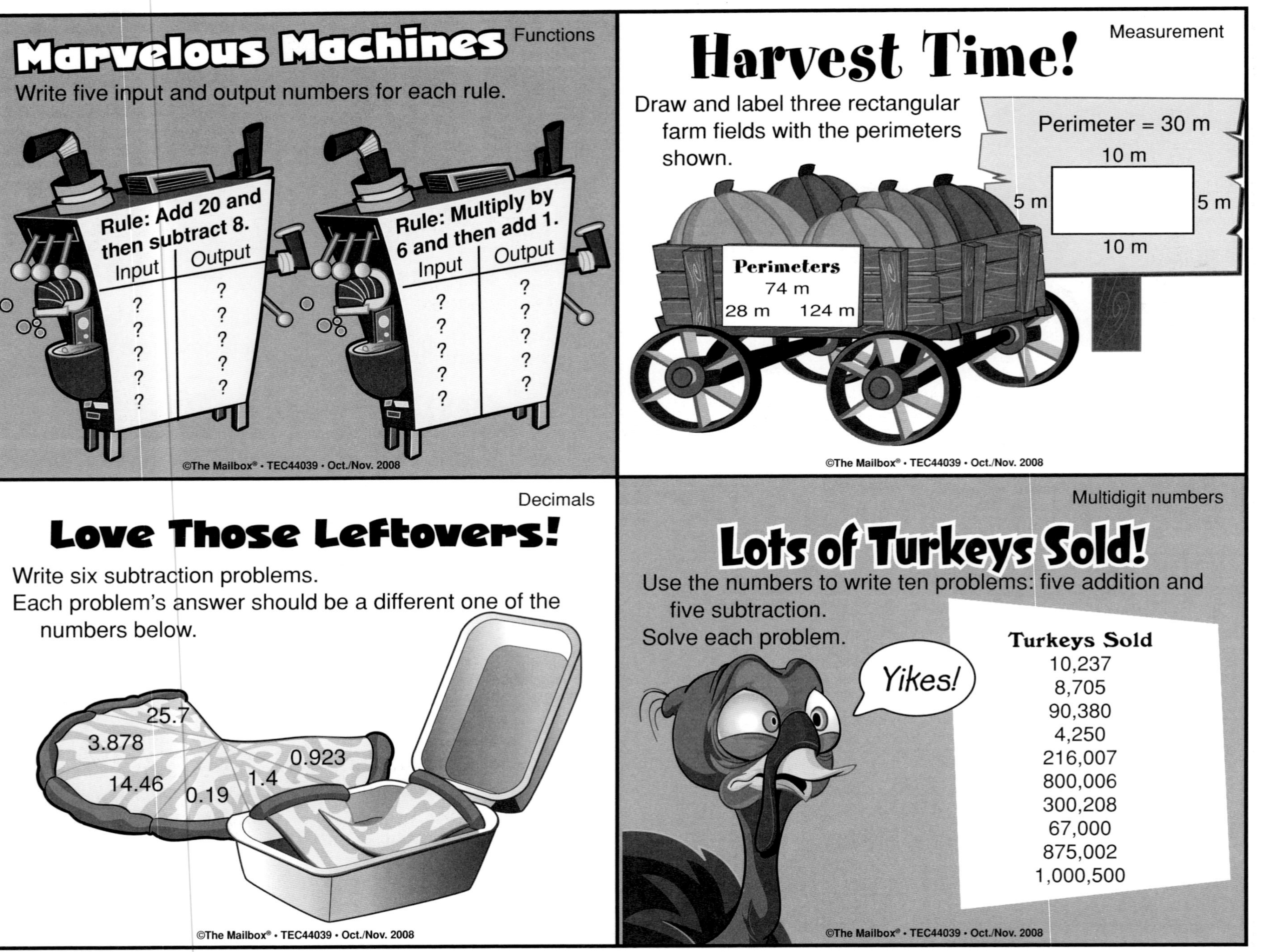

Marvelous Machines

Functions

Write five input and output numbers for each rule.

Rule: Add 20 and then subtract 8.
Input | Output
? ?
? ?
? ?
? ?
? ?
Rule: Multiply by 6 and then add 1.
Input | Output
? ?
? ?
? ?
? ?
? ?

Harvest Time!

Measurement

Draw and label three rectangular farm fields with the perimeters shown.

Love Those Leftovers!

Decimals

Write six subtraction problems.

Each problem's answer should be a different one of the numbers below.

Lots of Turkeys Sold!

Multidigit numbers

Use the numbers to write ten problems: five addition and five subtraction.

Solve each problem.

Turkeys Sold
10,237
8,705
90,380
4,250
216,007
800,006
300,208
67,000
875,002
1,000,500

Math Activity Cards

Copy and cut out the cards to use as center or free-time activities.

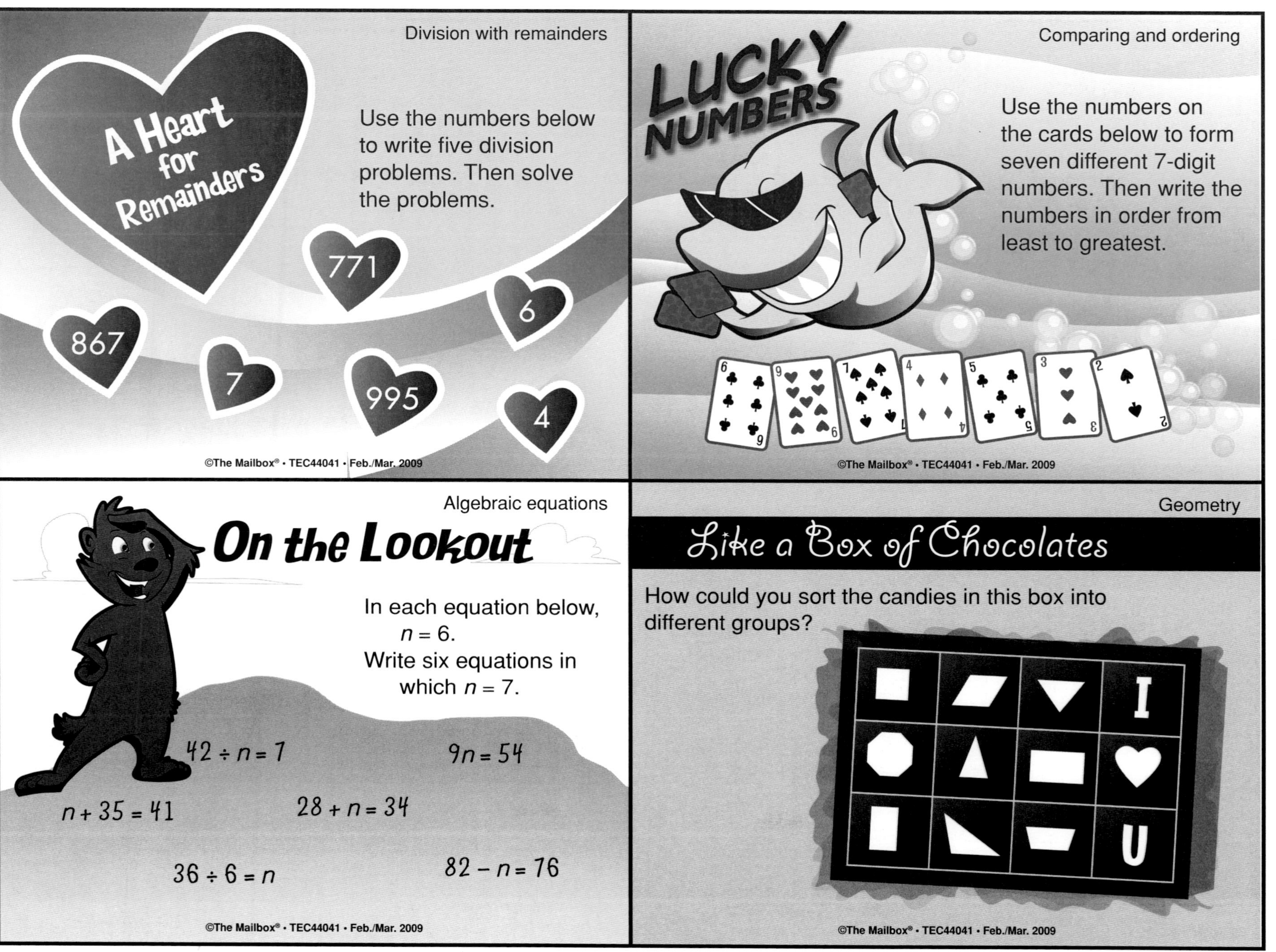

Division with remainders
A Heart for Remainders
Use the numbers below to write five division problems. Then solve the problems.
771
867
7
995
6
4
©The Mailbox® • TEC44041 • Feb./Mar. 2009
Comparing and ordering
LUCKY NUMBERS
Use the numbers on the cards below to form seven different 7-digit numbers. Then write the numbers in order from least to greatest.
6
9
7
4
5
3
2
©The Mailbox® • TEC44041 • Feb./Mar. 2009
Algebraic equations
On the Lookout
In each equation below, n = 6.
Write six equations in which n = 7.
42 ÷ n = 7
9n = 54
n + 35 = 41
28 + n = 34
36 ÷ 6 = n
82 – n = 76
©The Mailbox® • TEC44041 • Feb./Mar. 2009
Geometry
Like a Box of Chocolates
How could you sort the candies in this box into different groups?
I
U
©The Mailbox® • TEC44041 • Feb./Mar. 2009

Math Activity Cards

Copy and cut out the cards to use as center or free-time activities.

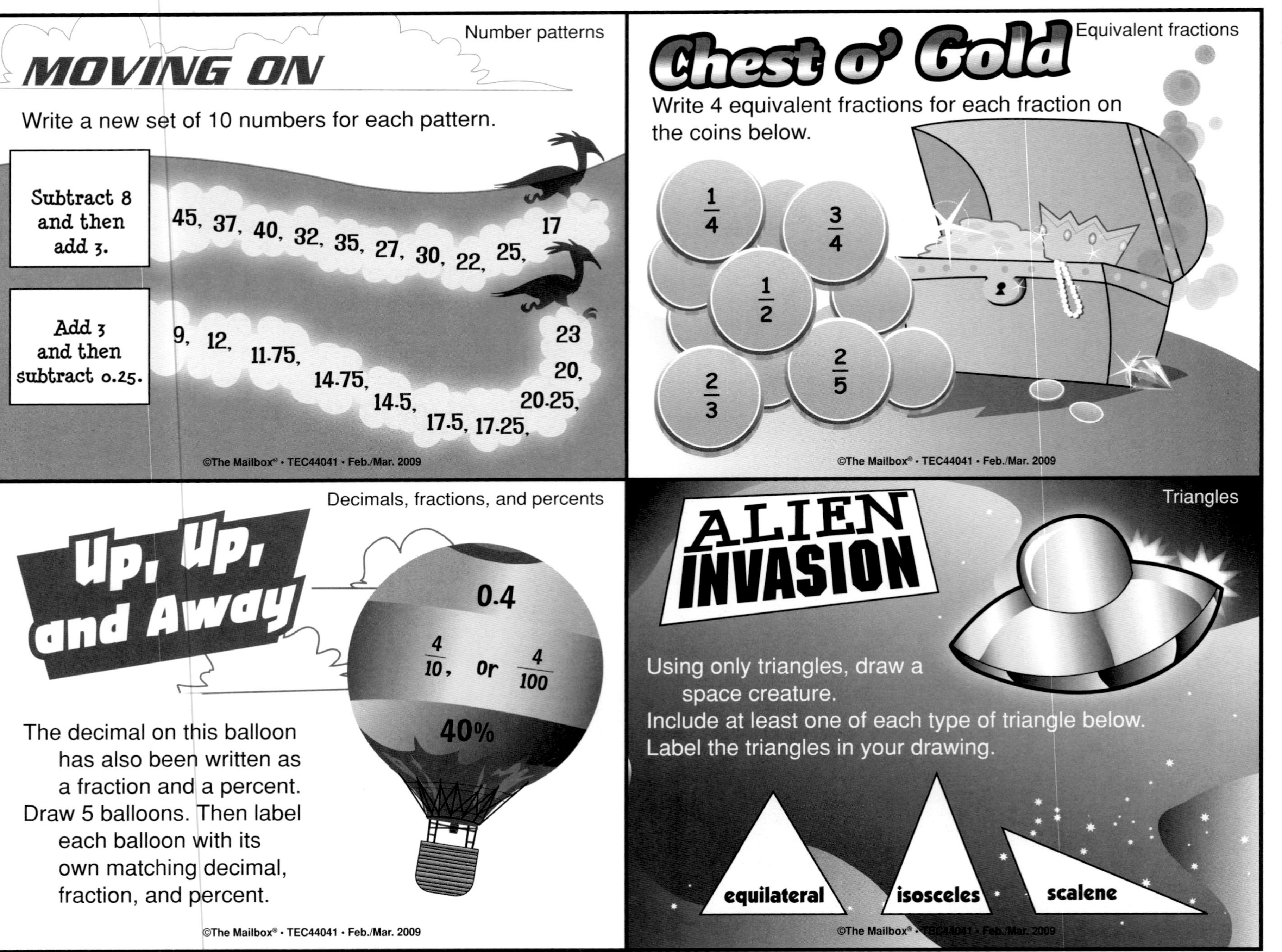

Number patterns
MOVING ON
Write a new set of 10 numbers for each pattern.
Subtract 8 and then add 3.
45, 37, 40, 32, 35, 27, 30, 22, 25, 17
Add 3 and then subtract 0.25.
9, 12, 11.75, 14.75, 14.5, 17.5, 17.25, 20.25, 20, 23
©The Mailbox® • TEC44041 • Feb./Mar. 2009
Equivalent fractions
Chest o' Gold
Write 4 equivalent fractions for each fraction on the coins below.
1/4
3/4
1/2
2/3
2/5
©The Mailbox® • TEC44041 • Feb./Mar. 2009
Decimals, fractions, and percents
Up, Up, and Away
0.4
4/10, or 4/100
40%
The decimal on this balloon has also been written as a fraction and a percent. Draw 5 balloons. Then label each balloon with its own matching decimal, fraction, and percent.
©The Mailbox® • TEC44041 • Feb./Mar. 2009
Triangles
ALIEN INVASION
Using only triangles, draw a space creature.
Include at least one of each type of triangle below.
Label the triangles in your drawing.
equilateral
isosceles
scalene
©The Mailbox® • TEC44041 • Feb./Mar. 2009

Elapsed time

Waiting in Line

You are the 7th person in line to buy a concert ticket.
Roll two dice to determine how many seconds you must wait before you can move up one space.
Then calculate how long you'll wait until you're first in line.
Write your answer in minutes and seconds.

TEC44043

Adding fractions

What a Catch!

Choose a fraction. Use it and another addend to write a problem whose sum is less than 1.
Repeat with each remaining fraction until you have written six different problems.

TEC44043

Averages

Time Me!

List five different decimals between 2.9 and 8.6.
Find their average. Round the quotient to the nearest tenth.
Repeat the steps using seven different decimals between 5.7 and 6.45.

TEC44043

Problem solving

Use numbers from the boxes to write four word problems.
Write one addition problem, one subtraction problem, one multiplication problem, and one division problem.

TEC44043

Math Activity Cards

Copy and cut out the cards to use as center or free-time activities.

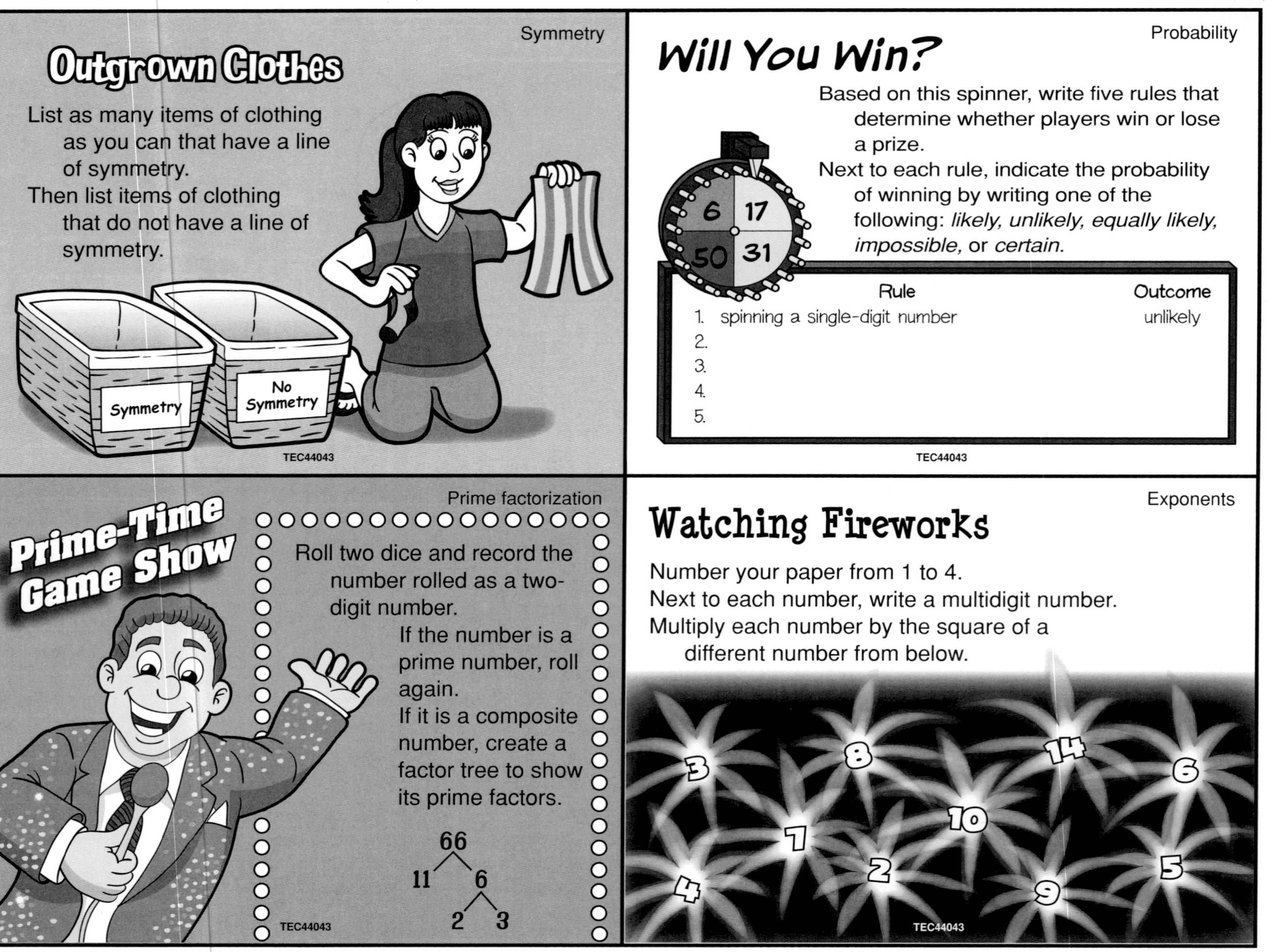

Symmetry

Outgrown Clothes

List as many items of clothing as you can that have a line of symmetry.

Then list items of clothing that do not have a line of symmetry.

TEC44043

Probability

Will You Win?

Based on this spinner, write five rules that determine whether players win or lose a prize.

Next to each rule, indicate the probability of winning by writing one of the following: *likely, unlikely, equally likely, impossible,* or *certain.*

Rule	Outcome
1. spinning a single-digit number	unlikely
2.	
3.	
4.	
5.	

TEC44043

Prime factorization

Prime-Time Game Show

Roll two dice and record the number rolled as a two-digit number.

If the number is a prime number, roll again.

If it is a composite number, create a factor tree to show its prime factors.

TEC44043

Exponents

Watching Fireworks

Number your paper from 1 to 4.

Next to each number, write a multidigit number.

Multiply each number by the square of a different number from below.

TEC44043

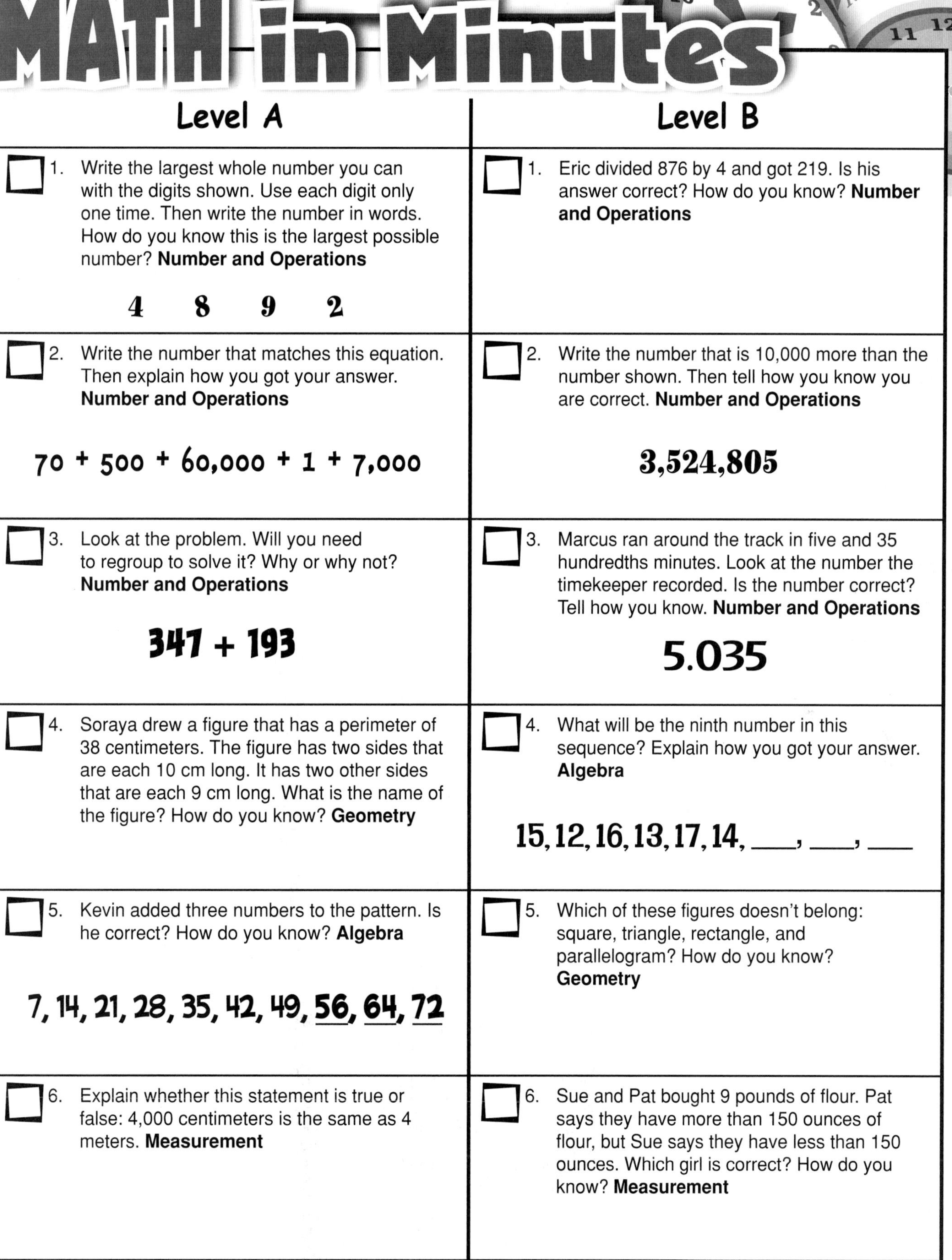

MATH in Minutes

Name

Level A	Level B
1. Write the largest whole number you can with the digits shown. Use each digit only one time. Then write the number in words. How do you know this is the largest possible number? **Number and Operations** **4 8 9 2**	1. Eric divided 876 by 4 and got 219. Is his answer correct? How do you know? **Number and Operations**
2. Write the number that matches this equation. Then explain how you got your answer. **Number and Operations** **70 + 500 + 60,000 + 1 + 7,000**	2. Write the number that is 10,000 more than the number shown. Then tell how you know you are correct. **Number and Operations** **3,524,805**
3. Look at the problem. Will you need to regroup to solve it? Why or why not? **Number and Operations** **347 + 193**	3. Marcus ran around the track in five and 35 hundredths minutes. Look at the number the timekeeper recorded. Is the number correct? Tell how you know. **Number and Operations** **5.035**
4. Soraya drew a figure that has a perimeter of 38 centimeters. The figure has two sides that are each 10 cm long. It has two other sides that are each 9 cm long. What is the name of the figure? How do you know? **Geometry**	4. What will be the ninth number in this sequence? Explain how you got your answer. **Algebra** **15, 12, 16, 13, 17, 14, ___, ___, ___**
5. Kevin added three numbers to the pattern. Is he correct? How do you know? **Algebra** **7, 14, 21, 28, 35, 42, 49, 56, 64, 72**	5. Which of these figures doesn't belong: square, triangle, rectangle, and parallelogram? How do you know? **Geometry**
6. Explain whether this statement is true or false: 4,000 centimeters is the same as 4 meters. **Measurement**	6. Sue and Pat bought 9 pounds of flour. Pat says they have more than 150 ounces of flour, but Sue says they have less than 150 ounces. Which girl is correct? How do you know? **Measurement**

Note to the teacher: Photocopy the entire page, one level, or selected problems to distribute to students. When a student solves a problem, he checks its box.

Name

MATH in Minutes

Level A

☐ 1. Chad's dad changes the oil in his car once every 3,000 miles. Since the last oil change, the car has been driven 1,268 miles. How many more miles can the car be driven before its oil is changed? Explain how you solved this problem. **Number and Operations**

☐ 2. Carrie's neighbor is younger than 50 but older than 30. The product of the digits of her age is a multiple of five. The digits in her age are not the same but both are odd numbers. How old is Carrie's neighbor? How do you know? **Number and Operations**

☐ 3. Erin wants to pack 330 cookies in eight boxes. If each box can hold exactly 36 cookies, does she have enough boxes? Explain. **Number and Operations**

Cookies

☐ 4. The length of a school sidewalk is 9,000 centimeters. Renee thinks this measurement is the same as 9 meters. Patrick says it's 90 meters. Who is correct? How do you know? **Measurement**

☐ 5. Lewis drew a scalene triangle. One side measures 22 centimeters. Another side measures 14 centimeters. Brad knows the length of the third side is neither 14 centimeters nor 22 centimeters. How does Brad know this? **Geometry**

☐ 6. Study the line plot. Based on its data, about how many text messages should you expect to get in a day? How can you tell? **Data Analysis and Probability**

7	8	9	10	11	12	13
				X		
				X	X	
		X	X	X	X	X
X	X	X	X	X	X	X

Number of Text Messages per Day

Level B

☐ 1. What is the sum of eight and nine tenths and nine and eight tenths? Explain how you know. **Number and Operations**

☐ 2. In this subtraction problem, 6.4 is written as 6.40. Could it also be written as 6.04? Explain why or why not. **Number and Operations**

$$\begin{array}{r} 15.69 \\ -6.40 \\ \hline \end{array}$$

☐ 3. There are 2,000 athletes entered in a state gymnastics contest. There are 12 boxes of ribbons with 175 ribbons in each box. Are there enough ribbons for each athlete to get one? How do you know? **Number and Operations**

☐ 4. Lexie and Ava bought 160 ounces of sugar to make fudge for a school carnival. Ava thinks they have ten pounds of sugar. Lexie thinks they have five pounds of sugar. Which girl is correct? Explain your answer. **Measurement**

☐ 5. A triangle, an octagon, a trapezoid, a hexagon, and a quadrilateral are in a row. The figure with the most sides is first. The figure with just one pair of parallel sides is second. The figure with six sides is right after the trapezoid. The figure with the least number of sides is right before the quadrilateral. What is the order of the shapes? How do you know? **Geometry**

☐ 6. This stem-and-leaf plot shows the number of pies the local baker baked last week from Monday to Saturday. How many pies were baked in all? How do you know? **Data Analysis and Probability**

Number of Pies Baked

Stem	Leaves		
1	2	4	
2	4	6	7
3	5		

Note to the teacher: Photocopy the entire page, one level, or selected problems to distribute to students. When a student solves a problem, he checks its box.

Name

MATH in Minutes

Level A	Level B
☐ 1. A roller coaster has a minimum height restriction of 48 cm. Jeff is 44.6 cm tall. How much must he grow to be able to ride? Explain how you know you are correct. **Number and Operations**	☐ 1. The starting number is $\frac{3}{4}$. Cory multiplied it by $\frac{1}{2}$ and got $\frac{3}{8}$. Is his answer larger or smaller than the starting number? How do you know you are correct? **Number and Operations**
☐ 2. What is the largest four-digit number that will round to 1,000? Tell how you know you are correct. **Number and Operations**	☐ 2. Find the largest possible product of a 3-digit number and a 2-digit number. Explain how you know you are correct. **Number and Operations** ☐☐☐ x ☐☐
☐ 3. Can the product of 499 and 49 be greater than 25,000? Why or why not? **Number and Operations** 499 x 49	☐ 3. The tallest giraffe in a zoo stands 14.8 meters tall. The shortest giraffe measures 11.45 meters tall. Is the difference in their heights greater than 3.25 meters? Tell how you know you are correct. **Number and Operations**
☐ 4. A pitcher of lemonade holds 6 pints. There are 10 guests at a party and each party cup holds 8 ounces. Can each guest be served a full cup? How do you know you are correct? **Measurement**	☐ 4. Can both a rectangle and a square have an area of 36 square units? Draw pictures to show your answer. Explain how you know your answer is correct. **Geometry**
☐ 5. What numbers can replace each shape to make both equations true? Explain how you got your answer. **Algebra** ♡ + ☺ = 15; ♡ − ☺ = 3	☐ 5. Write the next two numbers in the pattern shown. Is there more than one correct answer? Why or why not? **Algebra** 1, 2, 4, ____, ____
☐ 6. List three common attributes of a square and a rectangle. **Geometry**	☐ 6. Devin collected water from a leaky bathroom faucet in the amounts shown. Did the faucet leak more than a gallon of water? How do you know you are correct? **Measurement** 2 cups, 1 pint, 3 cups, 8 ounces

Note to the teacher: Photocopy the entire page, one level, or selected problems to distribute to students. When a student solves a problem, he checks its box.

Name

MATH in Minutes

Level A	Level B
☐ 1. The middle digit in the number below has been erased. If the number were divisible by 3, which digits could fit in the erased space? How do you know you are correct? **Number and Operations** 4 _ 1	☐ 1. If the mystery number below is divisible by 9, what is the smallest 4-digit number possible keeping the given digits? The largest number possible? Explain how you got your answer. **Number and Operations** 2, ? ? 4
☐ 2. Colin ran 4.65 miles. Jaden ran 0.2 miles farther than Colin. How far did Jaden run? Explain how you solved this problem. **Number and Operations** DISTANCE TRAVELED 0.2 Miles	☐ 2. Write these numbers in order from least to greatest to show how the number line below should be labeled. Explain how you know where each number should be. **Number and Operations** 0.75 0.5 0 1 0.25 0.8 0.19
☐ 3. Angie is making 3 batches of chocolate chip cookies for a bake sale. The recipe calls for $\frac{2}{3}$ cup of flour. She has $1\frac{3}{4}$ cups of flour. Does she have enough flour to bake all 3 batches? Explain your answer. **Number and Operations**	☐ 3. Write a 3-digit number and a 2-digit number whose product is 36,000. How do you know your answer is correct? **Number and Operations** ☐☐☐ x ☐☐ = 36,000
☐ 4. If x is greater than 8.5 but less than 8.6, what number could x be? How do you know you are correct? **Algebra** x=?	☐ 4. Which event below has the greater probability when rolling a die? Explain how you got your answer. **Data Analysis and Probability** a. getting an even number that is a multiple of 3 b. getting an even number or a multiple of 3
☐ 5. To decide who goes first in a board game, Hannah suggests flipping a coin and calling heads or tails. Megan insists that rolling a die and calling even or odd will have the same result. Is Megan correct? Explain your answer. **Data Analysis and Probability**	☐ 5. According to this graph, was the yearly rainfall more than one meter? How do you know your answer is correct? **Measurement** Rainfall (cm): 0–20; Month: Jan. Feb. Mar. Apr. May June July Aug. Sept. Oct. Nov. Dec.
☐ 6. Kara measures a window that is $1\frac{1}{2}$ meters wide. She finds blinds in 3 widths at the store: 80 cm, 120 cm, and 150 cm. Which blinds should she buy? How do you know? **Measurement** Window Blinds	☐ 6. One angle in a triangle measures 100°. If the triangle is isosceles, what are the measurements of the other two angles? How do you know? **Geometry** 100°

Note to the teacher: Photocopy the entire page, one level, or selected problems to distribute to students. When a student solves a problem, he checks its box.

Name

MATH in Minutes

Level A	Level B
1. Is the product of this problem closer to 0 or 1? How do you know? **Number and Operations** **$0.5 \times 0.5 = ?$**	1. What number between 8 and 15 has factors whose sum is 28? Explain how you found your answer. **Number and Operations**
2. Bill is buying a used convertible for the price shown. If he also buys new tires at $100 per tire, which place values in the car's cost will change? Explain your answer. **Number and Operations** $19,748	2. Joey's mom ordered 8 pizzas for his birthday party. Joey and each of his guests ate $\frac{2}{3}$ of a pizza. If all the pizzas were eaten, how many guests came to Joey's party? How do you know? **Number and Operations**
3. Which of these numbers is not equal to $\frac{4}{3}$? Explain how you know. **Number and Operations** $\frac{8}{6}$ $1\frac{3}{6}$ $1\frac{1}{3}$ $1\frac{9}{27}$ $1\frac{5}{15}$	3. This is the cost to charter a bus for a field trip to the state capitol. If 24 students go on the trip, will each child pay more or less than $120? Why? **Number and Operations** $2,832
4. Joni adds 4 sit-ups to her workout each day. On Wednesday, she did 20 sit-ups. At this rate, will she be able to do 50 sit-ups by next Wednesday? Explain your answer. **Algebra**	4. A recipe for chocolate chip cookies calls for 12 ounces of chips. If a store has only 1-pound bags of chips, how many bags should Heather buy to make 4 batches of cookies? Explain your answer. **Measurement** CHIPS
5. Three boys are building a project with their scout troop. Mark is using a board that is $\frac{1}{2}$m long. Eric's board is 10 cm long, and Felipe's board is 200 cm long. Which boy is using the longest piece of wood? How do you know? **Measurement**	5. Based on this graph, what is the average number of fourth-, fifth-, and sixth-grade girls who own a horse? Explain how you found your answer. **Data Analysis and Probability** Horse Owners number of students: 0, 2, 4, 6, 8, 10 grade level: 4th, 5th, 6th girls, boys
6. What is the sum of the number of faces, edges, and vertices on a cube? How does this sum compare with the total number of faces, edges, and vertices on a rectangular prism? Explain your answer. **Geometry**	6. Cutting this square in half diagonally forms two equal triangles. What is the area of each triangle? What is the area of a triangle that has a 3-inch base and a height of 5 inches? Explain your answer. **Geometry** 4 in. 4 in.

Note to the teacher: Photocopy the entire page, one level, or selected problems to distribute to students. When a student solves a problem, he checks its box.

Name

MATH in Minutes

Level A

☐ 1. Susan's recipe for sugar cookies calls for $\frac{2}{3}$ cup sugar. If she sprinkles $\frac{1}{4}$ of that amount on top of the cookies, how much sugar will be sprinkled on top? Explain how you got your answer. **Number and Operations**

☐ 2. Students at Will's school visit a planetarium every 5 years and the state capitol every 2 years. If Will visited both places during the 2007–2008 school year, how many years will it be before both places are visited again during the same school year? How do you know? **Number and Operations**

☐ 3. If Jessie saves 25% of the $200 he needs to attend baseball camp, his parents will pay the rest. Jessie has $30. Has he saved enough? Explain how you got your answer. **Number and Operations**

☐ 4. This plot shows the rolls of wrapping paper sold by each student in Mr. Chesney's class. Tina sold 13 rolls. Becky sold the most. How many more rolls did Becky sell than Tina? How do you know? **Data Analysis and Probability**

Stem	Leaves
3	1 4
2	0 1 6 6
1	1 2 2 3 4
0	4 5 6 8

☐ 5. Brad thinks the boldfaced square in this grid was moved from position A to position B just using translations. Cindy thinks it was moved just using reflections. Chad thinks it was moved just using rotations. Who is right? Explain how you know. **Geometry**

A	
	B

☐ 6. If this sign were next to a bridge, would a 10-ton truck be able to cross the bridge safely? Why or why not? **Measurement**

Weight Limit
18,000 lb.

Level B

☐ 1. The student council is covering 22 cafeteria tables with plastic for a teacher appreciation party. If each table needs 8.5 feet of plastic, will a 200-foot roll of plastic be enough? Why or why not? **Number and Operations**

☐ 2. Forty percent of Ms. Johnson's 30 students earned perfect attendance for the school year. The school record in any classroom is 13 students. Did her class break the record? How do you know? **Number and Operations**

☐ 3. If the estimated product of 98 and a number is 3,000, what is the number? Explain your thinking. **Number and Operations**

$$98 \times ? \approx 3{,}000$$

☐ 4. Study the balance scales. What is the missing number? How do you know? **Algebra**

● = 12 ■ = 4 ▲ = 3

3■ | 4▲ 8▲ | 2● 1● | ?■

☐ 5. An ice cream shop offers 12 flavors of ice cream on sugar cones, waffle cones, or plain cones. If Emily picks 1 flavor of ice cream and 1 type of cone, how many possible combinations can she choose? Explain how you know. **Data Analysis and Probability**

☐ 6. Abby and Joel are on the same track team. If Abby runs the 5-kilometer cross-country event and Joel runs the 1,600-meter event, which team member runs the longer distance? How do you know? **Measurement**

Note to the teacher: Photocopy the entire page or one level to distribute to students. When a student solves a problem, he checks its box.

SIMPLY SCIENCE

Layer by Layer

Earth science

These edible models invite students to explore the three main layers of soil. In advance, prepare a package of chocolate pudding. For the activity, give each student two chocolate sandwich cookies, a clear plastic cup, and a plastic spoon. Instruct each student to place one cookie in his cup (bedrock) and then coarsely crumble his other cookie on top (subsoil). Next, place a dollop of chocolate pudding in each student's cup (topsoil). Have the student use his spoon to eat his soil and explore the layers' properties. Follow up by discussing how the food items represent the layers in real soil. *(The uncrumbled cookie is hard and solid like bedrock, the crumbled cookie resembles small rocks like those found in subsoil, and the pudding is soft and dark like topsoil.)*

Samantha Mongrain, Mount Savage Elementary, Mount Savage, MD

Interesting Interviews

Life science

Interview With a Cactus

Reporter: So tell me, where do you like to live?

Cactus: I like to live in places that are hot and dry. I especially enjoy Mexico and the southwestern states like Arizona.

Reporter: What are some things that help you survive, especially in such a dry climate?

Cactus: Well, I have a thick, fleshy stem with waxy skin. My stem holds lots of water, and my skin keeps the water from evaporating from the heat. I also have really long roots, which help me collect water for storage. My spines help protect me from animals.

Reporter: What kinds of things are you used for?

Cactus: Many small animals build their nests in me or use my spines to hide from their enemies. I also provide food for people. Some people eat my fruit, and some people grind my seeds into a kind of meal for cakes. People all over the world also grow

To begin this fun partner activity about plants, have each pair of students choose a plant they would like to learn more about. Then have each duo research its plant to discover the plant's habitat, needs, uses, problems, and other interesting information. Direct each pair of students to write the dialogue from an interview between a reporter and the plant, using their research to generate questions and answers. Finally, have one partner play the role of the reporter and the other the role of the plant as they perform their interview for the class.

Mary Ann Etling, St. Louis, MO

Marker Mixes

Physical science

This small-group activity helps students explore the properties of mixtures. To begin, explain that a *mixture* is a substance made of two or more different kinds of matter, each of which keeps its own physical properties. Give each group a copy of page 234 and the materials listed on it. Direct students to follow the steps on page 234 to complete the activity. Follow up by asking, "Does a watercolor marker contain a mixture?" Guide students to conclude that the answer is yes because the ink from a marker separates into more than one color when wet.

Dr. Barbara B. Leonard, Winston-Salem, NC

Name ____

WHEN IT STRIKES!

Lightning is a powerful force. A single lightning bolt can be more than five miles long. When lightning strikes, it can release up to 100 million electrical volts. It can heat up the air around it to near 50,000°F. Because of lightning's power, people have to stay out of its way. If you are in a house during a thunderstorm, stay there. If you are outside but can get inside a house or other building, go. If you are inside a metal car, close the windows and stay there. If you get caught in a field or open area, sit down or squat to stay low. Don't hide under a tall tree. Don't stand on top of a hill, on the beach, or in a field. Finally, stay away from water until the storm has cleared.

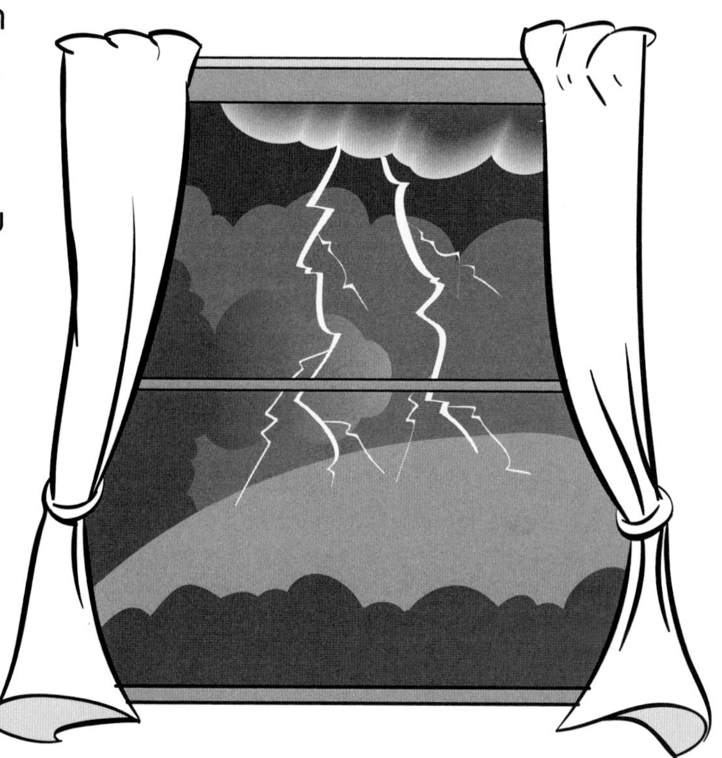

A lightning bolt is just about one to two inches wide!

Decide whether each sentence is true or false. Then color the correct lightning bolt.

1. A lightning bolt can be more than five miles long.
2. We use lightning to make electricity.
3. It is safe to stand under a tree in a thunderstorm.
4. A lightning bolt can let go millions of electrical volts.
5. You should stay low to the ground in a thunderstorm.
6. Lightning can heat the water around it up to more than 50,000°F.

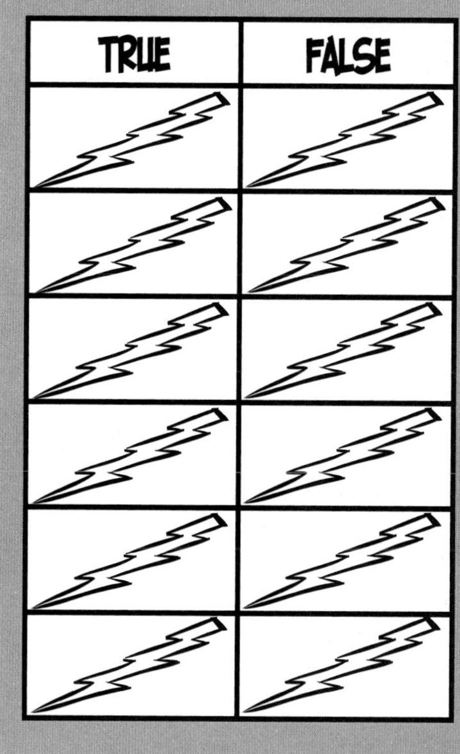

Name ______________________________

Marker Mixes

Materials:
3 different watercolor markers
scissors
coffee filter
ruler
small cup of water

Steps:

1. On the chart below, list each marker. Then predict which colors you think make up each marker's ink.
2. Cut the coffee filter into three strips.
3. Using a different-colored marker for each strip, draw a dot about a half inch from the bottom of each strip.
4. Place the marked end of one strip in the container of water. Make sure the water does *not* touch the colored dot.
5. After the absorbed water reaches the dot, set the strip aside to dry. When it's dry, observe the colors and record the information on the chart below.
6. Repeat Steps 4 and 5 with each remaining strip.

Marker	Color	Prediction	Actual
1			
2			
3			

 Note to the teacher: Use with "Marker Mixes" on page 232.

Simply Science

Battle of the Bones
Skeletal system

Review the major bones of the body with this fun game. Give each team a copy of page 238 to cut out and assemble as a human skeleton. Next, call out the name of a bone. Have a member from each team find that bone in its skeleton and point it out to you. Award a point to the first student who points out the correct bone. Continue in this manner, having team members take turns finding the bones. The team with the most points when all bones have been identified wins.

Juli Engel, Tyler, TX

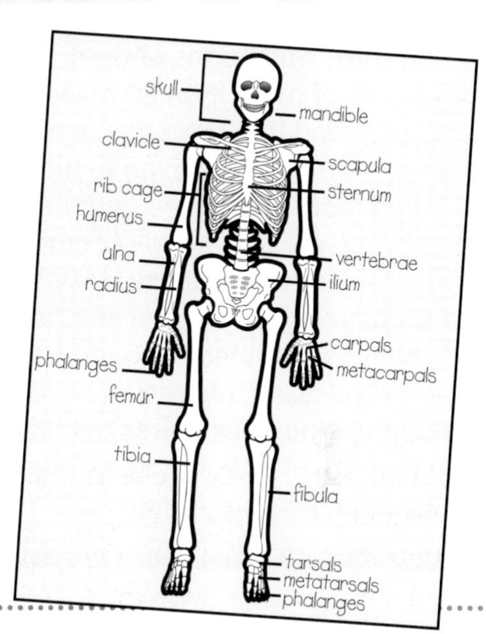

Totally Tubular!
Sound

For this cool hands-on experiment with sound reflection, arrange the listed materials in a quiet location as shown. Then guide pairs of students through the steps below.

Materials: cookie sheet; two paper-towel tubes; resealable plastic bag filled with several pairs of textured items (tissues, pipe cleaners, balloons, paintbrushes, toothpicks, cotton swabs, or feathers)

Steps:
1. One child places his ear where indicated and closes his eyes, while his partner lightly rubs each item pair together where indicated.
2. The listener then records his observations on notebook paper.
3. The pair repeats the experiment without the cookie sheet and records any new observations.
4. The child explains on his paper why he only heard sounds with the cookie sheet; then he switches places with his partner. *(The cookie sheet is a smooth surface, so sounds reflect more clearly from it than they do from a rough surface or without using the cookie sheet.)*

Jennifer Otter, Oak Ridge, NC

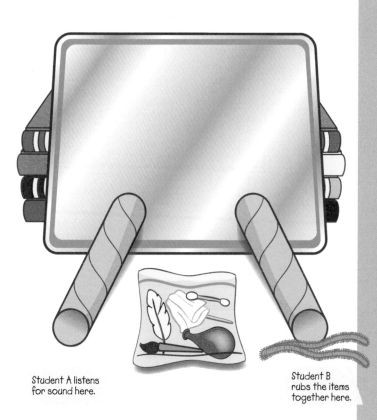

Student A listens for sound here.

Student B rubs the items together here.

Name ______________________________

Batty Behaviors

Even though they can fly, bats are not birds.

Bats are small, furry animals. They are warm-blooded and nurse their young with milk. This means that bats are mammals, but they are the only mammals that fly. Bats can have wingspans of up to $6\frac{1}{2}$ feet and can also fly at speeds of more than 30 miles per hour! They can even digest food in 20 minutes, which helps them carry less weight while flying. Even though only the largest bats weigh more than three pounds, all bats are still quite impressive. Bats usually come out only at night. To help them survive in the dark, they have excellent vision and a great sense of smell. Their hearing isn't too bad either. Bats use echoes of sounds they make to explore their surroundings. Bats rest during the day. Many bats hang upside down to rest, while others have been known to rest upright or even sideways. For such small animals, bats sure are remarkable mammals!

Word Bank

mammal	blind	largest
fly	echo	digest
wingspan	survive	thirty
night	upside down	smell
six	warm-blooded	sideways

Use the word bank to complete the puzzle. Some words will not be used.

Down

2. Bats _____ food quickly to fly better.
3. A bat's _____ can be as wide as a human is tall.
5. Bats are the only mammals that can _____.
7. Some bats rest _____ instead of upright or upside down.
10. Bats are not _____. They have excellent vision.

Across

1. Many bats like to hang _____ to rest.
4. An _____ is a repeating sound caused by reflected sound waves.
6. The _____ bats weigh more than three pounds.
8. Some bats can fly at speeds of over _____ miles per hour.
9. A _____ is an animal that feeds its young milk.
11. Most bats usually come out at _____.
12. To help them _____, bats have good sight, good hearing, and a good sense of smell.

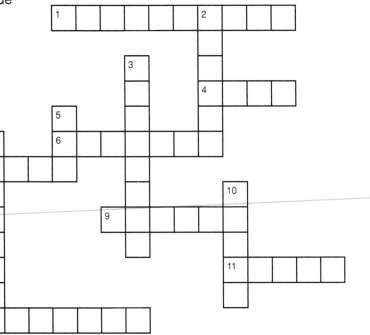

Name ____________________

SPACE EXPLORERS

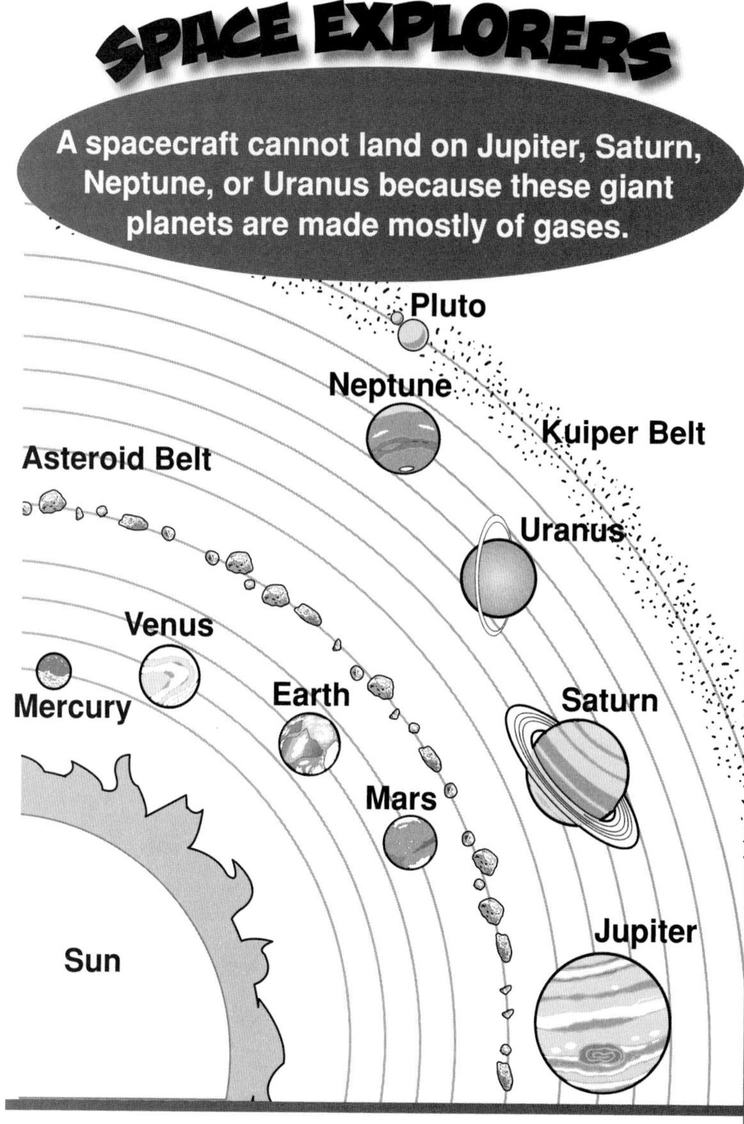

People have been exploring space for many years. Shuttles have been sent into space. Space stations have been built. Men have even landed on the moon. From all these efforts, scientists have learned many facts about our solar system. They know that the sun contains 99.8% of the mass of our solar system. They now know that the four planets closest to the sun, including Earth, are made mostly of iron and rock while the outer planets are made mostly of gases. They also know that the Asteroid Belt divides the inner planets from the outer planets. Scientists have even found the Kuiper Belt, a region of space where dwarf planets like Pluto orbit the sun. Just imagine what else they might learn about our solar system in the future!

Use the passage and the diagram to answer the questions.

1. What are the four inner planets? ____________________
2. What are the four outer planets? ____________________
3. What do we know about the sun? ____________________
4. Where is the Asteroid Belt located? ____________________
5. What is the Kuiper Belt? ____________________

Bone Patterns

Use with "Battle of the Bones" on page 235.

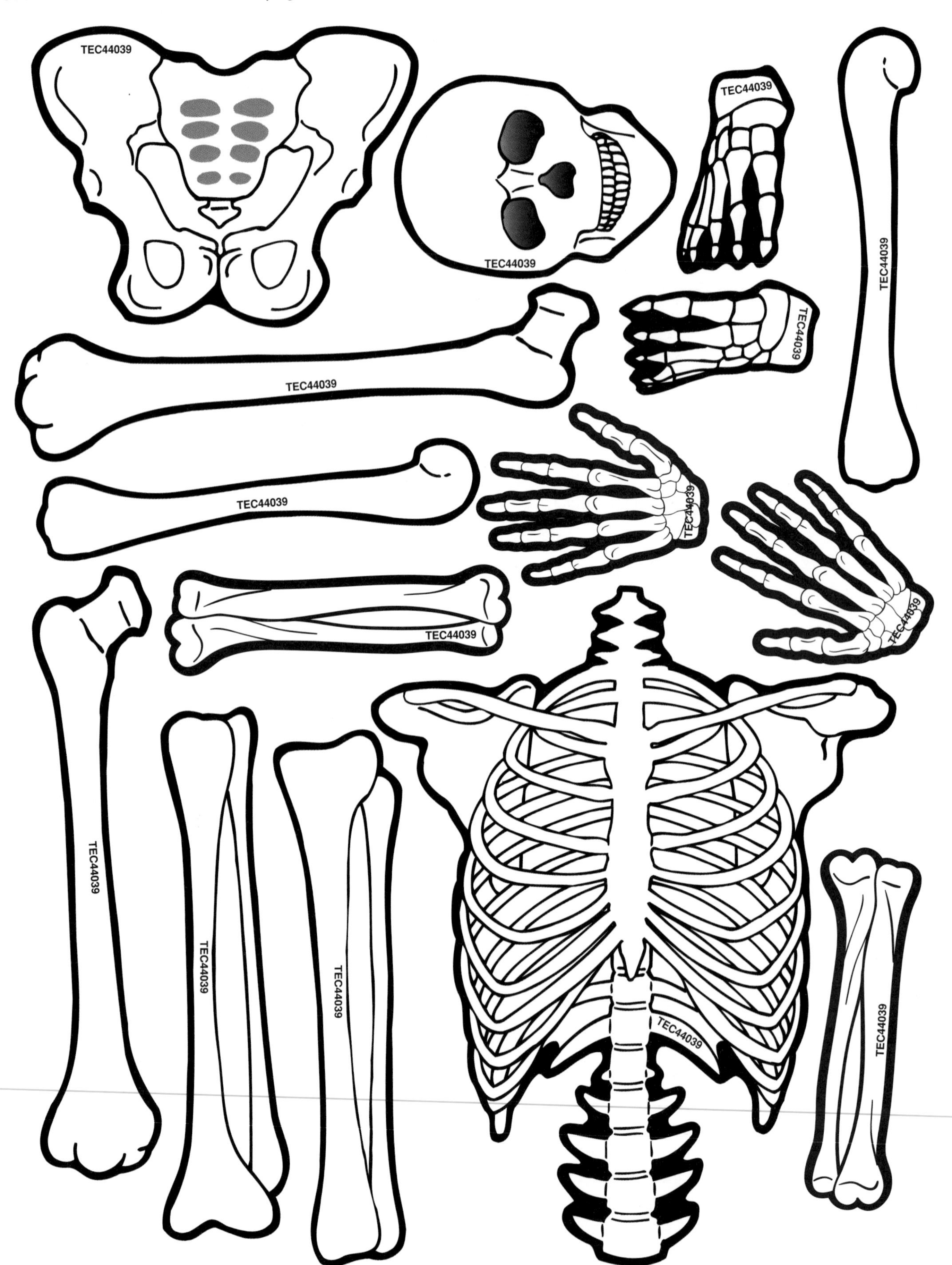

Molecules in Motion
States of matter

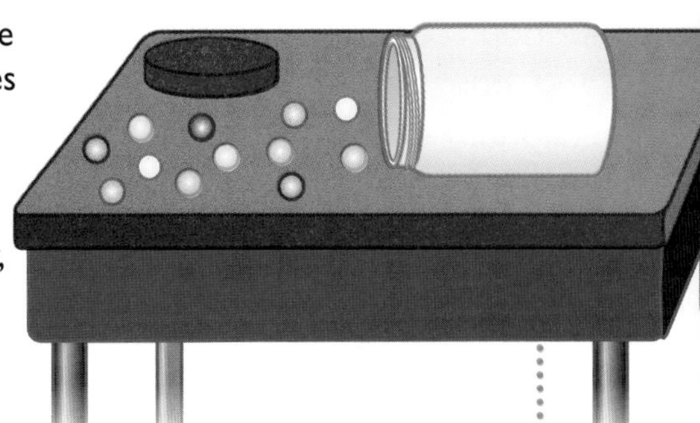

Use this simple demonstration to show students how molecules move in different states of matter. Fill a small lidded container with marbles (molecules). Gently shake the container to show students how the molecules barely move, similar to when matter is in a solid state. Next, remove and set aside about a third of the marbles. Then shake the container again to show how the marbles move about like the molecules in a liquid. Finally, pour the remaining marbles onto a flat surface to demonstrate how the molecules in a gas spread out and move freely in all directions.

Sharon Vandike, Visitation Inter-Parish School, Vienna, MO

Name *Manuel*

Trait	Yes	No
Do I have dimples?		X
Can I roll my tongue?	X	
Do I have a widow's peak?	X	
Are my earlobes unattached?	X	

Dominant or Recessive?
Genetics

Discuss with students how scientists think some traits—such as dimples, tongue rolling, widow's peaks, and earlobe attachment—are determined by a dominant or recessive form of single genes. Have each student determine whether he has the dominant or recessive form of each of these genes by working with a partner to answer the four questions shown. Explain that each *yes* means the student has the dominant form of the gene for that trait and each *no* means he has the recessive form. Encourage students to share their findings with family members.

Never-Ending Journey
Water cycle

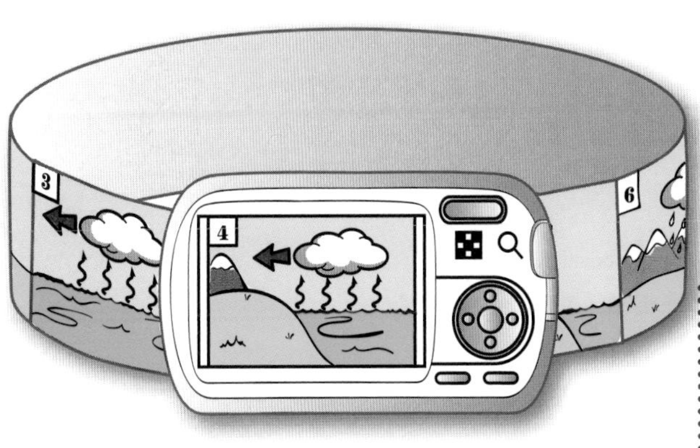

This project helps students review how water moves from the oceans and back again. First, each child colors and cuts out the photostrips and camera pattern on a copy of page 242. Next, she glues the tabs on the four photostrips together in sequential order to form a single strip. The student then cuts slits along the camera's two dotted lines. To make a loop, she slides the strip through the slits and glues photo 12 to photo 1 at the tab. Finally, she uses her finished project to write a paragraph about the water cycle.

Name ____________________

It's "Snow" Big Deal!

Crud, corn, and *mashed potatoes* are all types of snow.

Snow comes in many forms, and skiers and snowboarders have many names for it. Since the early 1900s, skiers have created their own vocabulary for snow. Long ago, *fluffy snow, powder snow,* and *sticky snow* just about covered it. But since then, much more descriptive words are heard on the slopes. These terms include *crud, corn,* and *mashed potatoes.* Read the skier's dictionary to learn more about these types of snow as well as a few others.

The Skier's Dictionary

corn: hard pellets of snow that have refrozen
crud: snow that has been skied over but is still soft and chunky
crust: hard, packed snow that's frozen
dust on crust: a small amount of powder snow on top of crust
grapple: snow that looks like sleet but is rounder and thicker
mashed potatoes: melting snow
powder: fresh snow that is loose and dry
sierra cement: wet, heavy snow

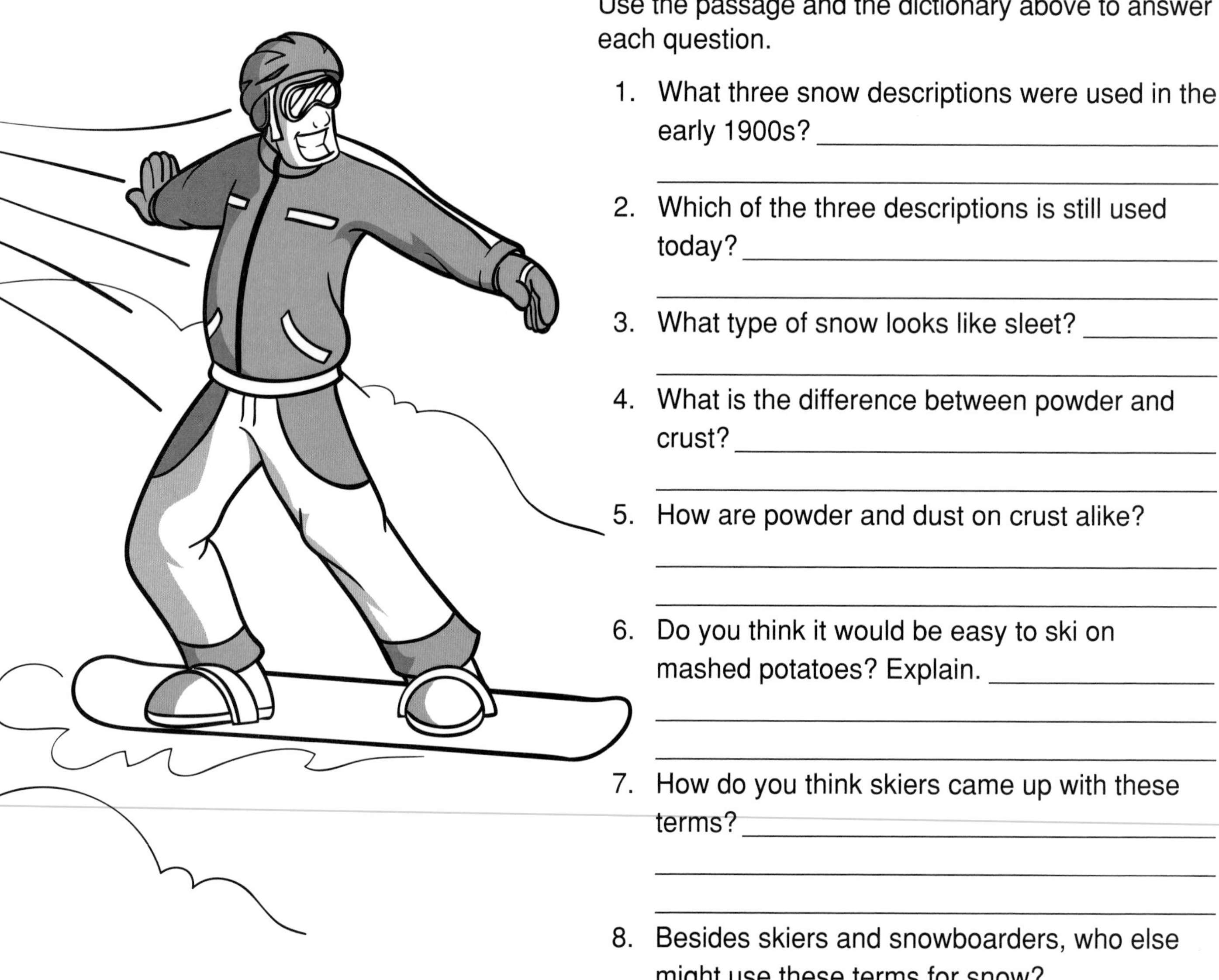

Use the passage and the dictionary above to answer each question.

1. What three snow descriptions were used in the early 1900s? ____________________
2. Which of the three descriptions is still used today? ____________________
3. What type of snow looks like sleet? ____________________
4. What is the difference between powder and crust? ____________________
5. How are powder and dust on crust alike? ____________________
6. Do you think it would be easy to ski on mashed potatoes? Explain. ____________________
7. How do you think skiers came up with these terms? ____________________
8. Besides skiers and snowboarders, who else might use these terms for snow? ____________________

Name ____________________

Real Reindeer

When a reindeer walks, a bone and a tendon in each ankle rub against each other. This makes a clicking noise.

It has never been proven that reindeer can fly around this time of year. However, we do know a few other cool facts about them. For example, reindeer are the only members of the deer family whose females grow antlers. Reindeer shed their antlers every year. They then regrow new ones.

Reindeer also have thick fur and extra wide hooves. This helps them survive in the cold Arctic. The fur helps keep the reindeer warm. The wide hooves prevent reindeer from sinking into the deep snow as they walk.

Perhaps one of the most unique reindeer features is the clicking noise their ankles make as they walk. Scientists believe that this adaptation helps reindeer stay in herds during blizzards. During migration, several thousand reindeer may be found within a herd.

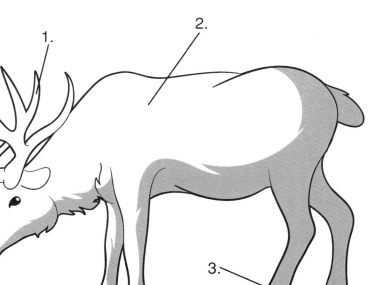

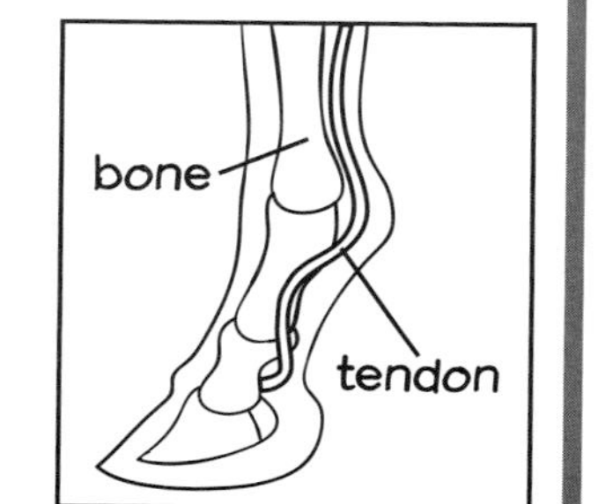

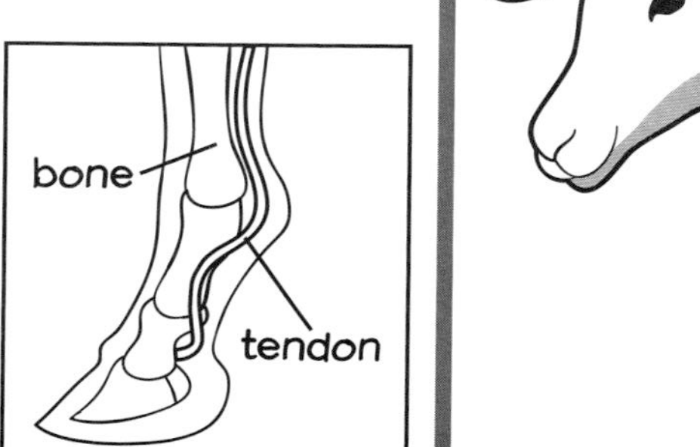

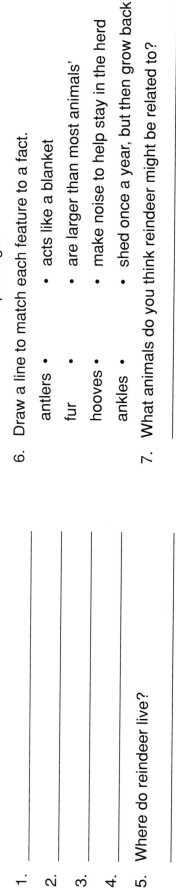

Write the name of each reindeer feature shown above. Answers can be found in the passage.

1. ____________________
2. ____________________
3. ____________________
4. ____________________
5. Where do reindeer live?

____

6. Draw a line to match each feature to a fact.

antlers •	• acts like a blanket
fur •	• are larger than most animals'
hooves •	• make noise to help stay in the herd
ankles •	• shed once a year, but then grow back

7. What animals do you think reindeer might be related to?

____

Photo and Camera Patterns

Use with "Never-Ending Journey" on page 239.

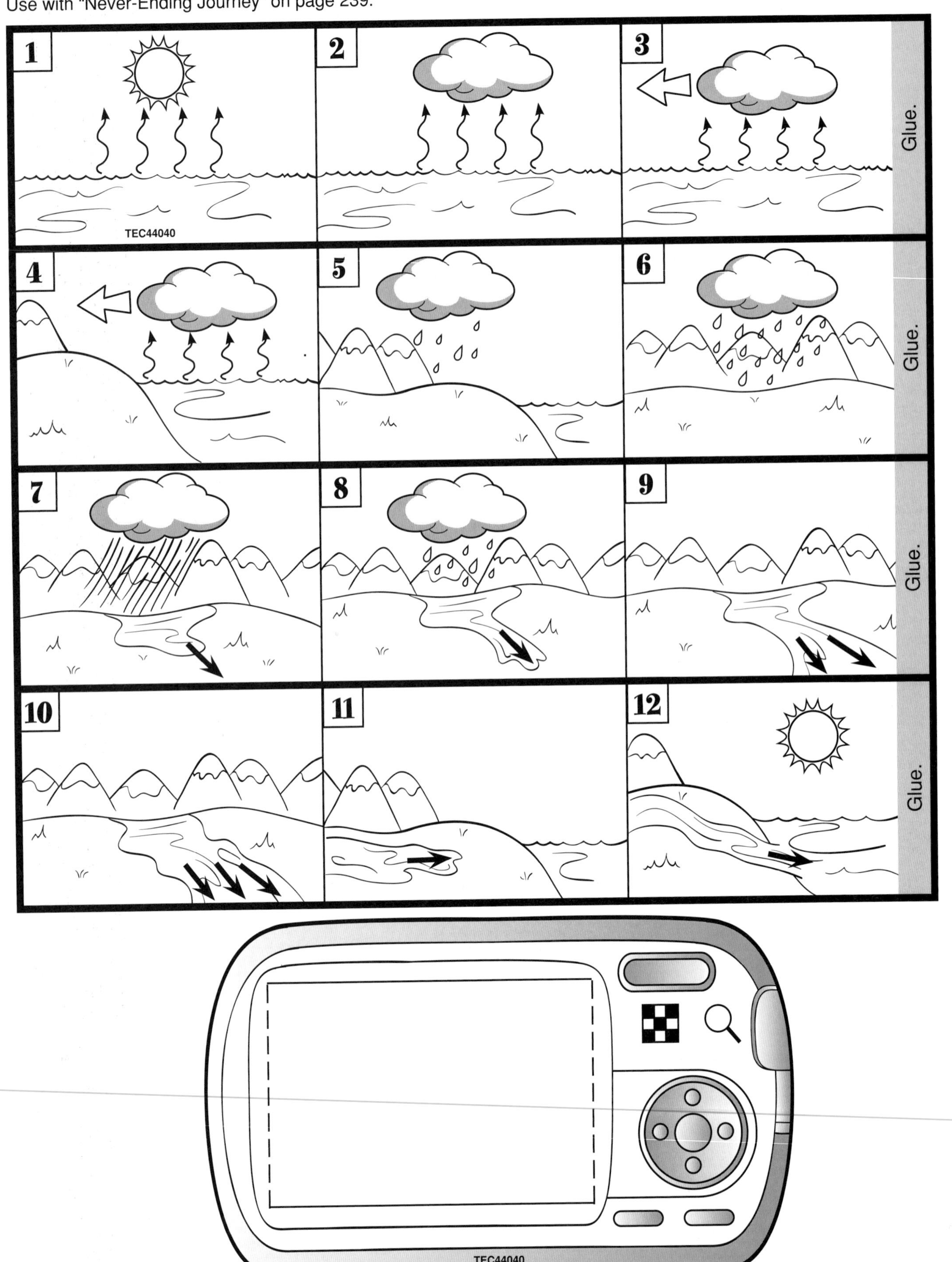

Many Moons
Phases of the moon

Transform students into moon gazers by giving each small group of students ten chocolate sandwich cookies (two extra in case of breakage). Have the group leave one cookie intact to represent the new moon and then carefully remove seven of the cookie tops. Using plastic knives, group members scrape away portions of the cream filling to represent each moon phase. Then they glue the phases in order on black paper and label them with a white pencil as shown.

Kenzi Neuman, Burt Elementary, Clarksville, TN

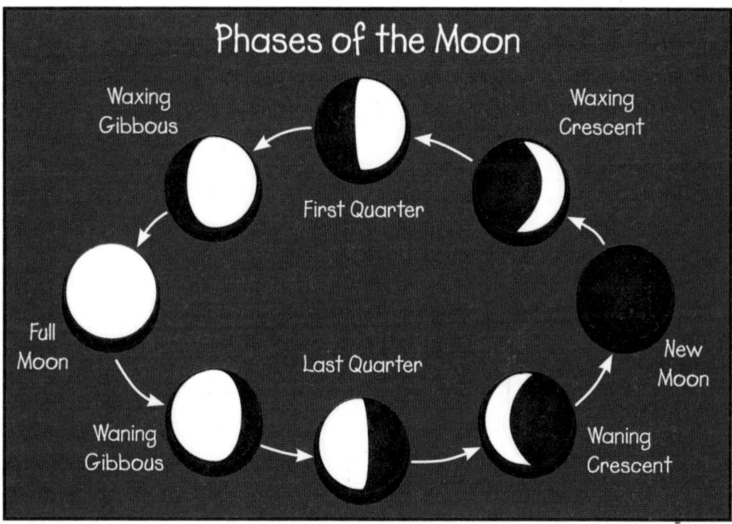

Name Cameron
Dates March 9–15
DAILY HIGH TEMPERATURES
Montpelier, VT
NORTHERN CITY AND STATE
34°F MON. 36°F TUES. 35°F WED. 38°F THURS. 40°F FRI. 42°F SAT. 41°F SUN.
Lake Charles, LA
SOUTHERN CITY AND STATE
62°F MON. 61°F TUES. 66°F WED. 65°F THURS. 66°F FRI. 61°F SAT. 60°F SUN.

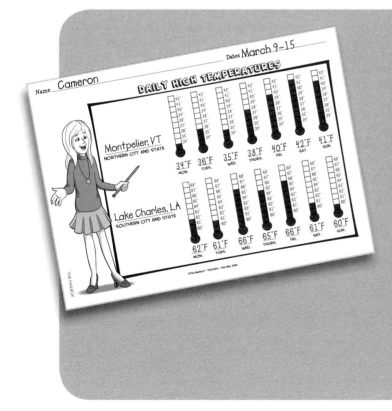

How's the Weather?
Air temperature

Compare daily temperatures in different regions of the United States by assigning each child one city from a northern state and one from a southern state. Have the student write her assigned cities and states on a copy of the recording sheet from page 246. Each day, have her use the Internet to find the daily high temperature for each city and shade the corresponding thermometer accordingly. Then have her create a double-bar graph to compare the high temperatures for her two cities and write a paragraph summarizing the results.

Jennifer Otter, Oak Ridge, NC

Name ____________________

A Computerized Heart?

The first artificial human heart was attached to large computers by seven feet of tubing.

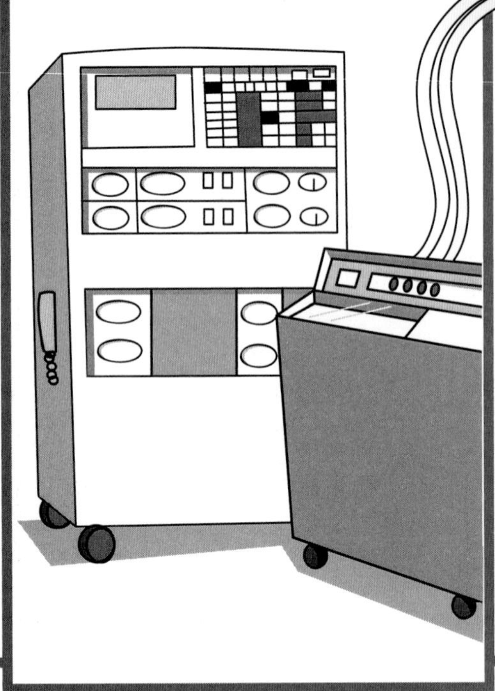

The heart is a major organ in the human body. It is the supply center for sending blood through the body. Sometimes when a heart becomes sick, it must be replaced. There are not enough real human hearts available for transplants. So Dr. Robert Jarvik designed the first permanent artificial human heart. He called it the Jarvik 7. In 1982, the Jarvik 7 was implanted in a human patient for the first time. The Jarvik 7 was attached to Barney Clark's circulatory system. Seven feet of tubing ran from Barney's heart, through his body, and connected to large computers in his room. With these computers, Barney's doctors could control his heart rate. Even though his artificial heart was still running well, Barney passed away 112 days later. Barney Clark and Dr. Robert Jarvik helped pave the way for future heart transplant patients.

Use the passage to find a word for each definition. Write the word in the blank.

1. ____________________: one of the major organs in the human body
2. ____________________: to move from one place to another
3. ____________________: man-made, not made by nature
4. ____________________: the first permanent artificial human heart
5. ____________________: to place in living tissue
6. ____________________: a system of the body that includes blood, blood vessels, and the heart
7. ____________________: a series or system of tubes
8. ____________________: designed to last for a long period of time
9. ____________________: a part of the body made up of tissues that performs a specific job
10. ____________________: someone in need of medical help

Name ____________________

"Bee-utiful"!

Bees can see ultraviolet colors that humans cannot see.

Bees are unique insects that can be found almost anywhere in the world. A bee's body is covered with tiny hairs. It is not like a human's hair, but it is similar. A bee uses its antennae to smell. It uses three small eyes and two compound eyes to see and distinguish between colors. Bees even see colors that humans cannot see. Each bee has three pairs of legs. Its front legs can be used as antennae cleaners, and its hind legs have pollen baskets, which are used to carry pollen back to the hive. Bees have four wings. The two in the front are larger than the two in the back. The wings allow bees to fly forward, backward, up, down, and even sideways. A female bee's stinger is used for self-defense. All female bees except the queen bees lose their stingers when they sting someone. Male bees do not have stingers.

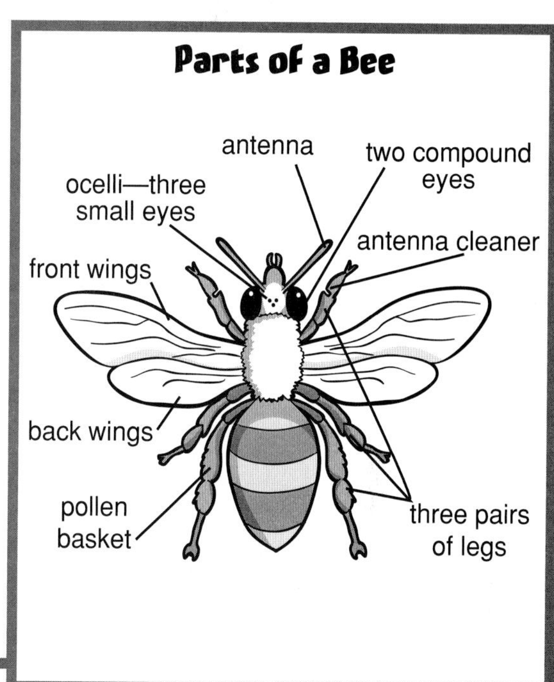

Read the information. Use the words from the passage to complete each honey-splattered sentence.

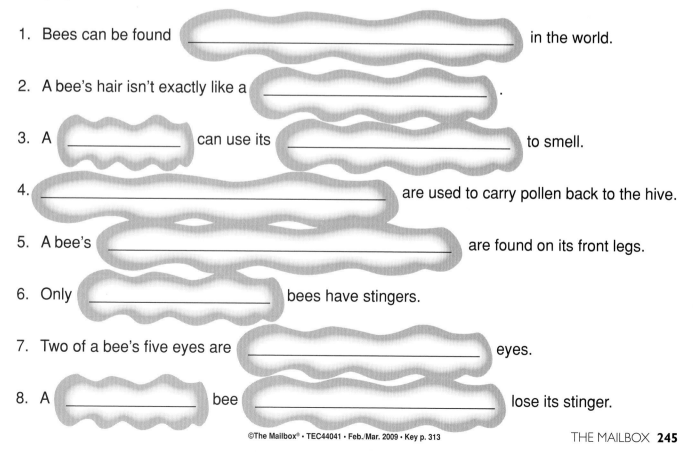

1. Bees can be found ____________________ in the world.
2. A bee's hair isn't exactly like a ____________________.
3. A ____________ can use its ____________________ to smell.
4. ____________________ are used to carry pollen back to the hive.
5. A bee's ____________________ are found on its front legs.
6. Only ____________________ bees have stingers.
7. Two of a bee's five eyes are ____________________ eyes.
8. A ____________ bee ____________________ lose its stinger.

Name ______________________ Dates ______________

DAILY HIGH TEMPERATURES

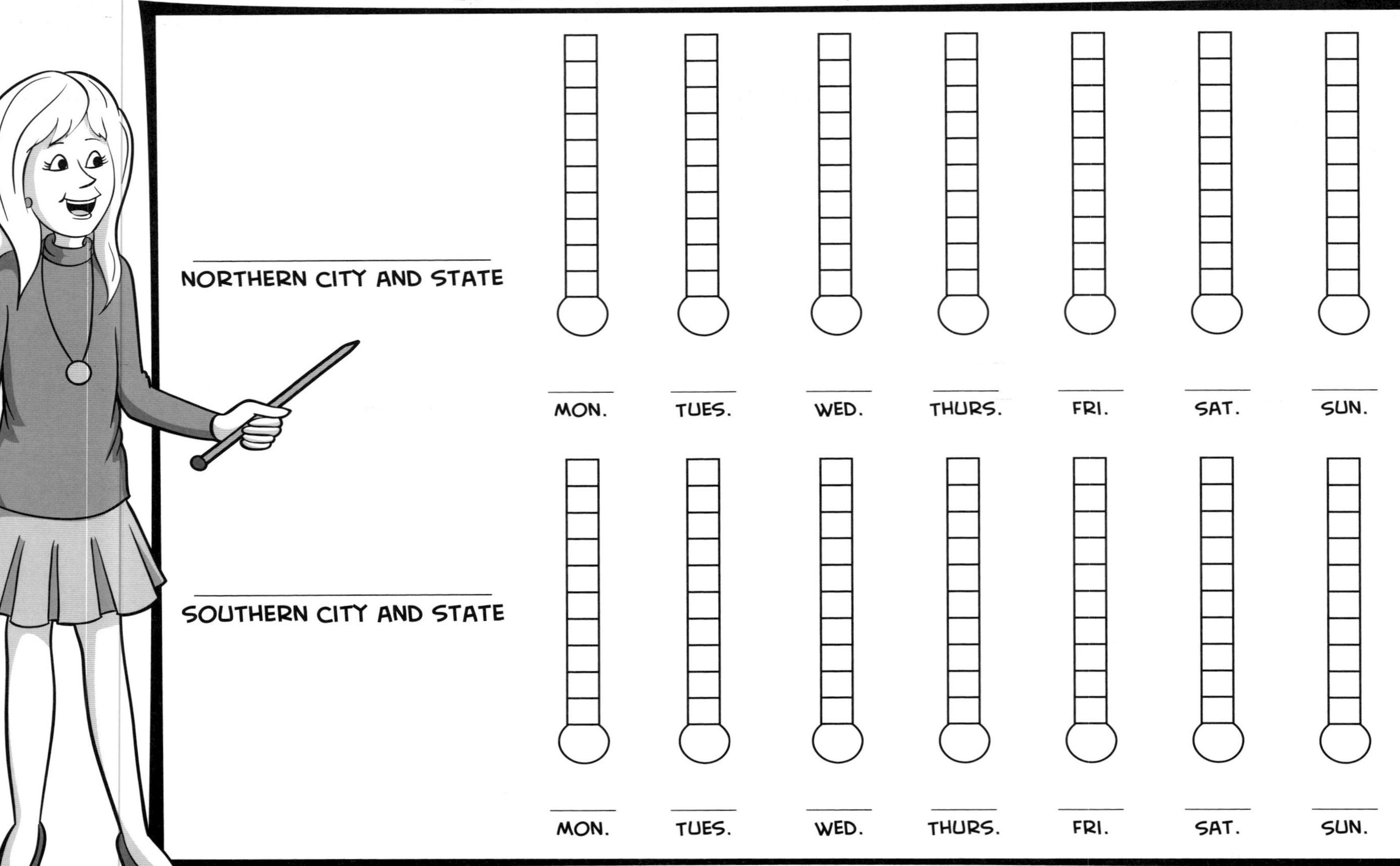

Note to the teacher: Use with "How's the Weather?" on page 243. Have each student determine appropriate increments for the thermometers and label them accordingly.

SIMPLY SCIENCE

Prepare for Take-Off

Flight

Use this handmade airplane activity when studying aviation or even the Wright Brothers. Provide each student with a copy of page 250 and the materials listed. Have students follow the steps on page 250 to complete their airplanes. (They will need your help with hot-gluing.) Then find an open space and let the flying begin. To incorporate math skills, have students measure the distances their airplanes travel.

Robert J. Windt, Cordova, IL

TIP
This activity also incorporates reading comprehension and following directions skills and can be used as an introduction to how-to writing.

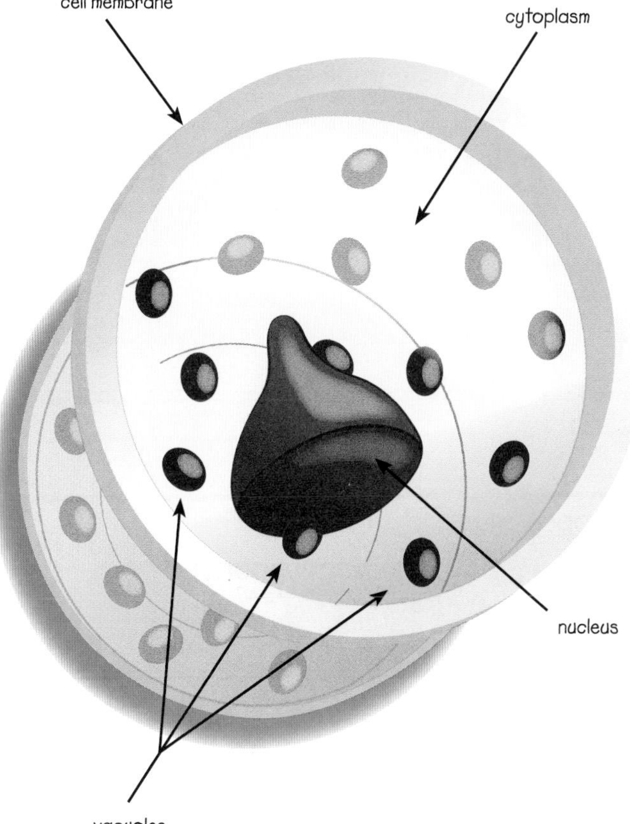

Cellular Gelatin

Parts of a cell

Create this tasty treat as a review of the parts of an animal cell. Give each student an individual container of gelatin, several pieces of small candy, and one piece of a larger candy. Explain to students that the container represents the cell membrane. Then instruct each student to press the large piece of candy in the middle of the gelatin, or cytoplasm, to represent the nucleus. Continue by having students press the smaller candies into the gelatin to represent the vacuoles. Modify this activity to review the parts of a plant cell by adding a green candy to represent the chloroplasts and placing the container on a paper plate to represent the cell wall.

Kimberly Creel, Brush Arbor Christian School, Orlando, FL

Name ______________________________

Shifting Shape

The earth is changing shape because of global warming.

For more than 200 years Earth has been getting warmer. Lately it seems to be happening more quickly. Since 1998 we have had the eight warmest years on record. What we are experiencing is called global warming.

Scientists believe this warming is partly due to the fossil fuels we are burning. Materials like coal and oil clog our air when they are burned. They increase the amount of greenhouse gases in our atmosphere. These greenhouse gases keep heat from escaping into space. We need some greenhouse gases to keep Earth's surface warm enough to sustain life. But higher amounts of these gases cause Earth's temperature to rise.

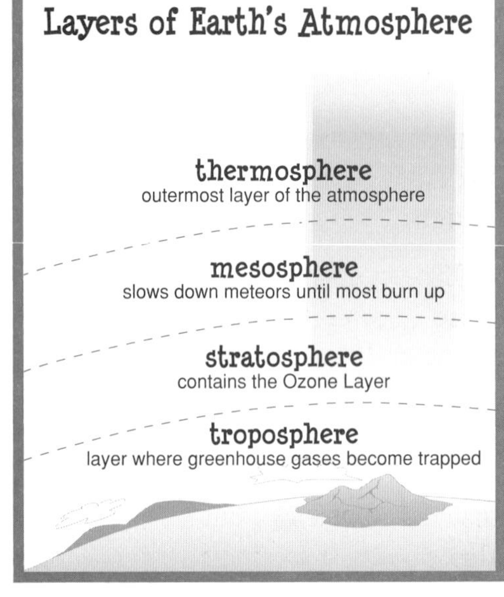

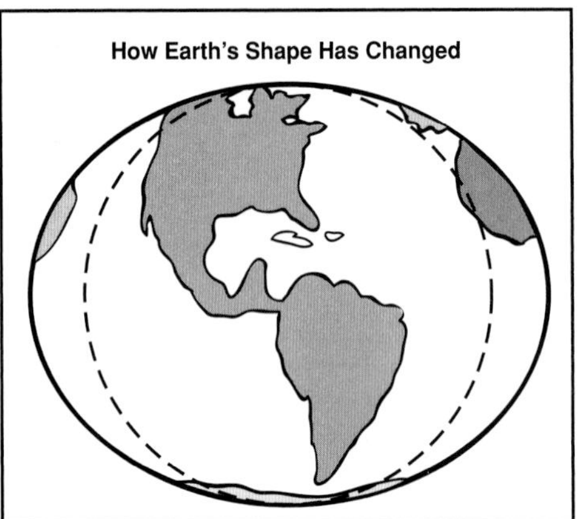

Deforestation is also adding to global warming. We are cutting down many trees. Trees remove carbon dioxide, a greenhouse gas, from the air. With fewer trees on Earth, more carbon dioxide is left to trap heat in the air.

This global warming is taking a toll on our planet. As Earth is warming, the glaciers are melting. In fact, so much of the ice has melted that more water is flowing into the oceans than normal. Some scientists think this has caused the planet to change its shape. It is now wider than it was before 1998. The earth is getting fatter!

The underlined words are in the wrong sentences. Write the correct word on each blank.

1. A rise in Earth's temperature is called atmosphere. ____________________
2. Mesosphere become trapped in our atmosphere. ____________________
3. The deforestation includes the layers of air surrounding our planet. ____________________
4. When many trees are cut down, it is called stratosphere. ____________________
5. The outermost layer of the atmosphere is called the troposphere. ____________________
6. The global warming is directly below the thermosphere but above the troposphere. ____________________
7. The Ozone Layer is found in the greenhouse gases. ____________________
8. The thermosphere is where greenhouse gases become trapped in the atmosphere. ____________________

Name ____________________

Kings of the Forest

A giant sequoia, which can tower 100 feet or more, grows from a seed that is only $\frac{1}{4}$-inch long.

Read the passage. Then follow the directions to cross out locations in the box below. The remaining locations will tell where sequoias can be found today.

If sequoia trees could talk, they would have a lot to say because these huge plants have been around for thousands of years. Sequoias are named for Sequoyah, a Native American who invented a written alphabet for his Cherokee tribe. These hardy trees, also known as redwoods, have thick reddish-brown bark on their trunks that protects them from fires. Giant sequoias do not die from disease, insects, or old age, but they are targets for lightning. They are also sensitive to air pollution. Until the last ice age, sequoias grew throughout North America. Now only three species survive. Extinct sequoias can be seen in Arizona's Petrified Forest National Park.

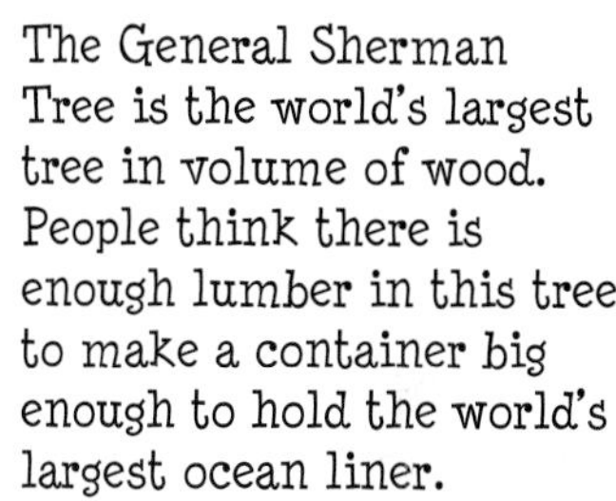

The General Sherman Tree is the world's largest tree in volume of wood. People think there is enough lumber in this tree to make a container big enough to hold the world's largest ocean liner.

Scientists can tell how old a tree is by counting the number of growth rings in its trunk. Each ring equals one year of growth. The General Sherman tree is thought to be almost 2,500 years old.

It is against the law to cut down a sequoia tree.

1. If a sequoia is also known as a redwood, cross out India.
2. If each tree ring equals one year of growth, cross out Canada.
3. If sequoia trees can talk, cross out eastern California on the western slopes of the Sierra Nevada mountains.
4. If sequoias are likely to be injured by fire, cross out northern and central California along the Pacific coast.
5. If it is not a crime to cut down a sequoia, cross out southern Oregon along the Pacific coast.
6. If sequoias are named for a famous Native American, cross out North Carolina.
7. If sequoias cannot resist insect attacks, cross out Sichuan province in China.
8. If glaciers did not cause sequoias to become extinct, cross out Sequoia National Park in central California.
9. If sequoias are not bothered by air pollution, cross out Hubei province in China.
10. If sequoias once grew all over North America, cross out South America.

The three surviving species of sequoia trees can be found in...

- Canada
- South America
- Sichuan province in China
- North Carolina
- Hubei province in China
- eastern California on the western slopes of the Sierra Nevada mountains
- Sequoia National Park in central California
- India
- southern Oregon along the Pacific coast
- northern and central California along the Pacific coast

Name ______________________________

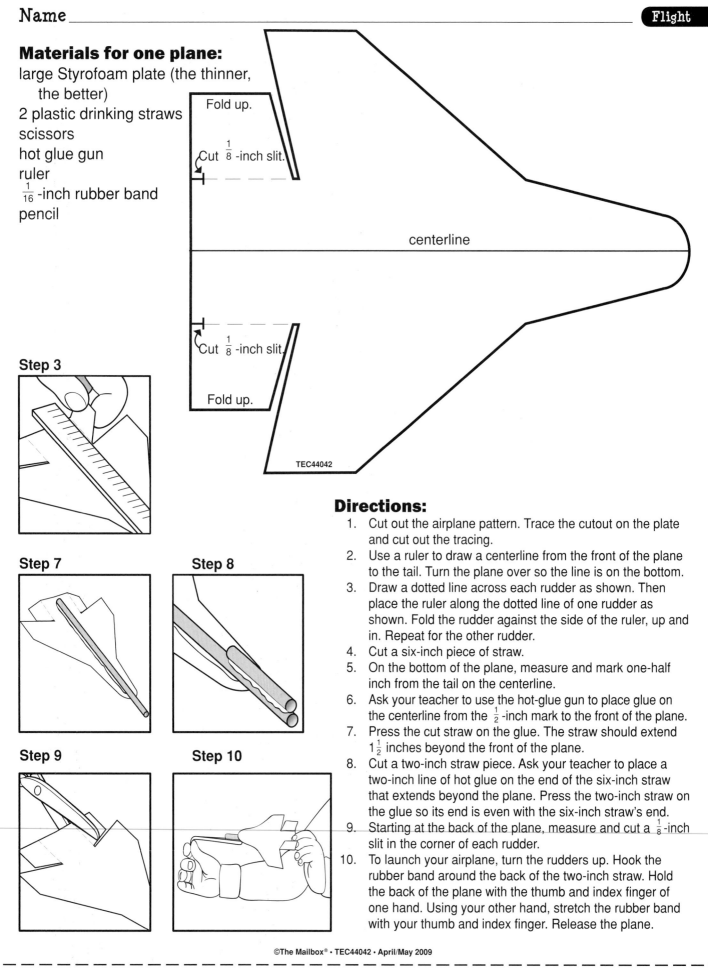

Materials for one plane:

large Styrofoam plate (the thinner, the better)
2 plastic drinking straws
scissors
hot glue gun
ruler
$\frac{1}{16}$-inch rubber band
pencil

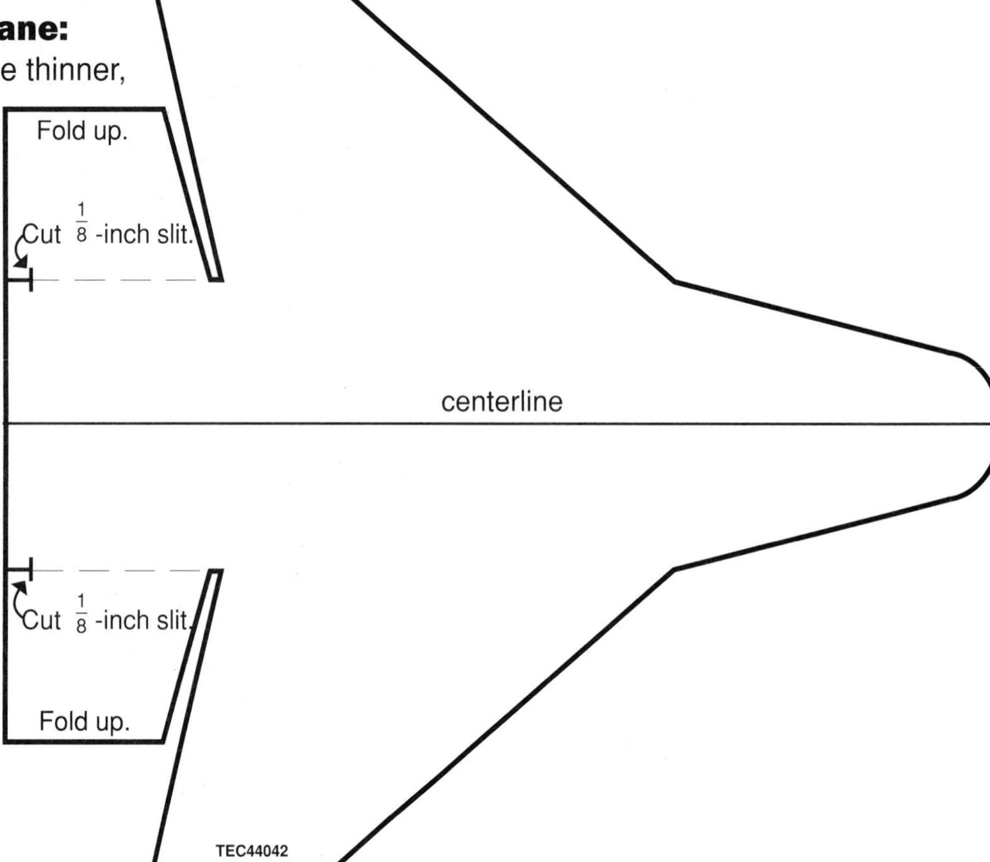

Step 3

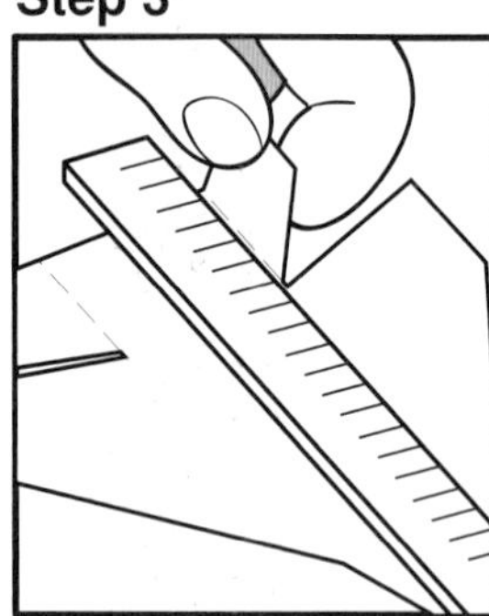

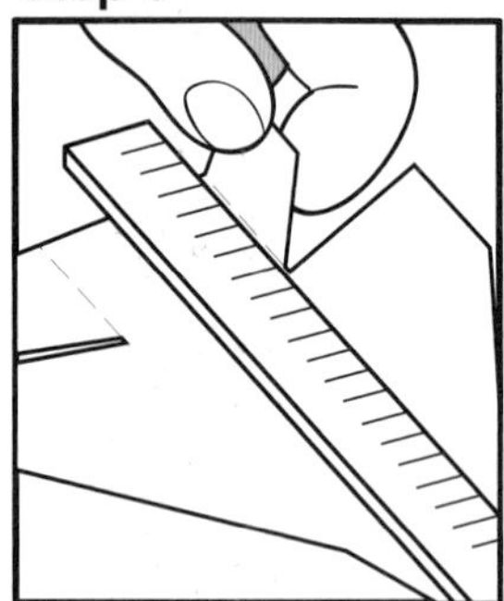

Step 7

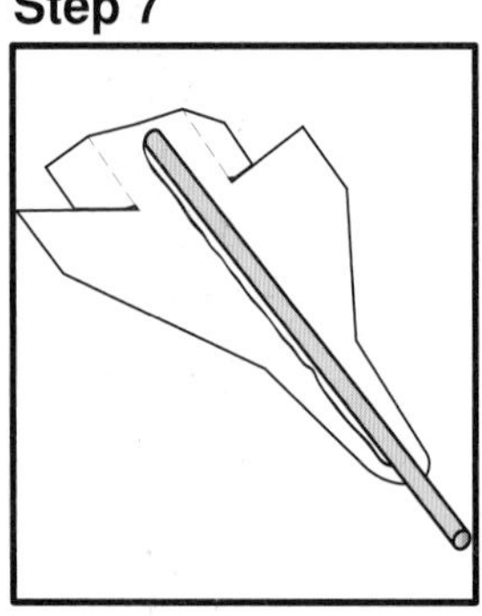

Step 8

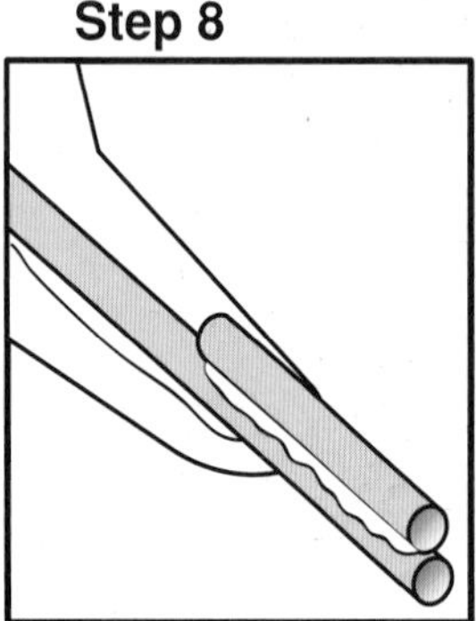

Step 9

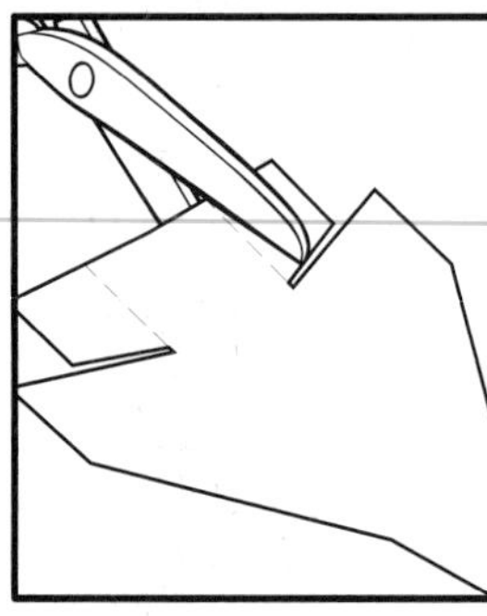

Step 10

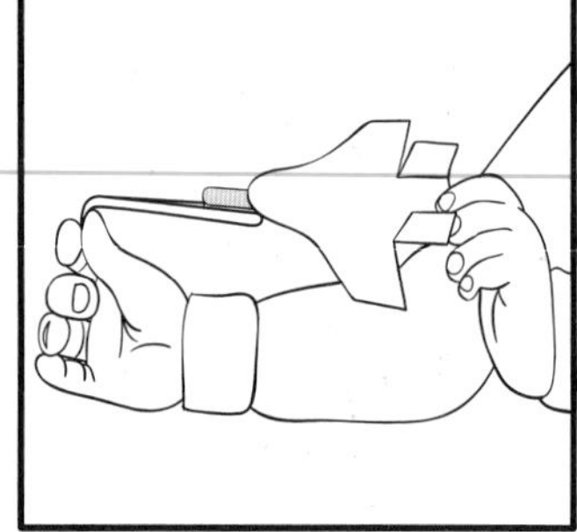

Directions:

1. Cut out the airplane pattern. Trace the cutout on the plate and cut out the tracing.
2. Use a ruler to draw a centerline from the front of the plane to the tail. Turn the plane over so the line is on the bottom.
3. Draw a dotted line across each rudder as shown. Then place the ruler along the dotted line of one rudder as shown. Fold the rudder against the side of the ruler, up and in. Repeat for the other rudder.
4. Cut a six-inch piece of straw.
5. On the bottom of the plane, measure and mark one-half inch from the tail on the centerline.
6. Ask your teacher to use the hot-glue gun to place glue on the centerline from the $\frac{1}{2}$-inch mark to the front of the plane.
7. Press the cut straw on the glue. The straw should extend $1\frac{1}{2}$ inches beyond the front of the plane.
8. Cut a two-inch straw piece. Ask your teacher to place a two-inch line of hot glue on the end of the six-inch straw that extends beyond the plane. Press the two-inch straw on the glue so its end is even with the six-inch straw's end.
9. Starting at the back of the plane, measure and cut a $\frac{1}{8}$-inch slit in the corner of each rudder.
10. To launch your airplane, turn the rudders up. Hook the rubber band around the back of the two-inch straw. Hold the back of the plane with the thumb and index finger of one hand. Using your other hand, stretch the rubber band with your thumb and index finger. Release the plane.

 Note to the teacher: Use with "Fascinating Flight" on page 247.

Ups and Downs

Temperature, conducting an experiment

Sharpen students' observation skills with this small-group activity. Give each group a copy of page 254 and the materials listed on the page. Guide the groups through the steps, having students record their observations. Then discuss their findings. *(Step 3, water level in straw is even with water level in jar; Step 4, water level in straw rises above water in jar because the bubble-blowing increases the number of air molecules, which increases air pressure inside the jar; Step 5, water level in straw rises slightly due to added heat from hands; Step 6, water level in straw drops below jar's water level due to ice causing the water temperature to drop.)*

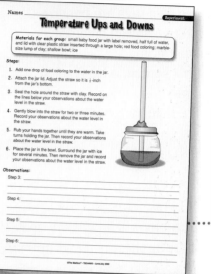

Names ________________

Experiment

Temperature Ups and Downs

Materials for each group: small baby food jar with label removed, half full of water, and lid with clear plastic straw inserted through a large hole; red food coloring; marble-size lump of clay; shallow bowl; ice

Steps:

1. Add one drop of food coloring to the water in the jar.
2. Attach the jar lid. Adjust the straw so it is $\frac{1}{2}$-inch from the jar's bottom.
3. Seal the hole around the straw with clay. Record on the lines below your observations about the water level in the straw.
4. Gently blow into the straw for two or three minutes. Record your observations about the water level in the straw.
5. Rub your hands together until they are warm. Take turns holding the jar. Then record your observations about the water level in the straw.
6. Place the jar in the bowl. Surround the jar with ice for several minutes. Then remove the jar and record your observations about the water level in the straw.

Observations:

Step 3: ________________

Step 4: ________________

Step 5: ________________

Step 6: ________________

It Takes Concentration!

Nervous system

This investigation of human brainpower tests students' abilities to perform two motions simultaneously. Ask each child to rub his tummy and pat his head one at a time and then at the same time. Point out that it is easy to do these actions one at a time but difficult to do them simultaneously for long because the brain then has to process two patterns of movement. Next, have small groups of students create their own patterns of two different movements that must be performed simultaneously. Allow each group to perform its motions, inviting classmates to join the action.

Bonnie Pettifor, Urbana, IL

Everyday Electricity

Forms of energy

Use this partner activity to reinforce the concept that electric energy can be changed into other forms of energy, such as heat, light, chemical, or mechanical energy. For each letter of the alphabet, have each pair of students write the name of something that runs on electricity. Then challenge the partners to tell what type of energy the electricity converts to. That'll charge their brain cells!

Juli Engel, Santa Teresa, NM

Kara and Abby

A–answering machine, mechanical
B–blender, mechanical
C–curling iron, heat
D–dryer, heat and mechanical
E–electric pump, mechanical
F–fax machine, mechanical
G–griddle, heat
H–hair dryer, heat
I–ice maker, mechanical
J–jukebox, sound
K–kitchen fan, mechanical
L–lamp, light
M–microwave, heat

N–night light, light
O–oven, heat
P–popcorn popper, heat
–quesadilla maker, heat
–radio, sound
steam iron, heat
toaster, heat
PC scanner, light
era, light and mechanical
asher, mechanical
ray machine, light
ht's motor, mechanical
ive on a computer, mechanical

Look on pages 252 and 253 for two reproducible comprehension pages about fascinating science facts.

Name ____________________

Seeing Things Clearly?

Mirages can be photographed.

mirage: an image that appears when light rays are bent by layers of air with different temperatures
optical illusion: a misleading image
refraction: the bending of light rays

In the hot summer, you can often look down the road and see a puddle of water. But as you get closer, the puddle disappears. Why? The puddle was a *mirage*, a type of optical illusion.

In a mirage, things are not the way they appear to be. A mirage occurs when layers of the atmosphere near the earth are different temperatures. When light rays pass through air with different temperatures, they bend. This is called refraction. Refraction causes an object to look like it is in one place when it is really in another. In the case of the puddle, light rays from the sky bend upward, so it looks like the rays are coming from the ground. What you see is a reflection of the sky. Refraction makes the sky look like it is on the ground. Even though the puddle is not really there, the light rays that make the mirage are. Since the light rays are real, the mirage can be photographed.

The next time you see a puddle up ahead on a warm, sunny day, look a little closer. It may just be nature playing a trick on you!

A Mirage

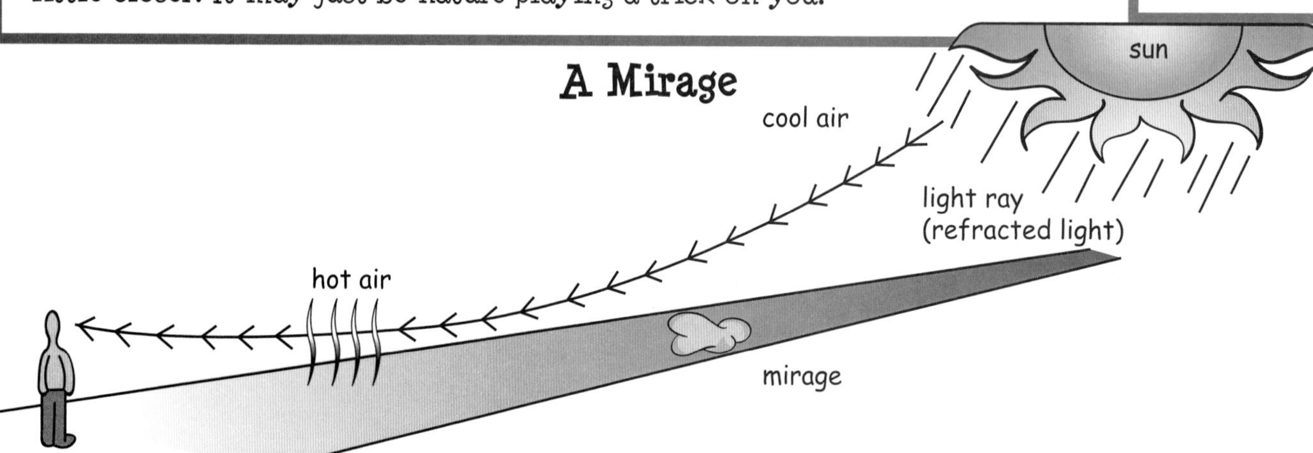

Change one or more words in each sentence to make the sentence true.

1. The bending of light rays is called a mirage.
2. An optical illusion is an accurate picture of an object.
3. In a mirage, the layers of air are similar temperatures.
4. A refracted image is always seen in the same spot as the actual object.
5. Mirages can bend when they pass through materials at different temperatures.

Name ______________________________

Here We Grow Again!

Some animals can lose body parts and regrow new ones.

Animal is attacked

Body part breaks off

Animal regrows body part

The starfish belongs to a unique group of animals. If a predator attacks the starfish and grasps one of its arms, the arm can break off. The starfish can then escape from the predator. A crayfish's claws can break off during an attack too. Another member of this unique group is the glass lizard. The tail of the glass lizard can break off during an attack. When the glass lizard loses its tail, the tail still wiggles. This distracts the predator while the lizard escapes.

Another special feature about these animals is that they can regrow the body parts that break off. The ability to regrow a body part is called regeneration. Many animals can regenerate body parts. Even humans can shed and regrow hair, nails, skin, and some other tissues.

Circle the best answer or answers to complete each sentence. Then answer questions 7 and 8.

1. Losing and regenerating body parts helps some animals ____________.
   A. eat B. survive C. sleep
2. A ____________ is an animal that eats other animals.
   A. prey B. pal C. predator
3. The glass lizard's broken-off tail ____________ to distract predators from attacking.
   A. lays there B. wiggles C. smells
4. Both ________ and ________ can break off body parts to escape from a predator.
   A. humans B. crayfish C. starfish
5. Humans shed and regrow ____________ and ____________.
   A. nails B. arms C. hair
6. ____________ is the act of regrowing a body part.
   A. Regrowth B. Renewal C. Regeneration
7. If *re-* means "again" and *generate* means "to bring into existence," how would you define regenerate? ______________________________
8. What other animals could benefit from the ability to regrow body parts? Explain on the back of this page.

Names ______________________ Experiment

Temperature Ups and Downs

Materials for each group: small baby food jar with label removed, half full of water, and lid with clear plastic straw inserted through a large hole; red food coloring; marble-size lump of clay; shallow bowl; ice

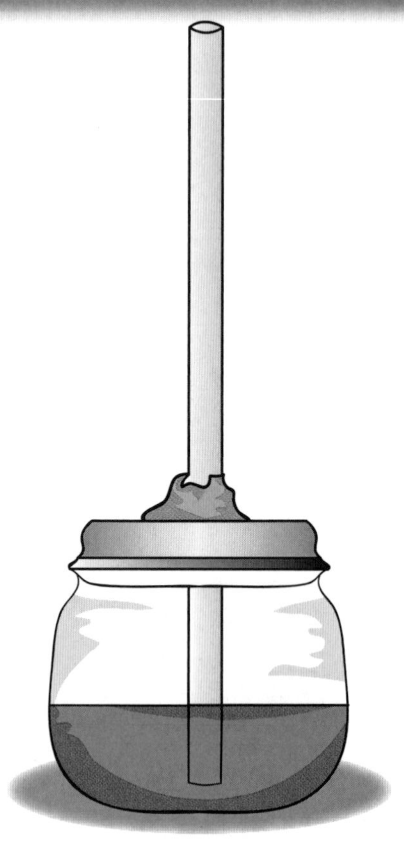

Steps:

1. Add one drop of food coloring to the water in the jar.
2. Attach the jar lid. Adjust the straw so it is $\frac{1}{2}$-inch from the jar's bottom.
3. Seal the hole around the straw with clay. Record on the lines below your observations about the water level in the straw.
4. Gently blow into the straw for two or three minutes. Record your observations about the water level in the straw.
5. Rub your hands together until they are warm. Take turns holding the jar. Then record your observations about the water level in the straw.
6. Place the jar in the bowl. Surround the jar with ice for several minutes. Then remove the jar and record your observations about the water level in the straw.

Observations:

Step 3: ______________________

____

____

Step 4: ______________________

____

____

Step 5: ______________________

____

____

Step 6: ______________________

____

____

 Note to the teacher: Use with "Ups and Downs" on page 251.

Exploring Social Studies

EXPLORING Social Studies

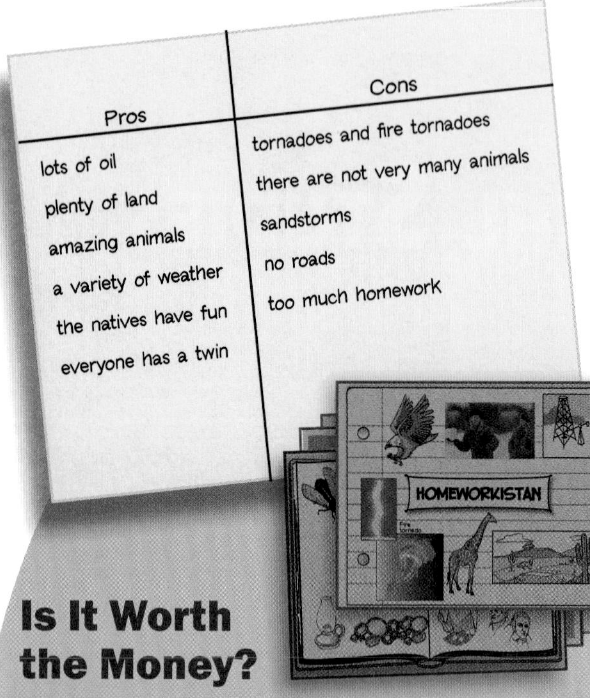

Pros
Cons
lots of oil
plenty of land
amazing animals
a variety of weather
the natives have fun
everyone has a twin
tornadoes and fire tornadoes
there are not very many animals
sandstorms
no roads
too much homework
HOMEWORKISTAN

Is It Worth the Money?

Explorers

To help students understand the connection between explorers and the rulers whom they depended on to finance their trips, give each small group a copy of a discovery card from page 258. Explain that each group has just discovered the area pictured on its card. Have each group study its card and then create a large T chart, similar to the one above, listing the pros and cons of further exploration of the area they discovered. Then have the group write a persuasive letter convincing a ruler to either fund or pass on funding future expeditions to their discovered area.

LaVone Novotny
Liberty Elementary
Caledonia, OH

Foldable Facts

Historical documents

Use these handy study aids to help students compare and contrast key historic documents. Provide each student with an 8.5-inch square of paper. Have the student fold the paper into fourths and then unfold it. Next, have the student fold each outer corner to the center as shown. Once the foldable has been created, have the student label each flap with the name of a historic document. Under each flap, have the student write the date the document was passed into law, the document's authors, and its significance in history.

Marsha Erskine, Dillard Elementary, Madison, NC

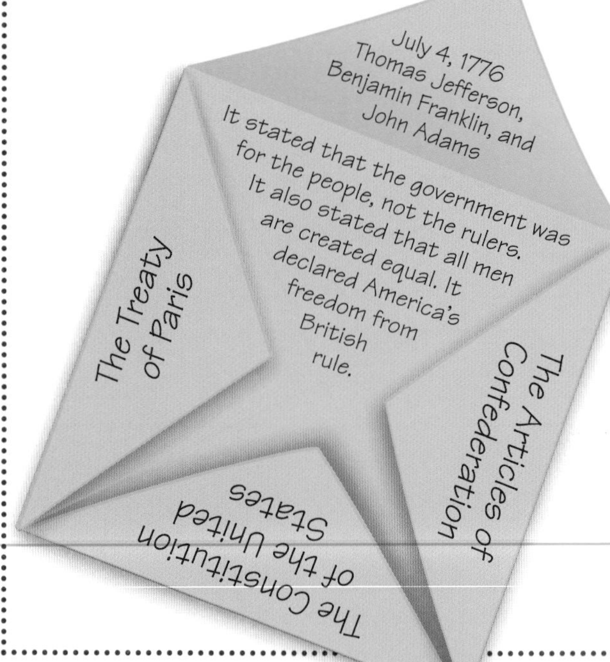

July 4, 1776
Thomas Jefferson,
Benjamin Franklin, and
John Adams
It stated that the government was for the people, not the rulers. It also stated that all men are created equal. It declared America's freedom from British rule.
The Treaty of Paris
The Articles of Confederation
The Constitution of the United States

Name ______________________________

LET'S CELEBRATE!

Read the information and then answer the questions.

Gouverneur Morris was in charge of writing the final draft of the Constitution.

George Washington was the first delegate to sign the Constitution. The delegates then signed the Constitution in order by state from north to south, starting with New Hampshire.

The original Constitution is displayed in the National Archives Building in Washington, DC.

Every year our government observes the anniversary of signing into law the Constitution of the United States on September 17. This day is called Constitution Day. More than 200 years ago, men like George Washington and James Madison signed the Constitution of the United States into law. The main reason for creating the Constitution was to set the rules for our country's government. It also helped outline the rights and freedoms of American citizens. The amazing thing about this document is that it can change with the times. Because of this, the Constitution is still in use more than two centuries after its creation. Happy anniversary to you, the Constitution of the United States!

President Harry S. Truman first declared September 17 as Citizenship Day on July 25, 1952.

In December 2004, President George W. Bush renamed September 17 as Constitution Day and Citizenship Day.

Constitution Day and Citizenship Day are observed each year on September 17.

1. What does Constitution Day celebrate? ______________________________

____

2. Who first declared September 17 as Citizenship Day? ______________________________

3. Who first declared September 17 as Constitution Day and Citizenship Day? ______________________________

____

4. Where is the original Constitution displayed? ______________________________

____

5. What was the main reason for creating the Constitution? ______________________________

____

6. Is the Constitution still in use today? ______________________________

Discovery Cards

Use with "Is It Worth the Money?" on page 256.

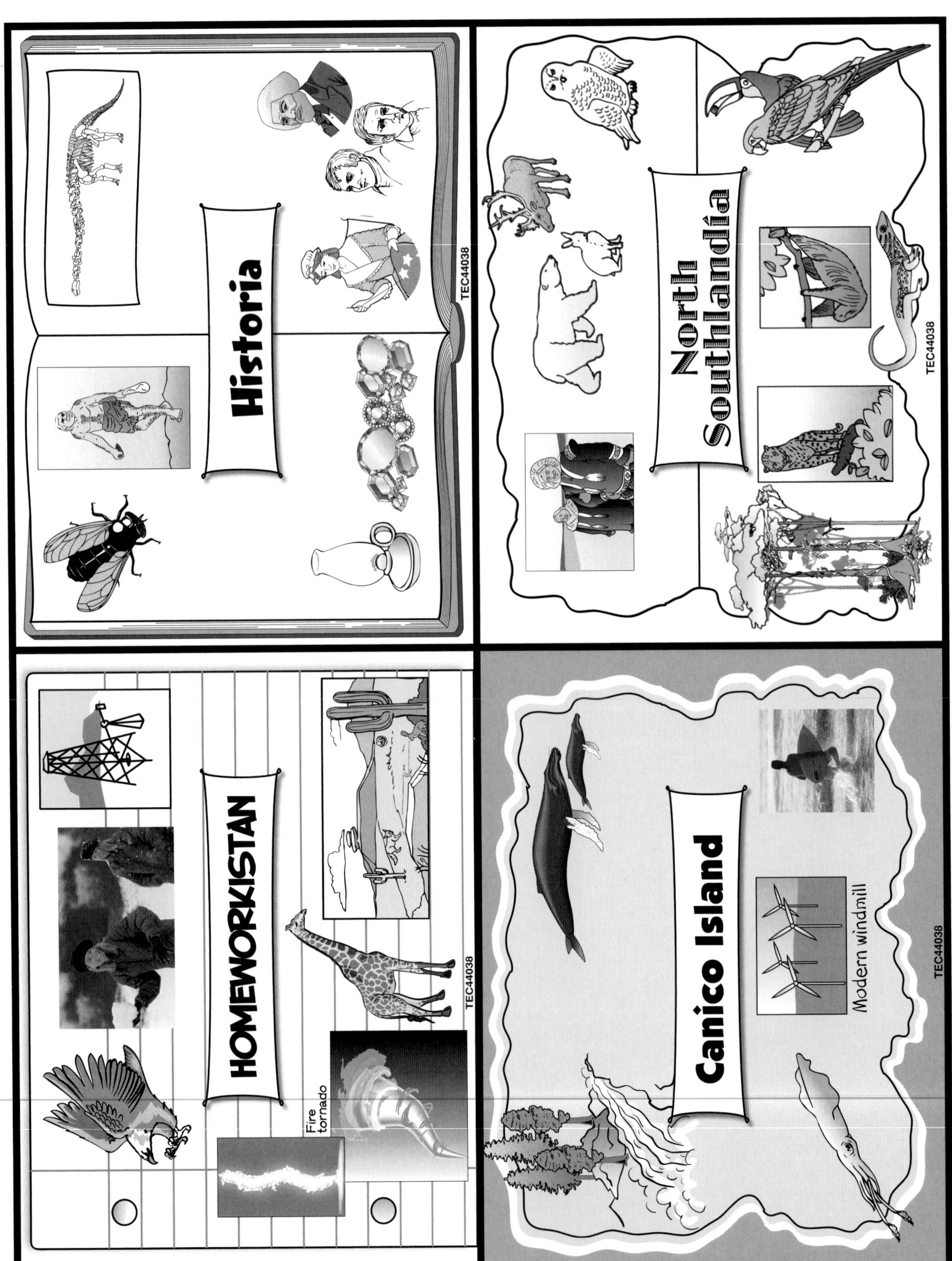

EXPLORING Social Studies

Here Lies...
1451–1506
In search of Asia, he came to
America, it's true;
Then many more trips he made
across the ocean blue.
Famous people in history

Review the contributions of historical figures with this simple display. Provide each pair of students with a colorful copy of the tombstone pattern on page 261 and then assign each duo a historical figure. Have the partners label their tombstone with their person's name, dates of birth and death, and a short epitaph telling of the person's contribution to history. Display the tombstones throughout the year, adding more tombstones with each new unit of study.

Marsha Erskine, Madison, NC

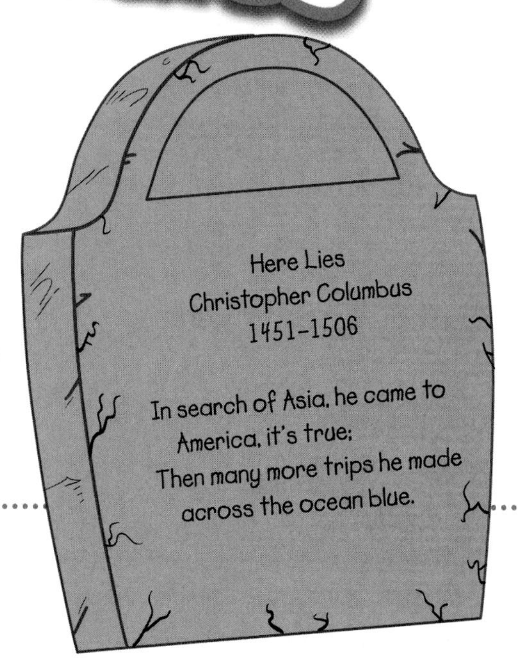

Job	Description
1. Chief Executive	enforce federal laws, treaties, and court rulings
2. Commander in Chief	decide whether to use nuclear weapons
3. Foreign Policy Director	propose laws dealing with foreign aid and international activities make treaties
4. Legislative Leader	deliver the State of the Union address sign bills into law or veto bills
5. Party Head	help form the party's position on important issues
6. Popular Leader	serve the interest of the entire nation
7. Chief of State	attend historical celebrations and dedications present awards to war heroes and honor distinguished Americans

enforce federal laws, treaties, and court rulings

Hang Your Hat
U.S. government

Use this sorting activity to help students understand some of the many different jobs and responsibilities of the president of the United States. To begin, program each of seven colorful paper hats with a presidential duty from the chart provided. Next, program the front of ten index cards with the descriptions listed in the chart. On the back of each card, write the corresponding job number. Place the hats and index cards at a center. Challenge small groups of students to correctly place the cards under the hats. Finally, have students turn over each card to check their answers.

Simone Lepine, Fayetteville, NY

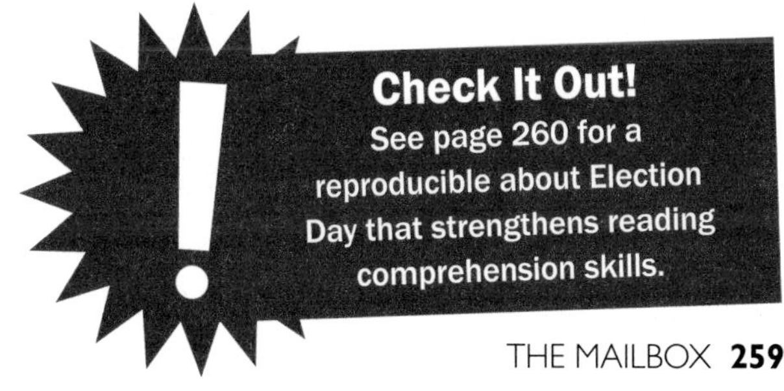

Check It Out!
See page 260 for a reproducible about Election Day that strengthens reading comprehension skills.

Name ____________________

Why Tuesday?

Read the information. Match each subject and predicate below to form a true statement. Then answer the questions.

Why is Election Day always on the Tuesday after the first Monday in November? The answer is simple. For most of our history, we have been a country of farmers. Long ago, lawmakers felt that November was the best month in which to hold elections. By then most crops had been planted and harvested. Plus, the weather was still mild in most of the nation. People who lived out in the country were still able to travel even on dirt roads. But lawmakers did not want Election Day to ever fall on November 1. It is All Saints Day, an important religious holiday for many people. Also, many businesspeople were known to settle their store bills on the first day of every month. So the Tuesday after the first Monday in November became known as Election Day in the United States.

___ 1. Election Day

___ 2. Lawmakers

___ 3. The weather in November

___ 4. Some people

___ 5. November 1

___ 6. In November most crops

___ 7. Many businesspeople

___ 8. The Tuesday after the first Monday in November

A. had to travel on dirt roads.
B. felt that November was the best month for Election Day.
C. have been planted and harvested.
D. is the day on which elections are held.
E. is mild in most of the country.
F. settled their store bills on the first day of the month.
G. is Election Day.
H. is All Saints Day.

9. What happens on Election Day? ____________________

____

10. How many times a year is Election Day observed in the United States? __________

11. What do you think would happen if Election Day were held in January? __________

____

12. If you could pick any day of the year to be Election Day, what day would you choose? Why?

____

Tombstone Pattern

Use with "Here Lies…" on page 259.

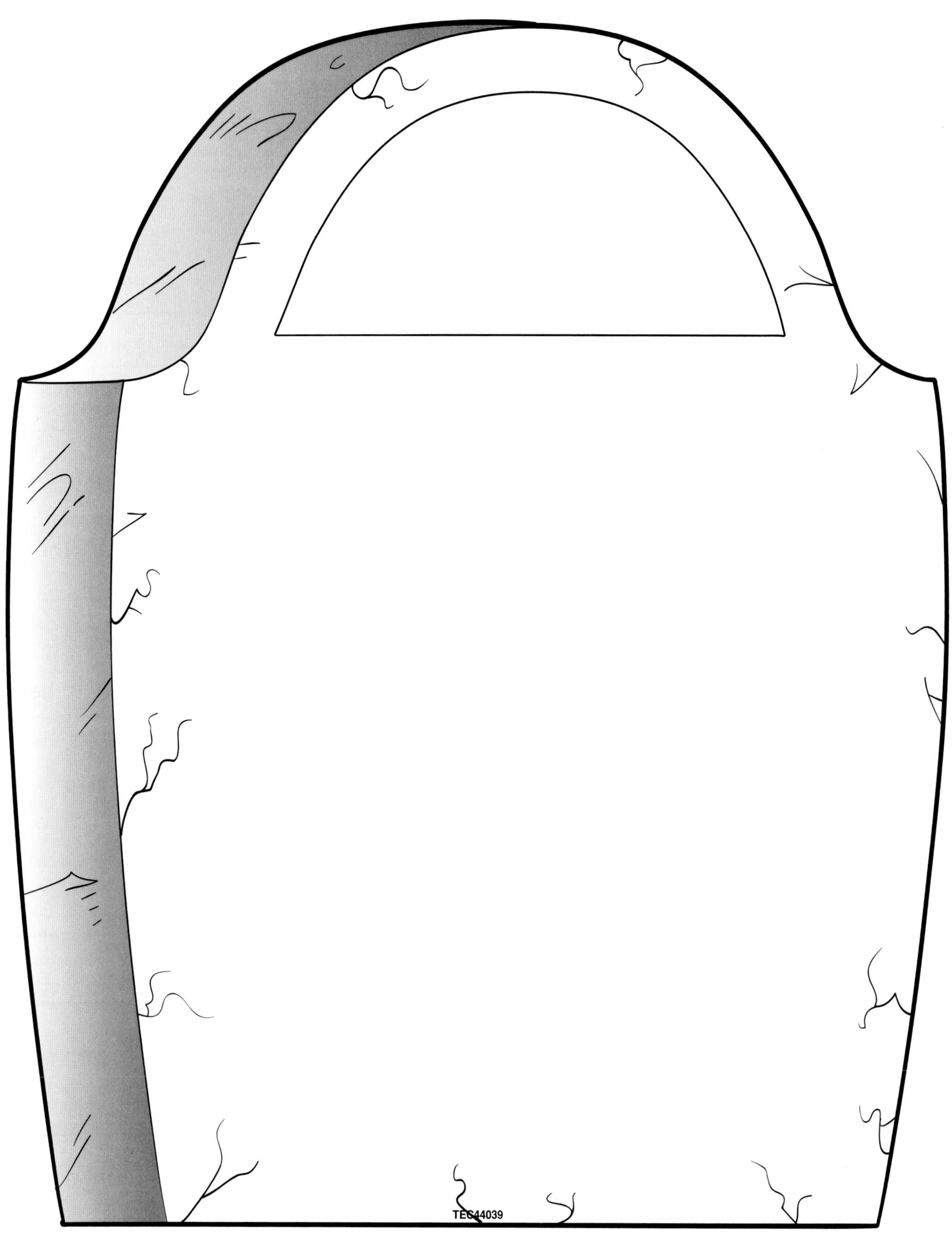

EXPLORING Social Studies

Fantastic Flags

Research

Use this activity when studying specific states, countries, or a unit that explores your students' cultural heritages. Provide each student with a manila file folder. Have the student draw her assigned state or country's flag on the outside of her folder as shown. Next, have the student record information about her state or country on a copy of the bottom half of page 264. Finally, have her glue her completed sheet inside her folder as shown. Display the flag folders on a board titled "Fantastic Flags."

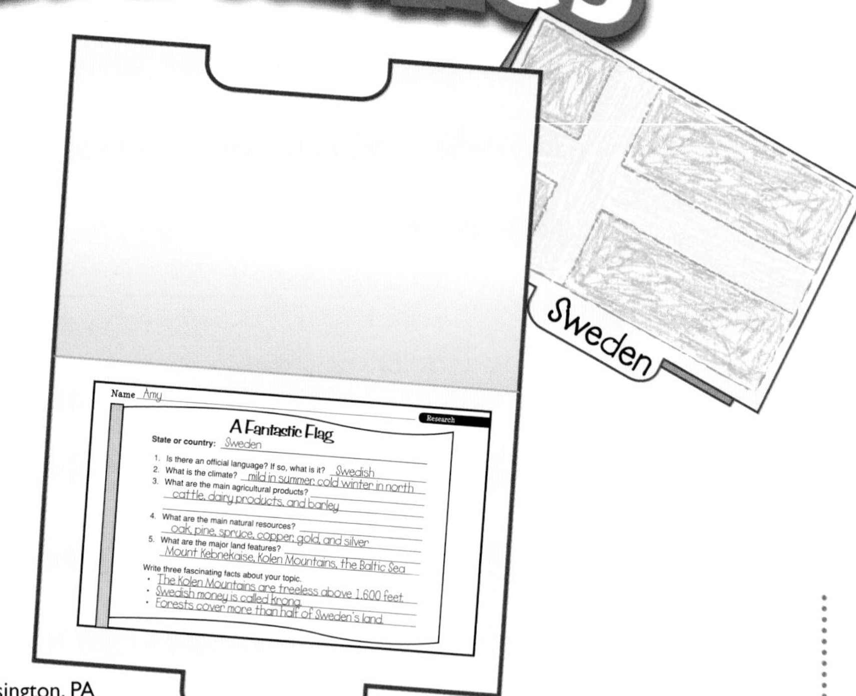

Sweden
Name Amy
Research
A Fantastic Flag
State or country: Sweden
1. Is there an official language? If so, what is it? Swedish
2. What is the climate? mild in summer, cold winter in north
3. What are the main agricultural products? cattle, dairy products, and barley
4. What are the main natural resources? oak, pine, spruce, copper, gold, and silver
5. What are the major land features? Mount Kebnekaise, Kolen Mountains, the Baltic Sea
Write three fascinating facts about your topic.
• The Kolen Mountains are treeless above 1,600 feet.
• Swedish money is called krona.
• Forests cover more than half of Sweden's land.

Colleen Brodbeck, Center for Student Learning, Fallsington, PA

Famous Quotes From the American Revolution

- "I have not yet begun to fight!"
  John Paul Jones
- "I only regret that I have but one life to lose for my country."
  Nathan Hale
- "There! His majesty can now read my name without glasses. And he can double the reward on my head!"
  John Hancock
- "Don't fire until you see the whites of their eyes! Then fire low."
  Israel Putnam
- "The distinctions between Virginians, Pennsylvanians, New Yorkers, and New Englanders are no more. I am not a Virginian, but an American!"
  Patrick Henry
- "They that can give up liberty to purchase a little temporary safety, deserve neither liberty nor safety."
  Benjamin Franklin
- "I know not what course others may take, but as for me, give me liberty or give me death."
  Patrick Henry

What Did They Mean?

American Revolution

In advance, program several index cards with famous quotes from the American Revolution (see the list), leaving out the speakers' names. Make one colorful copy of the pattern on the top of page 264 for each quote. Display each quote and pattern as shown. Then have each small group research one quote to find out who said it and what it means. Once all groups have finished, review the findings as a class. Select one student to record each correct name on its matching sign.

Terri Myers, Dalton, GA

Name ______________________________

Thank You, Ancient Greece!

The United States was not the first country to give rights to its citizens.

Read the passage. Then use the words from the word bank to complete each sentence.

Many people know that the Bill of Rights in the United States Constitution gives rights to the people. It also controls the power of the government. But did you know that the concept of people's rights goes back to the ancient Greeks? More than 2,500 years ago, the rulers of Greece wanted to make sure that no one person or group became too powerful. They began to give rights to the people. Free Greek men were allowed the right to bring cases to court and even had the right to vote.

America's forefathers took notes from older documents in use around the world. James Madison used ideas from the English Bill of Rights as well as the Virginia Declaration of Rights.

In America, Bill of Rights Day is observed on December 15. This is the anniversary of the day the first ten amendments were added to the Constitution.

1. _ (_) _ _ _ _ _ observes Bill of Rights Day on December 15.
2. The _ _ _ _ _ _ of ancient Greece did not want _ _ (_) _ _ _ to become too powerful.
3. America's (_) _ _ _ _ _ _ _ _ _ who wrote the Bill of Rights used ideas from _ _ _ _ _ _ the world.
4. James Madison used the Virginia Declaration of (_) _ _ _ _ _ as a reference.
5. The _ _ _ _ (_) _ _ Greeks introduced the _ _ _ _ _ _ _ of people's inalienable rights.
6. The Bill of Rights gives power to the _ _ _ _ _ (_).
7. The Bill of Rights is meant to _ (_) _ _ _ _ _ the power of the government.
8. James (_) _ _ _ _ _ _ also used the _ _ _ _ _ _ _ Bill of Rights as inspiration.

Word Bank
America
ancient
anyone
around
concept
control
English
forefathers
Madison
people
Rights
rulers

Write each circled letter from above in order on the lines below to reveal a special message.

_ _   _ _ _ _ d _ _

Revolutionary War Character Pattern

Use with "What Did They Mean?" on page 262.

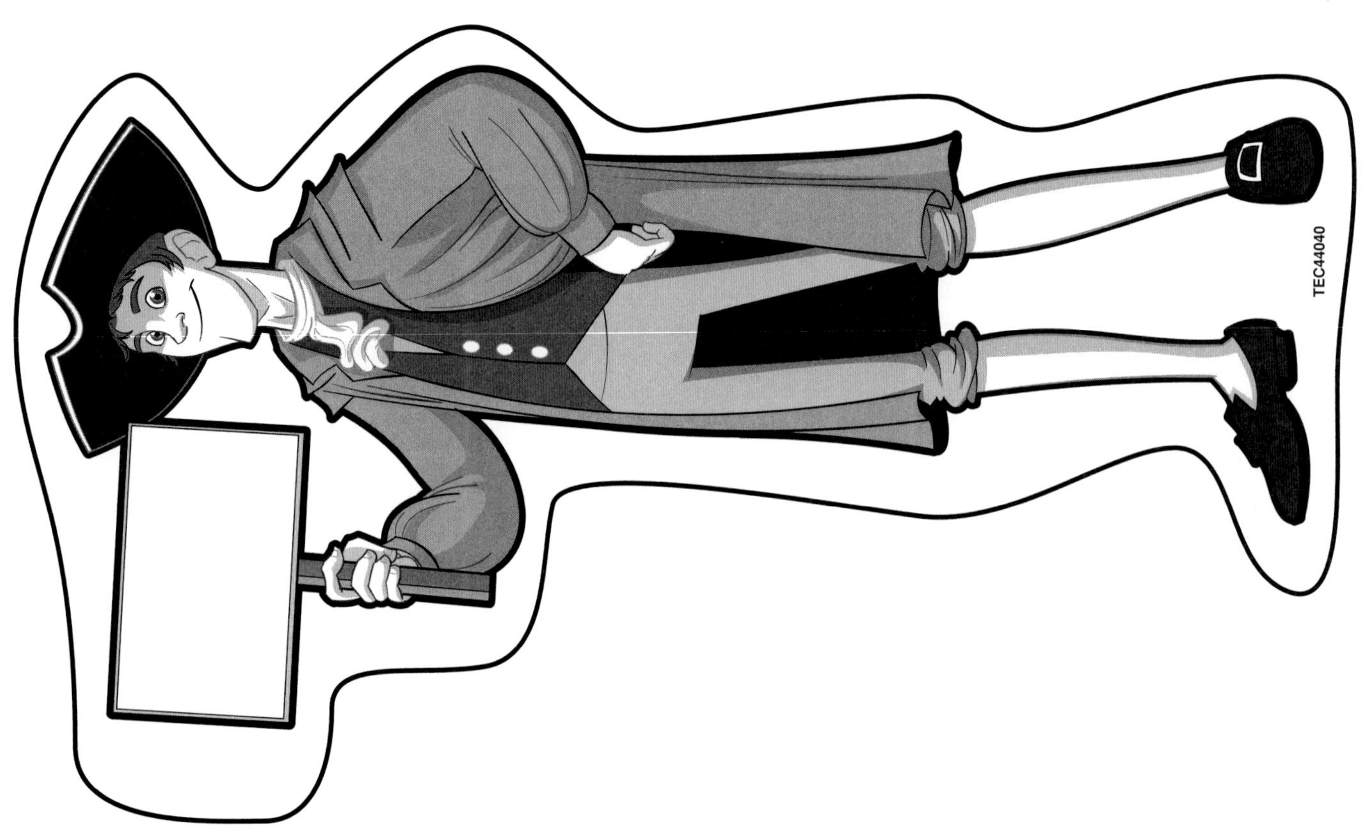

Name ____________________ Research

A Fantastic Flag

State or country: ____________________

1. Is there an official language? If so, what is it? ____________________
2. What is the climate? ____________________
3. What are the main agricultural products? ____________________
4. What are the main natural resources? ____________________
5. What are the major land features? ____________________

Write three fascinating facts about your topic.

- ____________________
- ____________________
- ____________________

 Note to the teacher: Use with "Fantastic Flags" on page 262.

EXPLORING Social Studies

Chief Executive Chronology

U.S. presidents

Help students study the presidents of the United States with this handy timeline. Divide the class into eight groups and give each group a large sheet of red, white, or blue construction paper. Assign each group a span of years shown. Then have the group program its timeline section with the names and terms of the presidents inaugurated during that time period, along with any other significant historic events. Finally, tape the sections together in order, end to end, to create a large timeline to display in your classroom.

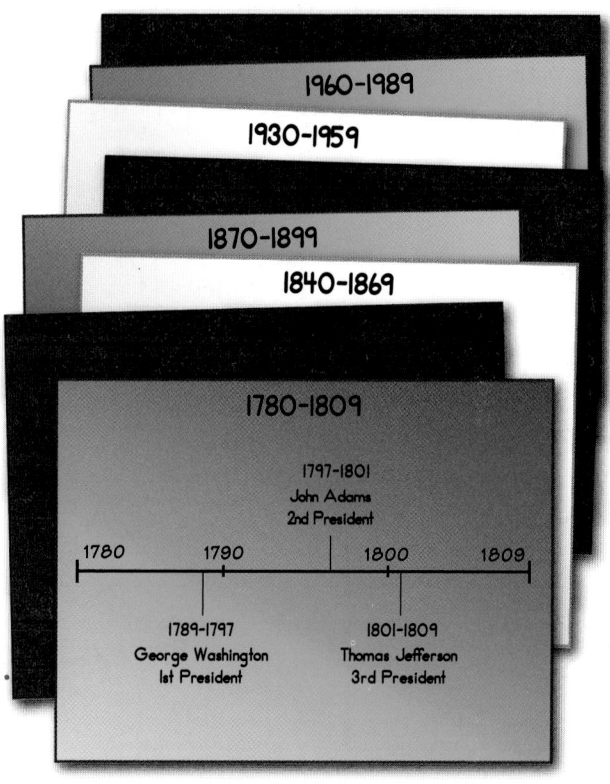

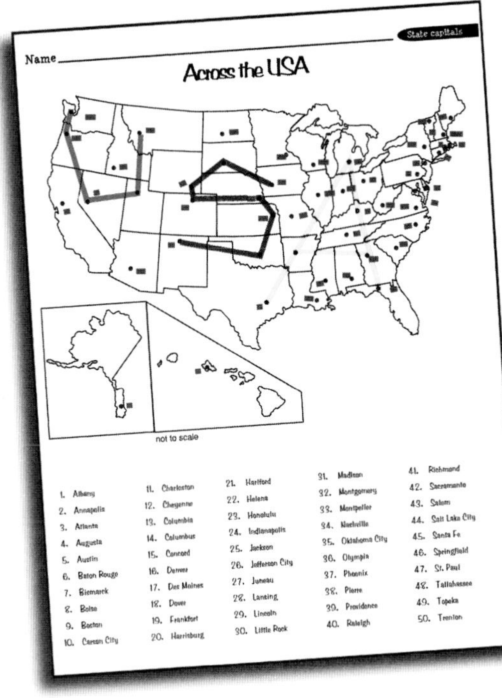

Name

State capitals

Across the USA

not to scale

1. Albany
2. Annapolis
3. Atlanta
4. Augusta
5. Austin
6. Baton Rouge
7. Bismarck
8. Boise
9. Boston
10. Carson City
11. Charleston
12. Cheyenne
13. Columbia
14. Columbus
15. Concord
16. Denver
17. Des Moines
18. Dover
19. Frankfort
20. Harrisburg
21. Hartford
22. Helena
23. Honolulu
24. Indianapolis
25. Jackson
26. Jefferson City
27. Juneau
28. Lansing
29. Lincoln
30. Little Rock
31. Madison
32. Montgomery
33. Montpelier
34. Nashville
35. Oklahoma City
36. Olympia
37. Phoenix
38. Pierre
39. Providence
40. Raleigh
41. Richmond
42. Sacramento
43. Salem
44. Salt Lake City
45. Santa Fe
46. Springfield
47. St. Paul
48. Tallahassee
49. Topeka
50. Trenton

Across the USA

State capitals

Provide each pair of students a copy of page 266. Have the partners work together to find each capital on the map. As they find each answer, have them write the capital's number by the star in the matching state. Once all stars are labeled, have students check their work by drawing a blue line to connect stars 36, 43, 10, 44, and 22 in the order listed. Next, have them draw a red line to connect stars 17, 38, 12, 29, 49, 35, and 45 in the order listed and then draw a yellow line to connect stars 5, 30, 28, 19, 3, 48, 3, and 30. Students will love the surprise answer that is revealed!

adapted from an idea by Liesa Owens and Rebecca Becker
W. C. Petty Elementary, Antioch, IL

Name ______________________________ State capitals

Across the USA

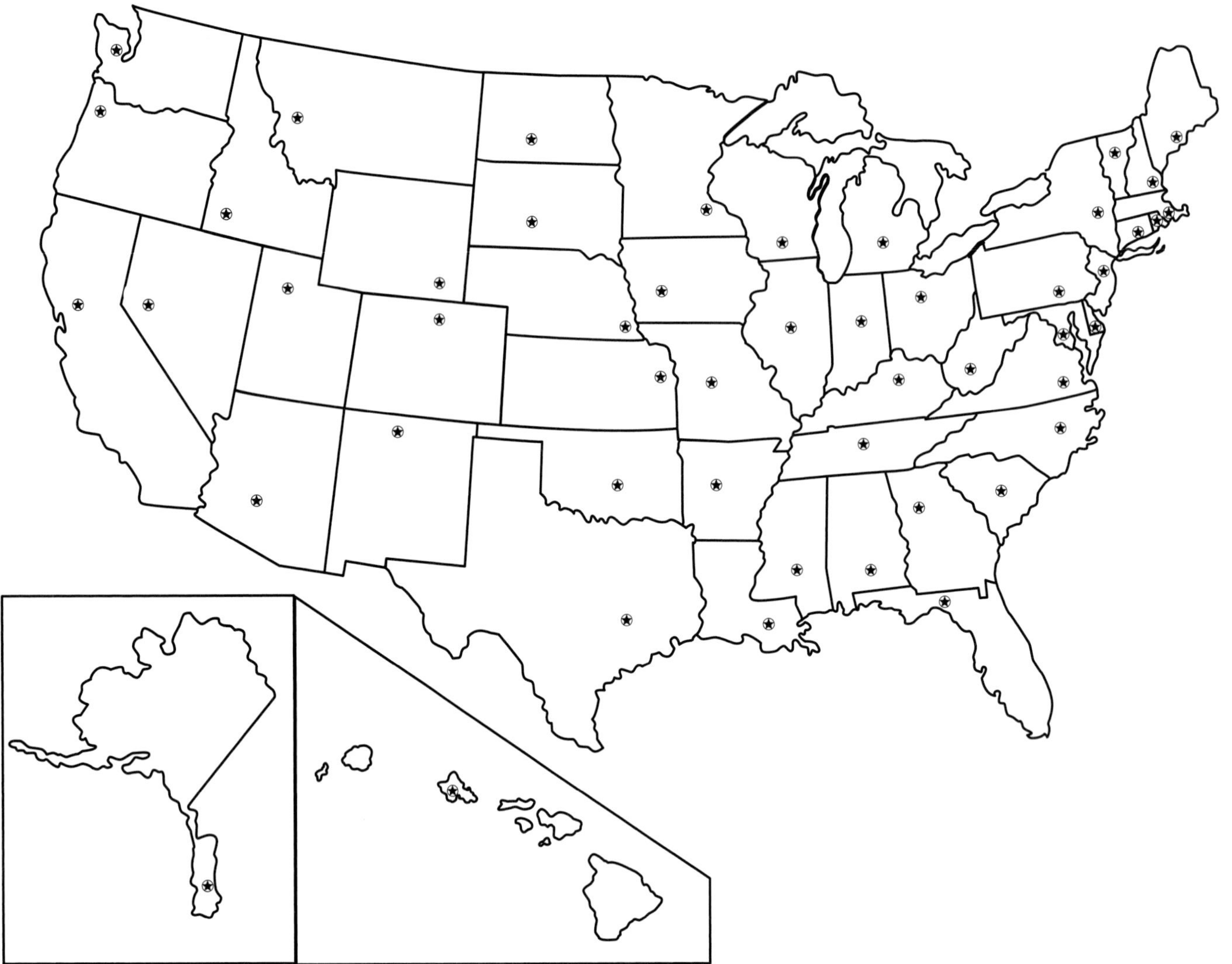

not to scale

1. Albany
2. Annapolis
3. Atlanta
4. Augusta
5. Austin
6. Baton Rouge
7. Bismarck
8. Boise
9. Boston
10. Carson City
11. Charleston
12. Cheyenne
13. Columbia
14. Columbus
15. Concord
16. Denver
17. Des Moines
18. Dover
19. Frankfort
20. Harrisburg
21. Hartford
22. Helena
23. Honolulu
24. Indianapolis
25. Jackson
26. Jefferson City
27. Juneau
28. Lansing
29. Lincoln
30. Little Rock
31. Madison
32. Montgomery
33. Montpelier
34. Nashville
35. Oklahoma City
36. Olympia
37. Phoenix
38. Pierre
39. Providence
40. Raleigh
41. Richmond
42. Sacramento
43. Salem
44. Salt Lake City
45. Santa Fe
46. Springfield
47. St. Paul
48. Tallahassee
49. Topeka
50. Trenton

 Note to the teacher: Use with "Across the USA" on page 265.

EXPLORING Social Studies

What Would We Do Without You?

Inventions

Practice inference skills with this easy-to-use center. Make a copy of page 269 (laminate the copy if you wish). Cut apart the cards and place them in a resealable bag at a center. To use the center, a student randomly selects an invention card and answers the questions on her paper. At the end of the week, set aside time for students to share their responses.

Ann Fisher, Toledo, OH

incandescent lightbulb
Thomas Alva Edison
1879
telephone
Alexander Graham Bell
1876
Questions
1. What is the name of the invention?
2. Why was this invented? What problem did it solve?
3. How have people benefited from this invention?
4. How could this invention be improved? Draw a diagram of your improvements on the back of your paper.
5. How would you rate this invention: useful or not important? Explain your rating.

The Important Thing…

Research

Begin this easy-to-adapt idea by having each child research three or four facts about a place, event, person, or topic currently being studied. Next, share with students *The Important Book* by Margaret Wise Brown. Students will quickly catch on to the repetitive text that ends each page: "But the important thing about…is that…" Next, instruct each child to write and illustrate several sentences about the topic she researched, as shown. Then compile students' papers into a class book.

Courtney Miller
Sienna Crossing Elementary
Missouri City, TX

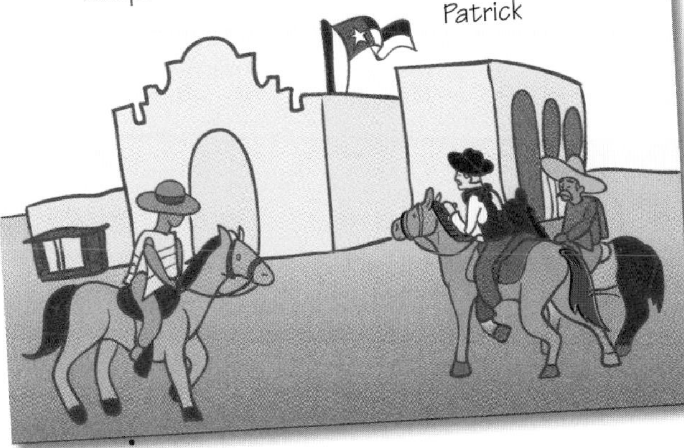

The Alamo
The Alamo is an important part of Texas history.
The old mission is located in San Antonio, Texas.
A band of Texans, led by William Barret Travis, fought hard there for 13 days.
The Texans lost the battle on March 6, 1836, after running out of ammunition.
But the important thing about the Alamo is that this is where 189 brave Texans fought for independence against the Mexican army.
Patrick

TIP
Repeat the activity to create similar books for math and language arts topics, such as geometry and parts of speech!

Name ____________________

Four Great Americans

The faces of the presidents on Mount Rushmore are larger than any statue in the world.

Read the passage. Then answer the questions.

Mount Rushmore, a national memorial to four American presidents, is a huge carving on a cliff in South Dakota's Black Hills. It is taller than the Great Pyramid of Egypt. Off and on between 1927 and 1941, 400 workers used drills and dynamite to cut the faces of George Washington, Thomas Jefferson, Theodore Roosevelt, and Abraham Lincoln in the mountain's granite. Each figure's head is as tall as a five-story building. Using this scale, a man with a head that size would stand 465 feet tall! Gutzon Borglum, an American sculptor, designed the memorial and oversaw most of the work. He chose this mountainous site because of its height, its soft grainy granite, and the long hours of sunlight it gets each day. This memorial is part of America's National Park System.

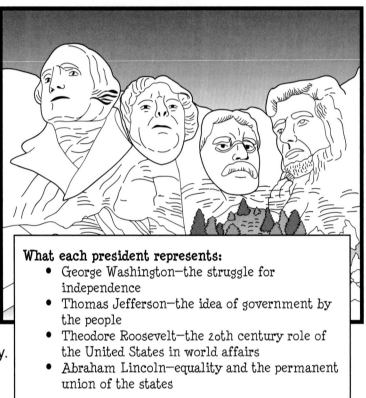

What each president represents:

- George Washington—the struggle for independence
- Thomas Jefferson—the idea of government by the people
- Theodore Roosevelt—the 20th century role of the United States in world affairs
- Abraham Lincoln—equality and the permanent union of the states

1. What is Mount Rushmore and where is it located? ____________________
2. Who designed this memorial? ____________________
3. Whose faces are carved on Mount Rushmore? ____________________
4. Why were these men chosen for the memorial? ____________________
5. Why was Mount Rushmore chosen as the site for the memorial? ____________________
6. How were the presidents' faces carved? ____________________
7. Why do you think it took so long to complete the memorial? ____________________
8. If another president's face were to be added to Mount Rushmore, which president do you think it should be? ____________________ Why? ____________________

Use the back if you need more space.

Use with "What Would We Do Without You?" on page 267.

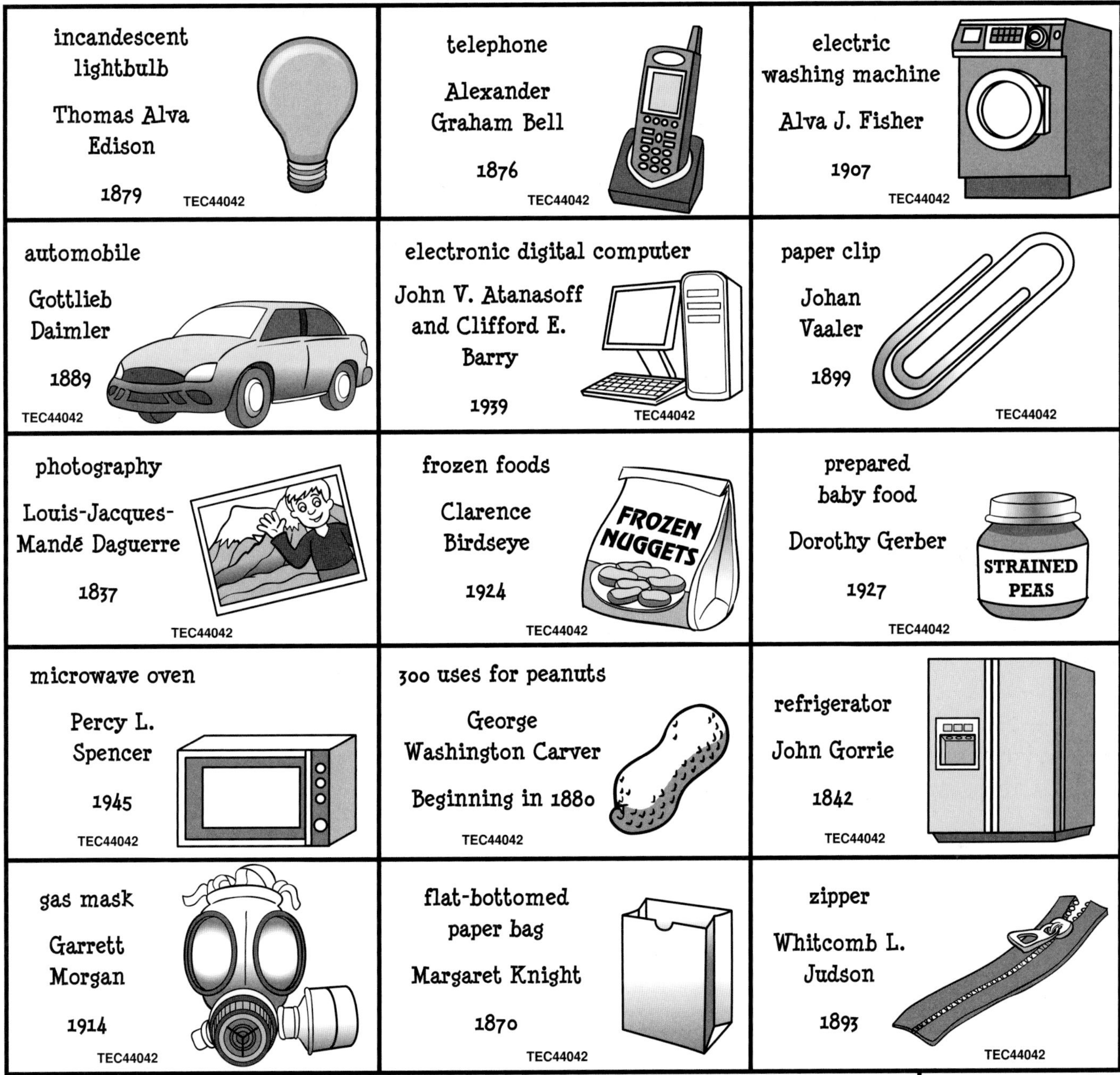

incandescent lightbulb
Thomas Alva Edison
1879
TEC44042
telephone
Alexander Graham Bell
1876
TEC44042
electric washing machine
Alva J. Fisher
1907
TEC44042
automobile
Gottlieb Daimler
1889
TEC44042
electronic digital computer
John V. Atanasoff and Clifford E. Barry
1939
TEC44042
paper clip
Johan Vaaler
1899
TEC44042
photography
Louis-Jacques-Mandé Daguerre
1837
TEC44042
frozen foods
Clarence Birdseye
1924
FROZEN NUGGETS
TEC44042
prepared baby food
Dorothy Gerber
1927
STRAINED PEAS
TEC44042
microwave oven
Percy L. Spencer
1945
TEC44042
300 uses for peanuts
George Washington Carver
Beginning in 1880
TEC44042
refrigerator
John Gorrie
1842
TEC44042
gas mask
Garrett Morgan
1914
TEC44042
flat-bottomed paper bag
Margaret Knight
1870
TEC44042
zipper
Whitcomb L. Judson
1893
TEC44042

Questions

1. What is the name of the invention?
2. Why was this invented? What problem did it solve?
3. How have people benefited from this invention?
4. How could this invention be improved? Draw a diagram of your improvements on the back of your paper.
5. How would you rate this invention: useful or not important? Explain your rating.

TEC44042

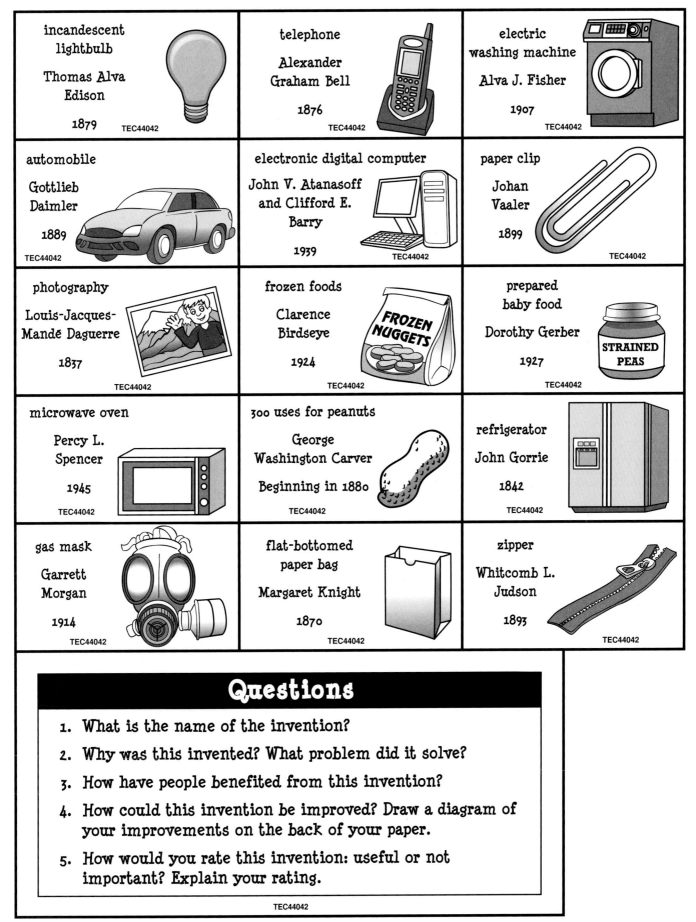

EXPLORING Social Studies

Money Matters

Economics vocabulary

Review economics jargon with this fun whole-class activity. Make a copy of the cards on page 272, cut the cards apart, and distribute them in random order. Have the student with the starred card read only its question aloud. Instruct the child holding the matching term to respond and then read her card's question aloud. Continue, using the key on page 313 as a guide, until the student with the starred card uses the term on his card to answer the final question.

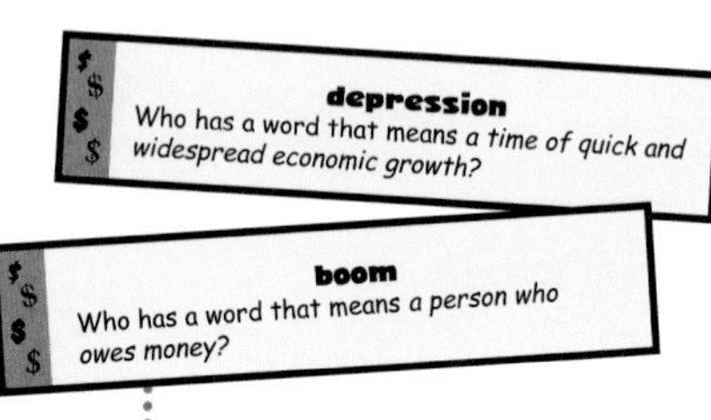

depression
Who has a word that means a time of quick and widespread economic growth?
boom
Who has a word that means a person who owes money?

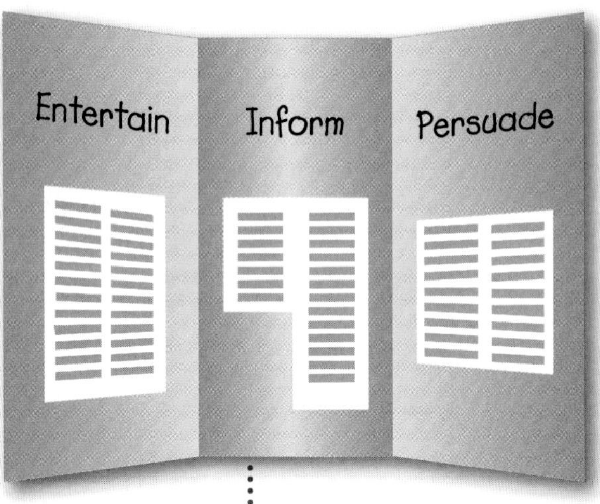

What's the Reason?

Current events, author's purpose

Help students identify an author's purpose by examining current events. Point out that news writing can entertain, inform, or persuade. Then direct each child to fold a large sheet of construction paper into thirds and label each section as shown. Have her search a newspaper or magazine for an example of each type of writing, cut out the example, and glue it in the appropriate column of her paper. As each student shares her articles with the class, discuss the characteristics of these three types of writing.

Who Am I?

Historical figures

To review the famous people students have studied this year, use this riddle-writing activity. Secretly assign each child a different person and number. Have the student write his number and three clues about his person on the front of an index card and the person's name on the back. Collect and shuffle the cards. Then tape one card (question side out) to each child's back. Have students number their papers and then move about the room to read the clues and record their guesses. If desired, give the student with the greatest number of correct guesses a treat.

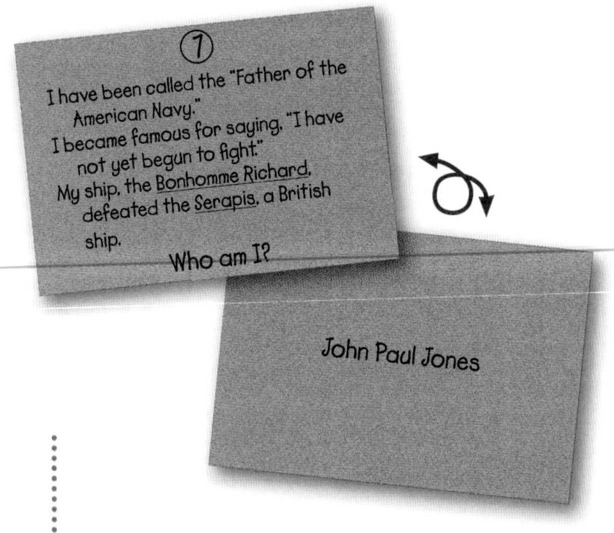

7
I have been called the "Father of the American Navy."
I became famous for saying, "I have not yet begun to fight."
My ship, the Bonhomme Richard, defeated the Serapis, a British ship.
Who am I?
John Paul Jones

Marsha Erskine, Dillard Elementary, Madison, NC

Name ____________________

From Rebellion to Revolution

John Hancock, one of the colonists most wanted by England's King George III, was the first man to sign the Declaration of Independence.

One of the most important documents in U.S. history is the Declaration of Independence. Richard Henry Lee was a delegate to the Second Continental Congress in Philadelphia. On June 7, 1776, he proposed that the 13 American colonies declare themselves free of England's rule. The Congress then asked a group of five men to draft a resolution. These men worked for 17 days and then sent a final draft to the Congress. The Congress debated the resolution for two days and then passed it on July 4, 1776.

The next step was to get all 13 colonies to approve the resolution. This took five days. The Congress then wanted an official copy of the document to be made. Almost a month after being approved, the Declaration of Independence was finally signed on August 2. John Hancock, president of the Second Continental Congress, was the declaration's first signer. In all, 56 representatives signed this important document.

- Thomas Jefferson, a member of the drafting committee, was chosen to do the actual writing of the Declaration of Independence.
- The first part of the Declaration of Independence explains the colonies' reasons for separating from England. It also outlines peoples' natural rights. The second part lists complaints against King George III.
- The official copy of the Declaration of Independence was handwritten with a quill pen.
- The signers' names are grouped by geographic location, which was a common practice at that time.
- Visitors can view the Declaration of Independence at the National Archives in Washington, DC.

1. Why do you think it took so long for Jefferson's committee to draft the Declaration of Independence? ____________________

2. What information does the Declaration of Independence include? ____________________

3. Why are the signers' names grouped as they are at the bottom of the document? ____________________

4. Why was the Declaration of Independence not signed until August 2, 1776? ____________________

5. Why was John Hancock the first signer of the Declaration of Independence? ____________________

Note to the teacher: For a math activity involving the signers of the Declaration of Independence, see "Signers' Likelihoods" on page 41 and the list of signers on page 47.

Economics Cards

Use with "Money Matters" on page 270.

★ **demand** Who has a word that means *more than is needed?* TEC44043	**surplus** Who has a phrase that means *the lowest pay a worker can receive by law?* TEC44043
minimum wage Who has a phrase that means *an economic system in which businesses are free to offer for sale many kinds of goods and services?* TEC44043	**free enterprise** Who has a word that means *a period in which there is little economic growth and a high rate of joblessness?* TEC44043
depression Who has a word that means *a time of quick and widespread economic growth?* TEC44043	**boom** Who has a word that means *a person who owes money?* TEC44043
debtor Who has a word that means *a written plan for managing money?* TEC44043	**budget** Who has a word that means *the way people produce, distribute, and consume goods and services?* TEC44043
economy Who has a word that means *a product brought into a country from another country in order to be sold?* TEC44043	**import** Who has a word that means *not plentiful?* TEC44043
scarce Who has a word that means *the state of being jobless?* TEC44043	**unemployment** Who has a word that means *a share in a company or business?* TEC44043
stock Who has a word that means *money that is paid by people to support the work of the government?* TEC44043	**tax** Who has a word that means *to trade with people by exchanging goods?* TEC44043
barter Who has a word that means *a budget shortage caused by spending more money than is earned?* TEC44043	**deficit** Who has a word that means *an economic condition in which it takes more and more money to buy the same goods?* TEC44043
inflation Who has a word that means *a product sent from one country to another to be sold?* TEC44043	**export** Who has a word that means *money that is leftover after a business has paid all its costs?* TEC44043
profit Who has a word that means *to buy a share of a business in the hope of making a profit?* TEC44043	**invest** Who has a phrase that means *a place where people can buy and sell stocks in businesses?* TEC44043
stock market Who has a word that means *a time of quick economic decline?* TEC44043	**bust** Who has a word that means *someone who buys goods and services?* TEC44043
consumer Who has a word that means *the amount of goods and services available for sale?* TEC44043	**supply** Who has a word that means *the need for goods or services to be produced or offered?* TEC44043

What Works For You?

What Works For You?

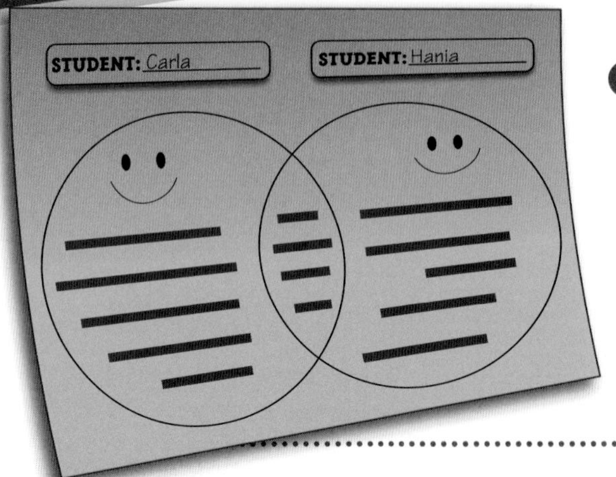

I have student pairs talk for ten minutes about each other's hobbies, families, favorites, and other topics. Then I give each pair a copy of the **Venn diagram** shown. Each student writes her name above a face. Then the partners fill in the diagram with ways they are unique and alike. Each duo shares its diagram with the class.

Shirley D. Jenks, Sabal Palm Elementary, Jacksonville, FL

On that important first day, I have each student complete an **interest inventory** (see page 275) that asks thought-provoking questions. This is a great activity for students to start as soon as they arrive in my classroom.

Lisa Rogers, Austin, TX

I make a class supply of a small card labeled with my **contact information.** After laminating the cards, I add magnetic tape to the back of each one. Then I send the magnets home on the first day of school for students to place on their refrigerators. Parents love having this information at their fingertips!

Roberta Swanson
Muscatine, IA

Ms. Brenda Case
McLean Elementary School
2515 Broad Avenue
Jackson, NV 00000
333-555-0111 ext. 11
bcase@jackson.k12.nv.us
Grade 5, Room 230

On the first day of school, my students and I **get acquainted** by playing Take a Stand! I ask yes-or-no questions, such as "Do you play a musical instrument?" and "Do you own a pair of red shoes?" The students and I stand whenever the answer to a question is yes.

Lisa Ford, Chicago, IL

Name ____________________

WHAT'S THE SCOOP?

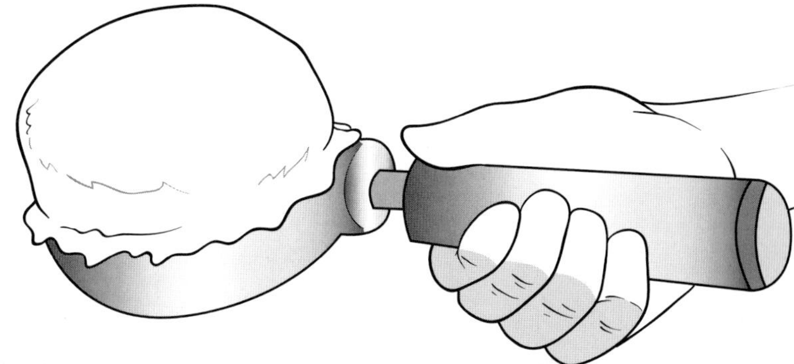

Finish each sentence.
Use the back of this page if you need more space.

1. Someday I hope to meet ____________________
2. I am very good at ____________________
3. If I could go anywhere, I'd go to ____________________
4. The greatest thing I could do with my life would be to ____________________
5. I get angry when ____________________
6. Sometimes I have to ____________________
7. Life is ____________________
8. I admire ____________________
9. I was embarrassed when ____________________
10. I've always wondered ____________________
11. The best day of the year is ____________________
12. I am happiest when I am ____________________
13. School is ____________________
14. I used to believe that ____________________
15. I need help with ____________________

Note to the teacher: Use with the second idea from "What Works for You?" on page 274.

What Works For You?

Parent Conferences

Parents often have no idea what their child's work should look like at your grade level. At conferences, I share with parents a binder of average-to-superior **work samples** with students' names whited out. As a parent compares work from her child's portfolio to the samples, she can more easily understand her child's effort and ability level.

Angela Falter Thomas, Tiffin, Ohio

Student Work Samples
Name
Survey
WHAT'S UP?
My favorite part of the school day is
because
My favorite subject in school right now is
because
The toughest subject for me is
because
I've done really well in
because

To occupy parents who arrive early for a conference, I run a PowerPoint **slide show** on a computer outside my classroom. As they wait, the early arrivals view their children participating in classroom activities, plus postings of upcoming classroom events, tests, and projects.

Brooke Beverly, Dudley Elementary, Dudley, MA

Before a first conference with parents, I have each student complete the **survey** on page 277. I then share the child's answers with his parent at the start of the conference. It's a positive way to begin our conversation about the child's academic strengths, weaknesses, and behavior.

Dana Johansen, Greenwich Academy, Greenwich, CT

I end each conference on a positive note by giving the parent a simple **memento** to take home, such as a list of parent resources available at the school, tips for selecting books for his child, or suggestions for educational gifts for his child.

Julie Lewis, J. O. Davis Elementary, Irving, TX

Name ____________________

My favorite part of the school day is ____________________
because ____________________

My favorite subject in school right now is ____________________
because ____________________

The toughest subject for me is ____________________
because ____________________

I've done really well in ____________________
because ____________________

I want to improve in ____________________
because ____________________

What I've most enjoyed about school recently is ____________________
because ____________________

I'm looking forward to ____________________
because ____________________

The book I am reading independently right now is ____________________
It's about ____________________

My favorite reading genre is ____________________
because ____________________

The classmate I most like to work with is ____________________
because ____________________

Note to the teacher: Use with the third idea on page 276.

What Works For You?

Makeup Work

Stack It High!
Welcome Back!
We Missed You!

I assign a student to collect makeup work for absentees in a two-pocket **folder** labeled as shown. This student records the day's assignments on a designated sheet of paper and collects copies of the day's skill sheets for each absent child. At the end of the day, my helper tucks everything in the folder and places it in a prominent location. When an absent child returns to school, she removes her assignments from the folder and turns them in as she completes them.

Katie Brooks, St. Michaels Elementary, St. Michaels, MD

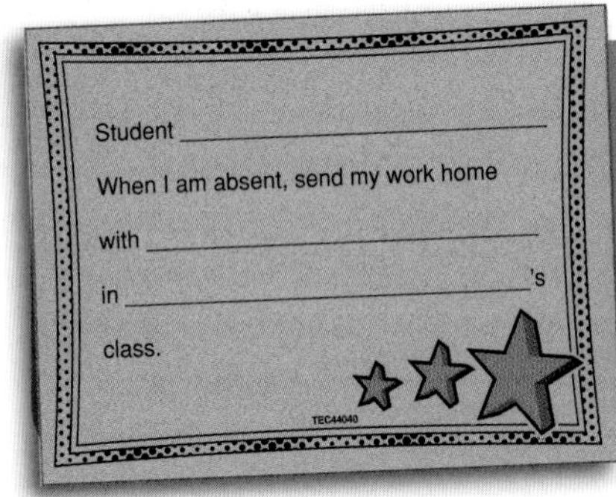

Student
When I am absent, send my work home
with
in 's
class.
TEC44040

To make it easier to **send work home** to a student who's sick, I have each child complete two cards from a copy of page 279 in advance. When a student is absent, I attach a card to her work. Then I have a student volunteer deliver the assignments to the designated person and classroom.

Joyce Hovanec, Glassport Elementary, Glassport, PA

Each morning, I write the day's assignments on a copy of my **class list.** As students turn in assignments, I check the appropriate boxes. During the week, I refer to the list to tell absent students which assignments must be made up.

Sheri Long, Sunflower Elementary, Gardner, KS

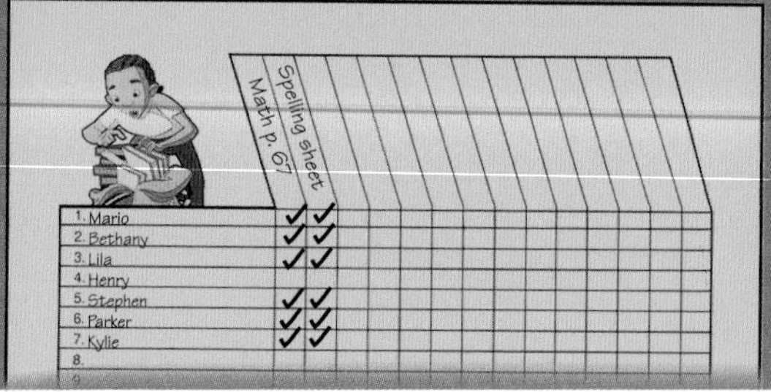

I created a **template** listing each subject area and saved it on my computer. Each day, I open the file and type the day's assignments in the corresponding sections. At the end of the day, I simply print a copy for each absent student.

Joyce Hovanec

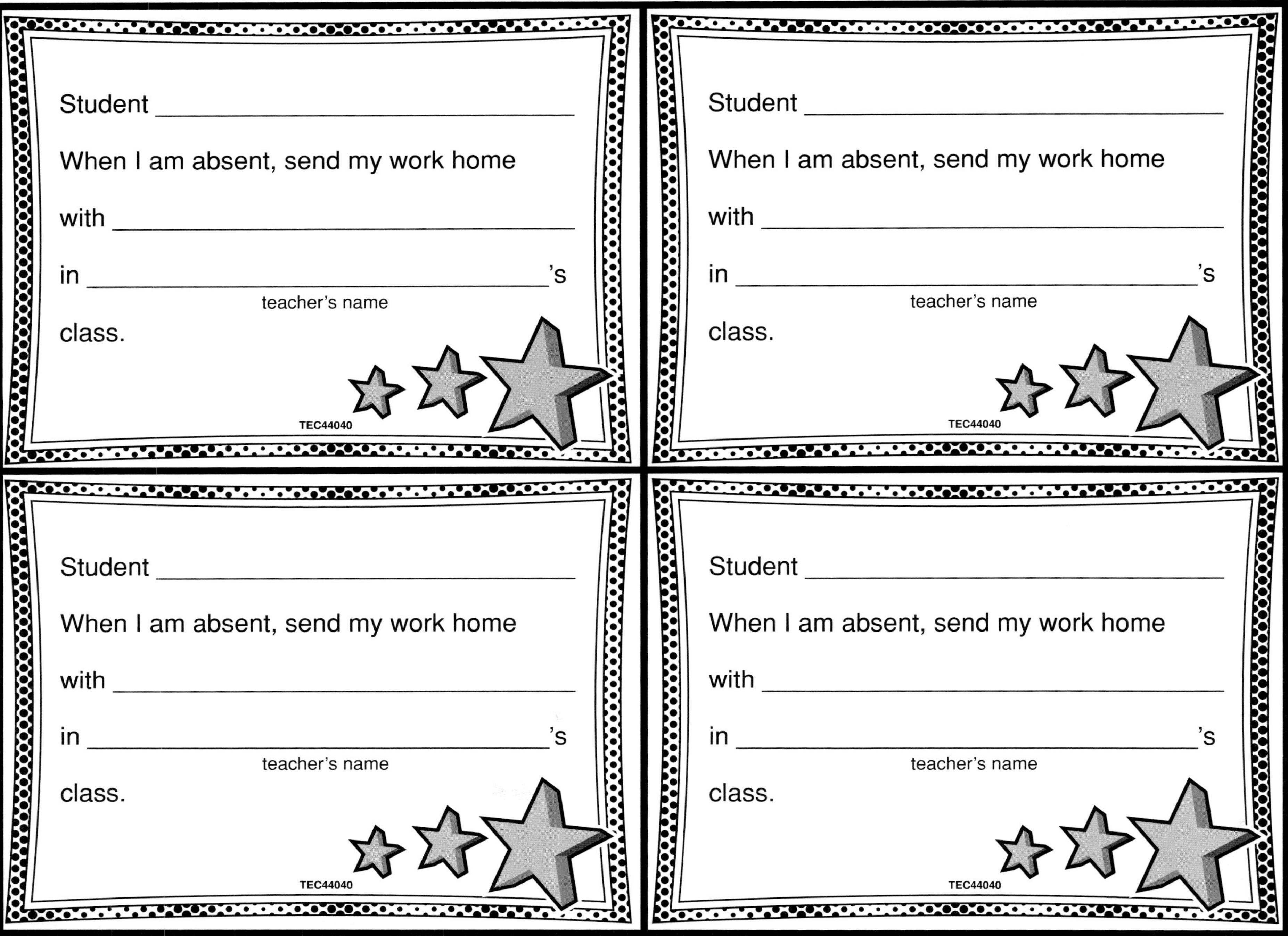
Student
When I am absent, send my work home
with
in 's
teacher's name
class.
TEC44040

Note to the teacher: Use with the second idea from "What Works For You?" on page 278.

I use movie **lingo** to help my students control their chattering. I have them think of our classroom as a movie set where I am the director. When I say, "Quiet on the set," they get the message. When I say, "Action," they're free to talk quietly.

Colleen Dabney, Williamsburg, VA

Chat Softly

Whisper

No Talking

To help me silently communicate my expectations about talking, I make three laminated signs backed with magnetic tape. Several times each day, I display the green sign on my whiteboard so students can chat with their chums for a minute or two. Anytime a child socializes while the red or yellow sign is up, I have her sign her name on the board under the appropriate sign. Then, the next time the green sign is up, anyone who doesn't have her name under a sign gets to socialize.

Pat Twohey, Smithfield, RI

To keep the rest of my class working quietly when I'm with a small group, we play Wipeout! If a child outside the small group talks, I cross his name off a laminated class list with a wipe-off marker. Between groups, I allow students a minute of talk time. Students whose names are not crossed off when group time ends are entered in a Friday drawing for a special treat or privilege. **For tickets to use in the drawing, see page 281.**

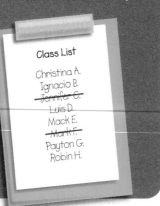

Class List
Christina A.
Ignacio B.
~~Jennifer C.~~
~~Luis D.~~
Mack E.
~~Mark F.~~
Payton G.
Robin H.

Kelly Dettinger, Riverview Elementary
Spanish Fork, UT

When student talking gets out of hand, I immediately stop what I am doing, look directly at the classroom **clock**, and start counting aloud increments of time, such as "five seconds…ten seconds…," until the talking stops. The accumulated time off-task is subtracted from recess or free-time activities. My students also know they can earn time back for being *on* task!

Kathleen Tulloss, Riverview Elementary
Spotsylvania, VA

Ticket Patterns

Use with the last idea on page 280. Have each child write her name on the back of a ticket before putting it in a container for the drawing.

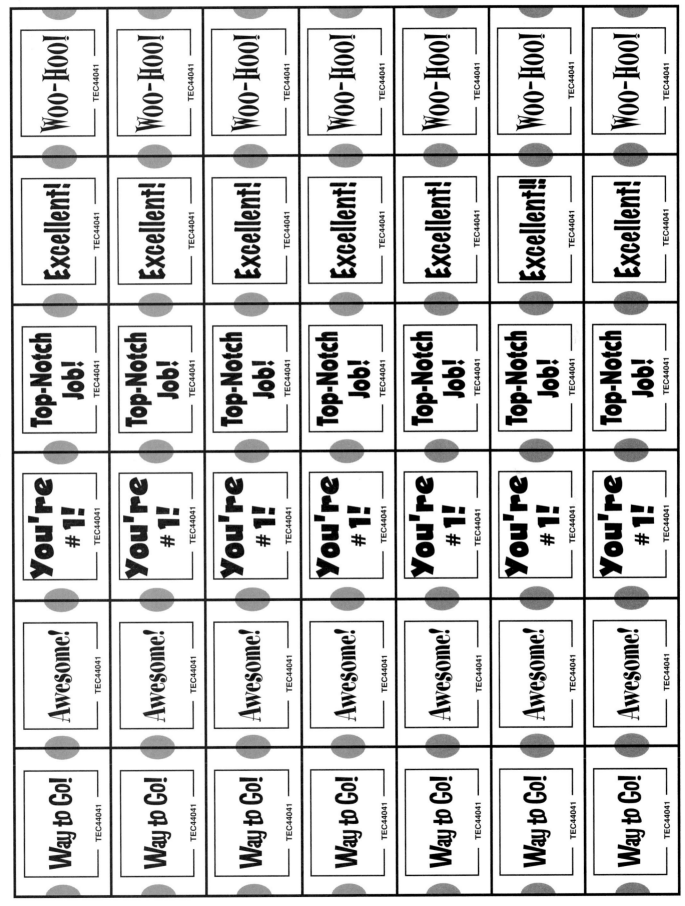

Woo-Hoo! TEC44041	Woo-Hoo! TEC44041	Woo-Hoo! TEC44041	Woo-Hoo! TEC44041	Woo-Hoo! TEC44041	Woo-Hoo! TEC44041	Woo-Hoo! TEC44041
Excellent! TEC44041	Excellent! TEC44041	Excellent! TEC44041	Excellent! TEC44041	Excellent! TEC44041	Excellent! TEC44041	Excellent! TEC44041
Top-Notch Job! TEC44041	Top-Notch Job! TEC44041	Top-Notch Job! TEC44041	Top-Notch Job! TEC44041	Top-Notch Job! TEC44041	Top-Notch Job! TEC44041	Top-Notch Job! TEC44041
You're # 1! TEC44041	You're # 1! TEC44041	You're # 1! TEC44041	You're # 1! TEC44041	You're # 1! TEC44041	You're # 1! TEC44041	You're # 1! TEC44041
Awesome! TEC44041	Awesome! TEC44041	Awesome! TEC44041	Awesome! TEC44041	Awesome! TEC44041	Awesome! TEC44041	Awesome! TEC44041
Way to Go! TEC44041	Way to Go! TEC44041	Way to Go! TEC44041	Way to Go! TEC44041	Way to Go! TEC44041	Way to Go! TEC44041	Way to Go! TEC44041

What Works For You?

Motivating Students to Do Their Best Work

This simple incentive encourages students to be intentional about doing their best work. From time to time, I attach a small reward, such as a piece of candy or a sticker, to each student work sample that exhibits qualities such as neatness, accuracy, and effort. Since students don't know when I'm going to distribute prizes, they are motivated to turn in top-notch papers every time.

Patricia E. Dancho, Apollo-Ridge Middle School, Spring Church, PA

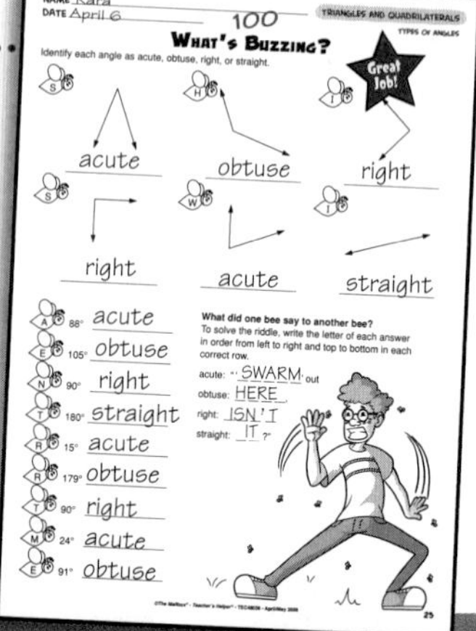

NAME Kara
DATE April 6
100
TRIANGLES AND QUADRILATERALS
TYPES OF ANGLES

What's Buzzing?

Identify each angle as acute, obtuse, right, or straight.

Great Job!

S acute
H obtuse
I right
S right
W acute
I straight

A 88° acute
E 105° obtuse
N 90° right
T 180° straight
R 15° acute
R 179° obtuse
T 90° right
M 24° acute
E 91° obtuse

What did one bee say to another bee?
To solve the riddle, write the letter of each answer in order from left to right and top to bottom in each correct row.

acute: "SWARM out
obtuse: HERE,
right: ISN'T
straight: IT?"

©The Mailbox® • Teacher's Helper® • April/May 2009
25

Membership Card
Right on Track Club
For Students Who Do Their Best Work
April 8
date
This is to certify that
Scott
student
is an official member of the Right on Track Club and is entitled to all privileges for one month from the date on this card.
Ms. Eller
teacher

Right on Track
Member in Good Standing
Club

I created a Right on Track club to prompt students to do their best work. Each month, I invite students who have consistently turned in quality work to join the club. I present each member with a copy of a membership card (see page 283) and a special treat to reward his efforts.

Amy Janak, Cypress Grove Intermediate, College Station, TX

To put motivation at my students' fingertips, I have each student write on a paper strip in block letters, "I am doing my best work." Then I attach each child's strip to her desk. When I see a student working accordingly, I instruct her to color a letter on her strip. After a child has colored all the letters on her strip, I present her with a special reward.

Kristin Payne, Sacramento, CA

I AM DOING MY BEST WORK.

When preparing to go to a much-anticipated activity or event—such as recess, lunch, or a special class—I use a recently completed assignment to determine the order in which students line up. I look at each paper and call the top ten students to the line. Students put forth their best effort every time to be the first in line!

Linda Teague, Randleman, NC

Membership Cards

Use with the second idea from "What Works for You?" on page 282.

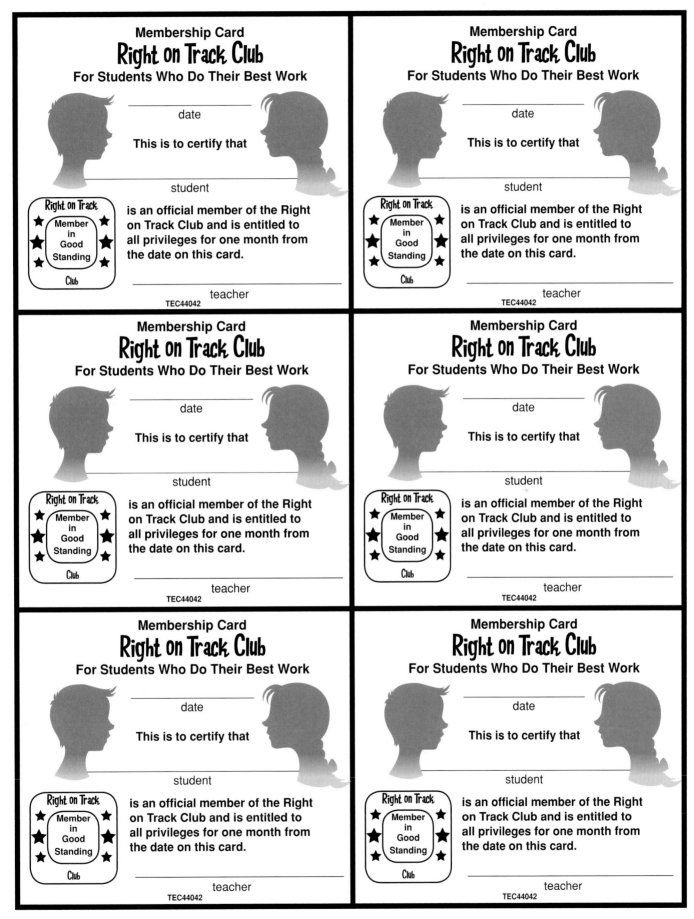

Membership Card

For Students Who Do Their Best Work

date

This is to certify that

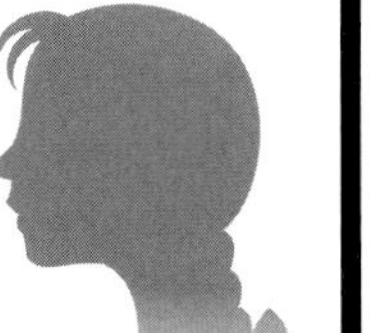

student

is an official member of the Right on Track Club and is entitled to all privileges for one month from the date on this card.

teacher

TEC44042

Membership Card

Right on Track Club

For Students Who Do Their Best Work

date

This is to certify that

student

is an official member of the Right on Track Club and is entitled to all privileges for one month from the date on this card.

teacher

TEC44042

Membership Card

Right on Track Club

For Students Who Do Their Best Work

date

This is to certify that

student

is an official member of the Right on Track Club and is entitled to all privileges for one month from the date on this card.

teacher

TEC44042

Membership Card

Right on Track Club

For Students Who Do Their Best Work

date

This is to certify that

student

is an official member of the Right on Track Club and is entitled to all privileges for one month from the date on this card.

teacher

TEC44042

Membership Card

Right on Track Club

For Students Who Do Their Best Work

date

This is to certify that

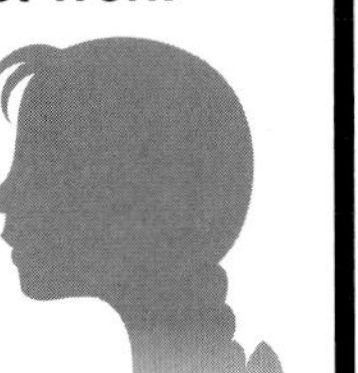

student

is an official member of the Right on Track Club and is entitled to all privileges for one month from the date on this card.

teacher

TEC44042

Membership Card

Right on Track Club

For Students Who Do Their Best Work

date

This is to certify that

student

is an official member of the Right on Track Club and is entitled to all privileges for one month from the date on this card.

teacher

TEC44042

What Works For You?

Early Finishers

Challenge 8
Sketch a new floor plan for your classroom.

Challenge 1
Write the numbers 1 through 100 on a sheet of paper. Find the sum of the numbers.

For students who finish work early, I post on a bulletin board six to ten **challenges** that review various subjects. Each activity uses a different learning style, and each student completes his work in a personal journal. Once a week, I reward those who successfully complete an activity.

Miriam Krauss, Bais Yaakov of Brooklyn, Brooklyn, NY

For 12 challenge cards, see page 285.

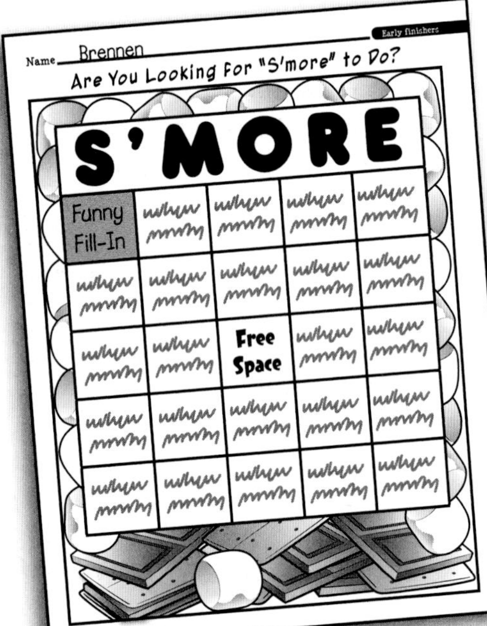

I place multiple copies of worksheets, activities from children's magazines, and old workbook pages each in their own labeled manila folder along with each answer key. Then I store the folders in a crate with hanging files. Next, I write the activities' titles on a copy of the **"S'more" grid** on page 286. I have each student place a copy of the grid in a pocket folder kept at his desk. Each time he completes an activity from the crate, he colors that square on his grid and places his work in his folder.

Jane Tauscher, Dallas Park Elementary, Ft. Worth, TX

To help students with their **creative writing** skills, I post on the board a large envelope and a funny or interesting magazine picture. When a student finishes her work early, I have her write a caption, poem, or story about the picture and then place it in the envelope. At the end of the week, I read aloud three or four of the best pieces.

Rifki Frieder, Masores Bais Yaakov, Brooklyn, NY

I have an early finisher pick a **die-cut shape** from an envelope and glue it to a sheet of paper. Next, I have him use markers or crayons to transform that shape into something else. I display completed projects around the room.

Linda Marshall, Poquoson Elementary, Poquoson, VA

Challenge Cards

Use with the first idea of "What Works for You?" on page 284.

Challenge 1
Write the numbers 1 through 100 on a sheet of paper. Find the sum of the numbers.
TEC44043

Challenge 2
Draw a picture that shows the meaning of this proverb: "Fish and visitors stink after three days."
TEC44043

Challenge 3
Write a song about your most recent science lesson. Use a familiar tune, such as "Row, Row, Row Your Boat" or "Jingle Bells."
TEC44043

Challenge 4
Write an essay explaining how to play your favorite sport or game.
TEC44043

Challenge 5
List words that can be formed using only the letters in the word *environment.*
TEC44043

Challenge 6
Describe what you think a classroom will be like in the year 2050.
TEC44043

Challenge 7
Write a poem about your favorite year in school so far.
TEC44043

Challenge 8
Sketch a new floor plan for your classroom.
TEC44043

Challenge 9
Measure and record the perimeter of ten objects in your desk.
TEC44043

Challenge 10
List words or phrases that rhyme with *cat.*
TEC44043

Challenge 11
Write a letter to convince your principal to help save an endangered animal.
TEC44043

Challenge 12
Write a summary about the best book you have ever read.
TEC44043

Name ____________________ Early finishers

Are You Looking For "S'more" to Do?

 Note to the teacher: Use with the second activity of "What Works for You?" on page 284.

Management Tips and Timesavers

Management Tips and Timesavers

Check the Pockets!

Monitor students' **comings and goings** with this unique idea. Attach to a bulletin board a personalized library pocket for each student. Direct each child to color and cut out a copy of the patterns on page 289, tape each of his cutouts to the top of a different jumbo craft stick, and then place the sticks in a container near the board. Each day when a student arrives at school, he places the "Present at School" stick in his pocket to indicate he is present. If a student leaves the room during the day, he places the appropriate stick in his pocket. You can tell at a glance who's absent and the whereabouts of a student who is temporarily out of the room.

Linda Masternak Justice, Kansas City, MO

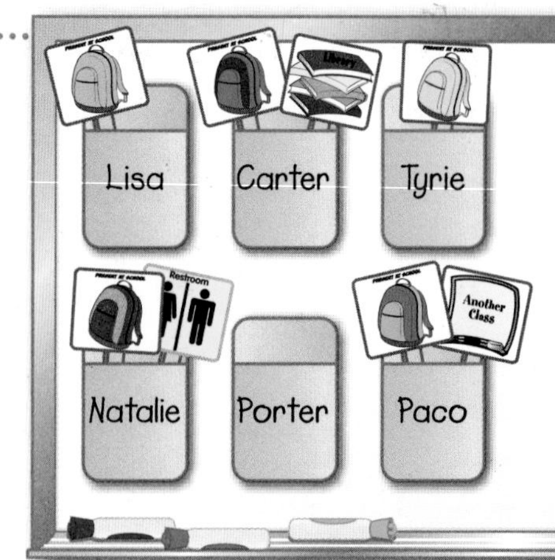

Name Buttons

For sturdy **nametags** even older kids will wear, obtain a class supply of inexpensive campaign-style buttons with pin backings. Cut out a class supply of paper circles sized to fit the buttons. Invite each student to decorate a paper circle as desired and glue it on a button. Use the nametags during field trips or when you have a substitute or visitor in your classroom.

Beth Ann Sadler, Bradley West School, Bradley, IL

Supply Buckets

Looking for a way to keep **supplies** organized and ready when students need them? Try inexpensive plastic buckets! Write each student's name on a separate bucket (plastic paint buckets work great). Then have each student personalize his supplies with a permanent marker and place them in his bucket. When supplies are needed, students simply grab their buckets and bring them to their seats. If a stray supply is found, a student just checks the name on the item and returns it to its bucket.

Julie Adams, St. Mary School, Elgin, IL

Location Patterns

Use with "Check the Pockets!" on page 288.

Management Tips and Timesavers

Letter by Letter

Help students recall **classroom rules and procedures** with acronyms. For example, use OYO as an acronym for independent work time. Explain to students that the letters stand for "On Your Own." Then assign acronyms to other rules and procedures (see the list) and share them with the class. When students need a reminder, simply say the appropriate acronym to get them back on track.

Shirley Kohls, Wilson Elementary, Beaver Dam, WI

Possible Acronyms

SIG = Silence Is Golden
SAL = Skip a Line
NOP = Name on Paper
ROS = Respect Other Students
SIS = Sit in Seat

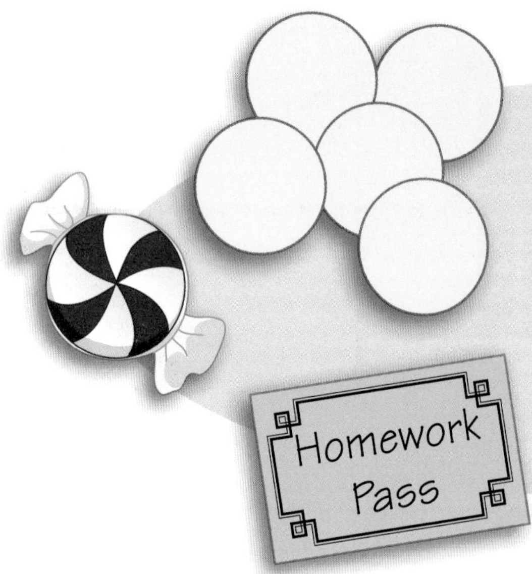

Participation Pays!

This rewarding idea encourages **student participation.** Laminate a supply of yellow paper circles (coins). Each time a student participates in a class discussion, give her a coin. When a child has collected a predetermined number of coins, reward her with a small prize or treat.

Tynisha Northcutt, Howard Kennedy Elementary, Omaha, NE

Check It Out!

Keep tabs on the books in your **classroom library** with student library cards! Invite students to personalize one library card (patterns on page 291) for each book you permit them to borrow at a time. Then laminate the cards for durability. When a student borrows a book, he writes the title and author's name on a sticky note and attaches the note to the back of one of his cards. He places the card in a designated location, such as a file box. When a child has used all his library cards, he must return a book before borrowing a new one. After he returns a book, he retrieves his card and removes the sticky note from the back.

Kim Minafo, Apex, NC

Library Card Patterns

Use with "Check It Out!" on page 290.

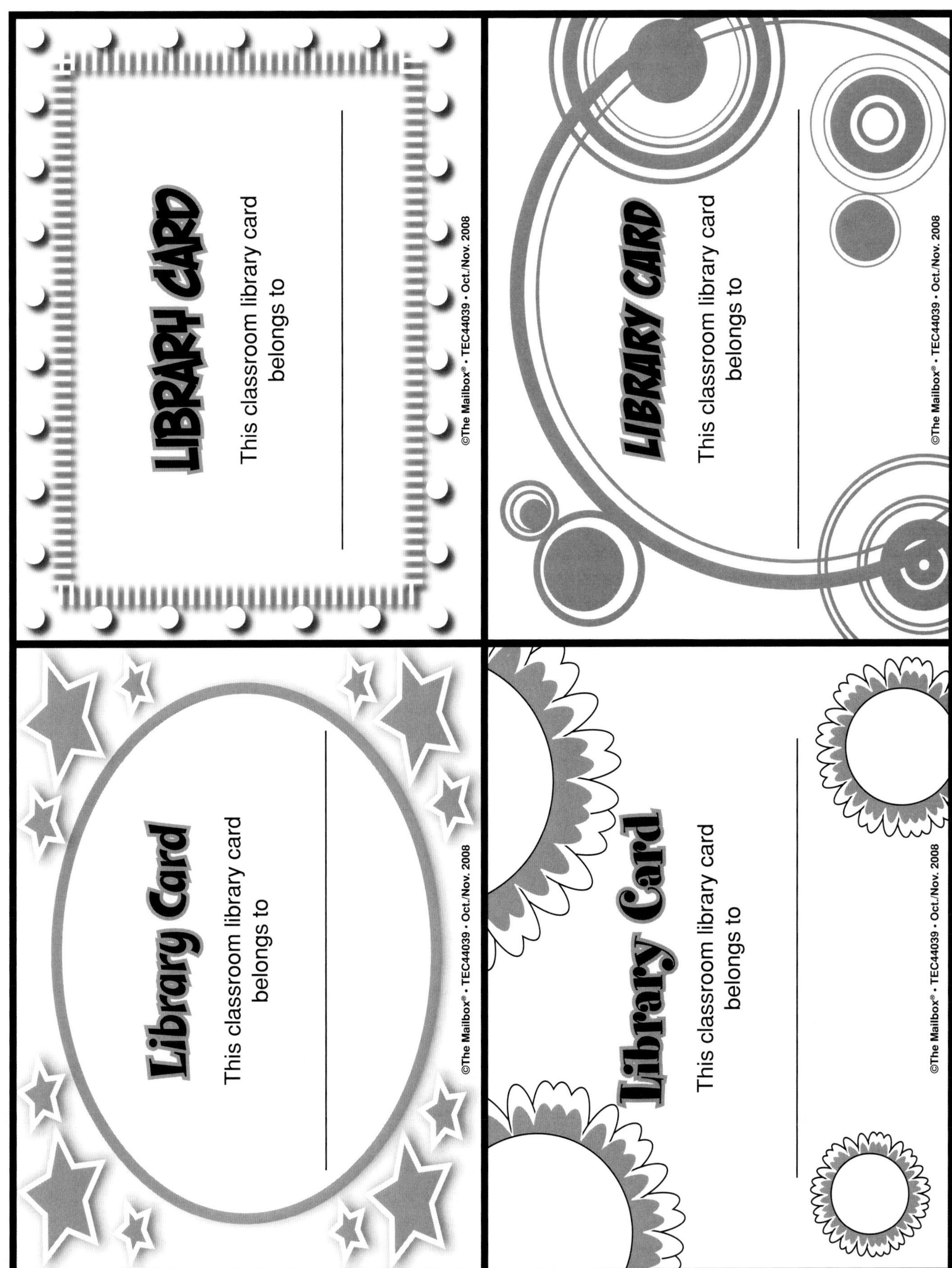

Management Tips and Timesavers

Lesson Plan Templates

Want to make quick work of planning for a **substitute teacher?** Create a computer template of boxes labeled with the subjects you teach, their time slots, and any important notes and information about your class. If your schedule varies, make a different template for each day. Keep several copies of the template on hand. When you need a sub, just jot down plans for each subject in the corresponding section.

Sherri Kilby, Royal Oaks Elementary, Kannapolis, NC

Substitute Lesson Plans

Thursday
Date <u>12-11-08</u>
7:45–8:30 Morning work
8:30–9:00 English
9:00–9:45 Writing
9:45–10:00 Break, students eat snacks and talk softly.
10:00–10:45 Reading
10:45–11:30 Science/Social Studies
11:30–12:15 Math
12:15–12:45 Lunch
12:45–1:10 Bathroom, pack up, novel
1:10–1:45 Recess
1:45–2:15 SSR
2:15 Dismissal

2nd Loaders:
(Use computer or play games quietly)
Bobby
Joel
Stephen
Areli
Arsenio

Morning Work
- Division worksheet

English
- Do the exercises on page 116.

Writing
- Write a persuasive paragraph about why people should or should not like cold weather.

Reading
- Read pages 142–157 in reading book.
- Discuss story.
- Answer activity questions.

Science/Social Studies
- Read pages 138–142 in science.
- Complete "After Reading" activity.

Math
- Review long division.
- Complete long division worksheet.

Novel
- Read Chapter 5 in <u>Tuck Everlasting</u>.
- Answer Chapter 5 discussion questions.

Free-Time Folders

Keep **early finishers** engaged by giving each child a personalized folder with a copy of page 293 stapled inside. When a student finishes his class work sooner than his classmates, he chooses an activity from the grid and completes the task on a separate sheet of paper numbered with the corresponding activity number. He stores the activities in his folder until they all are completed.

Elizabeth Loeser, Jacksonville, FL

Alternative Display Space

When you run out of wall space in your classroom, use your **window blinds.** Turn the blinds so that the curved side of each slat is next to the glass. Then hang posters, charts, or visual reminders from the slats with paper clips. The displays will be a cinch to change!

Gina Gottschalk, Wauconda Grade School, Wauconda, IL

Properties of Addition and Multiplication

- identity
  4 + 0 = 4 7 x 1 = 7
- associative
  (3 + 7) + 5 = 3 + (7 + 5)
  (2 x 3) x 4 = 2 x (3 x 4)
- distributive
  4 x (2 + 5) = (4 x 2) + (4 x 5)
- commutative
  7 + 9 = 9 + 7 3 x 5 = 5 x 3
- zero property
  8 + 0 = 8 8 x 0 = 0

Name ____________________ Activity grid

WHEN I FINISH EARLY, I CAN...

1. Use the digits 0, 3, 5, 6, and 9 to list as many five-digit numbers as you can.	2. If every person in the class had a dog, how many paws would there be altogether? 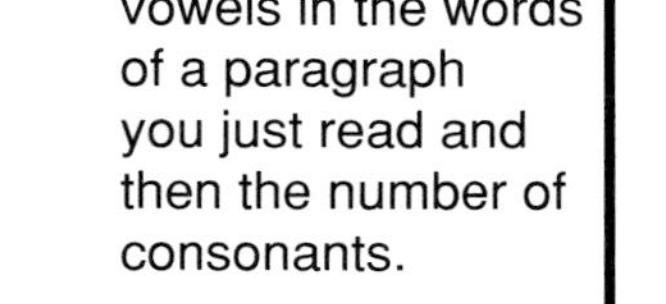	3. Write a poem about pizzas. 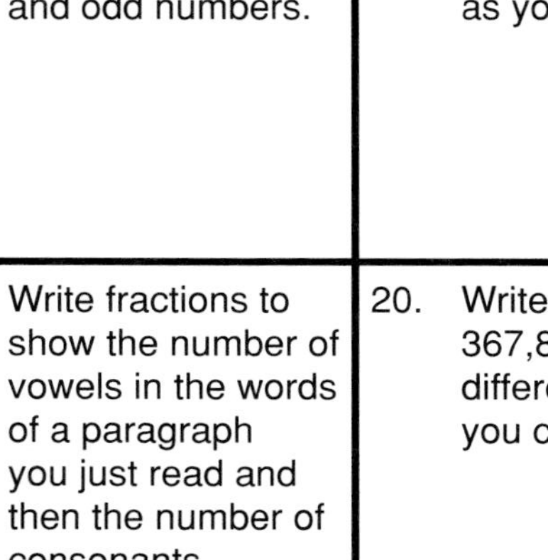	4. Use the letters in *computer* to write as many words as you can. 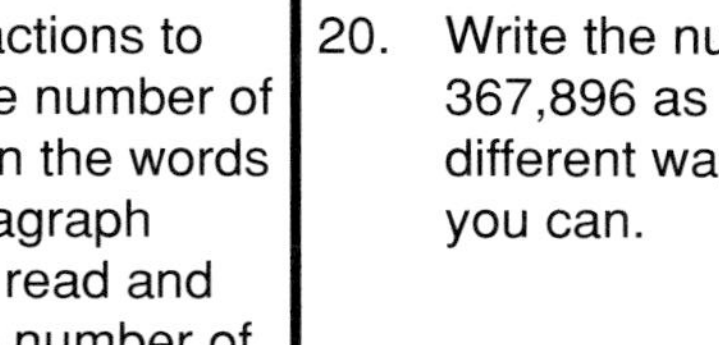	5. If each student in the class has two quarters, three dimes, five nickels, and four pennies, how much money does the class have altogether?
6. Look up *palindrome* in the dictionary and write its definition. List as many palindromes as you can.	7. Write three clues about your favorite animal. Have a classmate read your clues and guess the animal.	8. List at least ten foods that contain chocolate. 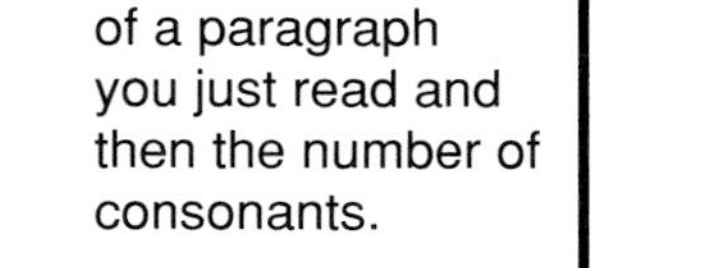	9. Write a persuasive paragraph about why people should or should not chew gum. 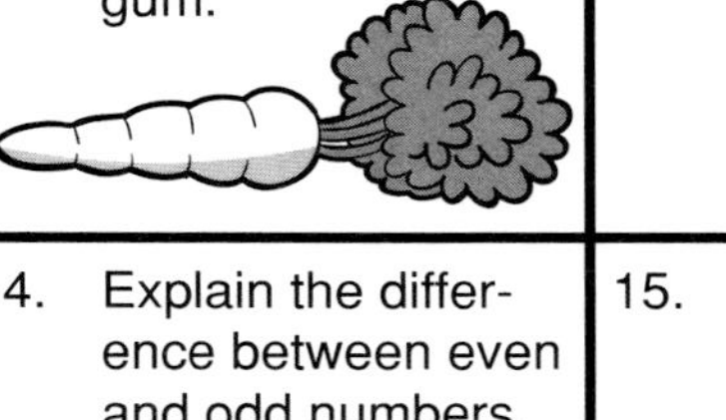	10. If you could choose only one food to eat for the rest of your life, what would it be? Explain why.
11. Is the number 688 divisible by 4? Tell how you know.	12. List some things you've learned in school this year.	13. Write a letter to someone thanking them for something they have done for you.	14. Explain the difference between even and odd numbers.	15. List as many states and their capitals as you can.
16. Describe your favorite thing about school. 	17. Think of 15 things you could do for fun after school that do not involve television, computers, cell phones, or video games.	18. Write five questions you would like to ask your teacher. 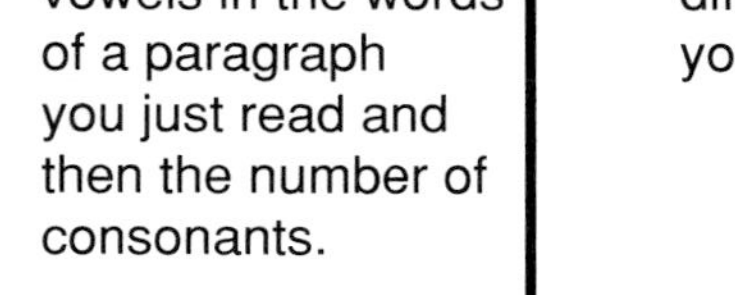 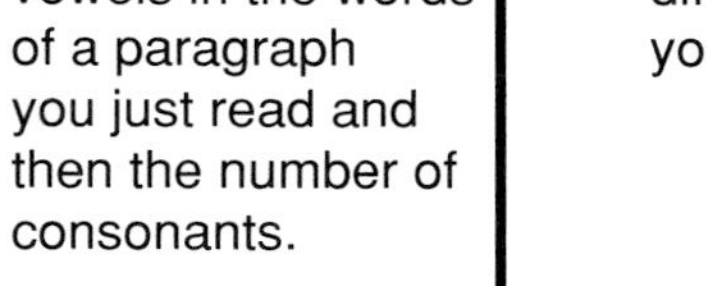 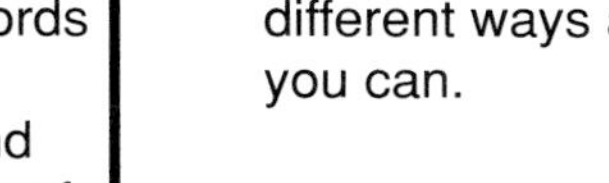	19. Write fractions to show the number of vowels in the words of a paragraph you just read and then the number of consonants.	20. Write the number 367,896 as many different ways as you can.

Note to the teacher: Use with "Free-Time Folders" on page 292.

Management Tips and Timesavers

A "Toe-rific" Tool

Foam toe separators help students keep **supplies** for projects at their fingertips. In each section of the spacer, a child slides an item such as a marker or a glue stick. The slots keep the supplies from rolling off students' desks onto the floor!

Colleen Dabney, Williamsburg, VA

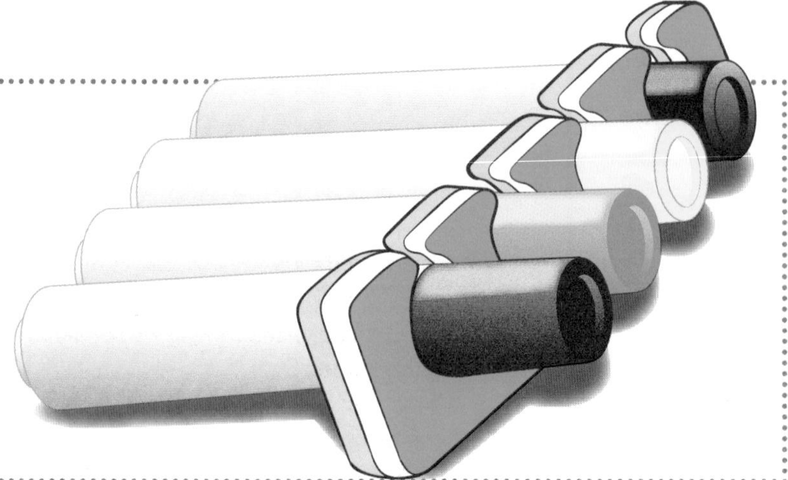

Special Delivery

Minimize trips to the office or other classrooms by hanging an inexpensive plastic envelope by your classroom door. Slip inside the envelope papers that need to be taken to other locations in the school. Each time you leave your classroom, check the envelope for any deliveries.

Samantha Call, Alva, FL

Daily Display

Instead of writing **morning routines and information** on the board every day, try this timesaving idea. Make a laminated sign for each regular task or request. Each day, display the desired signs on the board. If the day calls for something unusual, simply list it on the board.

Karen Hall, S. S. Dixon Intermediate, Pace, FL

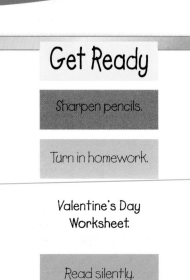

Get Ready

Sharpen pencils.

Turn in homework.

Valentine's Day Worksheet.

Read silently.

Management Tips and Timesavers

Write and Wipe

These easy-to-make **whiteboards** save both time and money! For each student, slip a sheet of plain white paper in a plastic page protector. If desired, place the paper back-to-back with a sheet of writing paper. Students write on either side with a wipe-off marker and then clean the surface for reuse. Not only do these boards cut down on the use of paper, but they can also be stored in students' desks to keep them easily accessible.

Ann Kennedy, Sangster Elementary, Springfield, VA

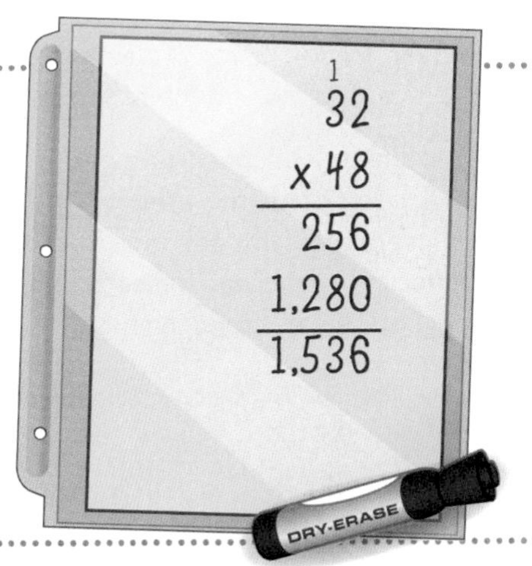

Many Markers

Looking for a way to organize your **dry-erase markers**? Try a shower basket with suction cups! Use the suction cups to attach the basket to your whiteboard. Then place your markers in the basket cap-side up to make it easier to grab the desired color.

Linda Bobbs, Christian Fellowship Academy, Jeanette, PA

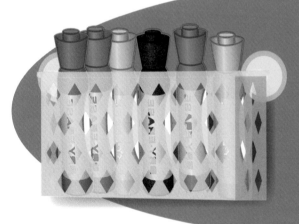

Equal Talk Time

Try this simple idea to ensure that all students have an opportunity to speak during **group time.** Give each child a small manipulative. Once he adds to his group's discussion, he places his item in a container. Then he quietly listens to the comments of other members of his group. If desired, increase the number of manipulatives per child to allow more opportunities to speak.

Deeann Schertz, Riggs Elementary, Gilbert, AZ

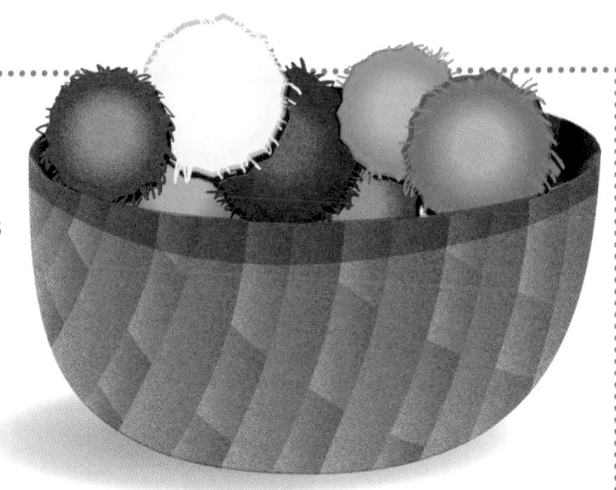

Management Tips and Timesavers

Cataloging Media Resources

Make **lesson planning** easier by writing on separate index cards the titles of videos, DVDs, and Web sites you use, along with any other pertinent information. Use a different card color for each subject. Then file the cards alphabetically by topic in an index card box as shown.

Maxine Gaul, Spalding Catholic School, Alton, IA

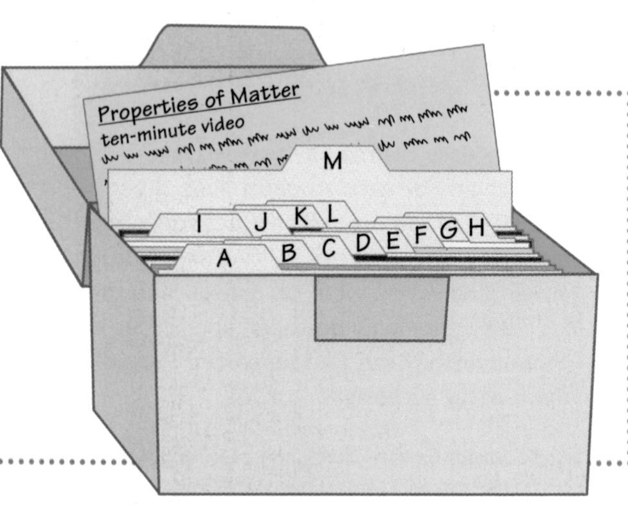

60, 59, 58...

Just a Minute

Use this silent game just before dismissal or anytime you need a quiet **time filler.** At your signal, have each student stand next to his desk with his eyes closed and faced away from the classroom clock until he thinks one minute has passed. Then have him sit down or kneel next to his desk. Allow the child who gets closest to the minute to line up first or assist you with the next activity.

Kristen Gober, Meadow Green Elementary, Whittier, CA

Right at Your Fingertips

Here's a way to organize the **differentiated materials** you've collected for each unit you teach. Put the materials in a colorful folder and place it inside the unit folder; then bind the two folders together with a rubber band. When you're ready to start a new unit, everything you need is right there!

Kim Helgeson, Pecatonica Elementary, Hollandale, WI

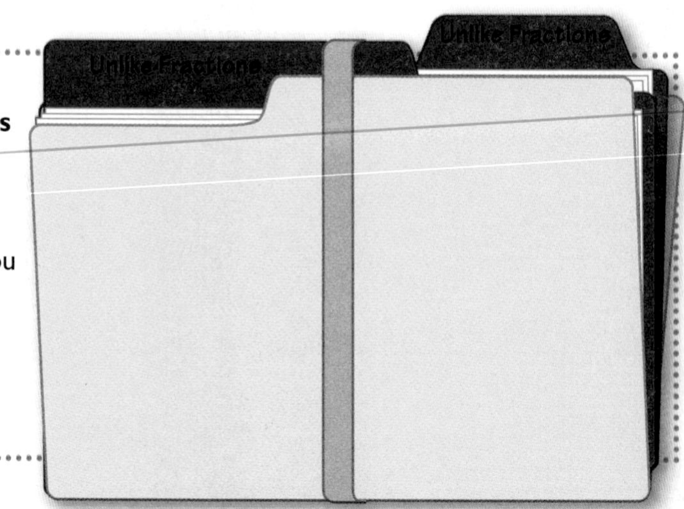

Our Readers Write

Textbook Scavenger Hunt

To familiarize my students with their **textbooks,** I have them participate in this small-group activity. I find interesting pages in each textbook and write one or two different clues to lead students to each featured page. I give each group a copy of the clues. Then I direct each group to use their textbooks to find and record the answer to each clue. Not only does this activity help my students get to know their textbooks better, but it also helps them be less intimidated by some of the larger books.

Stacy Krause, Blackstock Junior High School, Oxnard, CA

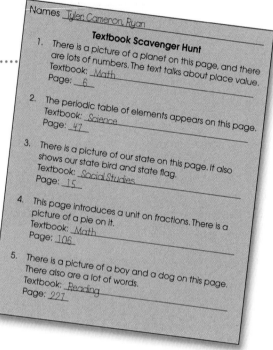

Names Tyler, Cameron, Ryan

Textbook Scavenger Hunt

1. There is a picture of a planet on this page, and there are lots of numbers. The text talks about place value.
   Textbook: Math
   Page: 6
2. The periodic table of elements appears on this page.
   Textbook: Science
   Page: 47
3. There is a picture of our state on this page. It also shows our state bird and state flag.
   Textbook: Social Studies
   Page: 15
4. This page introduces a unit on fractions. There is a picture of a pie on it.
   Textbook: Math
   Page: 106
5. There is a picture of a boy and a dog on this page. There also are a lot of words.
   Textbook: Reading
   Page: 227

Interactive Word Wall

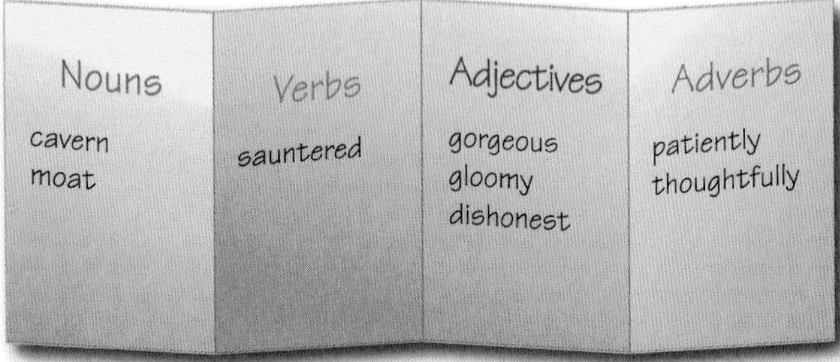

Nouns
cavern
moat
Verbs
sauntered
Adjectives
gorgeous
gloomy
dishonest
Adverbs
patiently
thoughtfully

Instead of a traditional **word wall,** I divide a sheet of bulletin board paper into four sections labeled as shown. Then I post the resulting word wall. As new words are introduced, I guide students to determine in which section I should write each word. To further involve my students, I give each child a vocabulary booklet divided into the same four sections as the word wall. As new words are added to the wall, my students record them in their booklets.

adapted from ideas by Cheryl Gaca, Manteno, IL, and Joyce Hovanec, Glassport Elementary, Glassport, PA

Place Value Caterpillar

A classroom caterpillar helps my students when studying **place value.** I glue together three green construction paper circles; label each section as shown; and add details, such as eyes, a mouth, and antennae. I explain to my students that the caterpillar has three body parts, just like each period of a number. We review that a zero in a number shows that place has no value. I display the caterpillar throughout our place value study as a helpful reminder.

Gretchen Gottschalk, Brookridge Elementary, Brooklyn, OH

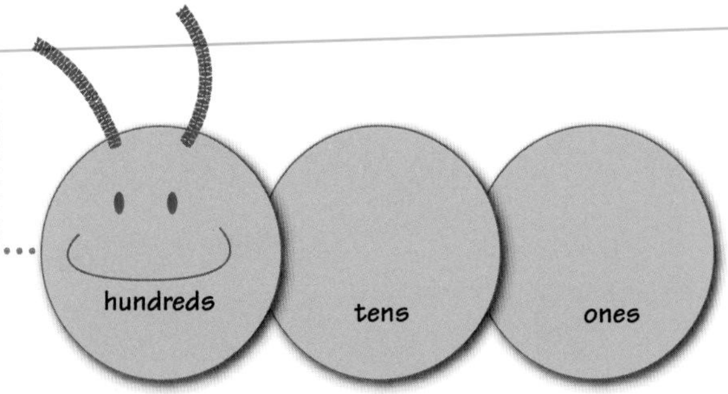

Super Slide Show

To free up my time at the **open house,** I use a slide show to share important information with parents. I use presentation software to create several slides with photographs of different classroom areas and daily activities, and slides programmed with helpful information. At the open house, I play the show on a television screen or computer monitor in a continuous loop for guests to view at their convenience. This leaves me free to greet parents and answer any questions they might have!

adapted from ideas by Betty Anderson, Skyview Elementary, Lizella, GA, and Melissa Boyle, Pleasant Grove Elementary, Mount Washington, KY

Lunch is from
12:30 PM to 1:00 PM

Up or Down?

This chant helps my students remember when to **round a number** up and when to round a number down. To begin, I review with my students that a number is rounded down if it ends in 0, 1, 2, 3, or 4 and rounded up if it ends in 5, 6, 7, 8, or 9. Then I lead students in the chant shown. For a visual reminder, I have my students give a thumbs-down during the first two lines of the chant and a thumbs-up during the last two lines.

Suzanne Darden, Carter Elementary, Strawberry Plains, TN

ROUNDING CHANT

Zero, one, two, three, four
Means we round down to the bottom floor.
Five, six, seven, eight, nine
Means we round up and all is fine!

Homework Buddy

At the beginning of the school year, I have my students make these furry friends to keep them company while completing **homework.** I have each student glue a large pom-pom on a tagboard heart as shown. I provide a variety of craft supplies for each student to decorate his buddy as desired. Before each child takes his buddy home, I attach a copy of the poem shown.

Sharon Vandike, Visitation Inter-Parish School, Vienna, MO

Catching Misspellings

As my students **edit** their writing, they often get so absorbed in the plot that they fail to notice any misspelled words. To make spelling errors easier to find, I suggest that they read their papers backward. This makes it easier for them to focus on each word instead of getting caught up in the details of the plot.

Jewell Flint-Stewart, Ellsworth, ME

I am your homework buddy,
As you can plainly see.
Set me at your workspace
Where you can look at me.
When your work's completed,
Back in the drawer I'll be
Just waiting for the next time
You bring homework home for me!

Starts Like *Left*

To help my students distinguish between the less than and greater than **inequality symbols,** I have them make the letter *L* with their left hands. I remind students that *left* and *less* both begin with *L*. Then I ask them to bend their wrists slightly to the right to form the corresponding symbol.

Beth Walsh, McMurray Elementary, McMurray, PA

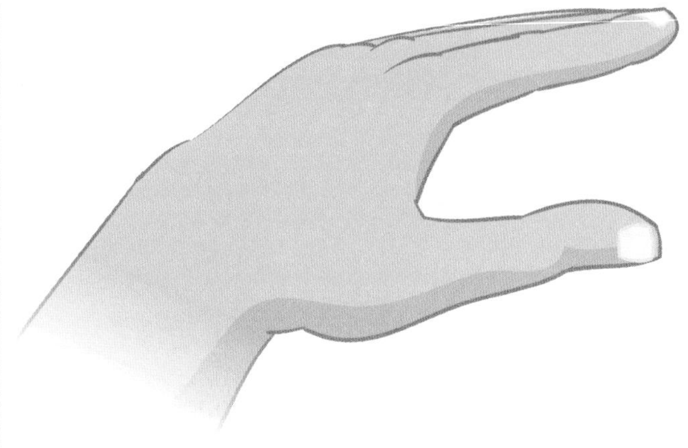

What's the Sign?

To help my students with solving **word problems,** I first review words and phrases that signal which operation to use. Then I teach them the hand motions below. To practice, I read aloud one word problem at a time. My students then find the identifying word or phrase and make the corresponding motion.

Lydia Beth Ouimet, Polaris Intermediate, Oak Lawn, IL

Addition—index fingers intersecting perpendicularly

Subtraction—index finger parallel to the floor

Multiplication—index fingers crossed to make an X

Division—closed fists, one on top of the other vertically

Spelling With a Twist

Before I give my **weekly spelling test,** I search the Internet to find an important event that occurred on the same month and day as the test. Before collecting the completed tests, I pose a question about the event for each child to answer at the bottom of her test. When I grade the tests, I award bonus points to each student who has the correct answer. Not only do my students love the possibility of receiving extra points, but they benefit from learning some historical trivia as well!

Theresa Suda, South Point Elementary, East Grand Forks, MN

Carter

1. stood
2. football
3. hood
4. pudding
5. shower
6. house
7. cloud
8. took
9. brook
10. cushion
11. power
12. crowd
13. outside
14. proud
15. wood
16. bush
17. butcher
18. however
19. loud
20. should

Bonus: World War I ended.

What important event occurred on November 11, 1918?

Poetry Party

Every year around Thanksgiving, I hold a **poetry reading** in my classroom. In advance, I have each student select his favorite poem (either one he wrote or one written by his favorite poet). I invite parents to this special reading. Then, as each child in turn reads his poem for the group, I serve pie or other tasty treats.

adapted from an idea by Amy Hoskins, Green Mountain Elementary, Lakewood, CO

Going Skiing

To help my students remember the difference between **parallel and perpendicular lines**, I invite them to go "skiing"! I tape sentence strips (lines) to the outsides of students' shoes (skis). To ski, a student makes parallel lines with her skis. To stop, she makes perpendicular lines.

Dana Johansen, Greenwich Academy, Greenwich, CT

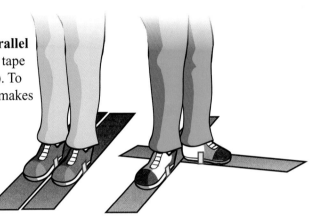

Colorful Quotations

When my students include **dialogue** in their writing, I have them underline each speaker's words with a crayon (a different color for each character). If a student spots more than one color in a paragraph, he knows he should start a new paragraph.

Doreen Placko, St. Patrick School, Wadsworth, IL

Carly
"Good morning!" called Linda.
"Humph!" growled Peter as he walked into the building.
"Why are you so grumpy?" asked Linda.
"Sorry. I left my homework at home again, and I dread having to tell my teacher. She'll think I'm not being responsible," replied Peter.

Classroom Webmasters

I have my students take over the task of updating our **classroom Web site**. I take a few minutes to demonstrate the process to my students. Then, each day, I assign a different pair of volunteers to post the day's homework assignments, news about upcoming events, and highlights from the day's activities. Not only do my students love to do this, but it gives me one less thing to do!

Julie Alarie, Williston, VT

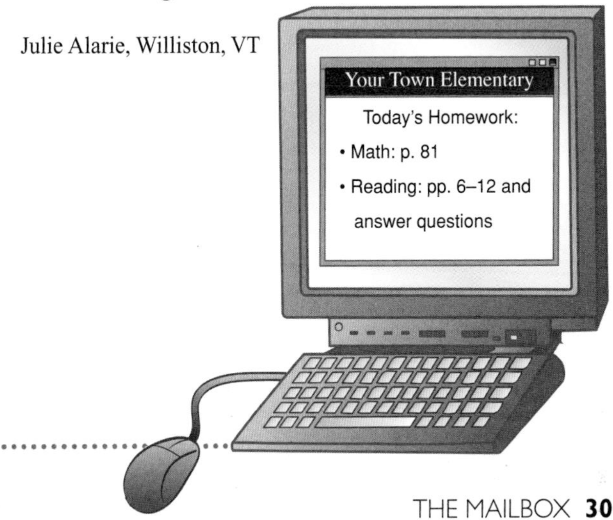

Your Town Elementary
Today's Homework:
• Math: p. 81
• Reading: pp. 6–12 and answer questions

Wipe-Off Puzzles

When my students finish their work early, they stay engaged by solving **reusable puzzles** from magazines and books. I mount each puzzle on construction paper and attach the corresponding answer key to the back of the paper. Then I laminate the puzzles and place them in a container along with wipe-off markers and tissues. A student simply chooses a puzzle to complete, checks his work, and wipes the puzzle clean for the next user.

Maranda Higgins, Massillon Christian School, Massillon, OH

Undercover Communication

To secretly **communicate** with parents about students who struggle with homework, I ask them to sign their child's daily planner in red ink if there were problems and another color if everything went smoothly. If I see red ink, I know the night before was stressful. This way, I can chat with the student about the situation without alerting him to the fact that his parent made me aware of it.

Kristi Titus, Leesburg Elementary, Leesburg, VA

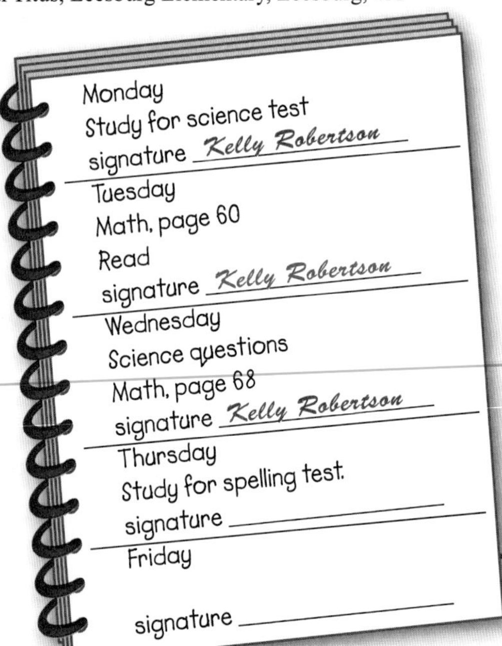

A Tic, a Tac, and a Zero!

My students sometimes forget to write **zero as a placeholder** when multiplying by two digits. To help them remember, I have the students use a special strategy. After they multiply the digit in the ones place by both digits in the top number, they "tic" it (cross it out). If a number was carried, they add it and then "tac" it (make a slash through it). Finally, they write a zero in the appropriate place and continue to solve the problem. To multiply by three digits, the last step becomes "a tic, a tac, and a double zero."

Kristin Oleary, Richard Henry Lee Elementary, Glen Burnie, MD

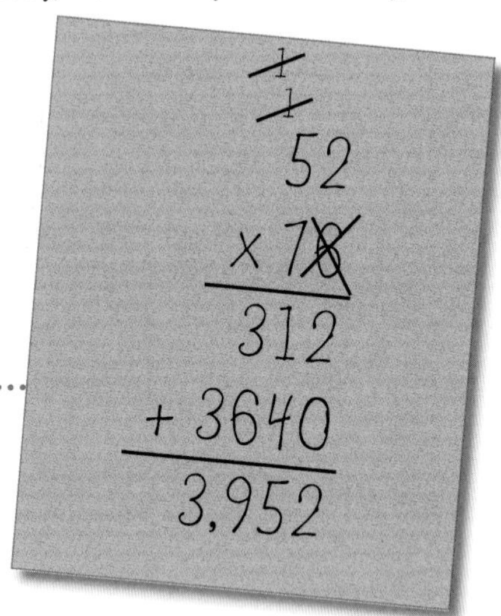

Sing a Song

To help my students remember the meaning of important **vocabulary** words, I sometimes challenge small groups of students to write songs about them set to familiar childhood tunes such as "Baa, Baa, Black Sheep" or "Three Blind Mice." Then I invite each group to perform its song for the class.

Angela Jefferies, Cowden Elementary, Cowden, IL

A Sweet Review

For a finger-licking good **geometry review,** I give each of my students an individual chocolate pudding cup. I call out a geometric concept such as parallel lines or quadrilateral. Each student then dips his finger in his pudding cup and draws the corresponding item on his paper. After I check for accuracy, I announce a different geometric concept. This activity not only provides a fantastic geometry review, but it works great with other math concepts as well!

Nicole Furfaro, St. Paul Catholic School, Guelph, Ontario, Canada

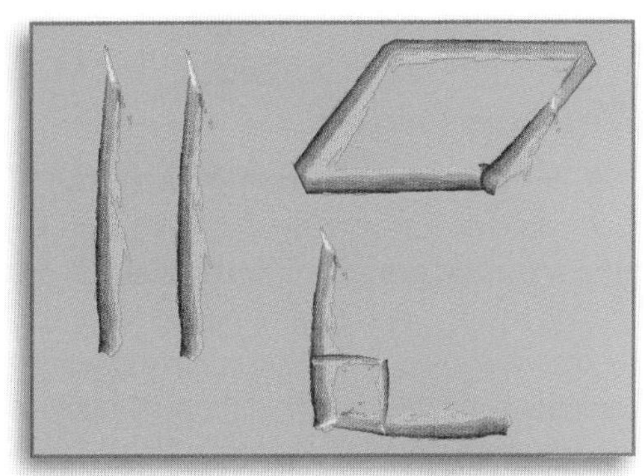

Climbing Up!

To help my students order numbers with **decimals,** I place a four-rung ladder cutout at a center along with a supply of number cards. A child chooses four cards and places them on the ladder's rungs, aligning the decimal points. Then she rearranges the cards until the numbers are in order from least to greatest, from the bottom rung to the top. When she is satisfied with her work, she lists the numbers in order on a sheet of paper.

Brooke Beverly, Dudley Elementary, Dudley, MA

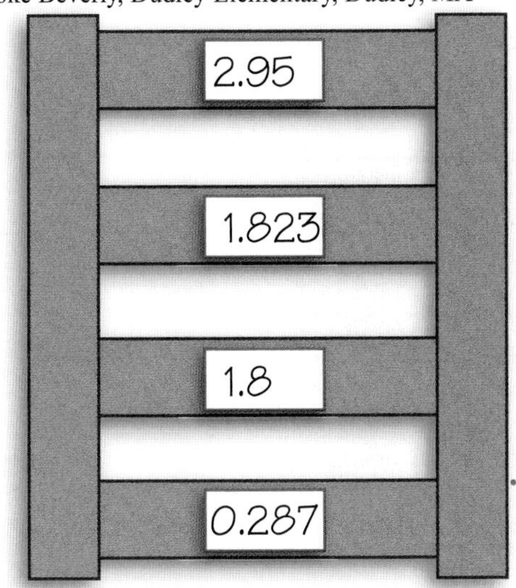

Interactive Map

This hands-on idea gives my students practice with **map skills.** I make a large map of our state and country and attach the hook sides of Velcro fasteners at the locations of major cities, lakes, or rivers. I attach the loop sides of Velcro fasteners to cutouts labeled with the names of the corresponding locations. A child then uses his social studies book or another resource to match each cutout to the correct location on the map.

Melanie Guido, St. Francis-St. Stephen School, Geneva, NY

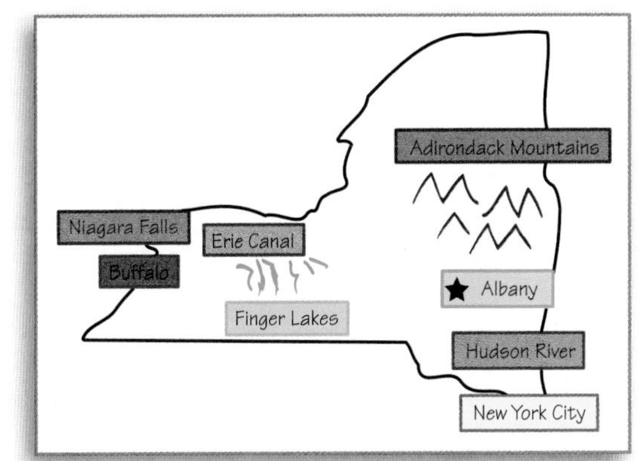

Tip-Top Order

This easy setup keeps my **classroom library** organized and student-friendly. First, I group all my books by genre and write the genre name—such as adventure, animals, biography, history, or humor—on the top edges of the closed books as shown. Then I arrange the books within each genre in alphabetical order by author. To make sure wandering books return to my classroom, I also write my name and room number on the bottom edges of the books.

Julie Alarie, Williston, VT

Editing Sleeve

To make **editing** fun and easy, I provide each student with a clear page protector to keep in her writing portfolio. When her writing is ready for editing, she places it in the sleeve and uses a wipe-off marker to practice her editing skills. When I conference with her, I look at the marks she made on the page protector. Then I pull out her original for me to edit. If the writing sample is two pages, the student can place the papers back-to-back in the sleeve.

Lora Bruker, Emerson Elementary, Parkersburg, WV

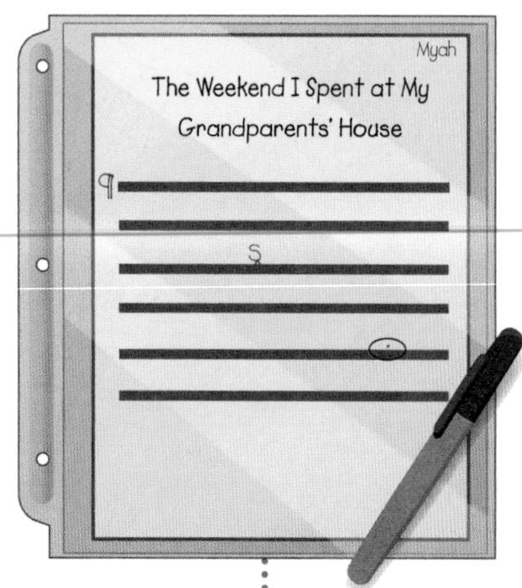

Musical Measurement

For a harmonious way to help my students remember the difference between **perimeter and area,** I teach them the song below. Before long, my kids have perimeter and area down pat!

Mindy Fulmer, Lakeview Elementary, Little Elm, TX

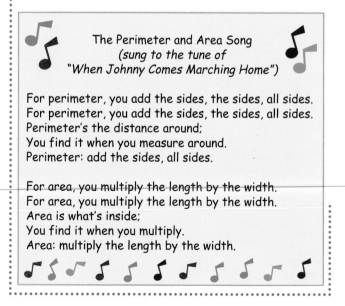

The Perimeter and Area Song
(sung to the tune of "When Johnny Comes Marching Home")

For perimeter, you add the sides, the sides, all sides.
For perimeter, you add the sides, the sides, all sides.
Perimeter's the distance around;
You find it when you measure around.
Perimeter: add the sides, all sides.

For area, you multiply the length by the width.
For area, you multiply the length by the width.
Area is what's inside;
You find it when you multiply.
Area: multiply the length by the width.

Fab Five Review

Each day I start **math** class by presenting five problems from math skills taught earlier in the year. I give students five minutes to complete the problems, and then we review the answers together. Students who solve all five problems correctly are invited to go around the room collecting high fives from their classmates. This activity really helps my students retain skills taught throughout the year.

Brooke Beverly, Dudley Elementary, Dudley, MA

1. $6\frac{1}{2} + 1\frac{5}{8} =$
2. What is a rectangle's perimeter if one side measures 6 cm and its area is 48 sq. cm?
3. 21.6 + 58.36 =
4. Find the mean of these test scores: 89, 96, 93, 75, 92, 88.
5. Draw an example of a right angle.

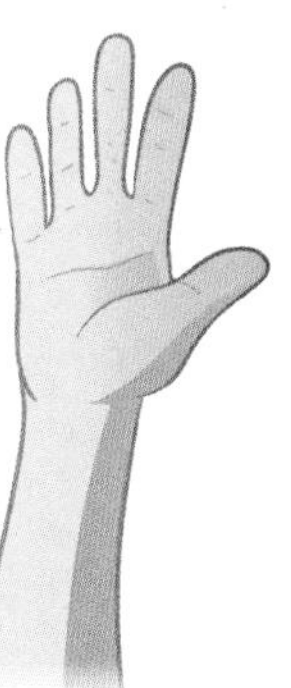

Whiteboard Scrabble

When I need a ten-minute filler, we play this **vocabulary game.** I write 15 letters on the board and have students write the longest words possible, using each letter only once. For scoring, I use multiplication doubles; for example, an eight-letter word is worth 8 x 8 points *(64 points)*. Each student totals his points, calculates the value of his left-over letters in the same way, and subtracts the leftover points from his total. If time remains, a student can try to form a second word for a higher score.

Julia Goodman, West Bloomfield, MI

W, E, R, T, O, U,
C, I, S, D, M, N,
A, F, H
fraction
8 x 8 = 64 points
W, E, U, S, D, M, H
7 x 7 = 49 points
64 – 49 = 15 points

Healthy Snack Jar

To promote **healthy eating** at school, I use a clear container and marbles as a motivator. Every day a student brings a healthy snack, she adds a marble to the jar. Once the jar is full, we celebrate with a healthy snack party! My students love to watch the jar as it fills and even remind their parents to pack healthier snacks.

Lina Miura, Livermore Valley Charter School, Livermore, CA

"SHO ME" the Great Lakes!

To help my students remember the names of the **Great Lakes,** I use the first letter of each lake's name to form the acronym SHO ME: the top lakes are Superior, Huron, and Ontario, and the bottom lakes are Michigan and Erie.

Fran Ross, Lee Academy, Clarksdale, MS

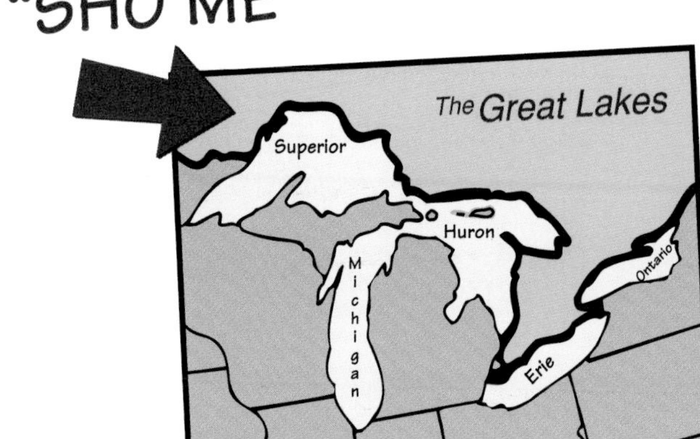

Sticky Solution

I use leftover stickers to make **review gameboards.** On a large sheet of construction paper, I use the stickers to create a path from Start to Finish. Next, I laminate the board. Then I create a set of question cards to use with the board to review a unit we are currently studying.

Leigh Anne Newsom
Cedar Road Elementary
Chesapeake, VA

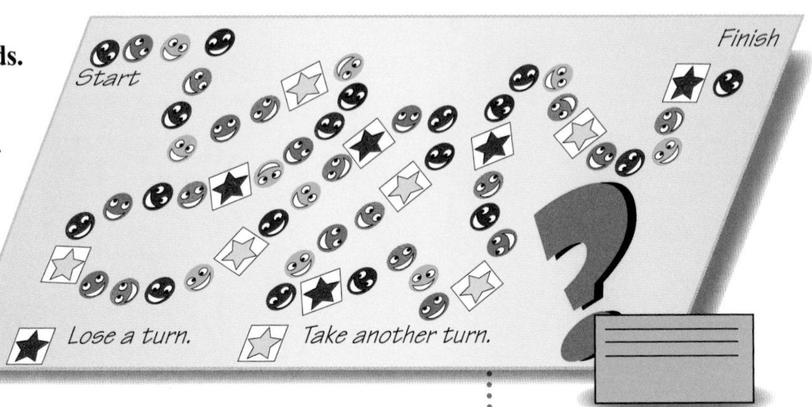

I've Got Your Number

On an enlarged outline map of the United States, I label each state with a number and designate the **time zones.** I display the map. Then I write several questions about the map on index cards and store them in a folder. When I have a few extra minutes, I ask my students a question and we discuss the correct answer. I even challenge my students to submit their own questions for us to use.

Carol Ann Perks, Comstock Elementary, Miami, FL

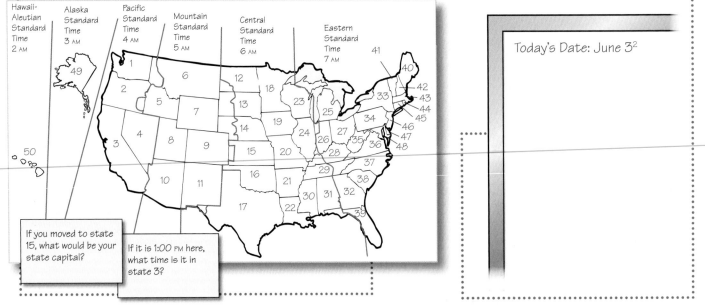

Hawaii-Aleutian Standard Time 2 AM
Alaska Standard Time 3 AM
Pacific Standard Time 4 AM
Mountain Standard Time 5 AM
Central Standard Time 6 AM
Eastern Standard Time 7 AM

If you moved to state 15, what would be your state capital?

If it is 1:00 PM here, what time is it in state 3?

What's Today's Date?

Instead of just writing the day's date on the board, I write it as a **math** equation. Once students get the hang of it, I have them take turns writing each day's equation.

Pamela Nesmith
Northside Middle School
West Columbia, SC

Today's Date: June 3^2

Around the Room

To practice **computation** and fill the final minutes of the day, I call out a number. Then I go around the room and have each student add an operation and number to it. The goal is to make it all the way around the room and end up with the original number.

Kathleen Butler, Meadows Elementary, Millbrae, CA

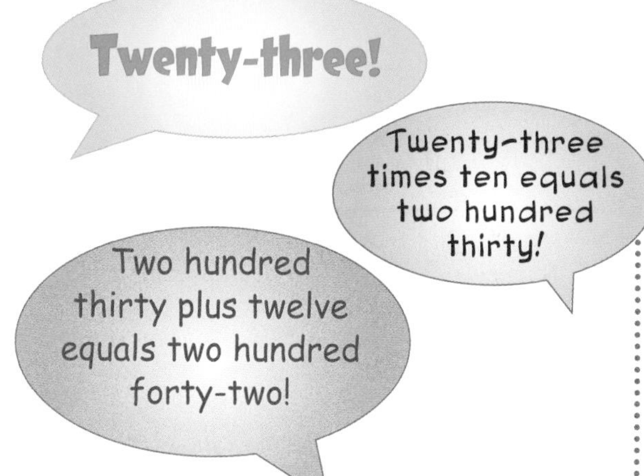

Twenty-three!
Twenty-three times ten equals two hundred thirty!
Two hundred thirty plus twelve equals two hundred forty-two!

Easy Assessment

To make **grading book reports** easier, I have my students use the computer. After reviewing how to use slideshow presentation software, I have my kids create one slide for each of the following parts of their reports: characters, setting, problem, solution, other major events, and a student rating of the book. As students present their reports, I grade each slide.

Brooke Beverly, Julia Bancroft Elementary, Auburn, MA

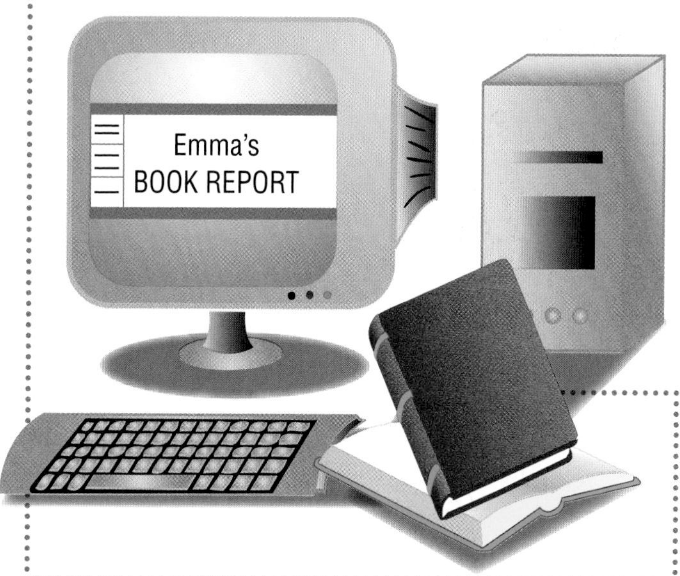

Rap Like You Mean It!

I teach my students the lyrics below to help them learn the differences among **mean, median, mode, and range.** They love to do the rap each day!

Barbara Majoy, Meadowlawn School, Sandusky, OH

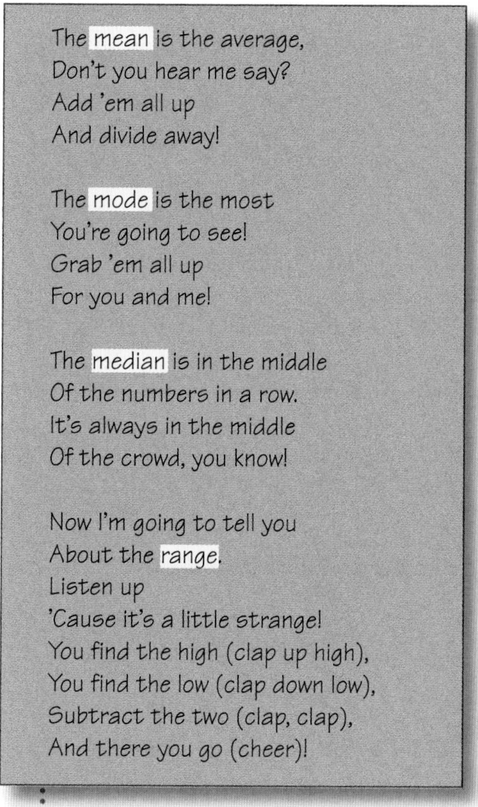

The mean is the average,
Don't you hear me say?
Add 'em all up
And divide away!

The mode is the most
You're going to see!
Grab 'em all up
For you and me!

The median is in the middle
Of the numbers in a row.
It's always in the middle
Of the crowd, you know!

Now I'm going to tell you
About the range.
Listen up
'Cause it's a little strange!
You find the high (clap up high),
You find the low (clap down low),
Subtract the two (clap, clap),
And there you go (cheer)!

Teacher's Top Picks

I use stands from old daily desktop calendars to **display books** I think my students will like. Instead of spending their time searching bookshelves for something to read, my kids tend to pick one of the display books.

Tish Paugh, South Putnam Central Elementary, Greencastle, IN

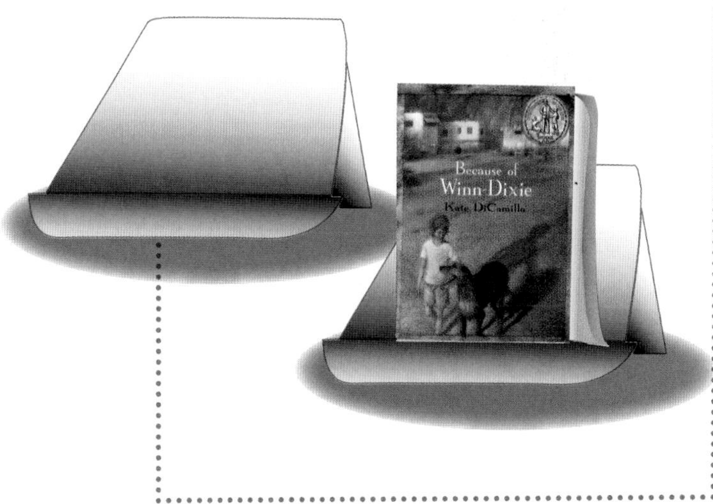

Answer Keys

Page 7

1. ten thousands, T
2. thousands, O
3. millions, D
4. hundreds, A
5. hundred thousands, G
6. ten thousands, T
7. tens, E
8. hundreds, A
9. millions, D
10. hundred millions, U
11. thousands, O
12. ten millions, I
13. ten thousands, T

A GOOD ATTITUDE

Page 8

1. dr. floss is my dentist. At every checkup he reminds me to floss.
2. The stylist who cuts my hair is named ms. clip.
3. mr. pipe is our plumber. He lives on leaky lane.
4. If I am sick, I see dr. well. He wants to keep me healthy and in school.
5. david digit is our banker. His house is on division street.
6. If we need someone to help clean the house, we call mr. sweep.
7. ms. english is my tutor. She lives in grammar, texas.
8. mike lube changes the oil in our car. He works at a place called quick change shop.
9. ima plant is our gardener. She is from new jersey, which is the garden state.
10. The best cookie maker I know is mom, and she lives with me on baker street.
11. bea a. teacher wrote a book titled homework, homework, and more homework.
12. The comedian named i. m. funny likes to tell jokes and make people laugh.

Yes, they match.

Page 9

1. cold cereal
2. pancakes and toast
3. 15
4. waffles
5. 100

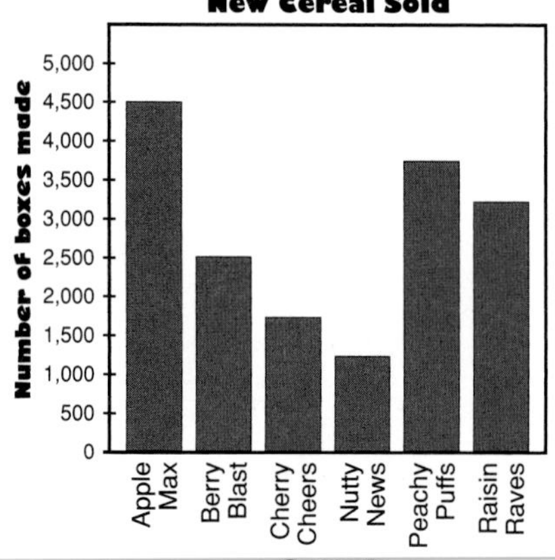

Page 14

A. 45
B. 315
C. 2,835
D. 5,670
E. 85
F. 680
G. 2,720
H. 8,160
I. 57,120
J. 248
K. 496
L. 3,968
M. 23,808
N. 119,040

Page 15

	Amos	Bernie	Camilla	Delphi
Homeroom 1	16	3	3	8
Homeroom 2	4	11	13	2
Homeroom 3	5	7	2	14
Total	25	21	18	24

1. Amos
2. Answers may vary. A possible answer is Homeroom 1, because that is where Amos received the most votes.

Page 16

Written answers will vary.

1. In 1621, Pilgrims and Native Americans planned an autumn harvest feast.
2. Men hunted wild turkeys and geese.
3. The women plucked and scrubbed the birds.
4. Men also slew deer for this meal.
5. Eel and clams may have been served.
6. The Pilgrims also may have caught lobsters.
7. They may have seasoned their food with liverwort.
8. Perhaps the children gathered walnuts and chestnuts.
9. The children may have also picked grapes and plums for the feast.
10. Someone might have pulled carrots from the ground.
11. Someone else might have peeled and chopped onions.
12. The Pilgrims did not bake pumpkin pies.
13. They also did not boil and mash potatoes.
14. They did not even eat corn on the cob, ham, or cranberry sauce.
15. Even without a modern menu of food, they enjoyed a great meal!

Page 20

A. Jen, 64 in.^{3}
B. Matt, 48 in.^{3}
C. Brad, 56 in.^{3}
D. Kel, 120 in.^{3}
E. Amy, 36 in.^{3}
F. Ian, 50 in.^{3}
G. Will, 60 in.^{3}
H. Meg, 24 in.^{3}
I. Todd, 30 in.^{3}
J. Jeff, 45 in.^{3}

Page 21

Corrections may vary.

Set 5: (29, 10) is incorrect. It should be (29, 5).
Set 4: (4, 7) is incorrect. It should be (4, 6).
Set 3: (20, 12) is incorrect. It should be (20, 13).
Set 2: (30, 17) is incorrect. It should be (29, 17).
Set 1: (11, 19) is incorrect. It should be (9, 20).

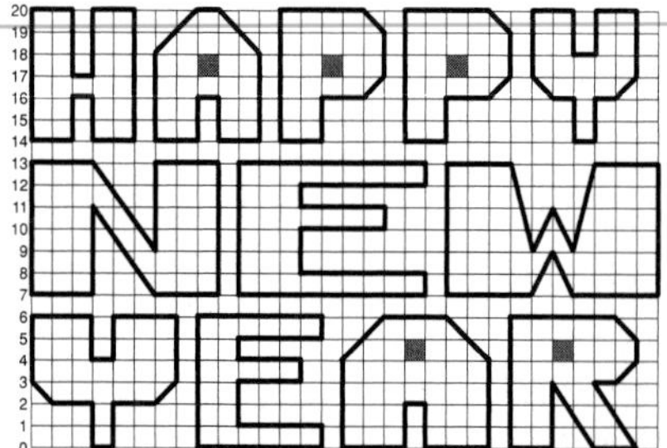

Page 22

5 similes

...like a(n) ___ in a(n) ___...
...as fast as a(n) ___ at a...
Like a(n) ___, I ran...
...he was like a(n) ___.
...like a bunch of ___ at...

5 metaphors

...playground, it was a(n) ___ made of...
...I was a really cold ___ and...
...was a snow-covered ___.
...hallway was a(n) ___ filled...
...sky was a dark ___...

Page 27

Order may vary.

1. frequent, seldom
2. common, rare
3. permanent, temporary
4. vague, clear
5. bravery, cowardice
6. natural, artificial
7. accept, refuse
8. safety, danger
9. departure, arrival
10. absent, present
11. generous, stingy
12. serious, jolly

I love you a ton!

Page 28

1. promised under oath
2. outside one's own country
3. buried
4. worked in office
5. children
6. first
7. brought into office
8. speech
9. wrote
10. worked
11. first
12. give up

Page 29

A. 1, 2, 5, 10
B. 1, 29; prime number
C. 1, 2, 4, 11, 22, 44

D. 12	36	E. 50	27	F. 40	16	G. 25	54	H. 31	62	I. 46	24
1	1	(1)	(1)	1	1	(1)	(1)	1	1	1	1
2	2	2	3	2	2	5	2	(31)	2	(2)	(2)
3	3	5	9	4	4	25	3		(31)	23	3
4	4	10	27	5	(8)		6		62	46	4
6	6	25		(8)	16		9				6
(12)	9	50		10			18				8
	(12)			20			27				12
	18			40			54				24
	36										

Page 30

E. 2½ in.
W. 1½ in.
T. 1 in.
D. 1¾ in.
E. 1¼ in.
W. 2¾ in.
G. 3 in.
H. ¾ in.
I. 2¼ in.
H. 4¾ in.
N. 1⅝ in.
T. ⅜ in.
I. 1⅜ in.
N. 2⅛ in.
O. 1⅞ in.

GONE WITH THE WIND!

Page 32

1. F
2. F
3. O
4. F
5. F
6. F
7. O
8. F
9. O
10. O
11. F
12. F
13. O
14. O
15. F
16. F
17. O
18. O
19. F
20. O

Page 36

Order may vary.

1. The data for writing elephant jokes is reversed.
   The number scale should go to 35.
   The shading of the bars for roller skating is reversed.
   The male elephant bar for art lessons is shaded to the wrong number.
   The bars for shelling peanuts are missing.

2. The dot for February is too high.
   April's dot should be connected between March and May.
   July's dot is on June's line.
   The dot for September is too low.
   The line connecting November's dot to December's dot is missing.
   The label for the y-axis should be "pies sold" instead of "dollars."

Page 37

1. hold, held
2. begin, began
3. bring, bringing
4. are, were
5. meet, met
6. take, took
7. bring, brought
8. win, won
9. tell, told
10. do, did
11. wear, wore
12. take, took
13. go, went
14. see, saw
15. shake, shook
16. leave, left
17. spend, spent
18. speak, spoke
19. forget, forget
20. keep, kept

Bonus Box:

1. will hold
2. will begin
3. will bring
4. will be
5. will meet
6. will take
7. will bring
8. will win
9. will tell
10. will do
11. will wear
12. will take
13. will go
14. will see
15. will shake
16. will leave
17. will spend
18. will speak
19. will forget
20. will keep

Page 38

1. 2/3
2. 1/6
3. 5/6
4. 1/2
5. 1/2
6. 1/2
7. 1/4
8. 3/4
9. 1/2
10. 3/8
11. 1
12. 1/4
13. 3/4
14. 1/5
15. 1/10
16. 3/10
17. 2/5
18. 0
19. 2/10
20. 1/10

Page 39

1. M, look
2. E, family
3. R, working
4. D, times
5. R, meals
6. M, people
7. U, hug
8. T, skills
9. È, watch
10. O, smile
11. A, clean
12. D, find

French = <u>MÈRE</u>
German = <u>MUTTER</u>
Swedish = <u>MODER</u>
Spanish = <u>MADRE</u>
Danish = <u>MOR</u>
Dutch = <u>MOEDER</u>

Page 43

N. 36 yd.^{2}; 36 yd.
F. 250 ft.^{2}; 70 ft.
O. 108 yd.^{2}; 64 yd.
E. 20 yd.^{2}; 26 yd.
A. 275 ft.^{2}; 104 ft.
T. 2,800 ft.^{2}; 256 ft.
W. 3,000 ft.^{2}; 350 ft.
D. 99 yd.^{2}; 40 yd.
R. 78 yd.^{2}; 38 yd.

Riddle: <u>IF TWO'S COMPANY AND THREE'S A CROWD, WHAT ARE FOUR AND FIVE?</u>
Answer: <u>NINE</u>

Page 44

1. antifreeze
2. bendable
3. bicycle
4. blockage
5. development
6. dishonest
7. ex-president
8. hopeful
9. kingdom
10. lengthwise
11. madness
12. malformed
13. misprint
14. neighborhood
15. nonfat
16. precut
17. self-help
18. teacher
19. unhappy
20. useless

Page 46

1. line symmetry
2. rotational symmetry
3. point symmetry and rotational symmetry

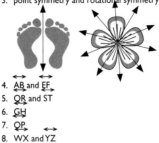

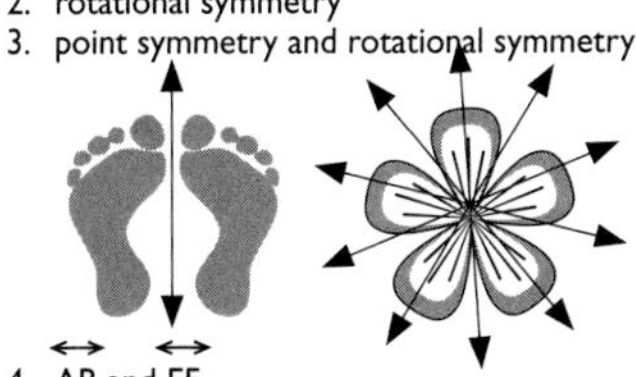

4. $\overleftrightarrow{AB}$ and $\overleftrightarrow{EF}$
5. $\overleftrightarrow{QR}$ and ST
6. $\overleftrightarrow{GH}$
7. $\overleftrightarrow{QP}$
8. WX and $\overleftrightarrow{YZ}$

Bonus Box: Answers will vary.

Page 71

1. blue
2. purple
3. blue
4. green
5. green
6. purple
7. purple
8. blue
9. green
10. blue

Bonus Box: Answers will vary.

Page 72

1. M
2. N
3. O
4. U
5. T
6. E
7. R
8. S
9. I
10. A

With all its little "<u>MOUNTAIN-EARS</u>"!

Page 82

1. D
2. A

<u>A "HEAD BAND"</u>

2. Renée answered, "Yes, I've always wanted to see this group in concert."
3. "We will go to the concert, watch the band, and then go get a bite to eat," Dad announced.
6. "It's going to start at 8 PM and should be over by 10 PM," I told everyone.
8. "My friend's band also is very good. Someday her band wants to put on a concert as well," added Kyle.

Page 88

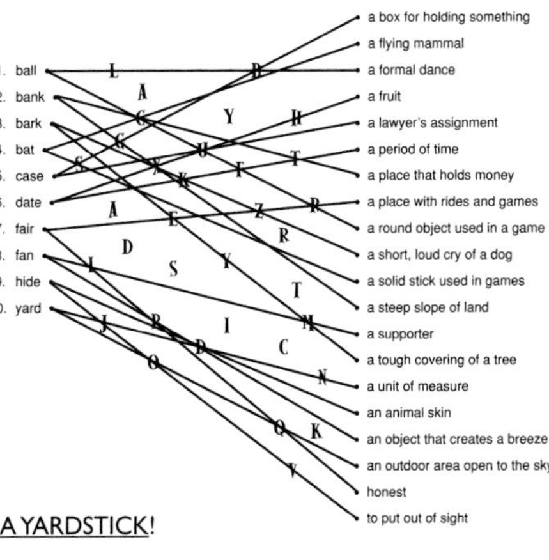

<u>A YARDSTICK!</u>

Page 89

1. For <u>three</u> (C) <u>long</u> (C) weeks, <u>the</u> (A) kids have not had <u>a</u> (A) <u>single</u> (C) <u>outside</u> (C) recess.
2. <u>Bad</u> (C) weather has kept <u>the</u> (A) kids indoors.
3. Today Ms. Brite said her <u>fifth-grade</u> (C) class could play <u>trash-can</u> (C) basketball in <u>the</u> (A) classroom.
4. Her <u>excited</u> (C) students liked <u>that</u> (D) idea.
5. Some of them hurried to move desks out of <u>the</u> (A) way.
6. <u>The</u> <u>Australian</u> (P) student put <u>an</u> (A) <u>empty</u> (C) <u>trash</u> (C) can near <u>the</u> (A) <u>front</u> (C) board.
7. Marty and Kendra used <u>yellow</u> (C) tape to make <u>a</u> (A) <u>free-throw</u> (C) line on <u>the</u> (A) <u>tile</u> (C) floor.
8. <u>The</u> (A) <u>smiling</u> (C) <u>American</u> (P) teacher listed <u>the</u> (A) <u>game</u> (C) rules.
9. <u>The</u> (A) goal was to toss <u>a</u> (A) <u>paper</u> (C) ball into <u>the</u> (A) <u>trash</u> can.
10. <u>Each</u> (C) player would stand behind <u>that</u> (D) <u>free-throw</u> (C) line to toss <u>the</u> (A) ball.
11. <u>Each</u> (C) basket would equal <u>one</u> (C) point for <u>the</u> (A) team.
12. She would keep track of <u>these</u> (D) points on <u>the</u> (A) <u>front</u> (C) board.
13. <u>The</u> (A) <u>eager</u> (C) students quickly formed <u>equal</u> (C) teams.
14. Ms. Brite named <u>each</u> (C) team after <u>those</u> (D) <u>four</u> (C) types of adjectives studied.
15. Then <u>the</u> (A) contest began.

Page 101

1. Kate was invited to a karaoke birthday party for her friend Chad.
2. She was nervous because she'd never been to a karaoke party before.
3. "Why are you nervous?" her mother asked. "You sing in front of your friends all the time."
4. "But I'm not sure I'll know the words to the songs we'll sing," Kate said worriedly.
5. "That won't be a problem," Kate's mother explained, "because you'll read each song's words from a video screen."
6. "Oh," Kate replied. "Then, yes, I *do* want to go to Chad's party!"
7. When Kate arrived at the party, her friends were eating chips, drinking sodas, and talking excitedly.
8. Chad's mom then set up the karaoke machine, and everyone cheered.
9. By 8:00 p.m., Chad and his guests had each sung two songs.
10. Kate performed so well that Chad gave her a nickname: Karaoke Kate.

Page 105

Answers may vary.

Far away in the village of Crunchopolis there lived a brave little band of cereal pieces. They feared only one thing: rain. One day a thundercloud appeared in the sky. Christy Crunchy-O ran to tell Sam Cinnamon Square about it.

"We would be safe from the rain if we could get into Baron Von Crisp's castle," she told Sam. "But he does not want to share. The baron has his castle heavily guarded by Shreddy and two of his buddies. What we need is a superhero to help us."

Just then a bright light flashed across the sky. Suddenly there appeared Supertoastie and his sidekick, Fred Flake.

"Never fear: Supertoastie is here!" the superhero announced. "Fred and I will get Shreddy and his buddies away from the castle because we are much stronger than they are. Follow us!"

Sure enough, the superheroes got Shreddy and his buddies to abandon their posts. As Shreddy ran, Christy pelted him with pebbles while Sam poured a whole pitcher of milk on his head.

Supertoastie and Fred Flake chased Baron Von Crisp out of his castle. Then they used the baron's own toaster oven to turn him to toast.

The brave little band of cereal pieces ran for cover in the castle just before the rain began to fall.

"Oh, thank you, Supertoastie. And thank you too, Fred! You defeated the selfish baron and saved us from becoming soggy heaps of cereal!" Sam said.

"It was nothing," the superheroes replied, and with a bright flash of light, they disappeared.

Bonus Box:

Subject Pronouns		Object Pronouns	Possessive Pronouns
They	they	it	his
We	they	us	his
we	You	us	his
she	It	him	his
he	they	him	his
we		you	their
I		you	his
we		us	his

Page 107

Sheet A

1. Last night I ate steak, mashed potatoes, and salad.
2. My littlest dog, Carleigh, likes to play with her toys.
3. We left for our vacation last year on June, 16.
4. Math is my favorite subject in school, but, I like reading too.
5. Have you ever been to Houston, Texas?
6. Max asked, "Do you know where the game is being played?"
7. When you are learning to play a new game, it takes time to memorize the rules.
8. For homework I had spelling, math, social studies, and science.
9. My family loves to eat out, but we also like to cook dinner at home.
10. When was the last time you saw your friend, Jamal riding his bike?
11. The camping trip will be on Saturday, May 23.
12. We are visiting my grandparents in Fort Myers, Florida.

Sheet B

1. My new school is located in Roanoke, Virginia.
2. Mom sent me to the store to buy, milk, bread, potato chips, and lunch meat.
3. Lucy, asked, "Did you know my favorite ice cream is strawberry?"
4. I was born on September 14, 1999.
5. The casserole we ate last night, chicken and rice, made my stomach hurt.
6. When the weekend finally arrives, I, want to play outside.
7. My dad said we had to go to sleep early, but, then he changed his mind.
8. When I was little, my favorite food was spaghetti.
9. I have saved my allowance since December, 26, 2008.
10. Payton, my best friend, had to move to a new state.
11. I thought all our games were over, but the last one is actually tomorrow.
12. Patrick, Roberto, and Cole are my three best friends.

Page 115

Answers may vary. Possible answers are listed.

1. next to the doughnuts, between the doughnuts and cinnamon rolls, above the turnovers
2. above the muffins, to the right of the cinnamon rolls, in the top right corner
3. above the round loaves of bread, beside the cookies, in the top left corner
4. on the bottom shelf, between the long loaves of bread and the pies, below the turnovers
5. on the top shelf, above the turnovers, to the left of the cakes
6. above the pies, on the middle shelf, below the cakes
7. below the doughnuts, above the long loaves of bread, next to the turnovers
8. between the round loaves of bread and the muffins, above the bagels, below the cookies and cinnamon rolls
9. in the bottom right corner, below the muffins, next to the bagels
10. in the bottom left corner, next to the bagels, two shelves below the doughnuts

Page 119

1. Arkansas, Indiana, Kansas, Louisiana, Maryland, Michigan, Montana, Pennsylvania, Rhode Island
4. *buy, by,* and *bye; pair, pare,* and *pear*
5. a. Snow White and the Seven Dwarves
   b. Goldilocks and the Three Bears
   c. Little Red Riding Hood
   d. Hansel and Gretel
   e. The Three Billy Goats Gruff
7. land: landslide, farmland, landmark, homeland
8. a. flowerpot
   b. rattlesnake
   c. homework
   d. scrapbook

Page 120

1. a. square
   b. Oval
   c. Triangle
   d. cube
   e. pyramid
   f. diamond
   g. cylinder
   h. Pentagon
2. In a **phone** call, Graham learns that his **dad** is bringing the **family** a **gift** when he returns from a **business** trip. But the **connection** is so bad, Graham can't understand what the gift is. He tells his **mom** that his dad is bringing a **poster**. When his dad arrived, he'd brought them a **toaster**.
3.

D	A	W	N
A	C	H	E
W	H	E	E
N	E	E	D

4. problem, solution
5. Answers may vary. One possible answer is *board, boar, oar, or, o.*
6. Answers may vary. Possible answers:
   a. This is our first heal in the new mouse.
   b. Do we reed nice for dinner?
   c. Don't bake the wear!
   d. You shouldn't sake tides.
7. a. She has eyes in the back of her head.
   b. searching high and low
8. a. buffalo
   b. panther

Page 121

1. Possible answers include *eleven, twelve, twenty, thirty, eighty, ninety, fourth,* and *eighth.*
2. a. dog
   b. bird, worm
   c. chickens
   d. cat, mice
   e. horse
3. a. fear of light
   b. fear of heat
   c. fear of animals
   d. fear of books
   e. fear of writing
4. blue, red
   Sentences will vary, but should include *blue* and *blew* in one sentence and *red* and *read* in the other.
5. I, he, his, she, it, its, we
6. Watch five foods magically appear! Line up each one carefully. When you're finished, clap, please. I'll be waiting around the corner near a spot at our favorite snack shop.
7. a. take
   b. look
   c. turn
   d. pull
8. LEFT
   LENT
   LEND
   LAND
   HAND

Page 114

1. octopus
2. oceanographer
3. Pacific
4. scuba
5. seahorse
6. submarine
7. intertidal
8. mussels
9. starfish
10. shark
11. crest
12. water cycle

Bonus Box: sound navigation ranging

Page 122

1. Alabama, Alaska; Wyoming
2. Answers may vary. Possible answers include *iota, mace, moan, more, mote, pace, pane, pore, port,* and *race.*
3. Nouns that can be verbs: time, bowl, snacks, thought
   Verbs that can be nouns: cut, can, watch, work, bear
4. Answers may vary. Possible answers include *I'll, you'll, she'll, they'll, he's, it's, here's, let's, who's, there's, they're, we're, you're, I've, they've, we've, she'd, he'd, you'd,* and *there'd.*
5. misspelled, separate, You're, likely, probably, different, doesn't, eighth
6. a. camel c. seal e. whale g. weasel
   b. mouse d. goat f. badger h. shark
7. Answers may vary. One possible answer is *wonderful.*
8. a. five, six, seven b. knife, fork, spoon
   c. black, white, gray

Page 123

1. A. potato salad
   B. grape juice
   C. pepperoni pizza
2. Answers may vary.
3. Answers may vary. Possible answers include *beg, crave, feed, rate, read, sag, see, tag, trade, tread, veer, wade,* and *wag.*
4. Answers may vary.
5. One set of double letters: Connecticut, Hawaii, Illinois, Minnesota, Missouri, Pennsylvania
   More than one set of double letters: Massachusetts, Mississippi, Tennessee,
6. January (The months are listed in alphabetical order.)
7. Answers may vary. Possible answers include *harsh, hatch, health, hearth, high, hitch, hogwash, hoorah, hunch, hush,* and *hyacinth.*
8. A. tip B. turf C. gripe D. pirate E. fatigue

Page 124

1. A. moose
   B. crises
   C. teaspoonfuls
   D. brothers-in-law
   E. oboes
2. Q: Why did the chicken cross the basketball court?
   A: It heard the referee calling fowls.
3. A. yellow jacket
   B. Purple Heart
   C. blueprint
   D. green thumb
   E. pink slip
   F. red carpet

Students' words will vary. Possible words include *yellow fever, yellow pages, blue cheese, blueberry, blue jay, blue ribbon, green bean, greenhouse, Red Cross, redhead,* and *red tape.*

4. Answers will vary. Possible synonyms include *excellent, extensive, fabulous, fine, sizable, splendid,* and *top-notch.*
5. Answers will vary. Possible answers include *bay, bayou, brook, creek, glacier, gulf, ocean, pond, river, sea, spring,* and *stream.*
6. Answers will vary. Possible answers include *antler, batter, crate, fewer, pigment, pupil, scallion, scatter, scrabble, share,* and *steel.*
7. Answers will vary. Possible answers include *accountant, architect, artist, custodian, dentist, electrician, flight attendant, judge, librarian, mechanic, nurse, physical therapist, physician, priest, rabbi, scientist,* and *travel agent.*
8. A. Montgomery
   B. Sacramento
   C. Charleston

Page 144

Mr. Cox: "Excuse me, waiter, is there spaghetti on the menu?"
Waiter: "No, sir, I wiped it off."

A student asked her teacher whether a person should be punished for something she hadn't done.

"No," replied the teacher, "of course not!"

¶ "Good," said the girl, "because I didn't do my homework."

"Doctor, doctor! I think ¶ I'm a dog!" exclaimed the patient.

"Well, come and sit on the sofa so we can about talk your problem," the doctor replied.

The patient answered, "But I'm not allowed on the sofa!"

A band class was just getting under way when a large insect flew (flu) into the room. The music students, eager to play their (there) shiny new instruments, tried to ignore the buzzing intruder. Eventually, one student, Greg, could stand it no more. He rolled up his music book and swatted the insect. Then he stomped on it to ensure its fate.

"Was it a bee?" another student asked.

"No," Greg replied. "Bee flat."

Page 149

I. Early Childhood
   A. Born on February 12, 1809, in Hardin County, Kentucky
   B. Moved with his parents from Kentucky to Indiana
   C. Borrowed neighbors' books to learn
II. Adult Life
   A. Married Mary Todd
   B. Had four sons
   C. Studied law and became a lawyer
   D. Became interested in politics
III. Life as President
   A. Was the 16th president of the United States
   B. Issued the Emancipation Proclamation to free the slaves
   C. Worked to reunite the nation after the Civil War
   D. Was assassinated on April 14, 1865

Page 150

Paragraph 1: A, C, N
Paragraph 2: O, D, F
Paragraph 3: P, R, Q
Paragraph 4: H, J, K, L
Paragraph 5: S, M, T

Unused sentences: E, G, B, I

Page 159

Having a pet requires many responsibilities. To begin, pets need special shots to help prevent illness and disease. In addition to shots, grooming your pet is important. Most pets can clean themselves, but others should be bathed occasionally. Besides grooming, pets must also have a proper diet. Pets need the right amounts of vitamins, minerals, and proteins. While eating is important, pets also need plenty of exercise. Lastly, all pets should have a good place to sleep.

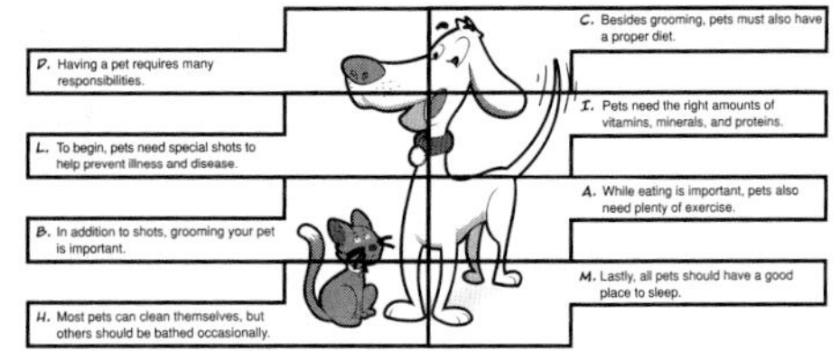

P. Having a pet requires many responsibilities.
L. To begin, pets need special shots to help prevent illness and disease.
B. In addition to shots, grooming your pet is important.
H. Most pets can clean themselves, but others should be bathed occasionally.
C. Besides grooming, pets must also have a proper diet.
I. Pets need the right amounts of vitamins, minerals, and proteins.
A. While eating is important, pets also need plenty of exercise.
M. Lastly, all pets should have a good place to sleep.

Page 170

1. 71,923 + 9,072 = 80,995
2. 434,443 + 38,177 = 472,620
3. 41,578 + 16,743 = 58,321
4. 151,617 + 155,753 = 307,370
5. 1,345 + 32,987 = 34,332
6. 17,846 − 3,936 = 13,910
7. 739,753 − 2,024 = 737,729
8. 508,608 − 32,273 = 476,335
9. 300,000 − 44,345 = 255,655
10. 800,743 − 318,484 = 482,259

Page 171

1. Length
1 ft. = 12 in.
1 yd. = 3 ft., or 36 in.
1 mile = 5,280 ft., or 1,760 yd.

2. Weight
1 lb. = 16 oz.
1 T = 2,000 lb.

3. Capacity
1 c. = 8 fl. oz.
1 pt. = 2 c.
1 qt. = 2 pt.
1 gal. = 4 qt.

4.

		Waldo	Amos	Baxter	Linus
Leash Length	2 yd.	X	X	🐾	X
	5 ft.	🐾	X	X	X
	48 in.	X	🐾	X	X
	$3\frac{1}{2}$ ft.	X	X	X	🐾
Dogs' Weights	160 oz.	🐾	X	X	X
	$\frac{1}{20}$ T	X	🐾	X	X
	8 lb.	X	X	🐾	X
	192 oz.	X	X	X	🐾
Water Bowl Capacity	3 qt.	🐾	X	X	X
	$\frac{1}{2}$ gal.	X	X	X	🐾
	3 pt.	X	X	🐾	X
	10 c.	X	🐾	X	X

9. 18½ feet
10. 2,080 ounces
11. 36 cups

Page 181

1. 54,642; 56,421; 504,142; 562,142
2. 98,988; 98,998; 99,989; 999,998
3. 241,504; 241,540; 504,142; 524,041
4. 76,452; 854,762; 867,542; 876,542
5. 201,206; 206,210; 210,602; 602,012
6. 36,652; 38,652; 378,652; 387,652
7. 498,889; 498,998; 499,989; 499,998
8. 56,677; 665,445; 667,654; 676,777
9. 70,001; 71,001; 700,001; 710,001
10. 181,188; 181,818; 188,188; 188,881

When she hands out lonG SENTENCES!

Page 182

17.087	0.01
520.493	0.02
510.886	78.13
795.77	10.8
791.97	100.09
80.95	167.14
109.14	1,330.82
689.29	523.7
666.11	816.458
92.08	1,979.266

Page 185

acute angle divisible by 11: 22°
even and prime acute angle: 2°
right angle: 90°
acute angle divisible by 3 and 7: 21°
half the measure of a right angle: 45°
largest whole-number acute angle: 89°
10° less than a straight angle: 170°
15° more than a right angle: 105°
twice the measure of a right angle: 180°
smallest whole-number acute angle: 1°
obtuse angle divisible by 11: 99°
smallest whole-number obtuse angle: 91°
5° more than the smallest obtuse angle: 96°
acute angle that is a multiple of 7 but not of 3: 14°
10° less than a right angle: 80°
largest whole-number obtuse angle: 179°

Page 188

S. 70	C. 51 R4
U. 103	E. 121 R8
I. 88	M. 423 R1
K. 2,630 R1	D. 1,241 R2
R. 1,018	T. 942 R6

Because the menu there does not include BEETS and DRUMSTICKS!

Page 189

1. 1.872
2. 38.25
3. 8.464
4. 343.2
5. 5.264
6. 50.82
7. 47.84
8. 4.770
9. 41.37
10. 2.870
11. 9.889
12. 5.700
13. 385.14
14. 7,123.44
15. 637.704

Page 194

1. P = 16 yd., A = 16 sq. yd.
2. P = 30 ft.
3. P = 32 ft., A = 60 sq. ft.
4. P = 36 yd., A = 77 sq. yd.
5. 3 ft. and 5 ft.
6. 36 ft.
7. 33 ft.
8. P = 92 yd., A = 528 sq. yd.

Page 195

S. green	O. green	B. green	N. blue
P. green	H. blue	I. green	L. green
C. orange	N. green	R. blue	L. green
O. green	E. blue	N. orange	E. orange
R. orange	A. orange	O. blue	

I see a CRANE! I see a HERON! I see a SPOONBILL!

Page 200

$\frac{1}{3} \times \frac{1}{2} = \frac{1}{6}$
$\frac{1}{3} \times \frac{1}{4} = \frac{1}{12}$
$\frac{1}{3} \times \frac{2}{3} = \frac{2}{9}$
$\frac{1}{3} \times \frac{3}{5} = \frac{1}{5}$
$\frac{1}{3} \times \frac{4}{5} = \frac{4}{15}$
$\frac{1}{3} \times \frac{5}{6} = \frac{5}{18}$
$\frac{1}{3} \times \frac{3}{4} = \frac{1}{4}$
$\frac{1}{3} \times \frac{4}{9} = \frac{4}{27}$
$\frac{1}{3} \times \frac{7}{10} = \frac{7}{30}$
$\frac{1}{2} \times \frac{1}{4} = \frac{1}{8}$
$\frac{1}{2} \times \frac{2}{3} = \frac{1}{3}$
$\frac{1}{2} \times \frac{3}{5} = \frac{3}{10}$
$\frac{1}{2} \times \frac{4}{5} = \frac{2}{5}$
$\frac{1}{2} \times \frac{5}{6} = \frac{5}{12}$
$\frac{1}{2} \times \frac{3}{4} = \frac{3}{8}$
$\frac{1}{2} \times \frac{4}{9} = \frac{2}{9}$
$\frac{1}{2} \times \frac{7}{10} = \frac{7}{20}$
$\frac{1}{4} \times \frac{2}{3} = \frac{1}{6}$
$\frac{1}{4} \times \frac{3}{5} = \frac{3}{20}$
$\frac{1}{4} \times \frac{4}{5} = \frac{1}{5}$
$\frac{1}{4} \times \frac{5}{6} = \frac{5}{24}$
$\frac{1}{4} \times \frac{3}{4} = \frac{3}{16}$
$\frac{1}{4} \times \frac{4}{9} = \frac{1}{9}$
$\frac{1}{4} \times \frac{7}{10} = \frac{7}{40}$
$\frac{2}{3} \times \frac{3}{5} = \frac{2}{5}$
$\frac{2}{3} \times \frac{4}{5} = \frac{8}{15}$
$\frac{2}{3} \times \frac{5}{6} = \frac{5}{9}$
$\frac{2}{3} \times \frac{3}{4} = \frac{1}{2}$
$\frac{2}{3} \times \frac{4}{9} = \frac{8}{27}$
$\frac{2}{3} \times \frac{7}{10} = \frac{7}{15}$
$\frac{3}{5} \times \frac{4}{5} = \frac{12}{25}$
$\frac{3}{5} \times \frac{5}{6} = \frac{1}{2}$
$\frac{3}{5} \times \frac{3}{4} = \frac{9}{20}$
$\frac{3}{5} \times \frac{4}{9} = \frac{4}{15}$
$\frac{3}{5} \times \frac{7}{10} = \frac{21}{50}$
$\frac{4}{5} \times \frac{5}{6} = \frac{2}{3}$
$\frac{4}{5} \times \frac{3}{4} = \frac{3}{5}$
$\frac{4}{5} \times \frac{4}{9} = \frac{16}{45}$
$\frac{4}{5} \times \frac{7}{10} = \frac{14}{25}$
$\frac{5}{6} \times \frac{3}{4} = \frac{5}{8}$
$\frac{5}{6} \times \frac{4}{9} = \frac{10}{27}$
$\frac{5}{6} \times \frac{7}{10} = \frac{7}{12}$
$\frac{3}{4} \times \frac{4}{9} = \frac{1}{3}$
$\frac{3}{4} \times \frac{7}{10} = \frac{21}{40}$
$\frac{4}{9} \times \frac{7}{10} = \frac{14}{45}$

Page 203

A. $\frac{3}{10}$
B. $\frac{7}{10}$
C. $\frac{2}{5}$
D. $\frac{1}{5}$
E. $\frac{9}{10}$
F. $\frac{1}{5}$
G. $\frac{2}{5}$
H. $\frac{4}{5}$
I. $\frac{1}{2}$
J. $\frac{3}{5}$
K. $\frac{4}{5}$
L. 0
M. $\frac{3}{5}$
N. $\frac{1}{10}$
O. $\frac{1}{2}$

Page 204

1. $\frac{1}{20}$, 0.05
2. $\frac{1}{2}$, 0.5
3. $\frac{3}{5}$, 0.6
4. $\frac{1}{25}$, 0.04
5. $\frac{1}{4}$, 0.25
6. $\frac{4}{25}$, 0.16
7. $\frac{3}{4}$, 0.75
8. $\frac{2}{5}$, 0.4
9. $\frac{3}{20}$, 0.15
10. $\frac{19}{20}$, 0.95

TO GET HIS TEETH CROWNED!

Page 209

1.

19	**22**	25	**28**
13	16	19	**22**
7	**10**	13	16
1	4	7	10

2.

51	**56**	61	66
43	48	53	**58**
35	**40**	**45**	50
27	**32**	37	**42**
19	24	**29**	34
11	16	21	**26**
3	8	**13**	18

3.

14	**18**	**22**	**26**	**30**	**34**	**38**
11	15	**19**	**23**	27	**31**	**35**
8	**12**	16	**20**	**24**	**28**	**32**
5	9	13	**17**	**21**	**25**	**29**
2	**6**	**10**	14	18	**22**	**26**

4. Answers may vary. Possible answers include the following:
   Drum 1:
   Each row from left to right: Add 3.
   Each column from top to bottom: Subtract 6.
   Diagonally from the top left corner to the bottom right corner: Subtract 3.
   Diagonally from the bottom left corner to the top right corner: Add 9.
   Drum 2:
   Each row from left to right: Add 5.
   Each column from bottom to top: Add 8.
   Each diagonal from bottom left to top right: Add 13.
   Each diagonal from top left to bottom right: Subtract 3.
   Drum 3:
   Each row from left to right: Add 4.
   Each column from bottom to top: Add 3.
   Each diagonal from bottom left to top right: Add 7.
   Each diagonal from bottom right to top left: Subtract 1.

Page 210

Arrangements of specified shapes within each square may vary. Possible arrangements are shown.

Page 211

Always congruent: 1, 5, 6, 9, 10
Sometimes congruent: 2, 3, 4
Never congruent: 7, 8, 11, 12

Page 213

1. $99\frac{99}{99}$
2.

2	7	6
9	5	1
4	3	8

4. 124 pairs of socks (8 legs x 31 days = 248 socks ÷ 2 = 124 pairs)
5. 14
6. 7 x 7 + 7 – 7 = 49
   9 + 9 x 9 ÷ 9 – 9 = 9
7. New York City, 168
   basketball, 85
   country, 116
8. The number in the middle column is formed by multiplying the digits on its left and right and then reversing the digits in the product. (Example: 9 x 7 = 63, reversed to 36.)

Page 214

1.

26	19	20
25	18	21
24	23	22

or

18	19	20
25	26	21
24	23	22

2. It belongs below the line since all numbers above the line have only straight lines and no curves.
3. ;The dark triangle is rotating around the square.
4. 3
5. a. DCLXXIX
   b. CMXXXVIII
   c. MMMDCXXXVI
   d. DCLXVII
6.
7. 14; A times B divided by C equals D.
8. 9

Page 215

1. 70 + 36 + 42 = 148; 109 + 6 + 16 + 17 = 148
2. 4 ways
   - 3 quarters + 1 dime + 3 nickels
   - 2 quarters + 5 dimes
   - 1 half-dollar + 4 dimes + 2 nickels
   - 1 half-dollar + 1 quarter + 5 nickels
3. Questions will vary. Possible questions include the following:
   - What kind of milk do you drink?
   - 2 is what percent of 100?
   - 4 is what percent of 200?
4. February
5. a. 3 b. 12 c. 2 d. 3
6. $\begin{array}{r}32\\7\overline{)224}\end{array}$ and $\begin{array}{r}74\\3\overline{)222}\end{array}$
7. 9
8. Answers will vary.

Page 216

1. Thursday
2. a. weeks in a year
   b. seconds in a minute
   c. ounces in a pound
   d. centimeters in a meter
   e. pounds in a ton
   f. quarts in a gallon
3. 1 + 4 + 6 = 11, or 2 + 3 + 6 = 11
4. c
5. Answers may vary. One possible solution is given.
   a. 18, 27, 45 b. 3, 11, 21 c. 6, 9, 15
6. 14
7. 3 days
8. a. 8 b. 24 c. 5

Page 217

1. 390 yd.
2. 14 squares
3. 4 factors: 1, 3, 5, and 15
4. 671 + 329 and 761 + 239
5. The clock says 8:30 AM when he wakes, but it really is 6:30 AM.
6. Answers will vary. One possible answer is 3 gallons – 2 quarts = $2\frac{1}{2}$ gallons.
7. ■, ★; A Zinkle is a solid shape with an even number of sides.
8. $3\frac{3}{4}$ dozen

Page 218

1. A. pineapple
   B. grapes
   C. pineapple
2. 100th day, April 10; 200th day, July 19
3. A. $\frac{1}{30}$
   B. $\frac{1}{2}$
   C. When there are four Sundays in June, the probability is $\frac{4}{30}$, or $\frac{2}{15}$. If there are five Sundays in June, the probability is $\frac{5}{30}$, or $\frac{1}{6}$.
4. No. Using equivalent fractions, Kyle had $\frac{24}{36}$ of the points. Kelsie had $\frac{9}{36}$, and Keith had $\frac{4}{36}$. The sum (24 + 9 + 4 = 37) of their points is greater than the total number of game points (36).
5. A. 3 x (15 – 9) = 18
   B. (6 x 10) ÷ 12 = 5
   C. (13 – 5) x (12 ÷ 6) = 16
6. 26; The rule is to add the sum of the digits in both addends.
7. Gertle, Myrtle, Bertle, Nurtle
8. 13 and 14

Page 225

Level A

1. 9,842; nine thousand, eight hundred forty-two; Because each digit can be used only once, the largest possible number that can be written is a four-digit number with its digits written in order from greatest to least.
2. 67,571
3. yes
4. rectangle
5. no; 64 should be 63 and 72 should be 70 because the pattern shows that the numbers increase by 7 each time.
6. false; 4,000 cm is equal to 40 meters

Level B

1. yes
2. 3,534,805
3. no
4. 19; The pattern is subtract 3, add 4.
5. triangle
6. Sue

Page 226

Level A

1. 1,732 miles
2. 35
3. no
4. Patrick
5. Each side of a scalene triangle is a different length.
6. 11

Level B

1. 18.7
2. no
3. yes
4. Ava
5. octagon, trapezoid, hexagon, triangle, quadrilateral
6. 138 pies

Page 227

Level A

1. 3.4 cm
2. 1,499
3. no
4. yes
5. ♥ = 9, ☺ = 6
6. Answers will vary. Possible answers include the following:
   - are quadrilaterals
   - have four congruent angles
   - have opposite sides that are parallel
   - have opposite sides that are congruent

Level B

1. smaller
2. 999 x 99 = 98,901
3. yes
4. yes; Each side of the student's drawing of a square should be labeled 6 units. The drawing of the student's rectangle should represent units of 1 x 36, 2 x 18, 3 x 12, or 4 x 9.
5. yes; The next two numbers can either be 7 and 11 or 8 and 16.
6. no

Page 228
Level A
1. 1, 4, or 7   2. 4.85 miles   3. no
4. Answers may vary.
5. yes
6. 150 cm

Level B
1. smallest: 2,034; largest: 2,934
2. 0, 0.19, 0.25, 0.5, 0.75, 0.8, 1
3. 900 x 40, 800 x 45, 600 x 60, 720 x 50, 500 x 72, 450 x 80, or 400 x 90
4. b   5. yes   6. 40° each

Page 229
Level A
1. 0
2. hundreds, thousands, and ten thousands
3. $1\frac{5}{6}$
4. no
5. Felipe
6. 26; The sum is the same.

Level B
1. 12
2. 11 guests
3. less than
4. 3 bags
5. 6 girls
6. 8 sq. in., 7.5 sq. in.

Page 230
Level A
1. $\frac{1}{6}$ cup
2. 10 years, during the 2017–2018 school year
3. no
4. 21 more rolls
5. All three students are correct.
6. no

Level B
1. yes
2. no
3. 30
4. 3
5. 36 choices
6. Abby

Page 233
1. true
2. false
3. false
4. true
5. true
6. false

Page 236

Page 237
1. Mercury, Venus, Earth, Mars
2. Jupiter, Saturn, Uranus, Neptune
3. It contains 99.8% of the mass of our solar system.
4. between Mars and Jupiter
5. a place beyond Neptune where dwarf planets orbit the sun

Page 240
1. fluffy snow, powder snow, and sticky snow
2. powder snow
3. grapple
4. Powder is loose snow and crust is packed snow.
5. Dust on crust has powder on top of it.

6–8. Answers will vary.

Page 241
1. antlers
2. fur
3. ankle
4. hoof
5. in the Arctic
6. antlers — shed once a year but then grow back; fur — acts like a blanket; hooves — are larger than most animals'; ankles — make noise to help stay in the herd
7. Answers will vary and may include deer and caribou.

Page 244
1. heart
2. transplant
3. artificial
4. Jarvik 7
5. implant
6. circulatory system
7. tubing
8. permanent
9. organ
10. patient

Page 245
Answers may vary.
1. almost anywhere
2. human's hair
3. bee, antennae
4. Pollen baskets
5. antenna cleaners
6. female
7. compound
8. queen, does not

Page 248
1. global warming
2. Greenhouse gases
3. atmosphere
4. deforestation
5. thermosphere
6. mesosphere
7. stratosphere
8. troposphere

Page 249
The three surviving species of sequoia trees can be found in eastern California on the western slopes of the Sierra Nevada mountains, Sequoia National Park in central California, southern Oregon along the Pacific coast, northern and central California along the Pacific coast, Sichuan province in China, and Hubei province in China.

Page 252
Answers may vary.
1. The bending of light rays is called **refraction**.
2. An optical illusion is **a misleading** picture of an object.
3. In a mirage, the layers of air are **different** temperatures.
4. A refracted image is **never** seen in the same spot as the actual object.
5. **Light rays** can bend when they pass through materials at different temperatures.

Page 253
1. B
2. C
3. B
4. B and C
5. A and C
6. C

7–8. Answers may vary.

Page 257
1. the signing of the Constitution of the United States into law
2. President Harry S. Truman
3. President George W. Bush
4. the National Archives Building in Washington, DC
5. to set the rules for our government
6. yes

Page 260
1. D
2. B
3. E
4. A
5. H
6. C
7. F
8. G
9. People vote for elected government officials.
10. once

11–12. Answers will vary.

Page 263
1. America
2. rulers, anyone
3. forefathers, around
4. Rights
5. ancient, concept
6. people
7. control
8. Madison, English

<u>my freedom</u>

Page 266

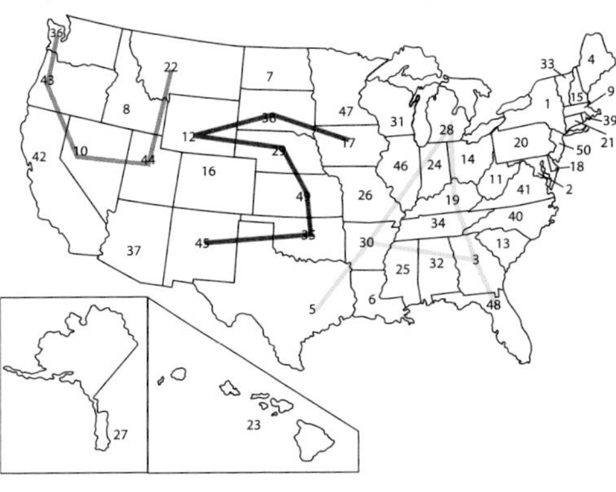

Page 268
1. a national memorial to four American presidents whose faces are carved on a granite cliff in South Dakota's Black Hills
2. Gutzon Borglum, an American sculptor
3. George Washington, Thomas Jefferson, Theodore Roosevelt, and Abraham Lincoln
4. Washington was chosen for the struggle for independence, Jefferson for the idea of government by the people, Roosevelt for the 20th century role of the United States in world affairs, and Lincoln for equality and the permanent union of the states.
5. because of its height, its soft grainy granite, and the long hours of sunlight it gets each day
6. workers used drills and dynamite
7. Answers may vary.
8. Answers may vary.

Page 271
1. Answers may vary.
2. The first part of the Declaration of Independence explains the colonies' reasons for separating from England. It also outlines peoples' natural rights. The second part lists complaints against King George III.
3. The signers' names are grouped by geographic location, which was a common practice at that time.
4. It took five days for all 13 colonies to approve the Declaration of Independence. It took more time to get an official copy made.
5. He was the president of the Second Continental Congress.

Page 272
more than is needed: *surplus*
the lowest pay a worker can receive by law: *minimum wage*
an economic system in which businesses are free to offer for sale many kinds of goods and services: *free enterprise*
a period in which there is little economic growth and a high rate of joblessness: *depression*
a time of quick and widespread economic growth: *boom*
a person who owes money: *debtor*
a written plan for managing money: *budget*
the way people produce, distribute, and consume goods and services: *economy*
a product brought into a country from another country in order to be sold: *import*
not plentiful: *scarce*
the state of being jobless: *unemployment*
a share in a company or business: *stock*
money that is paid by people to support the work of the government: *tax*
to trade with people by exchanging goods: *barter*
a budget shortage caused by spending more money than is earned: *deficit*
an economic condition in which it takes more and more money to buy the same goods: *inflation*
a product sent from one country to another to be sold: *export*
money that is leftover after a business has paid all its costs: *profit*
to buy a share of a business in the hope of making a profit: *invest*
a place where people can buy and sell stocks in businesses: *stock market*
a time of quick economic decline: *bust*
someone who buys goods and services: *consumer*
the amount of goods and services available for sale: *supply*
the need for goods or services to be produced or offered: *demand*

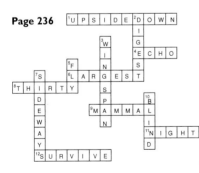

INDEX

ISBN-13: 978-156234924-0
ISBN-10: 156234924-4